# Education 3–13

Primary education is one of the most important phases of learning but there remains a scarcity of in-depth research on this vital topic. However, as the focus on improving outcomes increases there is a growing interest internationally in research that helps us to understand the best ways to help young children engage with the curriculum in order that they may have the best possible life chances. This text helps to address these issues and consists of seminal articles derived from the 40-year history of the journal *Education 3–13*, which can claim to be one of the most important and influential publications in its field.

The chapters included have been chosen carefully to represent a wide range of key topics in research on primary education and the text is sub-divided into five parts, each of which has been edited by leading academics who specialise in the topic under scrutiny. The parts include:

- Learning and teaching, including the psychology and philosophy of primary education;
- Key challenges in primary education, including changes to the governance of schools, and educational management and leadership;
- The primary curriculum, including Maths, Science, IT and Technology Education;
- The primary curriculum, including English, Humanities and the Arts; and,
- Primary teachers' work and professionalism.

Many of the contributions are written by seminal figures in academic research. The text will be especially relevant to students and researchers engaged in the study of primary education as well as to practitioners, advisers and policy makers and will prove an invaluable resource for those wishing to gain an overview of research into primary education. It is recommended especially for those who wish to understand the development of primary education and the many twists and turns in theory, practice and policy that have influenced its development over the period of a generation. Those who read the text will come across the origins of many of the ideas that continue to influence primary teaching today as well as very recent research on where we are now in this important subject area.

**Michael Bottery** is Professor of Education at the University of Hull. He is a member of the Board of Education 3–13.

**Mark Brundrett** is Professor of Education Research at Liverpool John Moores University and Editor of *Education 3–13: International Journal of Primary, Elementary and Early Years Education.*

**Neil Burton** is a university lecturer and currently Chair of the Association for the Study of Primary Education (ASPE), as well as a member of the Board of Education 3–13.

**Diane Duncan** is a consultant and writer on Education and former Principal Lecturer at the University of Hertfordshire. She is Vice-Chair of the Association for the Study of Primary Education (ASPE) and a member of the Board of Education 3–13.

**Peter Silcock** is Professor of Education at the University of Hertfordshire. He is a former Chair of the Association for the Study of Primary Education (ASPE).

**Rosemary Webb** is Honorary Professor of Education at the University of Manchester. She is a former Chair of the Association for the Study of Primary Education (ASPE).

**Wei Zhang** is a Lecturer in Education at the University of Leicester and a member of the Board of Education 3–13.

# Education Heritage Series

**Tracing Education Policy**
Selections from the Oxford Review of Education
*David Phillips and Geoffrey Walford*

**Rethinking Schooling**
Twenty-Five Years of the Journal of Curriculum Studies
*Ian Westbury and Geoff Milburn*

**Overcoming Disabling Barriers**
18 Years of Disability and Society
*Len Barton*

**From Adult Education to the Learning Society**
21 Years of the International Journal of Lifelong Education
*Peter Jarvis*

**Feminist Critique of Education**
Fifteen Years of Gender Development
*Christine Skelton and Becky Francis*

**Education, Globalisation and New Times**
21 Years of the Journal of Education Policy
*Stephen J. Ball, Ivor F. Goodson and Meg Maguire*

**Education and Society**
25 Years of the British Journal of Sociology of Education
*Len Barton*

**Curriculum and the Teacher**
35 years of the Cambridge Journal of Education
*Nigel Norris*

**Changing Educational Contexts, Issues and Identities**
40 Years of Comparative Education
*Michael Crossley, Patricia Broadfoot and Michele Schweisfurth*

# Education 3–13

40 years of research on primary,
elementary and early years education

**Edited by Michael Bottery,
Mark Brundrett, Neil Burton,
Diane Duncan, Peter Silcock,
Rosemary Webb and Wei Zhang**

Routledge
Taylor & Francis Group

LONDON AND NEW YORK

First published 2013
by Routledge
2 Park Square, Milton Park, Abingdon, Oxon OX14 4RN

Simultaneously published in the USA and Canada
by Routledge
711 Third Avenue, New York, NY 10017

*Routledge is an imprint of the Taylor & Francis Group, an informa business*

*British Library Cataloguing in Publication Data*
A catalogue record for this book is available from the British Library

*Library of Congress Cataloging in Publication Data*
Education 3–13 : 40 years of research on primary, elementary, and early years education / edited by Michael Bottery . . . [et al.].
    p. cm. — (Education heritage)
Articles originally published in the journal Education 3–13.
1. Education, Elementary—Great Britain. 2. Early childhood education—Great Britain. I. Brundrett, Mark. II. Education 3–13. III. Title: Education three to thirteen.
LB1556.7.G7E38 2012
372.941—dc23
                                                        2012021938

ISBN: 978-0-415-64515-7 (hbk)
ISBN: 978-0-203-07876-1 (ebk)

Typeset in Galliard
by RefineCatch Limited, Bungay, Suffolk


Printed and bound in the United States of America by Publishers Graphics, LLC on sustainably sourced paper.

# Contents

# Preface

*Education 3–13* was almost still-born in 1973. At that time the flurry of interest in English primary education kindled by the Plowden Report was being eclipsed by gathering economic problems which threatened the Conservative government's white paper, *A framework for expansion,* issued in 1972. The journal survived its difficult birth – just. The expansionist plans for the sector including a large increase in nursery education did not. Nevertheless high hopes accompanied the journal's arrival. It was launched by Professor Philip Taylor and others with the tacit support of Norman Thomas, Chief Inspector for Primary Education, to stress the fundamental importance of primary education and to subject the central issues and problems of 'education three to thirteen' to a many-sided scrutiny drawing on the resources of research, scholarship and reflection.

Those high hopes, intentionally set very high, have inevitably not been fully realised 40 years on (such is the fate of all such hopes) but considerable progress *has* been made. At present, in England, as in most of the 'developed' world, primary education still does not receive 'parity of esteem' with the secondary and higher education sectors. It still has fewer resources per head devoted to it; it still has few column inches written about it in the press; governments still spend more time (including focusing more criticism!) on other sectors; an 'expert' panel set up to advise government on a new English national curriculum still contains a majority of secondary specialists. But the profile and importance of primary education are far higher than they were. *Education 3–13* has played a significant part in this. As the articles in this book illustrate, many of its contributors (including its editors) have influenced opinion through their research and scholarship. The research the journal has reported and interpreted has entered the 'blood stream' of political and educational debate, at least to a degree.

But there is still more to do. Research, scholarship and reflection, fostered both nationally and internationally by a resurgent Education 3–13, still need to play a fuller part in informing policy and practice and in increasing our understanding of how to foster learning in that most receptive of age ranges, three to 13. The journal is 40 years young, not 40 years old; it has an exciting future ahead of it, as it reaches an ever-wider international audience. Who knows what progress and influence may be possible in another 40 years? Our high hopes remain undiminished, and must remain high, not only for research and study into primary education, but for the future education of every one of the world's children aged three to 13.

*Colin Richards, a former member of Her Majesty's Inspectorate of Schools, is Emeritus Professor of Education at the University of Cumbria and Honorary Professor of Education at the University of Warwick.*

# Acknowledgements

The production of this celebratory text has been a team effort based around members of the board of the journal. Whilst the editors of the sections in the text are all named on the front cover there are a number of colleagues on the board who took part in the discussions leading up to the proposal which subsequently became this work whose support needs to be acknowledged. They include Dr Paul Adams, of the University of Hull, UK; Professor Honqi Chu, of Beijing Normal University, China; Dr Megan Crawford of the University of Cambridge, UK; Dr Ruth Dann, of Manchester Metropolitan University, UK; Dr Christine Doddington, of the University of Cambridge, UK; Dr Chysanthi Gkolia, of the University of Thessaly, Greece; Mr Roy Hughes, of the University of Leeds, UK; Professor Anneli Sarja, of the University of Jyvaskyla, Finland; Dr Neil Simco, of the University of the Highlands and Islands, UK; Dr Gabriella Torstensson, of Edgehill University, UK; and Ms Sue Waite, of the University of Plymouth, UK.

In addition we would like to offer particular thanks to several academics who are associated with *Education 3–13* who kindly agreed to act as reviewers of the proposal. These include Dr Simon Clarke of the Graduate School of Education at the University of Western Australia; Professor S. Nayana Tara, of the Public Systems Management Area, the Indian Institute of Management, Bangalore, India; and Professor Linda M. Cameron, of the Ontario Institute for Studies in Education, University of Toronto, Canada.

*Education 3–13* is owned by the Association for the Study of Primary Education (ASPE) in the UK without whose support the journal could not have continued to exist during the 40 years of its publication. Limitations of space preclude the listing of all the members of ASPE but especial thanks are offered to the Executive Committee of the organization who regularly discuss matters associated with the management of the journal and whose unflagging work ensures the organization as a whole alive remains an influential voice for primary education.

Very great thanks are offered to the staff of Routledge who have been unfailingly kind, supportive and helpful during the very productive period of the association between the journal and that organization. Special thanks are extended to Katie Peace, who was managing editor during the period of gestation of this text, and to Vicky Quantrell, who took over in that role during the period when the project came to fruition. We also thank Anna Clarkson, Editorial Director at

Taylor & Francis, for her great kindness and support in encouraging and allowing us to develop this text.

We extend very great thanks to Professor Colin Richards, who was the first editor of *Education 3–13*, and who responded positively to our approach when we asked if he would be so kind as to write a preface to this text. His involvement is a great addition to the text which gives the perfection of circularity in returning the journal to its roots.

Finally, we wish to extend our gratitude to Miss Emma Fitzgerald, of Liverpool John Moores University, who has acted as the journal administrator for the last six years and who assisted in the production of this text. Rarely can an editor have been so blessed by the support of someone so calm, intelligent and efficient.

# Introduction

## The development of *Education 3–13*

*Education 3–13* was first published in 1973 and so, at the time of writing, is in its fortieth year of production. It is now the major publication of the Association for the Study of Primary Education (ASPE) and is read not only in England and the wider UK but is also distributed to academic institutions in many countries around the world. This text is a celebration of that 40 years of the publication of research on primary, elementary and early years education and this introduction sets out something of the history of the development of the journal, its links with the Association for the Study of Primary Education (ASPE), and the future prospects and challenges that the journal may face.

The journal was founded by the Primary Schools Research and Development Group in the West Midlands, and was the brainchild of Professor Philip Taylor. The first editor was a youthful Colin Richards, now Professor Colin Richards, who edited the journal for 10 years and went on to a distinguished career as an HMI, writer and academic. The first issues of the journal included short articles which were concerned with topics such as: the place of discovery learning; the issue of 'open schooling'; the role of the primary head teacher; reading; the aims of primary education; and 'children and their difficulties'.

The first editorial stated that 'the Journal will seek the central issues and problems of "education three to thirteen" and subject them to a many-sided scrutiny – scrutiny which has as its major goal the improvement of practice. Its purpose will be to promote an on-going debate, not assuming that the last word has ever been spoken but always probing the bases of current and future practice'. It concluded 'the Journal will stand or fall by the contributions it receives from all interested in the education of children three to thirteen'. Every issue of the journal is now available electronically in the archive on the journal website and those who may take the time to examine that invaluable resource will see that the journal has more than fulfilled those early aims since it has subjected the complex changes in primary education that have occurred since the early 1970s, both in the UK and internationally, to a sustained scrutiny.

The journal has also contributed positively to the complex and sometimes confusing discourse on how best to educate children from pre-school until the early years of secondary education. In this sense and many others the main values that underpin the content of *Education 3–13* have remained the same over its 40 years of existence. This stability of purpose is reflected in the continuity of policy and personnel that the journal has enjoyed and it is rewarding to note that many of those who worked with or on the journal in its early days remain friends or contributors to the journal to the present day. This feeling of continuity is exemplified by the fact that the journal has had only five permanent editors, each of whom undertook the role for a considerable period of time. The list of editors and their period in office is as follows:

Colin Richards 1973–1982
Guest editors/Jim Campbell 1982–1996
Colin Richards 1996–1999
Neil Simco 1999–2003
Rosie Turner-Bisset/Mark Brundrett 2003–2006
Mark Brundrett 2006–present.

In addition, the journal owes a great debt to the many 'guest editors', often but by no means solely, drawn from the Editorial Board of the journal, whose names are too numerous to state here individually.

This then, is a story of continuity and sustained engagement in the academic analysis of a key topic in education and it is undoubtedly true that the journal has benefited greatly from the long-term commitment and guidance of a number of individuals. Nonetheless, we must acknowledge that the history of the journal has been one of steady development and expansion. The first issue, one of two issues in that volume, consisted of an Editorial by Colin Richards, 12 articles and book reviews. The journal progressed to have two have three issues per year in 1987 and this was maintained until 2006 when the journal began a very productive relationship with its current publisher, Routledge, when it was soon found that more pages were required and the journal grew in the number of words contained in each issue. Since then, in 2007, the journal moved to four issues, in 2011 there commenced to be five issues and from 2013 the journal will move to six issues per year. These simple raw statistics would suggest that the journal is now very different from that first production of 40 years ago and that sense of change is enhanced by the fact that the physical shape of *Education 3–13* has changed several times over the years, as has the cover design. In addition, although there is more material in each issue, articles tend to be much longer at over 5000 words each so there are actually fewer items per publication, and the journal is now available online as well as in hard cover.

Throughout its history, *Education 3–13* has stood as one of the few journals dedicated to the work of teachers and other professional groups working with children in the years associated with pre-school, primary and middle schools. This makes it an unusual and important journal since it focuses on the one phase of schooling which is ubiquitous across all nations.

## The nature of this text

This text is a celebration of the 40th Volume of the journal *Education 3–13: International Journal of Primary, Elementary and Early Years Education* and includes seminal articles published over the 40-year history of the journal. It represents many of the key conceptual developments in the field of primary education during that period.

The rationale for the text was to provide a celebration of the work of an important journal that has acted as a focus for the publication of articles on research, policy and practice in primary education for four decades. The text consists of seminal articles chosen to represent the range of topics addressed in the journal and is sub-divided into parts on key issues in primary education, each of which has been edited by leading academics who are a specialist in the topic under scrutiny. The text is divided in five parts, each of which attempts to address a coherent conceptual area or set of issues in primary education. The parts include:

**Part I** – Learning and teaching (including psychology and philosophy of primary education)
**Part II** – Key challenges in primary education (including changes to governance, educational management and leadership)
**Part III** – The primary curriculum: Maths, Science, IT and Technology Education
**Part IV** – The primary curriculum: English, Humanities and the Arts
**Part V** – Primary teachers' work and professionalism

A considerable amount of time was spent in trying to define how best to represent the varied output of the journal and a number of issues were taken into account such as trying to reflect the range of material in the journal, the development of issues over time, and ensuring a gender balance of authors for the items included. For this reason, each section includes at least one article from each of the decades in which the journal has been published (1970s, 1980s, 1990s, 2000s) and at least one item from an 'international contributor' in order to reflect the international nature of the journal.

The editors of the sections within the text are all members of the Board of the journal or members of the ASPE Executive Committee and subject experts in the topic for which they have selected articles.

## The audience for the text

Education 3–13 has enjoyed wide appeal for practitioners, advisors, academics, and students undergoing initial teacher training or taking advanced degrees. For this reason the journal has always been of great relevance to higher education institutions involved in teacher education and educational research. The text should also have wide international appeal since the journal is popular in countries/regions as diverse as the UK, Scandinavia, Greece, India, Singapore,

Hong Kong, Australia, the USA and Canada. Thus, it is hoped that this text will appeal to the considerable number of institutional libraries worldwide who access the journal. It will be especially relevant to academic researchers and students engaged the study of primary education as well as to practitioners, advisers and policy makers.

## *Education 3–13* and ASPE

As noted at the start of the introduction, *Education 3–13* is owned by the Association for the Study of Primary Education (ASPE). ASPE was launched at a conference in Leeds in 1988 those present strongly endorsed the case for establishing a national association to help advance the cause of primary education by promoting its study. It was, of course, at that time that the 1988 Education Reform Act began to accelerate the pace of change in all phases of compulsory education. With these developments in mind it was felt that there was a need to provide a voice for those primary specialists working in *Schools, LEAs and Teacher Education* and this tripartite membership is still reflected in the organisation's membership as a whole and in the construction of ASPE's National Executive.

What distinguishes ASPE from other bodies with interests in primary education is its emphasis on reflective study and on collaborative activity between the groups it represents. ASPE is founded on the core purposes of advancing the cause of primary education and on supporting those most directly involved, through professional discourse, practice and study. ASPE holds conferences and seminars on primary education and is often consulted about proposed changes to primary education that will be of interest to all of the members of the constituencies it seeks to represent. The journal attempts to reflect the purposes of the Association and there is a close relationship between *Education 3–13* and ASPE with many of the members of the Association's Executive committee taking key roles with the journal. Anyone who is interested in the journal is encouraged to explore the work of the Association.[1]

## The future of *Education 3–13*

The history of *Education 3–13* has been once of steady development and expansion in terms of the amount of material that it contains. The defining feature of the journal in its current form is that it aims to publish refereed articles representing the highest quality research and analysing practice relating to children between the ages of 3–13, both in the UK and internationally, with a central focus on primary education. The status of the journal continues to rise and we seek to publish items from leading academics and researchers in the field whose work will be of interest to academics, students, teachers and advisers who seek perspectives on early years, primary and middle schooling.

The journal self-consciously seeks to have wide appeal whilst retaining a commitment to the highest standards of scholarship. This is because the policy context in which we operate remains as interesting and complex as it was in the founding year of 1973.

Over the last 40 years education has been subject to continuous change based on frequent intervention by policy makers, both in the UK and internationally, as politicians seek ways to improve school systems in order to make nations more economically competitive. Such change seems likely to continue unabated as governments seek to deal with the many and varied problems associated with a problematic international environment. The journal wishes to contribute to the debate that informs such change and in so doing hopes that it will stay true to the key purposes that were there at its inception.[2]

## Notes

1   More can be found out about ASPE, including how to become a member, on the ASPE website at www.aspe-uk.eu.
2   More details of the journal, its current policy and the ways in which to submit an article can be found on the journal website at http://www.tandf.co.uk/journals/titles/03004279.asp.

# Part I
# Learning and teaching

# 1 Discovery learning

## A personal view

*Alec Clegg*

'I am convinced that the way of teaching which approaches most nearly the method of investigation is by far the best since not content with serving up a few barren and life-less truths it tends to set the learner himself on the track of invention and to direct him into those paths in which the author has made his own discoveries.'

Edmund Burke

This statement of the case for learning by discovery was made by the great Edmund Burke many years ago and is re-echoed in the Plowden Report of 1967.

In its simplest terms it means that children's interests are more excitedly aroused and their minds set to work more effectively by things that they themselves find out than by things that they hear or see. It means that they understand things better if they can do them or take part actively in them. But if this is so, why the ebb and flow of conviction about activity and experience as a teaching method? Why the action and reaction ? The answer to this surely lies in the fact that it is far easier to tell a passive group of children all to do the same thing at the same time and see that they do it than it is to let each individual have some choice in what he does and to let each child in a class pursue a different line of interest carefully guided by the teacher. The former is a much more mechanical way of teaching – it is the job of the technician. The latter is much more demanding and is the job of the professional.

To anyone who has been watching results over recent years there is no doubt that the hard way gives both a better product in the quality of the children it produces and a better by-product in the quality of the work done by the children.

But there are dangers. Learning by discovery is a sensitive, individual approach to the business of learning. It cannot readily be reduced to a prescribed method of the kind that one can set down in a way that used to be demanded by the visiting College of Education lecturer of every student in training. So that what tends to happen today is that we evolve all-embracing and comforting clichés about what we proclaim to be the new ways of learning. A good teacher adopts the practice, whereby an older child helps along a younger one. It becomes a 'method' and we call it 'family grouping'. The idea gets around that this is the thing to do and if only all teachers will do it all will be efficient. Again one or two teachers find that they can work effectively together and do so, and before we know where we are there is a 'method' called 'team teaching' and another called 'open plan' teaching, and these become the latest bandwagon on which all climb whether they can play the instruments or not.

Many years ago I visited a school where there was one of the most gifted teachers I have known. She said, 'I don't bother with the bell any more. There is no sense in getting these children to break off when their interest is at its peak.' Two or three years later the Principal in the neighbouring College of Education told me that she had started a course of lectures on 'the integrated day'. I went back to the school where I had first seen this in operation years before and said to the teacher, 'Do you know what the integrated day is?' and she replied 'No. What is it?' I then described to her what she had been doing for a considerable time.

It is as well that we remember that first-rate teaching by discovery methods can occur in the old box-type schools, that an elderly teacher set in her ways may not want to work in a team, and that a young teacher may not be able to manage four-year-olds and seven-year-olds together. Given these reservations and precautions, there is no doubt that Edmund Burke and Lady Plowden are right.

# 2 'I suppose learning your tables could help you get a job'

## Children's views on the purpose of schools

*Cedric Cullingford*

It is easy for teachers to take schools for granted. Deeply immersed as they are in unique institutions they are kept so busy with the daily routine and the constant demands on their attention that it is very difficult for them to reflect on the fundamental purposes of schooling. Teachers instinctively react to the need for discipline and the fulfilment of social expectations, in raising academic standards and helping children pass exams. Even without the pressure of the examination system, or the concerns of parents, let alone the cajoling of the Department of Education and Science on the changing curriculum, teachers find themselves in a reactive role. Given the school as an institution in which pupils need to be organised this is not surprising. Teachers are expected to be able to control a variety of circumstances for a large number of individuals at the same time.

Nevertheless teachers, whatever type of school they are in, or whatever age range they teach, tend to hold consistent attitudes towards the purpose of schools.[1] They do not see themselves reacting to the demands of society by producing highly qualified manpower. They do not assume that they are there expressly to serve the state through the 'delivery' of an agreed curriculum. They see their role in more social and more subtle terms.[2] For them the purposes of education are to do with bringing out the best in each child so that each might be happy and able to mix easily with others. Teachers uniformly stress the importance of the individual child's 'autonomy' in the ability to learn and to strike up relationships with others.

For parents, the purpose of schooling is equally clear, and fundamentally different from the attitudes expressed by teachers. They are obviously concerned with their own children rather than with the whole school or the abstract concept of education as a whole, or as a means of improving society. For parents, schools exist to give their own children the best possible education so that they might acquire good jobs. Underlying their sympathy for teachers and the ideals of schools is a firm pragmatism that includes the desire that schools should impart discipline, use traditional methods of instruction and impart enough knowledge to secure employment and avoid what they see as social failure — not gaining at least as good a job as themselves. These attitudes naturally underly more complex concerns about school, and one can often discover what seems to be broad agreement between parents and teachers on several issues.

At a time of high unemployment one might have thought there would be less stress on the need to acquire jobs, but instead the sense of competition in parents' concern for their children is the more fierce as teachers reflect on the growing divergence between the idea of education for the sake of the individual and the idea of education as preparation for social life. There is, for them anyway, an ambiguity between the two views.

For children there seems to be no ambiguity. For those at primary schools, as well as those at secondary school, the purpose of education is quite clear. Children are at school to enable them to get jobs. The following article is based on extensive interviews with over sixty pupils, half of whom were in their last year in four different primary schools and half of whom were in their first year of the secondary school, in the Midlands. In discussing their attitudes towards changing from one school to another some very consistent and significant attitudes towards schools and teachers emerged, including strong beliefs in the purpose of schools.

Children of a variety of backgrounds are all agreed about the fundamental purpose of schools

> 'If I didn't go to school I'd know nothing and wouldn't be able to get a job or nothing . . .'
>
> girl (primary)

> 'To get a good job.'
>
> boy (primary)

> 'To get a good education so that you can get a good job.'
>
> boy (primary)

> 'If you want to get a job . . . it might help me with my job. Its important 'cos it helps to get jobs.'
>
> boy (primary)

> 'Its for teaching you to make sure you get a good job when you leave.'
>
> girl (primary)

Children repeatedly return to this theme. As they reflect on the variety of experiences in school, or the different methods of learning and the different expectations of teachers, they continually mention this ultimate purpose of school. It is the one thing which, to them, makes sense of the whole experience. It gives an insight into *why* they are learning the different subjects and why they are spending so much time on Maths and English. There is no evidence that the teachers ever mention employment, even as a threat that they will not get a job unless they work. It is however clear that this view of the purpose of school was *not* suddenly acquired just before entering secondary school.

'To learn things so you'll get a job.'

girl (primary)

'When you need a job and you hadn't been to school, it would be hard to get a job . . . Really you need to go to school to get a job when you're older.'

girl (primary)

'. . . because if you don't do it you won't get a job.'

boy (secondary)

'To learn, so that you can get a job later on. Other people might just say 'I'll not bother with school. Its not really worth it' . . . and later on they don't find a job.'

boy (secondary)

'. . . I suppose it is because it could be training me for a job I want to do.'

girl (secondary)

'It depends on the report you get at school to see if you can get a job or not.'

boy (secondary)

Whilst these are just a few examples, all the children stressed the same point. Some of them might include other reasons as well, but the fundamental vision of the school seen in terms of outcome, of result, was clear in them all.[3] Children in the primary schools saw their education not in terms of the present experience but in terms of the final result of schooling and their place in employment. The primary school was there to prepare them for the more serious purpose of the secondary school, and the secondary school's purpose manifested itself in their subsequent achievement.[4]

This instrumental view of the purpose of schooling pervades many of the children's other attitudes, like their attitudes towards the curriculum. If they concur with their parents in seeing improved qualifications towards employment as the aim of education, then they also assume that the curriculum should be relevant to this end. Interviews with people who have left school show that the majority of those who are not employed feel that the school was partly to blame, because of the fact that the curriculum seemed to have nothing to do with the world in which they subsequently found themselves.[5] Looking back, they wished that what they had learned had been directed towards the skills they would need in employment, and more particularly, directed towards an attempt to understand the political and social environment in which they lived. They wanted to know *why* they were in school, both then and afterwards. With hindsight the young unemployed interviewed by White and Brockington[5] in 1983 wished that school had been made more relevant to them all the time, from the primary phase onwards.

Children at school do not use terms such as, 'social relevance', but their insistence on the importance of jobs does suggest that they would all, on leaving school, have the same points to make about the curriculum and the sense of purpose in school. Those who would have gained a place in higher education would not feel the same lack of purpose as those who would be unemployed, but the interviews show that this sense is not only to hindsight or a feeling of betrayal. When children discussed the need for qualifications, one of the points that they mentioned was the utility of what they learned in school in terms of the job market. They implied that what they were learning should have a direct relevance in persuading someone to give them a job.

'I suppose learning your tables could help you get a job.'

boy (primary)

'To learn to get a good job, to help you learn to read and write.'

girl (primary)

'You do exams. That's about getting a job, though. Exams see how good you are on your tables, English, Maths and that . . . I'm really looking forward to getting a job.'

boy (primary)

'When you leave school and you're older and you can get a job, you'll know how to read and write and you'll know English and Maths and all that lot. To get a job you have to know English, Science, History, Maths and Spellings.'

boy (primary)

Whilst at school the children assume that the curriculum given to them *is* for the purpose of getting them jobs and to that extent do not question it, even if they subsequently discover that there was no such direct connection. They are somewhat muddled about the connections between the curriculum and examinations, and the curriculum and qualifications since there *are* correlations but these remain ambiguous.

'To learn about things, and history and science and that so that when you come out you'll be able to get a decent job.'

girl (secondary)

'It can help you get a job again because . . . like maths can help you get into computers.'

boy (secondary)

For most children the curriculum is at one level at least unquestionably 'relevant' because it is made up of the subjects that form the examinations. In taking qualifications seriously and in accepting that examinations are the real purpose of what they learn, children reflect the doubts of the educational system. They know their subsequent careers and employability depend on how well they do in examinations and they understand this point fully before they leave their primary schools.

> 'Learning so that when you grow up you'll learn how to find a job and add up things that are quite hard. Its for exams.'
>
> boy (primary)

> 'If I didn't go to school I'd know nothing and wouldn't be able to get a job or nothing . . . its really for people to learn things you didn't know before and when you are older you'll have so many 'O' levels you can get what you want . . . If you didn't go to school you wouldn't have no 'O' levels and you wouldn't ever get a job nowhere.'
>
> girl (primary)

> 'You've got to take all your exams so you can go into a job.'
>
> girl (primary)

> '. . . when you're about 16 you do your exams and then you leave school and try to get a job.'
>
> boy (primary)

> 'You've got to take all your exams so you can go into a job.'
>
> girl (primary)

> '. . . when you're about 16 you do your exams and then you leave school and try to get a job.'
>
> boy (primary)

> 'You do exams; that's about getting a job, though. Exams see how good you are on your tables, English, Maths and that . . . I'm really looking forward to getting a job.'
>
> boy (primary)

At primary schools the vision of schooling is that of preparation for secondary school, then preparation for exams followed by the job. At secondary schools the tone changes slightly; the examinations are more taken for granted and the purpose of getting a job looms so large that the necessary stage of passing an exam is less clearly articulated, except in terms of a certain amount of terror.

'. . . because it'll help me when I do exams in the fifth year.'

girl (secondary)

'So that when you come to exams if you haven't done it you won't know what to put down.'

girl (secondary)

'. . . it is when you get older and you need your 'A' levels and 'O' levels.'

boy (secondary)

'It depends on the report you get at school to see if you can get a job or not.'

boy (secondary)

The sense of purpose devoted to acquiring a job is strengthened by a certain amount of fear that they might be unemployed. Children hold no illusions about the job-market, or about the whole context in which their schooling is placed.

'Well, with today's unemployment you need so many 'O' levels and 'A' levels and degrees as you can get and the only way you can get these is to go to school. There are people paid to teach people. Its the only way you can learn. If your Mum and Dad were experts you have no problems about learning.'

boy (primary)

'The comp, tell you what kind of jobs you're fit for. If you want to get a good job you've got to really work hard at the comp. That's the kind of second step to being an adult and just before you finish they tell you what job you're qualified for, and then you can choose one of them. You're qualified when you learn most of your subjects and you've got 'O' levels and 'A' levels.'

girl (primary)

'Later in our life we would want to get a job and not just hanging around on the dole and we could have 'O' levels and 'A' levels and get good qualifications . . . It does prepare you for some jobs. If you forget everything your life is a misery and you won't be able to have a job or anything.'

boy (primary)

'The 'O' levels are important because if you don't get any you won't get a job or anything, and you'll be just on your own, nowhere really.'

girl (primary)

'To help you learn so that when you get older you'll be able to get a good job and be able to make money and you'll not be poor like a beggar or something.'

boy (primary)

It is instructive that primary school children feel so strongly about the importance of gaining qualifications and a job. Their vision of the purpose of schooling is particularly clear, and suggests that they view their own education at the time as a mere preliminary to the larger schools and the wider world. Those areas of learning that teachers insist they must know, like tables and spelling, are invoked on the grounds that without them, as with English and Maths, they will be unemployable. But they also realise that to be employed does not only depend on their qualifications on paper but on an interview. The girl who suggested that the school would tell her what kind of job she was fitted for had a very mechanistic view of the system. But others knew that schooling also included those other standards about which teachers and parents would talk in the same way as about tables and spelling; without tidiness and obedience there would be no progress.

> 'Teaching us what we might need to know when we get a job: how to be neat and have manners and how to behave properly.'
>
> girl (primary)

> 'You've got to learn things so that when you grow up you can know what things you need to when you're older. You've got to have the right education for a job.'
>
> girl (primary)

> 'Well, we have to come; its to teach you things. Manners and that. It does prepare you for some jobs.'
>
> boy (primary)

> 'Primary school was an introductory period to what you're going to be doing up here because we don't do handwriting or anything up here . . . learning, meeting friends . . .'
>
> boy (secondary)

Some of the children add that school is not only for the purpose of getting a job but for meeting other people. To this extent the idea of socialization was also in their minds, as in the minds of the teachers, although much more strongly in the sense of their own popularity and friendships with a variety of people. They saw school as the place where they could meet their friends, and where there would in consequence be much more entertainment than at home. To some of the children this was an additional purpose of the school. School is the great social meeting place, the supplier of friends and the opportunity to see them.[6]

> 'To learn things and to make new friends.'
>
> boy (secondary)

> 'To learn things and to meet people as well. To make friends.'
>
> girl (primary)

'To get a good education so you can get a good job. If you didn't meet anybody else you wouldn't be socialised.'

boy (primary)

If one of the prime motivations for doing well at school is to gain qualifications, another one is to be spared embarrassment. The children feel that just as they might be deemed stupid at school for not doing well so they would be made to feel silly for being incapable of getting a job or of handling themselves in a normal public way. Knowing the 'right things' could be bound up with the idea of an interview for a job, but was also seen to have a wider purpose.

'Because if you don't do it, you won't get a job . . . and they give you kind of things and say what kind of bus you go on and all that and if you don't know they won't give you a job.'

boy (secondary)

Underlying the children's realisation that they need to know is a fear of being embarrassed by their ignorance. The ability to gain a job does not depend, in their eyes, solely on qualifications, but on the way they conduct themselves. They realise that they need to know things to survive; they understand that knowledge of things like money and forms is a necessary part of their future equipment. But they also understand the wider dimensions of possessing knowledge.

'So that if you have children then you can tell them how to get a job and everything. To know things if anyone ask you.'

boy (primary)

Getting a job and knowing things are, of course, inextricably linked.

'To learn and to get a job. You wouldn't know anything if you'd stay at home.'

girl (primary)

'It's to learn things so that when you grow up you get a good education. The secondary school is for a good education. You wouldn't know anything if you didn't go to school and you wouldn't get a job.'

girl (primary)

But knowing things is also a necessity in itself, for the sake of avoiding embarrassment, or worse, a conflict with the teacher

'Learning . . . because you had to do handwriting and that . . . otherwise you're be in trouble.'

boy (secondary)

'You come for interest and learning things . . . its important because you want to get it right and nothing wrong and you want to impress the teacher and things like that.'

boy (secondary)

Teachers are not the only people who would look askance at any lack of knowledge.

'If you didn't do the work you wouldn't have no education at all and you would just go around dumb and not be able to write when you leave school.'

boy (secondary)

'Helping you to learn because if you didn't have school and someone said 'What's one and one'; if you didn't have school you'd just stay at home all the time and get really bored.'

boy (secondary)

'Someone might make fun of you when you're older if you're not good at maths or something.'

girl (secondary)

Children, therefore, seem to think of the purpose of schooling is to drive them to learn, to avoid embarrassment and to gain employment. Whilst there is a sense that schools are there for the wider aspects of learning, even in this aspect is an element of social pressure, of the need to keep us with other people, the need not to let themselves down. School might be a complete world in itself, a source of friendship and a place where boredom can be overcome, but in terms of purpose it is firmly embedded in the overall social context. Children do not generally approach the curriculum as a delight in learning, for its own sake. They know they *have* to learn, and they know that their learning has an ultimate and practical purpose. Underlying the purpose is the sense that

'You've got to do it or you'll never learn.'

boy (secondary)

'So we don't get into trouble and all that.'

boy (secondary)

The purpose itself is quite clear.

'To get me a job when I get older.'

girl (secondary)

'Well, if you stick it hard at school so you'll get a good job.'

boy (secondary)

'If you don't learn things you won't get a job or anything when you're older. When I'm older I'd like to be a poet.'

girl (primary)

Whatever they might think of as a job, a good speller or a poet being equally far-fetched, it is the sense of the job that seems to them the ultimate purpose of schooling. At first children take for granted that this is what schools provide. Later they begin to be restless when it doesn't appear to do this for them. Subsequently, as White and Brockington[5] show, they resent the fact that schools didn't.

## Discussion

### (a) Teachers' and pupils' points of view

Teachers very rarely have an opportunity to discuss the purpose of schools with each other or with the children. The time is taken up with the tasks of teaching, keeping up with meeting constant demands on their attention in what is one of the most demanding jobs in the world. But children want to be reminded of the important questions. They do not want to reserve discussion of the purposes of life to the sub-culture of peer groups and discussions with friends, when the discovery of attitudes depends so much on shared mythologies. The evidence that emerges from these interviews suggests that children feel a need to talk about the purpose of what they are learning. They fall back on the idea of employability not only because they are pragmatic, or because this view is socially pervasive, or held by their parents, but also for want of anything better. One implication for teachers is that more attention should be paid to discussing with children what schools are for.

### (b) The relevance of the curriculum

Children's sense of the supreme importance of the job market has other implications for teachers. Some might think that the education system had done itself a grave disservice by gaining the reputation of being a supplier of qualifications, so that the successful ones will be amply rewarded. At a time of high and continuing unemployment, schools cannot depend on this assumption alone, even if very many of them would anyway want to. But the children do see schools in terms of competition, whether some deliberately drop out or whether others are determined to make a success of it, whether they fear failure or are confident of success. The question is whether teachers can make more use of these attitudes, not by being more narrow in their own interpretation of what takes place in school as in a mechanistic 'core' curriculum, but through exploring the purposes of the curriculum more deeply. At the moment there seems to be a clear dichotomy between children's and teacher's attitudes towards school, and this is a dichotomy that is of benefit to neither one nor the other.

At a time when the curriculum is under so much discussion, in terms of its relevance, its 'delivery' and in the different aspects of learning it is supposed to take into account, one would have expected the debate to include a reappraisal of the purpose of the curriculum. But such a debate seems to be lacking (although there are many assumptions made about the curriculum) perhaps because little attention is paid to the pupils' points of view. And yet what they see as the purpose of the curriculum is crucial. Teachers know now how important motivation is, and how children react differently to their favourite subject. Understanding why a subject is relevant is part of such interest, not at the level of whether it gives certain skills, or whether everything in it is attractive to a potential employer, but at the more profound level at which one sees *why* each part fits, how it relates to other subjects and how it can be of interest and use outside the confines of the classroom and the school. It is in this sense of purpose in the curriculum that children understand that schools have a relevance to the world outside.

Teachers would find that it repays the time spent on it, to discuss with the children the reasons for taking the different parts of the curriculum, for it is one way to convey the excitement of learning. But this does, of course, depend on the teacher herself knowing *why* the subject is relevant and how it will help the individual child. Such a question can too easily be begged.

### (c) Teachers and the community

Teachers are always in a somewhat ambiguous position, both resented and respected by their 'clients' and the community. One of the many difficulties for teachers at this time is the increasing pressure on them to involve the community in school, as if teachers had deliberately avoided doing so. Parents are to be involved in classrooms, and to dominate the governing bodies. Teachers are to be answerable to the community, in the abstract and as embodied in parents. This makes teachers feel potentially vulnerable. They see their professional autonomy undermined. They sense that their teaching methods are not understood. And they do not feel that the demands parents make take in the complexities of being concerned for large groups of children.

Just as one of the answers to motivating children is to talk about the purpose of the curriculum, one of the ways in which teachers and parents can overcome some of their mutual suspicions is by discussing the purposes of schooling. Knowing that children share their parents' assumptions should make it more necessary to try to achieve a common aim. Even when schools, as so many do, try to involve parents at every level, this is easier said than done. Talking about connections between school and what children think of as relevant is a good way of creating a sense of real understanding, especially as children are so clear about the purpose of school. To 'bend' its curriculum towards employment ('the world of work') is not enough. If teachers had the opportunity to talk about the curriculum more perhaps the 'clients' in the community and in the school would begin to look at school rather differently.

# References

1 Cullingford, C. (1985) *Parents, Teachers and Schools*. Robert Royce. London.
2 For details of the evidence on parents' and teachers' attitudes see especially, 'The idea of the School: The expectations of Parents, Teachers and Children', in Cullingford op.cit., pp.31–152.
3 This is not dissimilar from the Government view of the purposes of education as seen in a curriculum designed to give the school leaver qualifications; a view of the curriculum that is implicit in primary schools as well as secondary.
4 Children were equally consistent in their view that primary school is less serious than secondary school, and that it is there to prepare them for the really important next stage.
5 White, R. with Brockington, D. (1983) *Tales out of School: Consumers' views of British Education*. Routledge & Kegan Paul.
6 Children say that one of the main pleasures of school is meeting their friends.

# 3 'Memories are made of this'

## Some reflections on outdoor learning and recall

*Sue Waite*

Potential benefits for learning that the outdoors may hold have been brought into increased focus in the UK by the recent introduction of a manifesto for learning outside the classroom (DfES, *Learning outside the classroom: manifesto*, Nottingham, Department for Education and Skills, 2006). This article draws on two recent studies of outdoor learning practices—a survey of 334 practitioners with children aged between 2 and 11, and a case study in a primary school in the West of England. The survey asked practitioners about their memories of outdoor experiences, and in the case study, the children talk of what they remember of their learning outdoors. With reference to relevant literature, the article reflects on how the quality of outdoor experience may sustain and support engagement and memory.

## Introduction

Many adults, when asked about a significant childhood memory, recount an outdoor experience, often in considerable detail and charged with highly positive affect (Chawla, 1990). The manifesto for learning outside the classroom (DfES, 2006) claims that 'the use of places other than the classroom for teaching and learning' (*ibid.*, p. 3) contribute to education because:

> These, often the most memorable learning experiences, help us to make sense of the world around us by making links between feelings and learning. They stay with us into adulthood and affect our behaviour, lifestyle and work. They influence our values and the decisions we make. They allow us to transfer learning experienced outside to the classroom and vice versa.
>
> (DfES, 2006, p. 3)

This article focuses on learning in outdoor contexts within this broader field, locates some recent research on outdoor learning in settings for children aged between 2 and 11 within the literature on memory and outdoor learning, and theorises what, in outdoor contexts, makes experiences memorable.

## Memory

Memory is a complex subject with distinct phases: perception, encoding, consolidation and recall (Sharot *et al.*, 2004). Neurological research (Phelps, 2006) has shown that the hippocampus is involved in the capture of memories but that these are then transferred to the cortex over a period of months for long-term storage. This process involves making links with existing knowledge and making sense of the event in relation to previous experiences. Memories are not located in single areas of the brain and the strength of memories relies on the number of connections forged, which is why meaningful learning is more enduring and easier to remember than rote. Links are made to existing memories and knowledge, which allows retrieval of that memory from several perspectives. Events with an emotional component are perceived as more vivid than neutral ones because they arouse another area of the brain, the amygdala, at point of perception and in the subsequent recall of such events (Phelps, 2006). This activation might explain an increased subjective sense of recall of emotionally charged events, although Anderson *et al.* (2006) suggest that systemic arousal may also be necessary.

Most research into emotion and memory has focused on the effect of negative emotions and their association with an apparent narrowing of attention, whereby peripheral details may not be remembered as accurately as the main event (Carver, 2003). This could have an adaptive purpose in highlighting salient features to avoid future danger, but in many modern situations, the effect of anxiety or negative affect is rather to impede learning (Shors, 2004). Positive emotion, on the other hand, is thought to have an opposite effect, broadening our attention so that more is noticed (Carver, 2003). It is also likely to increase our memory for participation of activities we have enjoyed (Bixler *et al.*, 2002).

Some experimental research, however, casts doubt on whether the accuracy of recall is better with emotional events, although the subjective sense of recall and its elaboration is often greater (Phelps, 2006). Our understanding of how perception works and our own epistemology affect how such studies might be interpreted. Experience may be seen as objective to be recorded or as subjective as perceived and constructed. A constructivist view also has implications for the nature of memory as re-construction rather than re-presentation of previously constructed meaning (Thompson *et al.*, 1996). In this sense, a mixture of imagination and memory is no less meaningful than an 'accurate' recollection of events as our experience of events is necessarily fluid and subject to re-interpretation in different contexts and at different times. Although some researchers (Borrie & Roggenbuck, 1995) express concern that reconstructive processes pose problems for valid and reliable evaluation of outdoor experiences, it could equally be argued that it is precisely these evolving understandings which make memories and learning important and influential for our present and future actions (Neisser, 1988). Furthermore, the 'new' memories are not necessarily purely cognitive 'post-hoc rationalizations' (Borrie & Roggenbuck, 1995, p. 2) but are also likely to involve post-hoc affective response, signalling continuing cognitive and emotional 'relevance' for individuals (Tarrant, 1996). Wang and Conway (2004) further suggest in their comparative study of autobiographical memories of Chinese and American individuals that there are strong socio-cultural influences on what is remembered.

Positive emotions may tend to reinforce our propensity to repeat experiences through a form of conditioning response (Turley, 2001; Bixler *et al.*, 2002) and may therefore act as a motivation for lifelong learning. Carver (2003) suggests that positive emotions offer feedback on our satisfactory performance, which increases our capacity to pay attention to any deficiencies or other opportunities in situations; thus providing another kind of motivation for learning. Enjoyment may therefore tend to 'spread' to other features associated with the source of positive affect and increase engagement.

## Outdoor learning

How then does learning outside the classroom fit into this relationship between positive affect and memory? There is a substantial literature about how the outdoors provides 'good memories' (Chawla, 1990; Berryman, 2000; Elliott & Davis, 2004), whether 'good' because they promote a sense of well being or 'good' because they are vivid and enduring (Knapp & Benton, 2006). In fact, it is suggested that these two aspects are related in that positive emotions contribute to enduring memories (Carver, 2003). However, Bixler *et al.* (2002) argue that much research fails to explain what it is in childhood outdoor experiences that might influence later adult behaviour (Ewert *et al.*, 2005). Social filtering of childhood play through the values and interpretations of parents and peers, for example, may also be influential (Berryman, 2000) and modify memory. Previous research suggests that the experiential nature of outdoor learning offers authenticity; opportunities for exploration and play; autonomy; freedom; creativity; novelty; incidental learning; enjoyment; and competency in social contexts (Beard & Wilson, 2002; Bixler *et al.*, 2002). Exploratory play and broader attention, allowing more incidental learning and creativity, appear to be supported by positive affect (Fredrickson, 1998). But it is not clear what amongst these qualities endure and may serve to influence later behaviour. Francis (1995) suggests it is the commonalities in memories of childhood gardens which point to what is important in making them significant through time, offering clues as to what it is in the outdoors which (a) makes it valued and (b) makes it an effective context for learning.

In this article, I report some commonalities in adult memories of outdoor experiences. I then turn to children's views on how they think the outdoors has helped them to learn; what features outside the classroom appear to be valued by children. In comparing these, features which may be important for successful outdoor learning are theorised.

## Research context

In 2005, the local Early Years Childcare Development Partnership funded a study of settings within Devon to find out what outdoor learning was happening in them and what aspirations staff had for improving their outdoor learning provision (Waite *et al.*, 2006a). Key issues in outdoor learning provision (Rickinson *et al.*, 2004; Dillon *et al.*, 2005; McKendrick, 2005) formed the basis for two questionnaires designed for settings with children aged 2–5 or 6–11 and distributed to 1933 early years' settings, primary schools and youth service providers in Devon, including childminders, private nurseries, pre-school and play groups, children centres, schools and out-of-school clubs. Areas of enquiry included practitioners' values and attitudes towards education outdoors, their current outdoor provision and practice and obstacles to further development to which they might aspire.

We attempted to achieve a balance between making the questionnaire short and easy to complete and obtaining rich qualitative data. However, the eventual length of the questionnaire (seven or eight sides of A4) may have depressed the number returned. Three hundred and thirty-four responses were received, an overall return rate of 17%. However, return rates for pre-schools and primary schools were somewhat higher at 26% and 28%. Qualitative software, N6, was used for exploration of the data. A framework for their responses to the question: 'Please describe in detail a memory you have from your childhood of a significant experience in an outdoor setting? Include details such as the type of environment, the level of enjoyment, things you learnt etc.' was developed by three researchers reading the comments and identifying seven emergent themes:

- social aspects—others included in the memory
- natural contexts—the environment in which the memory was formed
- active investigation—playful learning
- adventure/risk/challenge—exciting and risky activities
- space/freedom—sense of autonomy
- creativity—self-directed outcomes
- sensory experiences—multi-sensory appeal.

Comments were then coded according to these themes.

In addition to this survey, five case studies of a childminder, pre-school, private nursery, foundation stage and primary school were chosen from responses as exemplifying interest in and developing practice in outdoor learning (Waite *et al.*, 2006b). Each case study involved three visits for observations, the collection of documentary and photographic evidence, and interviews with key members of staff and children. Photographs that the children and researcher had taken were used as stimuli in focus groups held with 18 children at the primary school. These children aged between 8 and 11 contributed their views about what they retain from their outdoor learning and the values they place upon it. These were transcribed in full. Topics that were reiterated were deemed important for the children.

## The nature of memories reported by adults

Two hundred and forty-one (72%) of the 334 respondents to the survey shared memories of the outdoors. Table 1 shows sub-groups within four emergent

*Table 1*   Emergent themes in adult memories of outdoor experiences

| Theme | Theme indicators | Number of times reported |
|---|---|---|
| Social aspects | Friends | 46 |
| | Siblings | 32 |
| | More experienced person | 43 |
| | | (121) |
| Outdoor contexts | Woodland/trees | 50 |
| | Garden | 32 |
| | Water | 31 |
| | Farm | 27 |
| | Grassland | 25 |
| | Beach | 16 |
| | Park | 16 |
| | Countryside | 15 |
| | School grounds | 15 |
| | Waste ground | 6 |
| | Mountains | 2 |
| | | (235) |
| Active investigation | Playing | 48 |
| | Animals | 36 |
| | Plants | 8 |
| | Collecting | 8 |
| | | (100) |
| Adventure, risk and challenge | Exploring | 46 |
| | Tree climbing | 36 |
| | Camping | 12 |
| | Lighting fires | 11 |
| | Riding bikes | 11 |
| | Swimming | 11 |
| | Hiding | 8 |
| | | (135) |

Memories could be coded within several themes. As these examples show, there are complex and overlapping influences.

themes, which had 100 or more incidences in reported memories. Three other themes appeared less frequently: 'creativity' (73), 'sensory experiences' (51) and 'space and freedom' (42).

Of all the memories shared, only six reported a negative experience, 40 were neutral and 195 signalled positive affect. This suggests that, in line with previous research (Chawla, 1990; Elliott & Davis, 2004), memories of the outdoors are generally positive. Some memories are quoted in full to exemplify the interrelated nature of features that appeared to contribute to vivid recall and positive affect.

### Social aspects

While 123 responses did not explicitly detail others, many of these implied social involvement by the use of 'we'. There were 121 responses where 'others' were specified.

> My childhood was spent in the greater London area. I loved playing in the allotments with my siblings and neighbours. There were trees to climb and piles of wood and corrugated aluminium to make dens. There were seven children in our streets and our games continued on a casual basis for several weeks.

This memory conveys a sense of self-direction and social facilitation in wasteland areas (Pyle, 2002). Seventy-eight memories explicitly included references to peers and 43 mentioned adults.

> I used to spend a lot of time walking with my grandfather in the local area. He had grown up there as a boy and enjoyed being outdoors, pointing out wildlife, types of plants and trees etc. My local school was opposite a park which we used for nature walks and observations as well as sports practice. As a result I still seek to identify flora and fauna.

This sort of informal learning in the presence of a more experienced adult was often mentioned. Only six memories were about being on their own, and 15 emphasised that no adults were present. The vast majority of outdoor memories included a social aspect (Berryman, 2000). This is somewhat at odds with reported American cultural norms for autobiographical memories, which Wang and Conway (2004) found tended to be personal and autonomous in comparison to more socially positioned memories from Chinese respondents. A further point of interest is that 32 of the peer references were about siblings, which coupled with 35 references to older relations, including parents and grandparents, make family a strong feature of these memories. This influence has been relatively little considered (Berryman, 2000; Jeffrey & Woods, 2003; Ewert *et al.*, 2005) and it raises the question as to whether children today are building similarly rich memories of outdoor experiences within a family context (Turley, 2001)?

### Outdoor contexts

Natural contexts predominate in the adult memories, with wooded areas and trees being the most commonly reported (50). This prevalence of woodland is interesting as the Forest School movement[1] in some areas of Britain is developing regular access for children to woodland, claiming that it has cognitive and personal, social and health benefits (O'Brien and Murray, 2006; Waite & Davis, 2007). It may indicate that woodland has special qualities (Henwood & Pidgeon, 2001), which make it an effective learning environment. Some of the most commonly reported activities such as climbing trees and den building rely on trees and brush.

> At age of 8 my primary school class went on a nature walk on a piece of common land and woods. We were allowed to roam and collect items. The teacher named the items and gave details of the natural habitat etc. I still remember the names of plants we looked at even though that was 59 years ago!

Natural experiences appear to have produced long-lasting learning. Gardens (32) and farms (27) were also mentioned, suggesting that more remote locations are not necessary to create memorable outdoor experiences.

### Active investigation

Forty-eight memories were about playing, often including shared experience and autonomy (Waite & Davis, 2007). Many of the memories of active investigation featured animals (36), from worms to horses.

> Caravan holidays in west Wales, small site with no onsite entertainment so I spent many happy hours catching frogs, playing ball games, picking apples, blackberries. I often went to the beach, rock pool rambles with my brother and parents. I loved looking at nature, freedom to wander around the local fields. I learnt to love wildlife, family life and time to explore things for myself with no adult interruption.

This suggests that tangible contact rather than rarity may be important for memorability. Experience of real-life creatures seemed to have fostered learning about them. This has implications for environmental learning and science in schools as such contact appears to support engagement.

### Adventure, risk and challenge

Exploration (46) was the predominant sub-theme amongst those memories about challenge (135).

> Going for a walk up the local mountain, which we lived at the foot of, with my mates for the first time with no adults. It was a real adventure being able to explore with no-one telling you what to do. We stopped for a picnic in a very small old quarry which had grown over, which was just below the summit. 5/5 for enjoyment. The feeling of freedom was immense. This mountain is very special to me, the bonding with nature was strong and it often occurred in my dreams as a safe place.

Overcoming difficulty seems to confer more status to the activity. As another respondent noted:

> I grew up in the suburbs of Birmingham where there was still a great deal of 'wild areas'. We made our own games uncluttered by adult interventions. It is this feeling of excitement and risk taking I am trying to replicate in a structured environment.

Ewert *et al.* (2006) argue that early life experiences may have lasting effects on environmental activism. It would seem that positive outdoor experiences may influence teachers' pedagogical approaches (Bixler *et al.*, 2002). Excitement and enjoyment peppered most of the memories.

Extended play, social networking and invention were often mentioned. In den building activities (36), incidental learning appeared to occur. In one example, a shared language was created to maintain mystery. This seems to be linked to autonomy and exploratory learning not mediated by adults (Korpela *et al.*, 2002).

## Children's perception of what helps them learn in the outdoors

Children were asked to recall occasions when they had learnt outside, supported by photographs taken around the school site.

### *Active investigation*

Pupils aged about eight reflected on a geography trip undertaken in the previous year when they went around Barnstaple drawing pictures.

> Umm, because we could see what we were trying to think about. We could see the whole wide world and learn things like what might be in the future if something falls down or something and what it was like in the olden days because sometimes if you read it from a book, well I don't believe it but when you actually see it. Seeing is believing sort of thing.

> You also learn about being an adult.

> Yeah, so you know what's going to happen so you won't be scared of it happening.

This memory suggests that real-life experiences help to position their learning within a past, present and future context (Berryman, 2000). Incidental learning about becoming an adult or being responsible for oneself was also mentioned (Bixler *et al.*, 2002). The pivotal position of experience in a continuum of time, relating it to past events and to the future, was acknowledged for learning and to gain confidence as an adult.

*Multi-sensory experience*

Talking about a trip to a sculpture garden, children in the case study school suggested the three dimensional aspect of real life is crucial; a valuing of authenticity of experience.

> And that helps us learn, I can't remember but we have to make some sculptures I think in one class, we made sculptures and it helped us get the shapes right.

> If you just have pictures you don't think . . .

> If you have seen it, it might be like that or like that if you see it with just two faces.

*Attention to detail*

When prompted for what it was about the memories that they thought helped their learning, children aged 10 and 11 in the focus group suggested:

> Well, inside, like if you just hear of something you don't really know and like in reception you have never heard of tadpoles before and a teacher tells you about them, you wouldn't be able to see them for yourself. So we are quite lucky to have our own pond because if they tell us about them and we have never seen them, it is quite interesting to see them.

> Yeah and you can just go out and look I found one!

> You believe then.

This description of how they remembered the trip to the school pond had reinforced their learning was mirrored by an observation of a similar lesson taking place during the case study (Waite & Rea, 2007). The close attention given and level of engagement demonstrated meant that the features of frogspawn and other growing things were discovered, described and formed the basis for hypotheses, a process also of active investigation. Carver (2003) found a positive emotional association seemed to support noticing fine details and recall. Their comments also point to the value that they place on authenticity of outdoor experiences.

> I reckon it makes you understand more, it makes you . . . like some things you can't exactly go out and say there is a subtraction over there but some things when you look at stuff, it makes you look at it and perhaps describe it and try to remember it.

This child distinguished between some learning being more appropriate for experiential activities and supporting their memory.

## Enjoyment

In another child's memory from six years ago, positive feelings engendered by being outdoors or by the novelty of location appear to spill over into other aspects of learning, so the performance of a play in a natural amphitheatre conferred value despite some discomfort of feeling cold. Perhaps it is these other elements, although peripheral to the central experience, the play, which are perceived and registered emotionally at the time and add to its memorability (Phelps, 2006).

> I remember when we were only 5, the year somethings did a little play and we went to the wormy thing [others chant, wormy, wormy]

> I: Where is it?

> In the woodland. And they did a little play and I loved that. They did this wonderful play. It was so cool, that play. It was cold as well, you were shivering but it was really good.

## Social and emotional experience

Children aged 9 or 10, who had recently returned from a residential visit to a farm, also shared their views. Their tales were full of sensory and emotional details: mud, fear and arguments. In describing the residential aspect of their visit, it was clear that they had had the opportunity to air many personal and social issues.

> In our dorm we didn't get on very well, because everybody was arguing.

> They ran through the door and were screaming.

> And Miss E, every night she told us off.

> It wasn't all of us though.

> I: So what did you do about not getting on?

> We were arguing from the beginning until the end and then right at the unnecessary point when we were going home, we got friendly with each other.

Clearly, negative emotions might also contribute to the learning process (Phelps, 2006). The experience had been harrowing at times but problems had been resolved and the children were unanimous in their determination that they would repeat the experience. This accords with some adult memories, where pleasure lay in recollection rather than the experience at the time and suggests challenge was also valued by the children.

They also talked graphically about their witnessing the birth of lambs.

> Well the afterbirth, this little liquid bag came out and the umbilical cord was still attached and when the baby was born, he had to put this special thing on to make sure it was disinfected because when the umbilical cord snaps, it just dangles anywhere and this special liquid stuff was put on to stop it getting infected and after the lamb was born all the mother does is lick off, lick it.

> I: How soon did the lamb get up on its feet?

> About five minutes later.

> When the baby was born, there was this lamb where the head came out first and the feet are meant to come out not the head first, so he had to kind of rescue it.

> I: Really, I never knew that, that the feet came out first.

> They come out like they're diving.

The detail given and naming of parts indicate that this experience had been very effective for learning (Williams & Harvey, 2001). Both negative and positive emotional events were reported very vividly suggesting that detail had been noted and recalled. The information acquired first hand had been assiduously absorbed (Carver, 2003).

## Challenge

Another story, amongst several about things that frightened them, suggests that the challenge of the outdoors had meant facing and overcoming fears, increasing the children's sense of competence and confidence as well as developing practical thinking and reasoning skills (Waite & Davis, 2007).

> B was scared of the donkeys at first. She was scared if she stepped behind them too close they would kick. But actually there's a fact that if you stand really close to their rear they don't have the strength to stretch their leg and kick you, so they can't kick you. They can't really move their leg, so you don't get kicked. But if you stand far away, they will kick but it won't hit you. But if you are stood not too far away and not too near, they will swing their legs and kick you.

## A comparison of adult and children's memories

Authenticity, active investigation and challenge appeared important aspects of their memories for children in all the focus groups. For the adults, authenticity in contrast to classroom learning was not highlighted as there were few references to school-based outdoor learning, but 'real life' permeated their outdoor memories.

Challenge was predominant in the residential experience; the children appeared to have a strong sense of achievement, providing a motivation for future residential experiences. This positive view could be attributed to the experience being more recent, but this theory would not account for the strongly emotional content of the distant adult memories collected. Many of these shared positive emotional content with children's reports returning from their residential visit. This might indicate that alternative pedagogy employed in some outdoor settings is particularly powerful for learning (Davis *et al.*, 2006). Both the residential group and adults emphasise social influences (Berryman, 2000) in their stories, but these are less evident in on-site accounts.

Adult and residential trip memories also tend to show a playfulness in the way activities are conducted, which may also contribute to positive affect. This quality was not so apparent in the descriptions of outdoor learning from the other two focus groups. Despite reported enjoyment of outdoor learning, their accounts do not convey the same high level of engagement, perhaps suggesting that exploration and play should be utilised more to facilitate learning in outdoor curricular activities. Enjoyment activates the amygdala and raises levels of arousal, providing more links for recall (Phelps, 2006). In sum, many of the qualities suggested by Bixler *et al.* (2002), Berryman (2000) and Carver (2003) have also been observed in the memories reported in this study. A further outcome appears to be the affirmation of social bonds in family and community (Turley, 2001; Jeffrey & Woods, 2003). The multiple aspects of each memory illustrate rich contextualisation and different channels for recall of memories. The many neural links formed make the memories vivid and enduring (Phelps, 2006). However, more evidence is needed about how this may make a contribution to academic achievement; in line with Bixler *et al.* (2002), peripheral details were often as vivid as any central learning point.

Only outdoor memories were elicited so we cannot comment on whether these are qualitatively different from memories of indoor play. However, a comparison of the children's discussion about outdoor learning within the school grounds and those returning from the residential visit is interesting. It appears that children's talk of on-site activities uses school-based discourse; cognitive aspects are emphasised more than the sensory and emotional ones (Waite & Davis, 2007). However, the location of interviews in school and focus on outdoor *learning* rather than *experiences* may have led them to use school discourse and emphasise informal learning less than the adults. Further research using identical frames of references would help to disentangle this anomaly.

# Conclusion

While this small-scale study supports the view that memory for outdoor experiences does endure and is associated with positive affect for staff and children, it makes no claims for being representative. It did not seek comparison with the relative durability or lucidity of class-based learning, so provides no evidence of 'better' memory for learning outdoors. However, it points to some interesting areas for further research in the area of memory and outdoor learning. Many adult memories of the outdoors are detailed but global, perhaps indicating that peripheral factors (Carver, 2003) and incidental learning (Bixler *et al.*, 2002) are salient. In a similar fashion, children sometimes reported that outdoor learning was about 'art' if it involved drawing, regardless of the intended curriculum focus of the experience. If current dominant pedagogical principles that learning objectives and outcomes should be made explicit (DfES, 2004) are accepted, then arguably, links to the learning that it is intended to support with observational skills should be made plain. However, far more of the adult memories are concerned with informal learning and this itself may have significant implications for the importance of the use of alternative pedagogies within outdoor learning to make the most of its potential for self-directed learning. Care may need to be taken to retain the autonomy and interest-led learning which seems highly valued in these memories. Children's accounts highlight their appreciation of authenticity in learning outside the classroom, which may indicate that opportunities to incorporate such 'seeing is believing' more widely into the curriculum would be welcomed. Challenge and overcoming difficulty also appear important factors for the design of memorable outdoor learning experiences. Enjoyment and the positive outdoor memories so created appear to engender enthusiasm for repeating such experiences, a powerful motivation and potentially lifelong influence.

# Acknowledgements

I would like to thank the Devon Early Years Childcare Development Partnership for the funding which made our research possible and my co-researchers, Bernie Davis and Kylie Brown.

# Note

1 *Forest School*, as it has been developed in England from a Danish model of Forest kindergarten, is a particular kind of educational programme that takes place in the outdoors, preferably in a natural wooded area. It is characterised by positive relationships, achievable tasks and fun. It usually takes place in one session per week over a 6–10-week programme. The Forest School principles include building on an individual's innate motivation and positive attitude to learning, offering them opportunities to take risks and make choices and initiate learning for themselves.

# References

Anderson, A. K., Yamaguchi, Y., Grabski, W. & Lacka, D. (2006) Emotional memories are not all created equal: evidence for selective memory enhancement, *Learning and Memory*, 13(6), 711–718.

Beard, C. & Wilson, J. P. (2002) *The power of experiential learning: a handbook for trainers and educators* (London, Kogan Page).

Berryman, T. (2000) Looking at children's relationships with nature from a developmental perspective: towards an appropriate curriculum, in: P. J. Fonts & M. Gomes, *Environmental Education and the Contemporary World, Proceedings of the International Congress Environmental Education and the Contemporary World*, 19–20 October 2000 (Lisbon, Instituto de Inovacao Educacional).

Bixler, R. D., Floyd, M. F. & Hammitt, W. E. (2002) Environmental socialization: quantitative tests of the childhood play hypothesis, *Environment and Behaviour*, 34(6), 795–818.

Borrie, W. T. & Roggenbuck, J. W. (1995) *The use of verbal reports in outdoor recreation research: review, recommendations, and new directions*, paper presented at *Fourth International Outdoor Recreation and Tourism Trends Symposium and the 1995 National Recreation Resource Planning Conference*, St. Paul, Minnesota, 14–17 May 1995. Available online at: http://www. forestry.umt.edu/personnel/faculty/borrie/papers/Trends/(accessed 15 January 2007).

Carver, C. S. (2003) Pleasure as a sign you can attend to something else: placing positive feelings within a general model of affect, *Cognition and Emotion*, 17(2), 241–261. Available online at: http://www.tandf.co.uk/journals/pp02699931.html (accessed 12 November 2006).

Chawla, L. (1990) Ecstatic places, *Children's Environments Quarterly*, 7(4), 18–23.

Davis, B., Rea, T. & Waite, S. (2006) The special nature of the outdoors: its contribution to the education of children aged 3–11, *Australian Journal of Outdoor Education*, 10(2), 3–12.

DfES (2004) Excellence and enjoyment: learning and teaching in the primary years: assessment for learning (Nottingham, Department for Education and Skills).

DfES (2006) *Learning outside the classroom: manifesto* (Nottingham, Department for Education and Skills).

Dillon, J., Morris, M., O'Donnell, L., Reid, A., Rickinson, M. & Scott, W. (2005) *Engaging and learning with the outdoors*. Report of the Outdoor classroom in a Rural Context Action Research Project (Slough, NFER).

Elliott, S. & Davis, J. (2004) Mud pies and daisy chains: connecting young children and nature, *Every Child*, 10(4), 4–5. Available online at: www.earlychildhoodaustralia.org.au (accessed 12 November 2006).

Ewert, A., Place, G. & Sibthorp, J. (2005) Early-life outdoor experiences and an individual's environmental attitudes, *Leisure Sciences*, 27(3), 225–239.

Francis, M. (1995) Childhood's garden: memory and meaning of gardens, *Children's Environments*, 12(2), 1–16. Available online at: http://www.colorado.edu/journals/cye/(accessed 27 November 2006).

Fredrickson, B. L. (1998) What good are positive emotions?, *Review of General Psychology*, 2(3), 300–319.

Henwood, K. & Pidgeon, N. (2001) Talk about woods and trees: Threat of urbanization, stability and biodiversity, *Journal of Environmental Psychology*, 21(2), 125–147.

Jeffery, B. & Woods, P. (2003) *The Creative School: a framework for success, quality and effectiveness* (London, RoutledgeFalmer).

Knapp, D. & Benton, G. M. (2006) Episodic and semantic memories of a residential environmental program, *Environmental Education Research*, 12(2), 165–177.

Korpela, K., Kytta, M. & Hartig, T. (2002) Restorative experience, self-regulation and children's place preferences, *Journal of Environmental Psychology*, 22(4), 387–398.

McKendrick, J. H. (2005) *School grounds in Scotland research report* (Edinburgh, sportscotland) Available on line at: http://www.sportscotland.org.uk/Channel Navigation/Resource+Library/Publications/School+Grounds+in+Scotland.htm (accessed 17 July 2006).

Neisser, U. (1988) Five kinds of self-knowledge, *Philosophical Psychology*, 1(1), 35–59.

O'Brien, L. & Murray, R. (2005) *A marvellous opportunity for children to learn: a participatory evaluation of Forest School in England and Wales* (Farnham, Forest Research).

Phelps, E. A. (2006) Emotion and cognition: insights from studies of the human amygdala, *Annual Review of Psychology*, 57(1), 27–53.

Pyle, R. M. (2002) Eden in a vacant lot: special places, spaces, and kids in the neighborhood of life, in: P. H. Kahn & S. R. Kellert (Eds) *Children and nature: psychological, sociocultural and evolutionary investigations* (London, MIT), 305–328.

Rickinson, M., Dillon, J., Teamey, K., Morris, M., Choi, M. Y., Sanders, D. & Benefield, P. (2004) *A review of research on outdoor learning* (Shrewsbury, Fields Study Council).

Sharot, T., Delgado, M. & Phelps, E. A. (2004) How emotion enhances the feeling of remembering, *Nature Neuroscience*, 7(12), 1376–1380.

Shors, T. J. (2004) Learning during stressful times, *Learning and Memory*, 11(2), 137–144.

Tarrant, M. A. (1996) Attending to past outdoor recreation experiences: symptom reporting and changes in affect, *Journal of Leisure Research*, 28(1), 1–17.

Thompson, C. P., Skowronski, J. J., Larsen, S. F. & Betz, A. L. (1996) *Autobiographical memory: remembering what and remembering when* (Mahwah, NJ, Lawrence Erlbaum).

Turley, S. K. (2001) Children and demand for recreational experiences: the case of zoos, *Leisure Studies*, 20(1), 1–18.

Waite, S. & Davis, B. (2007) The contribution of free play and structured activities in Forest School to learning beyond cognition: an English case, in: B. Ravn & N. Kryger (Eds) *Learning beyond cognition* (Copenhagen, Danish University of Copenhagen).

Waite, S., Davis, B. & Brown, K. (2006a) *Current practice and aspirations for outdoor learning for 2–11 year olds in Devon*, July, report for funding body EYDCP (zero14plus) and participants.

Waite, S., Davis, B. & Brown, K. (2006b) *Five stories of outdoor learning from settings for 2–11 year olds in Devon*, July, report for funding body EYDCP (zero14plus) and participants.

Waite, S. & Rea, T. (2007) Enjoying teaching and learning outside the classroom, in: D. Hayes, *Joyful teaching and learning in the primary school* (Exeter, Learning Matters).

Wang, Q. & Conway, M. A. (2004) The stories we keep: autobiographical memory in American and Chinese middle aged adults, *Journal of Personality*, 72(5), 911–938.

Williams, K. & Harvey, D. (2001) Transcendent experience in forest environments, *Journal of Environmental Psychology*, 21(3), 249–260.

# 4   It is approaching breakfast and this is a campervan

## Weather, drawings and grandparenting in North-West England

*Tom Phillips*

An account is given of a series of drawings done by two boys (four and six years old) while staying with their grandparents. These are considered within a child development framework emphasising the place of context and the sociocultural theory of Wertsch. Context is explicated through looking at how household, local culture, mediated action and children's drawings can be connected. Links are made with the Early Years Foundation Stage and the championing of parent–teacher links within effective practice. Grandparenting is partly located within the generativity–stagnation arguments of Erikson in adult development.

**Keywords:** socio-cultural theory; contextualism; children's drawings; grand-parenting; household; mediated action; generativity; stagnation; meaning making

## Introduction

There are four good and equal reasons why this study was submitted to a journal. Firstly, there was my wife and I having two grandsons come to stay and be part of our household over two cold spring days in 2008, when some interesting early years phenomena emerged. Secondly, I am involved in teaching childhood studies and human development within undergraduate psychology and regularly supervise projects involving child study within natural environments. Thirdly, some data had presented itself featuring cultural practices of a grandparent's household. Fourthly, after an initial draft of this paper was presented to the boys, their parents and my wife, they agreed that I would have their support in seeking journal publication.

In what follows, 'I' refers to author, 'our' to author and Janet Phillips as grandparents; the boys are W (six years) and J (four years). My thanks to the boys, their parents, Catriona and Tony, and Janet for all their help in compiling this report.

## Conceptual point of departure

Key to these experiences becoming a study was my own special interest in what Mitchell (2002) identifies as contextualism, one of what she regards as the three basic views developmental psychology takes of the essential nature of humans.[1] In the mechanistic view, structures and functions are described, emphasised and explicated within a causal model of happenings. In the organismic view, it is within an organism's opening out, adapting and surviving within living systems that development articulates itself. The first of these creates its claims from among experimental and correlational data with Bandura a worthy exponent. The second in contrast creates its claims from observing patterns of adaptations of mind to ostensible intellectual problems with oneself and others and where Piaget excels. But in the view of contextualism, it is around the actions taken by maturing humans in describeable social and cultural contexts where explanations are sought about development. This perspective, deriving from the work of Vygotsky in the 1930s is today best illustrated in the socio-cultural and activity theory literature. At the heart of this theory is the simple idea that when confronted by a social situation:

> . . . human beings themselves create stimuli that determine their own reactions and are used as means for mastering their own behaviour. Human beings determine their behaviour with the help of artificial stimulus means. Free human activity is not the same as spontaneous behaviour of an animal. The former presupposes behaviour that is mastered and controlled. This is possible only by means of artificial stimuli, signs, and artifacts. Human freedom can exist only in the world of artificial things, in the sphere of mediated, interindividual activity.
>
> (Lektorsky 1999)

When researching in this perspective, the emphasis is on following and describing deliberative actions featuring the involvement of an individual making use of artefacts and which may be more properly described as mediated action or the activity of person-with-mediator. One influential promoter of this approach is Wertsch (1991, 8) who emphasises a wider notion of what is really being observed:

> When action is given analytic priority, human beings are viewed as coming into contact with, and creating, their surroundings as well as themselves through the actions in which they engage.

Prime data for this approach can come from any situation where a young person is engaging in actions of their own choosing, much of which will be away from schools or experimental set-ups or Piagetian type interview scenarios which characterise work in the other two perspectives. Such situations can arise very easily when a child is in a familiar setting such as being with grandparents, a context that is now being increasingly documented (Smyth 2005). Quantitative research has for some time been clarifying patterns in some specific areas here like custodial care or special needs (Tinsley and Parke 1984). Less common have been qualitative studies offering more immediate accounts of household activities directly involving grandchildren. It was these considerations along with an interest in culture and ethnography that drew me into drafting out an account of one area of these boys' activities that I felt was worth documenting. This involved taking some drawings J and W had done at this time and exploring their emergence within our everyday household setting and utilising some of these notions of mediated action. Before describing the drawings it may be worth expanding a little on why this set of circumstances and loose theoretical interests seemed promising.

Why drawings? The most immediate answer to this is that what I saw was not what any reading of the literature on children's drawing had prepared me for. This for the most part features the mechanistic and the organismic views and very little that drew attention to discovering the power of one of humankind's oldest cultural tools, mark making devices as used in depiction tasks and meaning making techniques. To see a child close up engaging in drawing as an action freely entered into, and following whatever emerged from this set me off thinking along lines Wertsch and others had been emphasising where the main point of interest was in how, through drawing, a child may be creating, as Wertsch suggested, 'a little bit of themselves'. Making a drawing of some object, event or living thing is a universal 'meaning making' human activity (Wright 2007), particularly as actions freely entered into and serving some purpose for the drawer. Developmental research on drawings is extensive and has given rise to some very interesting theories about perception, understanding, communication, psycho-motor skills, feedback and semiotic configuring and colouring, etc. Yet in the socio-cultural literature it has only a slight presence.

Why culture? While schools work to prescribed curricula, and hence what a child learns has already been largely chosen for them, within a family learning can be more enigmatic as local and regional culture is encountered as well as people's experiences of these. Here they can make discoveries, develop interests, produce responses and experience learning in a less formal way. A second reason such artefacts are treated as developmentally significant is that they help us appreciate how local culture can be encountered at this early age in a way that bears some resemblance with Geertz's (1973) celebrated notion that humans are animals 'suspended in webs of significance' which they themselves have spun, and where the analysis of it is not 'an experimental science in search of law but an interpretive one in search of meaning'.

And why action? It may sound a little strange to focus on an early years child's actions rather than the more typical research metrics of behaviour, cognition or impulse. The reason is that in socio-cultural theory, maturing is very much followed through a developing mind, where this is understood as emerging through sociogenesis, or as an outside-in dynamic as caught in Vygotsky's (1981b) famous statement:

> Any function in the child's cultural development appears twice, or on two planes. First it appears on the social plane, and then on the psychological plane. First it appears between people as an interpsychological category, and then within the child as an intrapsychological category.
>
> (163)

So actions engaged in lead to notions of these same actions becoming internalised in some way, and henceforth existing as an inferred mindfulness behind further repeats of similar actions. Some researchers like Rogoff (1990) or Lave and Wenger (1991) do not go as far as this, content instead to emphasise participation as sufficient evidence of maturing. For educationalists this framework has perhaps most relevance in how it raises issues about what constitutes the functional and nominal stimuli in any early years setting. As mentioned above, the socio-cultural perspective is very much intent on an active child creating their own functional stimuli rather than a passive child responding to what the teacher may create for them as an assumed functional stimuli but which may remain a nominal stimuli. In technical terms the child, in creating his or her own functional stimuli, is exemplifying Vygotsky's second signal system through which it becomes possible to follow activities in terms of multi-dimensioned action of the child's own construing rather than single dimensioned behaviour. As Kozulin (2000) shows, mediators are centrally involved in this through their apprehended utility of amplifying the powers of the individual, whether through tools (pen), semiotics (language) or supportive other (helper). What will be observed here, then, is action not in its full open philosophical sense but in the more restricted sense of mediated action identified by Wertsch (1998) that emerges from a child active in a setting with access to mediators to be found in this household.

Why household? This very inclusive term is favoured here because of its ability to suggest a background that brings together a physical setting, a location for activities with histories and involving limited participants known fully to each other as persons with personalities having both settled and emergent features. More specifically, household allows one to identify, after Fiese (2006), its two central active features of routines and rituals. Routines will refer to the regular ordered ways the work of the household is enabled and where communications are mainly instrumental, commitments are perfunctory and continuities are self evident. Meals, washing, cleaning and maintenance would be at the core of most routines. Rituals emerge more as activities reflecting the household group existing in a wider social and cultural world and may take the form of talk or argument or evaluative reflections of members' current, future and past experiences. Communication in these will be more expressive and symbolic, commitment reflecting enduring preferences and feelings, while continuities in these centre on meanings often stretching across generations. In particular, these two add considerably to our sense of how socio-cultural theory can illuminate development in the contextualist sense.

## Setting for study

Two areas of background are important to be clear about.

### *The household*

At the back of all this is an interest in understanding how our household has changed from empty nest to one increasingly predicated around diminishing involvement in work. A feature we both accept is that ours is a household good at maintaining what systems theory (Von Bertalanffy 1971) characterises as stable states. We had become predictable, creatures of habit and with a ready stock of devices to minimise openness to the wider world. The grandchildren challenged this in many ways and gradually over time the household has managed to adapt reasonably flexibly, though stable states are largely returned to each time they leave. If we are to fully analyse the situation then we would accept that the major dynamic coming into our lives now is the one identified by Erikson (1959) involving forces of stagnation vying with forces of generativity. This has also been recognised as determining how grandparenthoods can function as done by Thiele and Whelan (2006).

### *The permitting circumstances*

Our daughter, husband and their two boys, six and four, live three miles away and it has become a regular pattern for the latter to visit and stay over as part of the regular coming and going that can grow up between kin. The boys are our most frequent visitors and their knowledge of our household dates back to their earliest times. As the 'big jobs' of our working lives get replaced by less big ones we have more free time now to host visits during week days. The occasion for this visit was the pre-Easter school break of 2008 when Mum had a work commitment and arrangements had been made for the boys to come to us. The two days broke down like this:

- Tuesday: 10am arrival, thereafter in-house play/activities, expedition to neighbouring town (Blackburn) to swim, then back to in-house play/ activities, evening meal, more play/activities/tv, bed preparation and stories.
- Wednesday: from 7am to 9am early morning play/activities, breakfast, in-house play/activities, swimming at local pool, visit to ice-cream parlour, in-house play/activities, lunch, in-house play activities, evening meal and return to their house for about 7.30pm.

Throughout both days the weather was extremely cold and no outside activities were suggested, hence the inordinate amount of in-house time.

W at six years of age has very good drawing skills and allied with telling about his drawings finds this an immediate way of meaning making (Wright 2007) about his experiences with the objects, events and living things he encounters. In contrast, J at four years has up to this point shown little interest in drawing though in recent months he has been using his Lego to make representations of vehicles, houses and aircraft.

Our overall stance is one of allowing them to be able to freely choose an activity, have a reasonable expectation that either of us will join in if invited, and be there as a general point of reference on any topic that arises and on which there may be questions. While our own work can at times intrude, provision is always made for one grandparent to be on hand and give priority to any demand that may come from them. We may at times initiate an activity, but only when it is seen to add to the entertainment or interest; we seldom initiate anything if they are already engrossed. The television is usually off. While education is a faint theme in what happens, entertainment is perhaps more apparent, that is, engaging in fun things where there may be elements of game playing. Our interaction with the boys is of a coarser weave than what we observe between them and their parents. There is a greater sense of indulgence with us and we are possibly able to bring in a wider sampling of local and traditional British/English and Lancashire culture.

## Presenting a socio-cultural account of four drawing activities

As Wertsch indicates, socio-cultural work centres around episodes of mediated action and as this continues there should begin to come into focus a range of related features which are set off by this; it being the researcher's task to describe these. Two types of descriptive data will be presented under four scenarios: a brief account of events prior to the drawings and a loose description of the actions through which the drawings emerged. Essentially I will be seeking to follow a qualitative insider's perspective (Pelligrini, Symonds, and Hoch 2004).

### Scenario 1

(Of the two boys, W has been an active drawer since his third birthday. To the best of all our knowledge, J has never voluntarily attempted a drawing.)

### Background

It is approaching breakfast time. I am in kitchen, J has entered adjacent dining room, while across a hall W is in the lounge drawing. J declares he would like to do a drawing. I drop everything to find a jar of felt tip pens, but have no success finding a drawing book. Sensing no time must be lost I pick up a used envelope and point to its blank side which he immediately accepts, gets up on a chair and starts work. I return to the kitchen. Five minutes later comes an irritated comment: 'Its rubbish, I want to do it again, can I have more paper?' I can see that there has been considerable drawing activity on the envelope while quickly finding another one. I put the rejected effort to one side and return to kitchen. About two minutes later, we are still irritable: 'Rubbish, I can't do it . . . can I have more paper . . .?' Again evidence of something difficult being attempted is noted as another used envelope is provided. This too gets short shrift, effort abandoned; I quickly provide another envelope. In all, this is repeated five more times as he-with-pen-with-paper-with-me struggles to do something that plainly has significance for him. At the start of this episode I sought to keep up the tempo in the kitchen with porridge, croissants and boiling eggs on the go, but am now slowing things a little; whatever this is, the breakfast routine must not compromise it. I stand clear of his immediate working, but close enough to assure him of my availability. He uses the same brown pen throughout. I notice the sixth, seventh and eighth drafts take a little longer; there being that busy kind of silence familiar to junior school teachers. After about 12 to 15 minutes of working he finally has something he wants to show me:

J:   I'm finished . . .
T:   Whats that, eh . . .? [I say this to a not immediately recognisable figure]
J:   It's a campervan . . . yeah and these go up here.

After that he leaves the room and joins W, the episode over. I collect his 'envelopes' from the table and ready it for breakfast, reflecting intensely on all that has happened.

## *The mediated actions*

In producing the drawing J would seem to have been centrally involved in three sequential mediated actions:

(1)   Finding a helpful other to communicate a need to: Once J has formed a plan to do a drawing he has to think about where best he might start on this and it is plain that my presence in the kitchen emboldens him to open conversation. Over recent years J and I have often done things together within the universal format of the joint attentional scene (JAS), now so beloved of early years researchers such as Tomasello (1999). This is where two people, one there to give help and the other there to avail of it, engage with some object or other and explore typically its affordances or scripted uses and allow a mutual awareness of our respective trains of thought or felt intersubjectivity to develop. Hence his coming in to where I was, making a request, being assisted, using the table to work, with me not so far away is a variation and advance on earlier JASs. Evidence of such intersubjectivity is reflected in the dialogic type features in our interactions: he stated a wish which I took as a request; he declared his unhappiness about his efforts which met with my replacing the spoiled envelope; his moment of completion was an announcement to show me what he had done. These mediated actions then involve J-with-me.
(2)   Procuring suitable materials and working conditions: This also features J-with-me as a pen, paper, table and chair are provided to his satisfaction.
(3)   Engaging with the task of drawing: This is the major part of the action and featuring J-with-pen-with-paper-with-table. What now begins to emerge are marks on paper very much under J's control and allowing a series of drafts to emerge that help create a drawing that he regards as appropriate. This can be more fully understood by looking at the eight drafts:

Draft 1 (Figure 4.1): Clearly J may have believed at the start that all he had to do was a single draft. He gives this a good deal of time and produces good detail: a

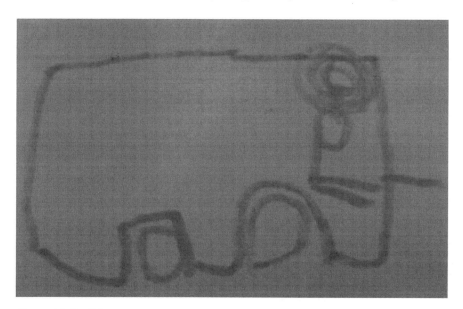

*Figure 4.1* Draft 1.

vehicular figure with wheel arches, each with a wheel, is plain to see. But there is also a partial human figure[2] or hufie and an unaccountable line from the front of the vehicle.

If, as we suspect, this is the first coming together of the sign making capacity of pen and paper as well as some notions J has of including signs that would make it a recognisable drawing, then this is an exciting moment. It is quite an achievement to create this degree of meaningful detail. So while he may be disappointed at not completing it, the striking detail must have been encouraging.

Draft 2 (Figure 4.2): Little time is spent on this draft as if he had made some discovery about how not to proceed.

He does not show any upset at doing this but cues me for another piece of paper, indicating an understanding that he can avail of paper being available.

Draft 3 (Figure 4.3): This is a return to first draft and some evidence that this vehicle outline or template may now be his way of starting the drawing: do the template first and then build up detail from there. This would in general terms equate to Vygotsky's second signal system, where instead of using the presented stimuli you create your own by which you can regulate your own actions. Draft 2 may have been rejected because the template had a flaw.

There is now something in this that has offended against his planning. The wheel arches seem ok but is that ball like figure the beginning of a hufie? Cox (1993) suggests that most hufie drawings begins with the head. Maybe the wheel arches are too far back? And the horizontal line at the front as seen in the first draft has returned.

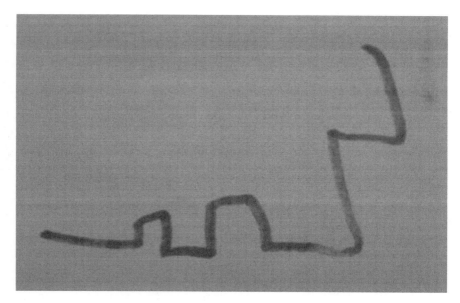

*Figure 4.2* Draft 2.

*Figure 4.3* Draft 3.

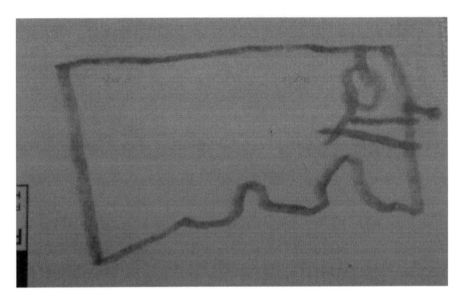

*Figure 4.4* Draft 4.

Draft 4 (Figure 4.4): While there's an untidy undercarriage, this has not upset the impulse to allow a hufie to start to emerge, as is exquisitely clear with its two arms.

But its dimensions are too much to keep within the outline. So there is now a definite order to how he draws: first comes the vehicular template and within this a head is placed, from which a hufie starts. But that puzzling short line at the front is included.

Draft 5 (Figure 4.5) confirms that the hufie figure is an essential part of the drawing and should have helped reassure him that he can achieve his goal. With the vehicular template and head formula comes better proportioning to now place the hufie more realistically within the whole.

Could he now be using a full mapping strategy from head to feet? The wheel arches here are more impressive. This draft reveals more control being exercised over details. It begins to show that he is somehow contending with a psychological complex that is part vehicle and part hufie. Again, the horizontal line at the front has gone missing.

Draft 6 (Figure 4.6): In Draft 6 the main development is the framing of the hufie in a square with further elaboration of a body. All the work is on the figure with the vehicular template again serving as a generative context.

There plainly must be some excitement on his part about the hufie as it has developed substantially from the previous draft. The framing may also be emerging as a challenge. And the horizontal line at the front again is back.

Draft 7 (Figure 4.7): The hufie now has a face with features, and arms and legs extending from the body, though the framing problem is not solved. Also the

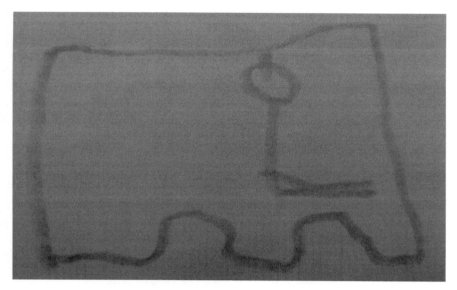

*Figure 4.5* Draft 5.

*Figure 4.6* Draft 6.

*Figure 4.7* Draft 7.

outline is no longer so rigidly adhered to; no wheel arches but there are two wheels! The horizontal line at the front has returned and some mysterious lines appear at the top.

There now seems some uncertainty about the vehicular template. Again it is now less a psychological complex and more a bringing together of vehicle and hufie.

Draft 8 (Figure 4.8): As seen above, this was an emphatic crystallisation of what each earlier draft seemed to be leading to. The hufie has now gone to the left; the wheels are properly in the wheel arches and the figure is reasonably well framed within what must be a window.

The perspective seems to be a view from the side and the emphasis is on presenting the hufie inside the vehicle. With this draft he ends the action; it seems to now sufficiently meet whatever criteria of depiction he was working to.

## Summary

This has been an attempt to describe J's struggle to achieve a depiction of an object familiar to him through appropriating such tools as pen, paper and a

*Figure 4.8* Draft 8.

number of semiotic devices from his culture. The actions he engaged in have connected him with these mediators and reflect much discovery, delight and satisfaction on his part as he discovers how the part depictions begin to emerge and grow into one satisfactory final draft. As the drafts show, this drawing process was not a simple affair of reading off some mental image and rendering it as a photographic likeness to the original object as say, Bruner (1996) implies in his notion of iconic representation. Socio-cultural theory instead sees the executing of a drawing as an exercise in integrating the different mediators and having a felt plan to work to. Plainly, it is an extended exercise in self regulation and self control and in the process more and more of J is made manifest to himself and others; there is his choosing this particular object, this particular time, there is a showing that he can now do drawings and there is his way of doing this. Finally, when J's Mum saw the drawings she immediately accounted for the campervan: this was the 'Peppa Pig' model of a campervan which she bought for J some months previously.

*Scenario 2*

(A common marker of a child's progress in drawing is the appearance of distinct human figures, or what are here called hufies, and for many these are the first identifiable figures that appear. In the drawing above J did a recognisable hufie but within the fuller figure of the campervan.)

*Background*

It is now late afternoon, lights are on, the boys are active in the lounge in a relaxed, idling sort of way. I join them with a newspaper under my arm and can see W is intent on some Lego pieces while J is animatedly engaged with drawing again, this time on a sheet from a pad W uses. J comments that this person is excited and shows me the sheet which consists almost entirely of short strokes, some dots, but also lodged in the middle and overwritten by these strokes is the vehicular template of this morning. He now moves to a new sheet and I notice how good his grip of the pen is, three fingers and good control. I get back to my reading, but after about five minutes, J is counting out loud some items on the drawing: 'One, two, three, four . . . five . . . . . . and six', after which he guffaws; there's something ha-ha funny here. I sneak a look and see that he has drawn some kind of hufie figure with hands! It is the fingers on one of these that he is counting. Could J be attempting to draw his first decontextualised human figure? No external template is being used and the figure emerges as a direct drawing. After about eight minutes he turns the sheet over and begins working on the other side. After about 10 minutes on this, he asks: 'How do you do faces . . .? I can't do a face!' I run my hands over my face and suggest: 'You do these and these and these . . .'.

It is when I touch my ears that he is triggered to resume, seemingly adding some detail to the figure he is working on. He then seems to start on a new figure, but after about three minutes gives up and hands me the sheet. He now draws my attention to the new sheet and tells me, 'It's a hand with fingers'. This refers to a drawing of just an arm shape with hand and fingers. He now draws out one full hufie and with colour fills in its body shape and soon abandons this sheet, drops the pen and moves off to do something completely different.

*The mediated actions*

Clearly J is dealing with some unfinished business from his drawing this morning and it seems to be about hufies. Of the four sheets he has worked on, only two have good detail. For me there is a very different feeling about his work here. Firstly, he has initiated this session himself, getting his own materials and proceeding to draw. Secondly, his use of the paper is different in that a number of drafts appear on a single side. Thirdly, I am not being as involved in this as in the morning. So it is primarily mediated action involving pen, paper and some semiotic devices he has encountered possibly in other drawing he has looked at.

*Figure 4.9* Second sheet.

In the second sheet (Figure 4.9) he has fully decontextualised the two hufie figures and he is attending to the detail of fingers.

In the left figure he is articulating the fingers but also doing it in a playful way, finding that it is possible for him to change the number of fingers, which is what he was finding funny. The face, the body and the legs do not come in for any fine work, but the sheet will have encouraged him in the belief that he can now produce identifiable human figures by availing of the same mediators.

It is in the next sheet (Figure 4.10) that he seeks to consolidate his growing ability by now focusing on the body, face and legs.

*Figure 4.10* Third sheet.

His working as I noticed it was from left to right with the central figure the culmination of his different moves with its face with features, head with features, arms with hands with fingers, and body with arms and legs beginning to be in the right places. There is also evidence of his ability to abandon drafts and move on as in the second and fourth figures.

*Summary*

Good evidence is emerging here of J now being able to draw a human figure at will (Matthews 1984). While this again shows him exploiting pen and paper as tools, the use of lines, closed shapes, having his figure erect and the degree of detail also show how he is exploiting semiotic mediation as his culture makes available such conventions for him to appropriate.

*Scenario 3*

(A common ritual in many British households today is looking at football on television which can often extend into discussions about teams and team loyalties. This can be an acute matter in North-West England where about a third of the top teams in the country are currently concentrated. When children like J and W join a household, they are often entering a cultural force field which sooner or later they may get caught up in.)

*Background*

On the way to swimming this morning at Blackburn, a neighbouring town famous for having a pool with a wave machine, W asked a number of pointed questions about football, but would not be drawn on what team he supported. As we talked W revealed a rather complicated three-way conversation he recently had in the school playground with two friends already with team loyalties, one a declared supporter of Bolton, one a supporter of Wigan (both local teams). The talk centred on a recent game when Blackburn beat Bolton and highlighted his not having a loyalty. The impression was tacitly being given then that maybe for him, Blackburn Rovers would be his team.

It is now evening of the same day, I am in the dining room readying the table for tea, J is playing with Lego bits, Janet is cooking in the kitchen. W comes in and pointedly asks me about the colours of Blackburn Rovers. This I am able to show him in a fixtures booklet for the season, that is always ready to hand. He returns to the lounge to whatever he is doing, but after about 20 minutes, just as we are about to sit down to tea, he returns with a large A3 sheet on which he has done an elaborate drawing as shown in Figure 4.11.

We fix it to a cabinet door so we can all have a good look and ask questions:

T:   It's a football game, and let's see what's happening . . .
W:   Blackburn have scored and these are the Bolton players and they are upset.

*Figure 4.11* Spontaneous drawing by W on A3 sheet.

T:    And who are these?
W:    That's the crowd and this man is saying Bog 'cos he supports Bolton . . . and this is the result here Bolton nil, Blackburn three.[3]

A basic assumption being made by W here is that we are interested in what teams he supports and that he perhaps needs to clear up the unanswered questions of the morning. It is yet another part of the common household rituals involving football where someone has to explain themselves. We are being cast in the role of audience to receive the completed drawing while being prepared to hear him out on all that he now wishes to say and express on the matter. In this drawing and telling, W is engaging in a meaning making exercise about what happens in a football game but done in such a way as to allow him also to making a personal statement about which team he supports.

## Mediated action

In common with how J has done his much simpler drawings, W also uses pens, paper and certain semiotic devices to get certain points across but with some significant differences. His choice of A3 paper reflects the imaginative scope needed to include both players and spectators and the number of pens allows colour to be included as a vital detail. At 6.5 years and with drawing a favourite way of his to represent experiences, W will in all likelihood have noticed in the work of others some of the different ways of approaching this kind of depiction task and hence be more sophisticated in the meanings he seeks to show. He is aware that there are different ways to delight in the triumphalism aroused. He also embraces the fuller sentiment that victory for one team is defeat for the other, with again some fulsome ways of representing this. Some thought is given to how it will reflect on this action: only a true supporter would be able to lavish such loving attention to detail of how badly the goal has gone down with the Bolton players and fans.

As a drawing, one can begin to see what Goodnow (1977) calls conventional equivalents of the comic strip creeping in, such as speech bubbles, the newspaper report format as in the headline and score line, all making for a visual story telling. This too reflects how semiotic devices associated with this genre help him towards a strong visual narrative. There is his choice of action, the dramatic event of a goal that is in his team's favour. Then there is the magnification of this in the delight of one section of the crowd and the misery of the other half. But he also goes for a mixed media approach when he features the use of spoken words to show how individual fans and players are registering the goal, a device which he will have encountered in comics. Finally, the comprehensive view enabled by the A3 sheet invites comparisons with murals celebrating local historical events which again he may have seen somewhere.

## Summary

As mediated action it is likely that just the doing of the drawing with these cultural mediators has helped W discover his true football loyalty. Certainly in this household he is now regarded as a Blackburn fan and through this will have a fuller way of participating in future household rituals involving football. Except for having the team colours shown to him, W, unlike J, has made relatively little use of a human mentor in doing the drawing. Finally, it could be said that W, through these mediated actions, is beginning to discover how to participate in football ritual, albeit for now within this household.

## Scenario 4

(Probably the best way to relate to a household is to begin to participate in its rituals and routines. These can have many functions, most of which only become understandable to a child with age and experience.)

*Background*

In the time a child spends at their grandparents', they are likely to be involved in some focus activities and some peripheral activities. These in turn are likely to generate odd by-products such as discarded sheets used in drawing or pen marks on leather upholstery or yellow plastic ducks in the bath or a football up a tree or a jump rope wound around a railing. Methodologists in ethnography such as Fetterman (2007) like to call these 'outcroppings', those odd incidentals that accumulate around local cultural practices and which to the trained eye can shed interesting light on these. Yet there is something in many households that cannot abide outcroppings and as soon as an activity is over, everything gets returned to its proper place, scraps get binned and no evidence is left of what may have happened. Among such discards will be children's drawings, some of which are likely to have been at some stage pinned up as part of a household ritual associated with wall displays. Family photos are most typical of these, with children's drawings often strongly in evidence during their early years. W's work has been such a feature for some time now, though any expressive marks that J makes would also go up. To finish, three of W's drawings, each one of which was rescued from a pile of old drawings that just seemed to accumulate in one corner of the lounge, will be looked at and related to this ritual in this household.

*Mediated action*

Each of these drawings reflects a visit W has been involved in, with this household being the place returned to after each one and where he found scope to reflect on each one by doing a drawing. As to why he did the drawing here, it may be due to him just feeling he wanted to do it or it could have been influenced by this household having some wall displays that are often used to talk about the past, people from the past and events relating to family members known to J and W. So it is entirely possible that W's drawings may have been motivated by his wishing to participate in the generation of wall displays, though this was never asked of him. As before, he is seen using meditational means as tools (pens, paper) and semiotic devices to achieve whatever meanings he wished to convey. In every case he did not interact with either grandparent when doing them but was always happy to show them to us when completed and then to see them displayed.

Drawing 1 (Figure 4.12): This was done soon after we made a trip to the seaside at nearby Southport. Here, the sea goes out a long way, there is a lot of sand and there are tides. It was J's first ever 'go' on a donkey and he liked it so much he had three. W who was 4 at the time had seen it all before; nonetheless he had two rides. We took photos and got to know the donkeys by name. In a drawing next day, W drew the image shown.

This subsequently got tidied away for some time before being found and put up on a wall. In it he scrupulously focuses on the two of them but also in that large brown foreground does a good job of getting the feel of Southport and its vast expanse of browny sand.

*Figure 4.12* Rescued drawing 1.

Drawing 2 (Figure 4.13): About one year ago we went camping in North-West England's famous Lake District with the boys, where they spent quite a bit of time on two swings in a quiet corner of the camp site. Within a few days of returning, W did a drawing of them on their separate swings – they can be identified by size.

This too got tidied away and was only picked out some weeks ago when I began working on this paper. While an interesting reflection on that visit, the fact that it features the two of them suggests a possible recurring theme in W's meaning making of capturing significant memories of this visit such as enjoyable moments involving both boys.

Drawing 3 (Figure 4.14): This, W tells us, is of two Vikings and is based on a visit to a museum where he had seen similar figures. Many North European children can get taken from an early age to a lot of museums featuring warrior pasts and you often wonder what they get out of it. Here we see W in meaning making mode concentrating on warrior details like the helmets, a standing spear and what looks like gun and holsters!

However, also interfering with the details of the Vikings are details from other warriors W has encountered a little closer to home such as the figures they interface with when playing with their Lego Star Wars. This game, with its psychological savvy function of allowing players to participate in a virtual world as two figures having travel adventures together, may also be influencing this. This

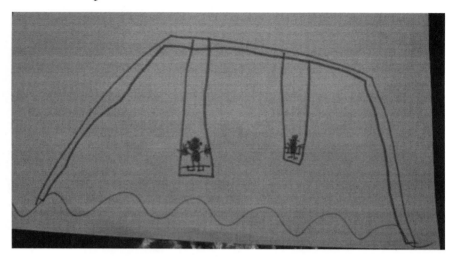

*Figure 4.13* Rescued drawing 2.

*Figure 4.14* Rescued drawing 3.

drawing was done by W on one visit, almost as soon as he was in the door. It can also be added in Piagetian terms that the figures here are being assimilated to an already existing 'partners' schema (Piaget and Inhelder 1969).

## Summary

These rescued drawings show W dealing with experiences which have made an impact or ones that have left him with a need, through reflection, to more fully understand them. They emerged spontaneously and feature quite different selections from the visits. Clearly there is a common theme of including another, whom we can assume is his younger brother, which may also be influenced a little by this household only ever having these boys together. There is also evidence of W's sensitivity to semiotics through what he chooses as signs, human figures, accessories, the framing, use of colour and the flexibility with which just enough detail is included to make a point. He is thus also doing lots of, what Cole (1996) calls, *appropriations* from local sources in his culture; a similar child in, say, Japan might well pick up a different set of meaning carriers. Behind this is also an awareness of assumed audiences who will find them meaningful as a wall display in this house.

## Conclusion

It is now recognised that effective practice in early years educational settings must have a place for parents as partners. While this is a worthy goal, it raises immediate challenges about how well each side understands the world of the other. In the Early Years Foundation Stage document that raises this, 'Effective Practice: Parents as Partners' (DfES 2007) the emphasis is very much on how educators should interface with parents. The teachers are advised to respect diversity, become attuned to the many forms communication can take on childhood matters, offer help and encouragement for parents to know their child as a learner and co-researcher and finally be mindful of finding ways for parents to be more directly involved in their setting's day to day work with the children. All of this is to be applauded but it is a little thin and very much one way traffic. Why not assume children also learn within households, get caught up in cultures after their own fashion, actually have cultures, develop interests and thus provide some means of traffic the other way: parents talking about their teaching, their mentoring, their nurturing for teachers to read? One disappointing absence in this document are grandparents whose involvement in children's lives is no longer an insignificant one, but this it seems, has yet to come to official notice.

If we are to be practical then it is time educational theorists and writers worked a little more on the import of different theories and initiate arguments at more general levels, after, say, the manner of Miller mentioned earlier. With early years children it is essential that distinctions are drawn between theories dealing with behaviourism and cognition through the mechanistic and organismic views on the one hand and the contextualist view as featured here on the other. Without such a contextualist perspective to take in things like a child's meaning making, their encounters with cultural artefacts, their engaging in mediated action or becoming active participants in a working household then it is likely that these and other features of the life outside the early years settings will remain undiscovered. It is hoped that documenting the drawings of these two boys will have shown how early years experiences in this wider social, cultural and historical world can be more concretely appreciated and related to.

And finally, if we are to be more specific about what grandparenting can be, then it is something symbiotic; as much about older lives being enriched as about younger ones being enabled: generativity and nurturance; nurturance and generativity.

## Notes

1  While these three categories produce some helpful order in dealing with the sheer volume and diversity of child development research, such contemporary researchers as Tomasello (2008) are less easy to hold in this framework.
2  I will call the human figure here a hufie to help us pick it out as something small and dynamic.
3  'Bog' is a term these boys share to refer to any frustrating experience, a kind of expletive!

## References

Bruner, J.S. 1966. *Studies in cognitive growth*. London: Harvard University Press.
Cole, M. 1996. *Cultural psychology*. London: Belknap Harvard.
Cox, M.V. 1993. *Children's drawing of the human figure*. Hove: LEA.
DfES. 2007. *The early years foundation stage*. Nottingham: DfES Publications.
Erikson, E. 1959. *Childhood and society*. London: Penguin.
Fetterman, D. 2007. *Ethnography*. 3rd ed. London: Sage.
Fiese, B.H. 2006. *Family routines and rituals*. London: Yale University Press.
Geertz, C. 1973. *The interpretation of cultures*. London: Fontana Press.
Goodnow, J. 1977. *Children's drawing*. London: Fontana.
Kozulin, A. 2000. *Psychological tools*. London: Harvard University Press.
Lave, J., and E. Wenger. 1991. *Situated learning: Legitimate peripheral participation*. Cambridge: Cambridge University Press.
Lektorsky, V.A. 1999. Actvity theory in a new era. In *Perspectives on activity theory*, ed. Y. Engestrom, R. Miettinen, and R. Punamake, 65–9. Cambridge: Cambridge University Press.
Matthews, J. 1984. Children drawing: Are young children really scribbling? *Early Child Development and Care* 18: 1–39.
Mitchell, P.H. 2002. *Theories of developmental psychology*. 4th ed. New York: Worth Publishers.
Pelligrini, A.D., with F.J. Symonds, and J. Hoch. 2004. *Observing children in their natural worlds*. Mahwah, NJ: Lawrence Erlbaum.
Piaget, J., and B. Inhelder. 1969. *The psychology of the child*. New York: Basic Books.
Rogoff, B. 1990. *Apprenticeship in thinking*. Oxford: Oxford University Press.
Smyth, P.B. 2005. Grandparents and grandchildren. *The Psychologist* 18, no. 11: 684–7.

Thiele, D.M., and T.A. Whelan. 2006. The nature and dimensions of the grandparenting role. *Marriage and Family Review* 40, no. 1: 93–108.

Tinsley, B.J., and R.D. Parke. 1984. Grandparents as support and socialization agents. In *Beyond the dyad*, ed. M. Lewis, 161–94. New York: Plenum.

Tomasello, M. 1999. *The cultural origins of human cognition*. London: Harvard University Press.

Tomasello, M. 2008. *Origins of human communication*. London: MIT Press.

Von Bertalanffy, L. 1971. *General system theory. London*: Penguin.

Vygotsky, L.S. 1981b. The genesis of higher mental functions. In *The concept of activity in Soviet Psychology*, ed. J.V. Wertsch. Armonk, NY: M.E. Sharpe.

Wertsch, J.V. 1991. *Voices of the mind: A socio-cultural approach to mediated action*. London: Harvester-Wheatsheaf.

Wertsch, J.V. 1998. *Mind as action*. Oxford: Oxford University Press.

Wright, S. 2007. Young children's meaning making through drawing and 'telling': Anologies to filmic features. *Australian Journal of Early Childhood* 32, no. 4: 37–49.

# Part II

# Key challenges in primary education

# 5 Challenges to primary education

## Colin Richards

### Three squirrels

Once upon a time when the curriculum world was younger, when England held the World Cup, when Harold Wilson wore a new Gannex mac and when Houghton was no more than a twinkle in a dreamer's eye, there were three squirrels — Comtail, Tradtail and Progtail. All were teachers: paid-up members of the NUTS — the National Union of Teacher Squirrels. As teachers they were responsible for initiating young squirrels into the valued aspects of squirrel culture and to prepare them for life in a high-rise society. In particular, they aimed to get as many squirrels as possible to the top of the tree. The main element in the squirriculum was tree-climbing, though nut collection and nut storage were also important components. There were subsidiary subjects, too, offered as options or as activities during the afternoons — activities such as teeth-sharpening, preening bushy tails or barketching for the aesthetically-inclined.

Progtail was a reddish-tinged squirrel: it was rumoured by his opponents that his lesson notes were contained in a little red book. He didn't believe that differences in colour or innate ability were major factors in influencing squirrel attainment in the basic skills: what was crucial, he believed, was the richness of the woody environment. Tradtail, on the other hand, was distinctly grey. His lesson notes were written on black paper, and he was a fierce believer in large natural differences in ability. In particular, he believed that grey squirrels were a class above the red variety. Comtail, our third squirrel and my hero, was a little bewildered: he didn't quite know where he stood or, to be more precise, where he sat. He didn't take either extreme position but believed that all young squirrels should be introduced to tree-climbing and the other basic skills, though he realised rather sadly that some would profit much more from these than others. His lesson notes tended to be written on the cuffs of his coat or on the back of envelopes — usually whitish in colour. They other two thought him indecisive — they criticised him for spending too much time sitting on fences rather than climbing trees.

Two other characters need to be mentioned. One was Adviserytail, a squirrel renowned for his course comments and for his inverse-Chameleon qualities: he was able to appear greyish when in the company of red squirrels and reddish when with grey! The other figure was Henry Hedgehog, a HEMIS — her majesty's inspector of squirrels. His opponents reckoned him to be a bit of a prickly customer, given to huffing and puffing, and liable to roll up into a ball when threatened with a direct question about the squirriculum. He stayed in the background a lot, guarding his nuts, in an enforced period of hibernation, but he was always likely to put in an appearance at the most unlikely time.

Tradtail, Comtail and Progtail all worked at different tree schools but within the same authority. At his school, Tradtail spent most of his time on tree-climbing. He had little time for the 'frills' of free play on the branches. He planned one way to the top, sorted out the nimble from the less nimble, and did his best to coax, cajole and sometimes shove his youngsters up the well-trodden climb. He provided plenty of footholds, made sure the youngsters knew how well (or badly) they were progressing, and gave them gold acorn shells for both effort and attainment. Progtail also believed that all ought to be given a chance to get to the top of the tree, but he didn't accept that that was the only goal of the tree-school. Squirrels ought to be encouraged to enjoy the view on the way up, they ought to have an opportunity to explore side-branches, they should be able to engage in activities such as nut-collection, barketching, and claw-sharpening on the way. He would help them on their way, prod them a little, ask them questions about their journey but wouldn't try to force the pace unduly. As usual, Comtail was far less dogmatic and more cautious than the other two. His goal was the same but he wasn't in the same hurry as Tradtail, nor did he want to give his charges the same degree of self-responsibility as Progtail. He tried different aspects of both their approaches, never being wholly satisfied with the outcome. Parents' reactions were interesting and predictable: many were fervently behind Tradtail: you see, they believed their red squirrels were really grey ones. Some supported Progtail: his efforts were widely disseminated by Adviserytail and his colleagues. Comtail tended to be rather neglected: he didn't get the praise from parents: he wasn't televised on England's smallest TV channel, Nutland TV.

It was at this point that Neville the Deville appeared on the scene. Like me, he was a strange, off-beat species of squirrel: a unisquirrel. Unisquirrels spend a lot of time charging up and down trees, looking rather bewildered, scratching their nuts, and all too often preening themselves. It was rumoured, however, among teacher-squirrels that they had never got to the top of any trees anywhere. Neville was a Lancastrian squirrel (you could tell that by the Blackpool rock he sucked). He'd been very active in another stretch of woodland investigating how 10–11 year-old North-western squirrels were taught to climb trees. He did this by posting letters to all the primary tree-schools in Lancashire and Cumbria and then selecting from these letters a small number of classes (less than forty) for further study. The trees were visited, their youngsters observed and tests administered. In large measure these were limited to basic skills such as clambering, clinging and digging-in of heels. He spent a lot of time adding up and taking away his results in his computer. He then went tramping the length and breadth of the land, proclaiming his 'massive' and 'unequivocal' results in forest glade after forest glade. 'The effect of teaching style is statistically and educationally significant in all attainment areas tested . . . formal teaching such as Tradtail's fulfils its aims in the tree-climbing area without detriment to nut collection and nut storage, whereas informal teaching as practised by Progtail only partially fulfils its aims in the latter area as well as engendering poorer outcomes in tree-climbing achievement'.

The news came at a time when another tree school was in the news. It was said that at the William Tyndale tree-school in Islington both teachers and young squirrels had been totally barking up the wrong tree. Progtail's methods had been misinterpreted and taken to an extreme. Some squirrels didn't have to climb trees at all if they didn't want to; some were virtually encouraged to burrow beneath trees. Others spent long periods picking dandelions or playing ping-pong on toadstools. It was clear, the basic squirriculum was not being taught.

It was about this time that Henry the HEMIS appeared from his enforced hibernation huffing and puffing and rubbing his eyes rather blearily and disbelievingly. In a book with a yellow cover, he put forward the suggestion for a common core to the squirriculum; soon modified in the squirrel context to a common kernel. He said nothing directly about Neville the Deville but did stress that in inexperienced paws the squirriculum could be adversely affected by Progtail's methods.

Other proposals were made in a series of meetings. Squirrel attainment ought to be assessed — perhaps by a team of monitor lizards from the mystical land of APU. Closer links ought to be forged between tree schools and the woods around since some young squirrels and their teachers, it was rumoured, couldn't see the wood for the trees. In-service training for teacher squirrels was to become a priority — to sharpen their claws and keep them up to scratch. After discussing these and other proposals with interested parties, Henry promised to go away and write up his proposals on green paper.

Which brings us to the present day (June). The green paper is awaited expectantly. All over the land, squirrels like Tradtail are rubbing their paws together with glee: their secret doubts about the effectiveness of their methods and their secret worries about the importance of offering squirrels some degree of self-responsibility have disappeared. Progtail has gone underground, has made himself far less visible but is seemingly more determined than ever to carry on. Which brings us to Comtail, and remember, the Comtails of the educational world are in the majority. Where does he stand?

Are Neville's findings conclusive? Will Comtail want to, or be forced to, adopt more of Tradtail's ways? Or are there other ways of providing the structure and guidance necessary to get pupils to the top of the tree? What part can, or should, Adviserytail play? Will he change his name to Tell-tail? How far will Henry the HEMIS want to, or be able to, press the common kernel on tree schools? Will activities such as bark-etching or teeth-sharpening be devalued or even removed from the squirriculum offered some pupils? When the APU lizards begin assessing squirrels' performance, will this deflect and disturb teacher squirrels? Will monitoring, plus the direction of tree-school managers, reinforce a move in Tradtail's direction? Will Comtail be willing or able to maintain his rather precarious position, or will he tend to take an easy way out?

What the end of the story is no-one knows, for the end is still to be written, but one thing is certain. The story is being written at this very time and all of us have a stake in the outcome.

## Over-simplification

Stories can reflect realities to varying degrees; to be meaningful they have to tie in with the readers' experiences or conceptions at some point, but being meaningful to this degree does not make them adequate reflections of the situations they attempt to portray. I want to contend that the tale of three squirrels captures many of the characteristics of current discussion on education but only a limited selection of the underlying realities and problems facing primary teachers at present.

Certainly the tale re-echoes the gross over-simplification characteristic of current discussion over-simplification which fails to do justice to the complexities, subtleties and richness of primary education. Despite Neville Bennett's research, primary teachers cannot be neatly and cleanly divided into those adopting formal, informal and 'mixed' styles; despite reactions to his supposedly 'unequivocal' findings, formal teaching (whatever that is) has not been proved superior to informal teaching; despite *Black Paper 1977* there is no conclusive evidence that large number of teachers are sacrificing the future achievement of their pupils in the pursuit of a transitory happiness in the here and now; despite Tyndale, progressive education (whatever that is) has not been totally discredited as an approach for working-class children; despite those regional conferences, educational issues (particularly curricular ones) remain stubbornly complex and not amenable to the kind of cursory treatment they're often given.

The enterprise in which we're engaged is hellishly complex — much more so that routine law or medicine. As an amalgam of value, preferences, hunches, intuitions, actions, intentions, knowledge and much more, it demands theory and deliberation of an equally subtle kind. Too often it is distorted by the educational simplifiers of the day. In the words of Elliot Eisner, 'they offer us a piece of the whole. They reduce the richness of educational problems to a size which fits a bubblegum wrapper'. Certainly during the last troubled year there has been 'bubblegum' aplenty wrapped in black, red and whitish paper, some at least of which ought to have found its way into our waste-paper baskets! In particular, Neville Bennett's research and the Tyndale Inquiry have generated a good deal of superficial comment in the press. What follows is one person's attempt to think rather less simplistically about *some* of the crucial issues raised.

## Bennett

Last April, amid a cascade of multi-media publicity not even accorded Plowden, came *Teaching Styles and Pupil Progress*[1] by Neville Bennett and his team. I don't intend to refer to it as the 'Lancaster Report' since this connotes a definitiveness and an authority unwarranted by the research itself. To many, as to the person writing advertising copy for its publishers, it represents 'the first hard evidence on whether progressive education works'. It has been seized on by some as a definitive evaluation of progressivism; it has been considered as an objective rebuttal of the woolly-minded, impractical idealism of Plowden. That Plowden was often woolly-minded cannot be denied, that teaching needs appraisal cannot be contested, but does Neville Bennett's work clearly and objectively demonstrate that formal teaching is more effective than informal teaching? . . . My firmly-held contention is that it does not: indeed, unless parties to to the educational enterprise agree on what effectiveness is (and they don't) and unless much more sophisticated measures are available (which they aren't) I can't see any piece of educational research demonstrating, let alone proving, the matter one way or the other. Although, as an ex-primary school teacher, I do intuitively support some, though not all, of Neville Bennett's findings (and then only to a certain extent) I have to admit that in the last analysis, the case against 'informal' teaching (whatever that is) remains 'not proven'.

A considerable number of shortcomings of the research have been detailed elsewhere, concerned with such aspects as sampling, statistical analysis and the measuring instruments employed. I want to look briefly at one particular weakness which has not received enough attention and which links in with something mentioned earlier. This concerns the adequacy, comprehensiveness and validity of the teaching 'styles' (originally twelve, later 'collapsed' into three) in relation to which attainment scores of pupils were computed. To take one example: how far does this 'capture' the essential elements of the teaching style of an informal teacher you know?

Type 2:

> These teachers prefer integration of subject matter. Teacher control appears to be low, but the teachers offer less pupil choice of work (than type 1). However, most allow pupils choice of seating and only one third curb movement and talk. Few test or grade work.
>
> (page 45)

In my opinion, none of Bennett's twelve types captures teaching 'style' at more than a superficial level. His 'styles' scratch the surface of classroom organisation instead of providing penetrating descriptions of teaching which hopefully could begin to provide convincing explanations for differences in pupil attainment.[2] The research begins by trying to encompass something of the complexity of teaching; it ends by reinforcing simplistic thinking by 'collapsing' twelve already inadequate characterisations into three even more inadequate ones — not surprising 'formal', 'informal' and 'mixed'. In short, Bennett's 'styles' are but caricatures, only somewhat less simplistic than those of Tradtail, Comtail, Progtail and Henry the HEMIS.

Having criticised the research but admitting my intuitive support for a moderate interpretation of some of his findings, I do believe the research is both important and suggestive. It should give us considerable pause for reflection on a number of counts. Initially it should alert us to the danger of making glib generalisations in primary education. Plowden was certainly misguided in asserting in paragraph 1233 that '"Finding out" has proved to be better for children than "being told"'; *Black Paper 1977*[3] is equally mistaken on page 13 in asserting that 'Bennett's Report is only one of many pieces of educational research which show the superiority of formal teaching'; Neville Bennett is himself at fault on page 162 in summarising boldly and baldly how formal teaching fulfils its aims whilst informal teaching only does so partially — in the passage I 'quoted' in the squirrel story. His own research indicates how pupil differences of attainment and personality affect the relationship between so-called teaching 'style' and pupil attainment: he himself acknowledges the importance of teachers' structuring and sequencing of material (not built into the research design) and there are, of course, a multitude of background factors, affecting both pupil and teacher performance. Although most of us prefer clear, straight-forward statements, school life does not lend itself to these. As teachers we have to live with the complexities and uncertainties of classroom life: we have to live with the complexities and uncertainties of explanation too.

The reception accorded Bennett also pinpoints the danger of adopting an uncritical attitude to educational research, either rejecting it out of hand as 'irrelevant' or uncritically accepting it as some form of received wisdom. Colin Lacey,[4] research director at the Schools Council, suggests there are two predominant models of educational research: a 'medical' model involving convergent problem-solving, and a 'divergent' model aimed at increasing understanding. He argues that in education we tend to expect definitive solutions to problems along the-lines of the 'medical' model, but research can rarely deliver such unequivocal messages. Most often, and here he includes Bennett, research contributes more to understanding situations than to providing a solution.

Clearly, we need to become more research-conscious in primary education, able to consider both its benefits and its limitations. There is a developing research base for our sector which does address the problems which concern us: I'm thinking here of the research discussed by Brian Simon in a recent issue of *Education 3–13*.[5] This needs to be incorporated into the knowledge-base of primary teaching along with the kind of rigorous thinking about issues characteristic of the work of Robert Dearden.[6] Instead of being uncritically applauded or ignored, Bennett's research ought to be a basis for further more refined research which will begin to accumulate as part of teachers' technical 'capital', a part of professional expertise grounded in knowledge as well as intuition, in reflection as well as in spontaneous action. Too often we still operate at the level of folklore, not far removed in sophistication from the tale of the squirrels and the hedqehog.

A third lesson to be drawn from reactions to Bennett is the necessity for much clearer thinking and much clearer communication of our thoughts concerning the theory and practice of teaching. The theories underlying our practices, the aims to which we subscribe, the practical principles we seek to apply, the organisation and teaching strategies we use, need to be much more closely related and clearly enunciated both for inexperienced teachers and the wider public. This is particularly important for those of a 'progressive' persuasion. It's no good the latter maintaining that Neville Bennett, Terry Ellis or the Black Paper writers misunderstand what progressivism entails: part of the blame must lie with their inability to provide carefully considered explanations, descriptions and justifications. Plowden has much to answer for in this regard.

Neville Bennett's research has implications too at classroom level: in particular, it should make us think very carefully about the forms of classroom organisation we employ. It could well be that some forms of classroom organisation are dysfunctional: they are so time and energy-consuming simply to maintain that teachers are unable to devote themselves to their major task: seeing that children are learning worthwhile things and acquiring worthwhile attitudes to learning. It could be that organisation is getting in the way of, rather than facilitating, the curriculum: perhaps as Makins[7] suggested in the TES, some teachers are getting the worst of both worlds by adopting a form of 'informal' organisation whilst still trying to teach the same body of knowledge as they did formally.

In particular, and here I'm mounting a particular hobby-horse of mine, we need to think hard about 'individualised learning', especially where this involves children working daily through a programme of work cards, work sheets, SRA cards, *Spelling Workshop* and so on — supposedly at their own pace but in reality at a pace dictated by the speed and success of the hard-pressed teacher in monitoring such work. Of course, not all 'informal' classrooms are like this, but a good many are. Does this form of organisation leave much room for teaching as opposed to management? Can it promote 'independence'? Does it provide children with the necessary stimulus for question-posing and problem-solving? Do children get enough exposure to the richness and flexibility of adult language which can help them acquire concepts and understand explanations? I have my doubts on all these points. Such an inadequately thought-through informality can result in stereotyped individualised learning, dominated by the inflexible and often sterile language of the work-card and work-sheet.

If nothing else, Bennett's work suggests that no one form of organisation is equally effective with all children, a fairly obvious point but one whose implications are not always worked through in practice. There is a place for individualised learning, but also a place for the shared experience of class teaching. In particular I would argue we need to give far greater attention to small-group teaching than we do. This is much neglected, but, I believe, does make much more economical and fruitful use of teachers' scarce expertise, time and especially, language than does over-reliance on other modes.

These then are some of my reactions to Bennett. He raises many other points, and certainly his work is important. It challenges us to go beyond teacher intuition and to strive to make our theory and practice of primary education more rational, less emotive, more readily communicable and more genuinely incremental.

## William Tyndale

Neville Bennett's research is timely and significant: most of the issues it raises are directed at, and can be resolved by, the teaching profession itself. William Tyndale raises some such similar questions, but to regard the affair as primarily an intraprofessional clash between proponents of traditional and progressive teaching is to miss its true significance. Tyndale is not particularly important in itself (except of course to the parents, children and teachers directly involved); its importance lies in the way it has brought to the surface, highlighted and focussed on a number of fundamental problems and tensions. Bennett's impact on primary education may well be short-lived, but I doubt if the same will be true of Tyndale.

Tyndale raises the fundamental problem of how far the curriculum and teaching methods employed in schools are matters for public, as well as professional, concern and control.[8] Professionalism, not just teacher professionalism, is being challenged by a developing and increasingly vocal consumerism: teachers are the most prominent targets for such a challenge at present but other professions are unlikely to remain unscathed in the years ahead. Values are at the heart of the educational enterprise, values regarding the worth-whileness of different activities, different parts of the stock of public knowledge, different skills, different modes of conduct, different forms of social arrangement. Such values are very fundamental; they cannot be avoided in schools. But are they too important and fundamental to be left to teachers alone, particularly in our pluralistic society? Tyndale calls into question what Philip Taylor and Frank Musgrove call the 'benevolent despotism' of teachers[9] who have taken on themselves the task of determining both means and ends in education. The managers of Tyndale were not just expressing concern at what they saw as the 'inefficiency' of particular methods being used on their children: they were articulating a growing concern that the curriculum, the heart of schooling, is a matter for public debate and decision-making. There is a fast developing belief that the curriculum is no longer a 'secret garden' tended by, and accessible to, professionals only; it is being seen as more akin to the grounds of some National Trust property, open to the public under certain conditions and managed on their behalf. It is these conditions and this form of management which are at the very centre of the educational debate today. In such matters virtually all parties concede that a balance has to be struck between professional rights to a measure of discretion in providing their services and the public's right to know what's going on and to be consulted.

Tyndale, the Taylor Report and DES proposals for a common core all promise (or threaten) a shift in that balance. Some of the discretion accorded us in primary education is likely to be removed; managers are no longer likely to be mere expressions of the local community's benevolence; greater accountability at local and national level is coming. Our much vaunted autonomy is being threatened, though to be frank, I think too many of us have been content to assert rather than to use it in the past. To my mind, the question of who controls the school curriculum, on what terms and to what degree is one of the most important issues in education today. It is one that did not face Plowden. But it faces us. It is very regrettable that it has to be faced at a time of widespread demoralisation in the education service: it couldn't have come at a worse time; what we're being asked to confront is the nature of the context of control in which most of us will spend the remainder of our teaching careers.

Implicit in what I've just said and highlighted by the Tyndale affair is a challenge to another dominant assumption about primary education. Those squirrels lived and worked in a non-political 'never-never' land; primary schools are often considered non-political, concerned simply with the job of teaching young children. Terry Ellis and other members of the Tyndale staff question this: they assert I think cogently,[10] that schools and their curricula haveinevitable political implications. Through schools, children form attitudes towards the exercise of power and authority, towards the state, towards organisations and institutions; they are introduced implicitly or explicitly to views of society; they are encouraged to acquiesce (or more rarely question) the social status quo, they develop (or fail to develop) a sense of power over their own environment and circumstances. All these are political with a small p – all are concerned with the distribution and exercise of power in our society, particularly power for different social classes.

In particular Tyndale makes us ask whether schools have done enough to give working-class people a sense of the possibility of self-determination. Terry Ellis and his supporters would argue firmly that schools are simply agencies for the reproduction of the cultural and social status-quo. They are agencies of social control, gentling the masses as they've always done since 1870, manipulating the working-class in the interests of capitalist society and the middle class. In their pursuit of equality and respect for children the Tyndale rebels claim to be taking Plowden to its logical conclusion; they argue (again cogently) that their opponents represent a political stance every bit as much as they do. The struggle over Tyndale is primarily a struggle between conflicting views of education and its relation to society, rather than a struggle between traditional and progressive teaching methods. Have we thought through the political implications of our work with young children? For too long those of us in primary education have been politically naive: we need to develop a far greater degree of political awareness and sophistication, both in terms of what we do with children and how we deal with the many groups and organisations claiming a legitimate stake in the educational enterprise.

Tyndale raises many more issues: the lack of staff-wide curriculum planning, the importance of careful structuring and sequencing of material in many curriculum areas (especially, I would argue, more advanced reading, social studies and science), the necessity for record-keeping systems, the balance to be struck between social and academic considerations, the dangers of individualised learning, the role of the local inspectorate, the celebration of learning as opposed to teaching. Because of limitations of space, I will close with a brief mention of one other vexed issue, which relates back to my comments on Bennett. This is the question of 'efficiency' in teaching. It took Robin Auld's inquiry many months and cost the ILEA over £50,000 to conclude that the teaching at Tyndale was not 'efficient' but even then this judgement can be contested. There are simply no agreed criteria for assessing the performance of Terry Ellis, Brian Haddow or any other teacher. Teacher 'efficiency', or more likely 'inefficiency', is going to be much discussed in the next few years of teacher re-deployment, but we are no nearer than we ever were in agreeing a meaning to 'efficiency' and in providing measures of it. Can we form a consensus on the basis of which we can draw up clear unambiguous criteria for assessing teacher performance? I doubt it. Teaching is too much of an art to be assessed, even indirectly, by the results of a Neville Bennett or by the latest tests from the NFER hurriedly introduced into schools by frightened LEA's. Pupil performance ought certainly to be monitored at national level, and then only in appropriate areas of experience, but emphatically this cannot be directly correlated with teacher 'efficiency'.

## Challenge

Of all the challenges levelled at primary education during the last twelve months, this challenge to teaching by the proponents of 'efficiency' is perhaps the most fundamental. Teaching, as opposed to information-transmission, is an incredibly complex activity, whether considered in practical or theoretical terms. It's an amalgam of so many elements — interpersonal, academic, physical, even aesthetic. It involves notions such as 'respect, 'concern', 'integrity' that cannot be captured by tests or observed unambiguously by researchers or advisers; its ends and means are inextricably interwoven; it is a moral enterprise as well as a practical activity.

I believe that it is this sense of teaching which above all else we need to protect in the years ahead. It was enshrined in Plowden but it is threatened now. Unlike those three squirrels, we cannot afford a prolonged period of hibernation!

## References

1. Bennett N. and others. 1976. *Teaching Styles and Pupil Progress,* Open Books.
2. See Richards C., 1976 'A sense of style', *Teachers World,* 2 July, 1976.
3. Cox C. and Boyson R. (eds.). *Black Paper 1977.* Temple Smith.
4. Lacey C., 'Research and education: a personal view', *Research Intelligence,* vol. 2, number 2, 1976.
5. Simon B. 1976 'Observational studies in the primary school', *Education 3–13,* volume four, number two.
6. Dearden R. 1968 *The Philosophy of Primary Education,* RKP.
   Dearden R. 1976 *Problems in Primary Education,* RKP.
7. Makins V. 1977. 'The worst of both worlds?', *T.E.S.,* 11 February, 1977, and 'On from the basics', *T.E.S.,* 18 February, 1977.
8. See Gretton J. and Jackson M., 1976. *William Tyndale,* Allen and Unwin.
9. Musgrove F. and Taylor P. 1969. *Society and the Teacher's Role,* RKP.
10. Ellis T. and others, 1976. *William Tyndale: The Teachers' Story,* Writers and Readers Publishing Cooperative.
11. Auld R. 1976. *William Tyndale Junior and Infants Schools Inquiry,* I.L.E.A.

# 6 Delegation

## Burden or empowerment?

*Rosemary Webb*

## Introduction

Delegation is 'the transfer of a task, or set of tasks, and the resources and responsibility to carry out the work from one person to another with appropriate professional support' (Bell and Rhodes, 1996, p. 157). It serves two most important inter-related purposes. Firstly, delegation allows a headteacher to share appropriate tasks and responsibilities with others thus creating more time for school development planning and evaluation and for those activities that only he or she can do. Secondly, delegation has the potential to enable those to whom the work has been delegated to develop new skills and abilities thus contributing to their personal and professional development and career prospects. When this occurs delegation is a vehicle for empowerment. However, if the work delegated is not supported by adequate training, resources and mentoring, it is likely to be perceived as an additional burden and possible source of resentment.

Since the Education Reform Act (1988) the roles and responsibilities of headteachers have increased exponentially with the result that many duties such as leadership in particular curriculum subjects, which headteachers might have undertaken themselves in previous decades, are now routinely delegated to teachers and incorporated in their job descriptions. However, the current educational culture is one where funds and opportunities for school improvement frequently arise through bidding successfully for projects. Such projects generally involve the allocation of new and additional tasks to teachers. In an evaluation of *Heads You Win* (HYW), an LEA programme of school improvement early years' projects in 20 schools, delegation emerged as an unanticipated but topical and important issue. This article draws on the evaluation data to examine headteachers' attitudes towards, and approaches to, delegation and to consider whether and why those to whom project tasks were delegated found this a burdensome or empowering experience.

The LEA secured funding from the Esmée Fairbairn Charitable Trust to support its HYW school improvement programme the main purpose of which, as stated in the programme proposal, was 'the development of head-teacher leadership and management skills through a school-based project designed to raise children's attainment through the direct involvement of parents/carers in their children's learning and development'. The aims and content of the programme related directly to the Teacher Training Agency's National Standards for Headteachers and the Leadership Programme for Serving Head-teachers (LPSH). The programme ran initially for the academic year September 1999 – July 2000 but with the expectation that some schools were likely to need longer to complete the full cycle of planning, implementation, evaluation and review of their projects.

## Evaluation

The evaluation, which was commissioned by the LEA, was of a year's duration and had both a formative and summative role (Webb and Sudworth, 2001). Data were gathered mainly through:

- an analysis of programme documentation such as schools' action plans, project Newsletters and teachers' professional development files;
- visits to the schools in the Spring Term 2000 during which semi-structured tape-recorded interviews were conducted with headteachers and other project staff;
- follow-up visits in the Summer Term 2000 for an update on progress, to observe project work and to collect parents' perspectives;
- final school visits in the latter part of the Autumn Term 2000 during which further semi-structured tape-recorded interviews were conducted with headteachers and other project staff;
- attendance at a a training day and meetings for headteachers; and
- ongoing dialogue with the LEA advisor who was the programme co-ordinator.

## School projects

Schools were identified by the LEA for participation in the programme based on their Key Stage 1 (KS1) results over a three-year period and Qualifications and Curriculum Authority benchmarking, which showed that they were underperforming relative to comparable schools in the county and nationally. The schools were pleased to be invited to participate viewing the invitation as further recognition by the Advisory Service of the challenging local circumstances in which they worked. Also, headteachers were attracted by the prospect of schools being able to devise projects to meet their own needs.

Twenty schools (19 primaries and 1 nursery and infant school) were involved in the programme. The schools were in three very different parts of the county where there is considerable social and economic disadvantage which detrimentally affects children's behaviour and attainment pre-school and at KS1. The schools ranged in size from five small schools (with less than 100 pupils on roll) the smallest of which catered for 42 pupils to four large schools (with over 400 pupils on roll) of which the largest had 625 pupils.

Twelve schools opted to carry out Share projects. Share is a national strategy which seeks to enhance the quality of parental involvement in children's learning.

Two schools implemented Steps projects (derived from an American personal and professional development programme for community application), one of which was also involved in Share. Seven schools took the opportunity offered by the HYW programme to design their own community projects, which often had several related strands either planned in parallel or sequentially, including the setting up of toy libraries, Story Sacks, a breakfast club, a parent mentoring scheme for pupils and a school website.

## Headteachers' attitudes to delegation

Essentially management is about making things happen and accomplishing tasks through, and in co-operation with, other people. Delegation is therefore essential to effective management. However, there appears to be considerable confusion and uncertainty about when and how to delegate which often results in managers undertaking themselves tasks that ought to have been delegated. Whitaker (1993) gives examples of commonly heard arguments that headteachers present for undertaking work that they ought to delegate;

- 'If you want a job done well, do it yourself'.
- 'This one is too hot for my staff to handle'.
- 'I want to keep my hand in'.
- 'It's easier to do it yourself than to delegate it.'
- 'I don't want to ask my staff to do anything I'm not willing to do myself'.

(p. 141)

However, such admissions by headteachers, while revealing some of the genuine dilemmas of delegation, should not constrain their approach to management.

In the HYW Programme the more recently appointed headteachers experienced the greatest difficulty in delegating. They gave two main reasons for this. First, they admitted finding it difficult to hand over project responsibilities to staff and in so doing vest the necessary degree of trust and reliance on colleagues. In part this appeared to be because teachers were likely to approach tasks differently from the way the head-teachers would tackle them and yet headteachers were ultimately accountable for project outcomes. Less experienced headteachers were uncomfortable with the notion that, providing project outcomes and success criteria for evaluating these outcomes were agreed, ownership of the processes for achieving them should be the preserve of the teacher running the project. However, a few headteachers had recently attended LPSH courses and they found the projects an opportunity to put into practice the advice offered on delegation:

I'm very hands-on. I like to do lots and lots of things and get involved. The LPSH started me off thinking that I've got to step back, let go and let things start to happen because the people I've got are more than capable and *Heads You Win* came in at the perfect time. It gave me the skills to learn how to let go and it's given us all a bit more awareness of what we are capable of doing ourselves.

(headteacher)

The second main constraint on delegation was because headteachers experienced feelings of guilt at 'downloading responsibilities', as one head described delegation, and so creating an additional burden of work for already overstretched teachers. In the current climate where teacher workload and government initiatives are the main reasons for new recruits and experienced teachers leaving the profession (Smithers and Robinson, 2001), teachers may be resistant to extra responsibilities and headteachers hesitant to broach the prospect with them. However, those heads expressing such views appeared to regard delegation primarily as a means to project implementation without having to take on additional work themselves. The possibility of teacher professional development and increased job satisfaction through project delegation appeared overlooked or perceived as unlikely to compensate adequately for the work involved.

The finding that willingness to delegate relates to previous management experience reflects the research findings of Bullock and colleagues (1997). They studied twenty-eight teachers drawn from primary and secondary education – half of whom were experienced managers and half of whom were newly appointed to managerial posts – in order to identify critical factors in the acquisition of educational management skills at different career stages. Experienced managers were confident about, and had clear strategies for, delegating responsibilities and were aided in this by their high level of interpersonal skills and an inclusive approach to decision-making. Several of the new-to-post managers admitted that they found delegation difficult. In part this was derived from a wish to be seen to generate successfully activity and make a recognisable contribution to the leadership and organisation of the school before identifying areas of development for others to tackle. Bullock *et al.* (1997) also speculate that perhaps the new managers 'did not have the requisite knowledge of their colleagues and the working context to construct the strategies to support delegation at a comfortable level' (p.56). This contrasted to the approach of established managers who recognised which tasks could appropriately be delegated to which staff, were confident in their communication skills and abilities to overcome any resistance to delegation and had no need to be seen 'as generators of activity'.

Heads of small schools in the HYW programme were also unaccustomed to the opportunity to delegate. One headteacher, who had moved to her present school with 4/5 members of staff after being head of a very small school for 9 years where there was only one other member of staff, described how in that situation she had become accustomed to taking responsibility for most initiatives. Consequently, she continued in a similar manner after she moved schools. As she explained, project funding enabled her to step back and delegate:

There's a point at which you can't actually cope with it all – but it's knowing that point before you become ill and I didn't. . . . So it was very good for me to be able to delegate it [Share], to feel 'No this is made for a teacher to run it. Let somebody else do it'. And I've been more than pleased to do that and just keep a casting eye over it and it's worked very well. . . . I've left it all to the classteacher but we have talked frequently about it and she has kept me in touch with what was happening – very much so – and I've talked to one or two parents when I've seen them around.

(headteacher)

In addition to the management experience of the head-teacher, the other two main factors determining the interpretation and practice of delegation were the familiarity of the school as a whole with the kinds of knowledge and skills involved in the project and the length of time in post and experience relevant to the project of the classteacher to whom responsibility was delegated.

## Supporting and reviewing delegated tasks

Bell and Rhodes (1996) argue that every act of delegation should be given considerable thought and that this is most readily achieved through a written plan. They suggest that this plan should clearly identify:

- what is to be delegated;
- the person to whom the work is to be delegated;
- the training required;
- the resources needed and deadlines to be met; and
- how progress will be monitored and reviewed.

Much of this initial information, which formed the context in which project delegation occurred, was contained in the schools' project action plans which were submitted at the inception of the programme and revised a term into it. These action plans took as their starting point an audit of existing provision, resources required to support the project and an analysis of the needs of participants. The plans also included strategies for monitoring project processes and success criteria for evaluating/measuring the achievement of project objectives. However, the depth and thoroughness with which headteachers tackled the action planning varied considerably and was influenced by factors such as pressures of other work, the number of other developments that were being managed simultaneously, the timing of co-ordinator visits and the importance that headteachers placed on using the projects to further their own professional development.

Identifying the most suitable person to take on delegated tasks generally involves posing questions such as who might benefit most from the challenge and who has the most time to devote to it. However, which teachers would be involved in HYW projects was largely predetermined by the programme's early years focus. For example, as Share projects were viewed as most appropriately located in Year 1 and taken by Year 1 teachers who knew the pupils and their parents, these teachers were the first to be approached and assumed project responsibilities in ten out of the twelve Share project schools.

All the projects required classteachers to some degree to acquire new knowledge and skills. As part of the programme the LEA provided preparatory in-service training to meet the needs of those teachers involved in Share projects. However, those schools carrying out individual community projects were responsible for identifying the means to meet their own needs. For example, a classteacher who was developing Story Sacks arranged to go to a training session by the initiator of Story Sacks and visit another school where a Story Sacks project was successfully underway. In a few cases relevant training was not available and teachers were unaware of any schools attempting similar initiatives from which they might seek advice.

Once project implementation got underway a few head-teachers provided further training and support through demonstrating, coaching and/or working alongside their junior colleagues. One primary school headteacher provided considerable support for the Year 1 teacher delivering the Share project because it was a completely new enterprise for the school and for the teacher who had only been in teaching for three years. She had non-contact time for the afternoons when Share sessions took place and was supported by the school secretary, who had experience of working in adult education, and the teaching assistant, who ran the creche for the parents' younger children. She also met regularly with the head-teacher to brainstorm ideas and review project progress. The head used the project to develop, and reflect critically on, the processes involved in delegation. For these reasons delegation changed the nature of her involvement in the project rather than substantially lessening the extent of that involvement.

Headteachers tended to characterise their delegator role as a facilitative one:

> I drew up the action plan, I've been in on two meetings and I did the questionnaire but I've certainly let it run without any interference. It was up to the classteacher to order resources, book a time with the supply teacher, things like that. I've been a facilitator to allow her to do that rather than thinking 'Oh this is another thing I've got to take on board'.
>
> (headteacher)

Striking a balance between totally giving up control and too much intervention and supervision is difficult. Ideally, delegation involves setting the parameters and then staying in touch with the project through reviewing progress and meeting with those to whom responsibility is delegated at critical junctures. Developing confidence in teachers to whom responsibilities have been delegated and establishing mutual trust between headteachers and their staffs takes time to establish. It has to be worked at through sharing and reviewing experience and learning from it. Inter-dependence is the ideal relationship for which to aim whereby 'interactions arise when the manager needs to check on progess and development and when the colleague needs to report or consult about specific issues' (Whittaker, 1993, p. 140).

The LEA envisaged that project funding would be used to provide supply cover for teachers running projects not only to facilitate training but also to enable some project planning and activities to be carried out during the school day. Where support through the provision of non-contact time was provided for classteachers to assist with the extra work and to allow Share meetings with parents to be prepared for and to be unhurried, this enabled tasks to be carried out both more thoroughly and creatively. The provision of such non-contact time was a very strong motivating factor as it was viewed by teachers as confirming status on their projects and acknowledging that they were new departures for the school. Teachers appeared very willing to devote weekend leisure time to project work when they felt that the school was recognising the effort involved and prepared to devote funds to support it. Also, as explained by the classteacher central to the website project, the time the project had given him to think through thoroughly what he was doing was particularly valued:

> It's been great because the funding has meant that I've had time out to do things and stop and think and reflect as well on what is going on – not just do it and walk away but sit down and think about it and write it down as well.
>
> (classteacher)

Some of the classteachers kept professional files on their projects which provided a detailed record of project processes and were viewed as a valuable resource for project replication. Some files also contained critical reflections on what worked and what did not and why:

> I kept a file and every time I did a newsletter I put it in and then after each meeting I'd just type what I felt went on and what I might do next. It's more like a diary I think and I've got photographs in and the things parents have done I've kept a record of. And I've constantly asked them for ideas and I've written these down so we can refer back to them. I mean towards the Summer last year it got a little bit harder to keep the diary thing going but luckily over the Summer I was able to get it all back up-to-date ready to start this September.
>
> (classteacher)

Professional files served as a as a useful vehicle for professional development. They also had the potential to provide a focus for project review meetings between headteachers and classteachers.

From the outset schools were aware that they would be asked to supply short 'case studies' of the key features and outcomes of their projects. Drafts for these provided a stimulus for discussion between headteachers and involved staff particularly on the ways in which schools had benefitted from the projects and how the developments begun by projects could be carried forward. The case studies were brought together in a glossy publication which was disseminated to all schools in the county and served to publicise and celebrate the teachers' work (Curriculum Management and Advisory Service, 2002).

It was important for the morale of those running projects that colleagues should be fully aware of their nature and rationale and thus be in a position both to provide encouragement and to answer any parent enquiries. However, knowledge of projects by colleagues, children, parents and governors was very variable. Agendas for staff meetings were generally full and teachers were unable to create a slot to talk about the projects. Where more than one teacher was involved, discussions were overheard and participated in by colleagues so heightening project awareness in the school. Generally staff found out about projects through Share displays to celebrate parental involvement and their children's achievements, 'good work' assemblies when children presented what they had done and through project events for the entire school community such as the launch of a toy library.

## A burden for the classteacher

As expressed below projects could provide excellent opportunities for teacher professional development:

> I think that it's an opportunity for these two young teachers to further their career – to take it [share] on board, claim ownership and take it forward which I think they are doing. They seem very keen. My involvement has been on the shop floor in offering them support, help, advice, encouraging them, going in looking at what they've been doing and talking to parents.
>
> (headteacher)

However, where the nature and outcomes of, and support for, the delegated work had not been fully discussed and understood by those to whom tasks were delegated, the perceptions of headteachers could be at variance with those of teachers. This is illustrated by the comments below of the two teachers to whom the headteacher is referring:

> Well really we weren't given an option. We didn't know anything about it [share]. We were sent on a two day course. Even when we came back we were still told basically 'You haven't got a choice . I've decided I want to take it on board. You are doing it – you teachers are doing it'.
>
> (classteacher)

They felt resentful at 'being dumped on' which became fuelled because the initial notion of the headteacher taking their two classes while they ran the Share session did not work out in practice. The two teachers found themselves taking turns in doing the session and having a double class which they found most unsatisfactory. Fortunately, intervention by the co-ordinator brought these issues out into the open enabling them to be discussed and resolved.

Where activities had to be 'squeezed in' and 'bolted on to everything else' – for example, taking Share sessions during an afternoon assembly – it was difficult for classteachers to give them maximum thought and effort, to go beyond what they were already accustomed to doing and as a consequence to develop professionally:

> It's just another thing to plan really. I mean it's not horrendous but it's just another thing. I feel that I can manage it quite spontaneously and so when I've got the subject it might be that I photocopy a couple of things but it's not like I plan what I'm going to say because I don't feel I need to. Were I to hand it over to somebody else, who wasn't quite as confident as I am in that sort of thing, then I think they might find it quite a heavy burden if they didn't have some extra time.
>
> (classteacher)

In about half of the projects headteachers had delegated project responsibilities to an individual classteacher who carried out much of the work for the project alone. One acting head, who was unused to delegation, felt on reflection that she could have devolved tasks to more people so making it more of a team project, spreading the workload and capitalising on staff expertise.

## A source of empowerment

The majority of the classteachers believed that participation in the projects had contributed considerably to their professional development. The development of skills in working with parents/carers, which was one of the programme's main objectives, was cited most frequently as the predominant gain. For most of the class-teachers the projects provided new and challenging opportunities: to gain confidence in addressing parents as a group; to communicate and negotiate sensitively with them taking into account their individual needs and circumstances; to devise appropriate activities and workshops for adult learners; and to deepen their understanding of the impact of parental involvement in their children's learning and on the children's attitudes, behaviour and attainment. With the exception of two extremely experienced infant teachers who were already confident about working with parents, teachers spoke very enthusiastically about the skills that they had learned through the projects:

> The main thing has been to gain the confidence to speak to adults and know how to address adults and how to work with adults as it's very different from working with children. It's dealing with them in a sensitive way, especially trying to make sure there's no competition, handling negative comments and drawing the positive out of them. . . . It's completely different to anything I'd ever done before and I wouldn't necessarily have volunteered myself for it. Those initial meetings I was petrified and I still get butterflies but obviously now my skills have developed.
>
> (classteacher)

> One of the best bits was that I got to go and address a conference in Newcastle for Share and took a parent with me. Share has been a wonderful experience for me, I feel it has given me a lot of extra confidence.
>
> (classteacher)

Also, over half the classteachers commented on how the appreciation of project provision expressed by parents had boosted their morale and increased their job satisfaction.

The second most frequently mentioned area of professional development for teachers was the acquisition of management skills in order to be able to accommodate successfully within their role an area of work in addition to their classroom responsibilities:

> I've developed management skills in dealing with parents, in planning and organising things. I think it taught me to organise myself because I've had that extra workload on top of Literacy and I've had to get things done, as and when they came up. I've had to try and organise myself so I don't have to work myself into the ground at home as well. Time management, a bit of delegation are things I've started to do.
>
> (classteacher)

Generally teachers may be given management tasks but with no power or opportunity to delegate aspects of the these. Consequently, unless they have acquired appropriate skills through other aspects of their lives, delegation will be an unfamiliar concept. In the same way as the headteachers had come to recognise that in implementing an innovation the responsibility can and should be shared, so some teachers were also experiencing the need to let go and to delegate aspects of their project work to parents. For example, following advice from the head during a second 'drop-in' workshop for making Story Sacks the teacher responsible created an opportunity for parents to organise their work for themselves rather than doing it for them.

The majority of teachers commented on how at certain points in implementing their projects they had been required to think reflectively and innovatively in relation to a range of issues. Some of the examples they gave were devising alternative ways of recruiting parents to projects when initial approaches were unsuccessful, organising creche provision for parents attending workshops, handling sensitively situations likely to lead to disagreements between parents and celebrating the work achieved by parents and/or parents and children.

It was not only teachers who reported benefits from the projects. Some projects also involved other staff and volunteer helpers in project development and monitoring. For example, in one school the infant teacher responsible for Share and the classroom assistant, who worked with her, had been able to develop their joint planning and practice through both attending Share training sessions and collaborating over project implementation. The assistant also collected and recorded evidence on project progress and became the 'think tank' of the project.

In addition the HYW funding enabled her to go on a two-day residential computer course. These opportunities made her feel more valued within the school, enabled her to assume greater responsibility and boosted her confidence in interacting with parents.

## Conclusion

As shown here the processes and relationships involved in delegation mean that it is a great deal more complex than the reallocation of tasks. Being able to delegate with confidence and success appears to be one of the hallmarks of an experienced and effective manager. According to Everard and Morris (1996) effective delegation depends on; clearly defined objectives with a timetable; clearly defined criteria which should be borne in mind in achieving the objectives; and review procedures or checkpoints (p.49). In the HYW programme most headteachers appeared to give much more attention to the first two of these than to making opportunities at key points for teachers to report back. In part this was probably because primary schools tend to be small informal communities and so heads could take advantage of chance conversations with teachers for a project update. However, using 'snatched time' for reviewing delegated tasks can adversely affect the morale of those to whom tasks are delegated and denies them the opportunity to share fully concerns and successes with headteachers and to learn from their experience. In the HYW programme the quality of preparation and support for teachers running the projects and the nature and extent of headteachers' mentoring and feedback proved crucial in determining whether delegation was experienced as a burden or empowerment.

Teachers begin to take responsibility for managing tasks which are likely to include the potential for delegation at an early stage in their careers. Consequently they need access to training both external and internal to the school. As suggested by Bullock *et al.* (1997), both schools and teachers might benefit from a more systematic approach to learning through delegation. Teachers in senior positions could relinquish aspects of their organisational responsibility and authority to less experienced colleagues but within a supportive structure offering opportunities for discussion and mentoring. Projects, such as those in the HYW programme, provide excellent opportunities for this to happen.

## References

Bell, L. and Rhodes, C. (J996) *The Skills of Primary School Management,* London: Routledge.

Bullock, K., James, C. and Jamieson, E. (1997) 'The process of educational management learning', in Kydd, L. Crawford, M. and Riches, C. *Professional Development for Educational Management.* Buckingham: Open University Press 50–59.

Curriculum Management and Advisory Service (2002) *'Heads You Win in North Yorkshire'.* Northallerton: North Yorkshire County Council.

Everard, K.B. and Morris, G. (1996) *Effective School Management.* (3rd edn) London: Paul Chapmen Publishing Ltd.

Smithers, A. and Robinson, P. (2001) *The Teacher Labour Market*. Paper given at the DfES Research Conference, 11 December, London.

Webb, R. and Sudworth, S. (2001) *Heads You Win, Final Evaluation of a Programme of Headteacher Professional Development in North Yorkshire*. York: Department of Educational Studies, University of York.

Whitaker, P. (1993) *Managing Change in Schools*. Buckingham: Open University Press.

# 7 Planning for leadership succession

## Creating a talent pool in primary schools

*Mark Brundrett, Christopher Rhodes and Chrysanthi Gkolia*

## Introduction

There is evidence that as many as one in three schools are now failing to appoint a head when they first advertise and this may be indicative of a potential crisis in leadership recruitment in the United Kingdom (UK) (Shaw, 2006). The impact of a 'retirement bulge' has also been identified by the Institute for Public Policy Research (IPPR) (2002) and Hartle and Thomas (2004), who indicate that many middle-level as well as senior leaders will retire over the next few years. There has been suggestion that falling applications for middle-level and senior leadership posts may be further exacerbated by a growing feeling of disenchantment with leadership based on the standards and standardization agenda (Fink & Brayman, 2006; Hargreaves & Fink, 2006). A shortage of school leaders is not a phenomenon limited to the UK. Fink and Brayman (2006) report on the increasing evidence of a potential leadership crisis in many Western educational jurisdictions with the potential to undermine their school improvement initiatives. For example, shortages of school principals have been reported in parts of Canada (Williams, 2003), Australia (Gronn & Rawlings-Sanaei, 2003), New Zealand (Brooking *et al.*, 2003) and the United States of America (Thomson *et al.*, 2003). Nor is concern about preparing the next generation of leaders limited to the education sector. For example, succession planning has been identified as an important strategy in nurse leadership education (O'Connor, 2004).

The research reported in this article formed part of a study that was commissioned by the National College for School Leadership (NCSL) to explore practices, drivers and barriers to leadership talent identification, leadership development, leadership succession planning and leadership retention within a group of contextually different schools. Understanding practices and potentialities with regard to these issues is important, as one possible solution to the leadership crisis is to emphasize the growth of leadership talent within individual schools (Rhodes & Brundrett, 2005, 2006).

In human resource management (HRM) terms, Coleman and Earley (2005) draw attention to the worldwide trend of decentralizing the management of schools that has moved the responsibility for managing people to the institutional level. This involves getting the right people in place to do the job (staffing the organization), making sure the job is done well (performance management) and supporting their ability to achieve organizational goals and promotion (development and succession). Leadership supply remains a vital element in the life of any school. The appointment of individuals to leadership positions within schools has potentially profound implications, not only for those individuals, but also for their colleagues and the schools in which they work.

## Perspectives on the recruitment and retention of staff in schools

The schools sector has tended to have a poor history of professional recruitment and retention of staff (DfEE, 2000; DfES, 2001; Dean, 2001; GTCE, 2002). These problems are especially severe for the recruitment of heads (Hartle & Thomas, 2004; Shaw, 2006). It has been established that the leadership crisis in schools is likely to be exacerbated by a forthcoming demographic downturn characterized by a retirement 'bulge' amongst senior and middle-level leaders over the next few years (IPPR, 2002; Hartle & Thomas, 2004). Stark headlines attract the attention of readers of the NCSL's magazine (*LDR*, 2004): 'If current trends continue there will be a recruitment crisis of heads and deputies in the next six to ten years' (p. 16).

Traditionally associated with a single individual, notably the head, leadership in schools has increasingly become associated with individuals at different levels in the school (Gronn, 2000; Gronn, 2003a, 2003b; Wallace, 2002; Harris, 2003, 2004; Muijs & Harris, 2003). Ensuring a supply of able middle-level and senior leaders in schools is of key strategic importance to individual schools and to national success. Given a national (IPPR, 2002; Hartle & Thomas, 2004; Shaw, 2006) and an international (Fink & Brayman, 2006) shortage of leaders, the notion of pro-activity in 'growing one's own' leaders within schools is rapidly emerging within the UK (Rhodes & Brundrett, 2005, 2006).

A recently reported study undertaken in the USA (Quinn *et al.*, 2006) has posed questions concerning the nature of knowledge, skills and experiences required to support leadership potential and desire. In suggesting a four-phase model of leadership development for new teachers, these authors are mindful that without talent development, a rich source of human potential remains untapped and untrained and may be lost. Supportive of the notion that leadership potential should not be lost, a recent document presented to the UK Parliament by the Secretary of State for Education and Skills (DfES, 2005) emphasizes that there is a need to develop better career paths for those with talent to be developed as the school leaders of the future.

Pro-activity in the development of leadership successors requires the recognition of potential leadership talent in others. In commercial organizations this typically involves the organization taking a longer-term view so that future requirements for leadership roles and skills can be addressed. It involves well-targeted career development for talented individuals and senior staff working together to recognize and value the leadership potential of others. Much commercial-sector literature emphasizes that the adoption of a *laissez-faire* attitude to future leaders is irresponsible, as performance, motivation and retention are seen as important outcomes of active succession planning (see Wolfe, 1996; McCall, 1998; Hirsch, 2000; Byham *et al.*, 2003; Rothwell, 2005). Hartle and Thomas (2004) have reviewed leadership succession practices in organizations outside the education sector and conclude that many organizations are now investing considerable resources in developing leadership talent in-house.

In comparison to commercial organizations, only limited information concerning leadership succession and succession planning practices within educational organizations is available in the literature. In the UK, a number of individual studies are beginning to offer a picture of issues in leadership succession and succession planning. For example, a study by Fletcher-Campbell (2003) has secured feedback on teacher perspectives of the advantages and disadvantages of seeking promotion to middle-level leadership posts. Castagnoli and Cook (2004) have emphasized the importance of training new staff so that they can replace other staff as they leave. Hayes (2005) has cautioned that the number of deputy heads not seeking headship and the interactions between heads and their deputies in terms of leadership succession requires further study. In a Scottish study, Draper and McMichael (2003) identified a number of problems in relation to headship recruitment. For example, the attraction of senior staff to other career opportunities in schools and in education other than headship is likely to occur due to individuals' reluctance to take on further responsibilities, to address burdensome bureaucracy and to lose control over life. There is evidence that some heads and local education authorities are becoming more aware of the notion of a developing leadership crisis and the possibilities and challenges associated with 'growing your own leaders'. The relatively neglected phenomenon of leadership succession in schools is now beginning to receive more attention.

## Methodology

### *Overall research project and sample*

The overall research project from which this article is derived was organized into three distinct but interrelated phases. First, a focus-group phase was conducted so that a second, questionnaire survey phase might be informed. Finally, a semi-structured interview phase was undertaken in order to capture narratives and create vignettes of practice. All phases drew upon a sample group of 70 contextually different schools located within the Midlands and north-west of England. It is the final-phase element of narratives on which this article draws in order to unpack some of the issues that are specific to primary schools.

Schools selected for the interview and subsequent narrative analysis phase were self-disclosing in one of two ways. Either it was apparent that good practices with respect to the issues under study were being identified by both heads and their staff in questionnaire returns from individual schools. Alternatively, heads directly invited researchers to contact their schools via a section included in the questionnaires. A total of nine schools took part in this final phase of the study. All data sources were brought to bear on the creative process. For example, while we listened to information provided by the respondents, we asked about the Office for Standards in Education (Ofsted) and other outturn data. In constructing accounts, all respondents were asked to tell the interviewer about:

1   The perceived strengths and mechanisms of their school in leadership talent identification.
2   What evidential base they had that the school was good at leadership development.
3   What role they perceived for the local authority (LA) or local education authority (LEA) in leadership development and succession planning.

### Narrative analysis

Narrative or story is becoming an established way of revealing the human scale of teaching (Clandinin & Connelly, 1991) and we have argued previously in this journal that story is an effective means of depicting the complexity of teachers' work (Brundrett, 2006). The aim of such narrative writing is to provide a lifelike account that is grounded in the everyday world of practice so that practitioners who read the accounts identify with or relate to the information. As themes emerged, we constructed narrative accounts, using as much as possible of the verbatim text from the interview material. Each narrative account was constructed after the interviews and a copy of the final report was sent to the respondents. In these ways we sought trustworthiness in matching the constructed realities of the participants with the leadership stories attributed to them (Lincoln & Guba, 1986; Connelly & Clandinin, 1990; Flinders & Eisner, 1994).

We argue that the narrative account conveys information that is complex and multifaceted in an integrated way. The accounts are written in the first person, in the voice of the respondent, since we prefer to write the accounts in the voice of the principal rather than using the voice of an assumed, omnipresent, academic observer (Eisner, 1998). Our aim is to convey the rich texture of the experiences of the participants in the study, without the explicit interpretation of the researcher. Although the accounts contain descriptive and factual contextual information, more importantly they each tell a story, using the devices of story-telling. For example, each account has a title or theme. Such story-telling is therefore a creative act, carried out by the researchers (Clarke & Wildy, 2004, pp. 561–562).

## The stories of two school leaders

A total of nine narratives were created in the process of research but limitations of space preclude the inclusion of all these interactions. Two narratives from contextually different primary schools are offered as examples of the technique and in order to elucidate the kind of responses gained by the researchers.

### School 1: linking the head and the deputy though shadowing

School 1 has 210 pupils on roll and is one-form entry. Its headteacher is in his 7th year in the school. He has spent three years as deputy, one year as acting headteacher and three years as headteacher. The school is Church of England voluntary controlled and lies in a suburban/urban location with under 8% of students receiving free school meals. The catchment area's population is mainly white and there are very few pupils who speak English as a foreign language. The narrative for this school is given below.

> We are very proud of our staff development. The school was awarded the 'Leading Achievement Award: Leading Learning through the Workforce' award in 2005 by Birmingham City Council—which is an award for good staff development for all staff from non-teaching, to Teaching Assistants, to NQTs, to teachers, to SMT. For example, the caretaker and school secretary have got NVQs and deputy has completed NPQH recently. We are pleased with a *shadowing* programme we have developed, which is designed to create a closer relationship between the head and the deputy. The deputy works very closely with me and we are currently working on school finance and the deputy comes to budget meetings with the governors. The deputy has 1 day week release from class, and had this before the remodelling agenda kicked in, so this allows us to meet on a regular basis. The deputy gets very involved with learning about all aspects of headship and is currently working on part of the school SEF, which is leading on the 'Healthy Schools Initiative'. I think the link between the head and deputy is a critical one. You have to accept there is an element of chance with a deputy—you may get a good one, or a bad one or not get to appoint one at all. The benefits of close work shadowing by the deputy mean a head can take risks in the knowledge that the deputy is secure and therefore that the school is secure so I can leave school and everything will keep running. I think that the head needs to let go sometimes and not be checking all the time or you just get into the habit of being very directive. Stepping back from trying to model everything for everybody is also developmental for the head. I expect that the deputy will leave in due course as he wants a headship but I'm OK with this because a legacy will be left behind.
>
> I think the LEA are good at this level because they provide opportunities for both deputies and headteachers for secondment. Here, I was acting head in this school for one year before taking over permanently while my own head had been seconded to another school. The LEA is not active enough in seeking leadership talent, despite the fact that they need heads in all their schools. Having said that the LEA is pro-active in the appointment of heads, they help the governing body make decisions regarding this and make

recommendations. They should also be more active in training governors but this is a problem because you can ask: Is it worth providing this training so that they can lead on the appointment—because probably they will only ever be doing this once?

### School 2: from high turnover to sustainability

School 2 is an urban, multicultural primary school with 370 pupils, which came out of special measures in November 2005. The headteacher has been in post for two years. The narrative is given below.

> I inherited a school in special measures with leadership and management as one of the key issues requiring improvement. In order to increase the rate of progress at the school, immediate action had to be taken. A review of the staffing structure, alongside the introduction of a whole school monitoring and evaluation programme led to an increased emphasis on staff accountability and consequently led to a large turnover of staff.
>
> During this period of change, we began to recruit staff to join the 'understaffed' School Leadership Team. We appointed a science leader and community leader. These were both internal appointments. Both members of staff developed very quickly and 'grew' into their roles. We also made a number of external appointments, a gifted and talented leader and two new 'learning leader' posts. These new posts were offered on a secondment or permanent basis. The 'learning leaders' were appointed to raise standards in literacy and numeracy and support staff development. The seconded learning leader left after a term. The community leader took on a number of the responsibilities.
>
> Our journey through special measures led to the creation of distributed leadership at the school. We created *action teams*—these involve all the teaching and support staff. The teams undertake projects and work related to priorities identified in the school development plan. The teams encourage a degree of flexibility, and give staff the opportunity to put forward development ideas—this gives a sense of ownership. The governors are very interested in what is happening in the action teams and ask for updates at each meeting. The teams are also a vehicle fro developments around the Every Child Matters agenda. When the teams were created, some staff needed encouragement to join a team, now most staff allocate themselves to a particular team. Every half term each team reports on the actions taken, outcomes for teachers, children or parents, and any new resulting actions. The meetings have become part of the school calendar—so staff know when they will be feeding back to each other. The teams have also led to greater collaboration within the school. It is wonderful to see teachers and support staff working to their strengths and helping the school to become a better place for the children.
>
> A further example of distributed leadership includes giving two learning support practitioners the responsibility for the day-to-day management of

special needs. With the introduction of the TLR structure, we have recently created a single *school improvement post*, which is a fixed term 'ghost post'. If there is a project in school needing additional time for a member of staff, other than an already designated leader, they can take leadership of the work—all members of main scale teaching staff can apply. Going through special measures and the introduction of TLRs has made us think more carefully about the way we work in this school—what is in place must be *sustainable*. I feel that sustainability has been achieved with the development of the action teams. Action teams are giving staff the opportunity to learn from each other and lead on school improvement priorities. They provide a way of 'growing' our own leaders within the school because if someone leaves—there is always someone to take over. We have to keep looking for the next layer of leaders; otherwise, we would always be fire-fighting to fill posts. We don't want to wait until someone leaves to start thinking about a replacement.

Leadership is good if it is having a positive impact on standards of learning and teaching. Leadership and management have to have a positive impact upon teaching and learning and to be effective over time it needs to be sustainable. Sustainable leadership is now such that if I left the school the school would still be able to continue to move forward—the systems and processes must not all depend on a single person to take the lead. However, a school will not continue to move forward without the right people. Sustainability is not just about systems and processes, you also need the right people with the right skills throughout the school to ensure effective long-term sustainability. In our school, leaders work-shadow the head and each other in order to increase their skills and deepen their understanding of school improvement issues.

The LEA has a deputy head group for networking. There are some good CPD opportunities.

## Summary of findings

One of the most striking features of the narratives is the extent to which all of the respondents were self-consciously engaged in staff development. Senior management teams, especially heads and deputy heads, build up pivotal relationships which are mutually supportive and assist in their own professional development and in the professional development of the wider staff. There is a strong commitment to leadership and management structures which encourage or require all staff to take on active leadership roles, and thereby to develop skills in decision-making and allied leadership skills. This may take the form of distributed leadership, but many heads seek to retain some element of hierarchical structure within which staff take on specific responsibilities. The mechanisms by which this culture was developed include work-shadowing, paired work with 'critical friends' or peer coaching.

Several schools suggested a direct link between high-quality leadership development and student outcomes. Other evidence included the notion that good staff development would inevitably lead to colleagues gaining promotion.

Nonetheless a high staff turnover was seen as a contra-indicator. The conception that the school would continue to function well after the head had left was seen as significant and several heads seemed to indicate that they felt that they were engaged in legacy-building in the attempts to enhance the leadership skills of the rest of the staff.

Local education authorities and local authorities are seen to be improving in their role in staff development but they are no longer seen as key agents. Nonetheless many LEAs were seen to be improving. The major role that school leaders perceived that LAs and LEAs can play in leadership development was the development of networks to facilitate interaction. The additional roles that could affect leadership development included functioning as a 'critical friend'.

In successful schools which consider themselves to be good at leadership development a number of key features arise:

1   Heads view themselves as key agents of staff development.
2   A culture of leadership distribution is engendered.
3   Staff are encouraged to work in task-oriented teams.
4   Leadership sustainability, staff promotions, a consistent but modest staff turnover, and high levels of pupil attainment are viewed as key indicators of robust leadership development systems.
5   Work-shadowing, coaching, the use of 'critical friends' and networking are seen as key mechanisms for leadership development.
6   There is evidence that NCSL programmes such as Learning from the Middle (LftM) are beginning to affect leadership development for middle-level leaders.
7   LEAs and LAs are seen to be improving in performance in relation to leadership development but their main role is seen as network facilitation rather than programme development and delivery.

## Conclusion

This potential crisis in leadership recruitment in schools is manifest in falling numbers of applicants for middle-level and senior posts and in a retirement 'bulge' amongst existing heads and middle-level leaders. Systematic national and local responses would entail the development of mechanisms based on good HRM practices to ensure rational decision-making with respect to leadership talent identification, development, succession and retention in all schools. Some of these mechanisms are already in place and are rooted in the effectiveness of some development mechanisms reported in this study. Other mechanisms, particularly around succession, succession planning and succession management, appear less well-developed and are a cause for concern at both national and local levels.

Although a complex nexus of personal and professional issues impinge upon an individual's desire to pursue leadership progression within their own school or at another school, local issues within the control of the local authority or the school itself are of significance. The mindset of heads and other senior leaders, the culture they have created within the school, the static influences of context such as school size and the more flexible immediate context of school performance all appear to be influential.

The study points to the importance of shared understanding between heads, middle-level leaders and classroom teachers of the characteristics of leadership talent identification. It is clear that schools need to ensure that a longer-term view of leadership requirements becomes part of school strategic thinking. Where appropriate, senior leaders need to actively and purposefully support leadership development through creation of a talent pool that encourages staff to take on new roles and to aspire to leadership positions. The narratives presented in this study point to some of the ways in which schools may enhance their position in 'growing their own leaders', such as leadership distribution, coaching, career planning and an active developmental relationship between the head and the deputy.

## References

Brooking, K., Collins, G., Court, M. & O'Neill, J. (2003) Getting below the surface of the principal recruitment 'crisis' in New Zealand primary schools, *Australian Journal of Education*, 47(2), 146–158.

Brundrett, M. (2006) The impact of leadership training: stories from a small school, *Education 3–13*, 34(2), 173–184.

Byham, W., Smith, A. & Paese, M. (2003) *Grow your own leaders* (London, Financial Times/Prentice Hall).

Castagnoli, P. & Cook, N. (2004) *Growing your own leaders: the impact of professional development on school improvement.* Full practitioner report (Nottingham, National College for School Leadership).

Clandinin, D. J. & Connelly, F. M. (1991) Narrative and story in practice and research, in: D. Schon (Ed.) *The reflective turn: case studies in and on educational practice* (New York, Teachers College Press), 258–281.

Clarke, S. & Wildy, H. (2004) Context counts: viewing small school leadership from the inside out, *Journal of Educational Administration*, 42(5), 555–572.

Coleman, M. & Earley, P. (2005) *Leadership and management in education: cultures, change and context* (Oxford, Oxford University Press).

Connelly, F. M. & Clandinin, D. J. (1990) Stories of experience and narrative inquiry, *Educational Researcher*, 19(4), 2–14.

Dean, P. (2001) Blood on the tracks: an accusation and proposal, *Journal of In-Service Education*, 27, 491–499.

Department for Education and Employment (DfEE) (2000) *Statistics of education: teachers in England and Wales 2000* (London, Stationery Office).

Department for Education and Skills (DfES) (2001) *Schools achieving success* (London, Stationery Office).

DfES (2005) *Higher standards, better schools for all: more choice for parents and pupils* (London, Stationery Office).

Draper, J. & McMichael, P. (2003) The rocky road to headship, *Australian Journal of Education*, 47(2), 185–196.

Eisner, E. W. (1998) *The enlightened eye: qualitative inquiry and the enhancement of educational practices* (Englewood Cliffs, NJ, Prentice-Hall).

Fink, D. & Brayman, C. (2006) School leadership succession and the challenges of change, *Educational Administration Quarterly*, 42(1), 62–89.

Fletcher-Campbell, F. (2003) Promotion to middle management: some practitioners' perceptions, *Educational Research*, 45(1), 1–15.

Flinders, D. J. & Eisner, E. W. (1994) Educational criticism as a form of qualitative inquiry, *Research in the Teaching of English*, 28(4), 341–357.

General Teaching Council for England (GTCE) (2002) *Teachers on teaching: a survey of the teaching profession.* Available online at: http://www.educationguardian.co.uk

Gronn, P. (2000) Distributed properties: a new architecture for leadership, *Educational Management and Administration*, 28(3), 317–338.

Gronn, P. (2003a) *The new work of educational leaders* (London, Paul Chapman).

Gronn, P. (2003b) Leadership: who needs it?, *School Leadership and Management*, 23(3), 267–291.

Gronn, P. & Rawlings-Sanaei, F. (2003) Recruiting school principals in a climate of leadership disengagement, *Australian Journal of Education*, 47(2), 172–184.

Hargreaves, A. & Fink, D. (2006) *Sustainable leadership* (San Francisco, CA, Jossey-Bass).

Harris, A. (2003) Teacher leadership as distributed leadership: heresy, fantasy or possibility?, *School Leadership and Management*, 23(3), 313–324.

Harris, A. (2004) Distributed leadership and school improvement: leading or misleading?, *Educational Management Administration and Leadership*, 32(1), 11–24.

Hartle, F. & Thomas, K. (2004) *Growing tomorrow's school leaders.* Available online at: http://www.ncsl.org.uk/researchpublications

Hayes, T. (2005) *Rising stars and sitting tenants: a picture of deputy headship in one London borough and how some of its schools are preparing their deputies for headship.* Summary practitioner enquiry report. (Nottingham, National College for School Leadership).

Hirsch, W. (2000) *Succession planning demystified.* Report 372 (Brighton, Institute for Employment Studies).

IPPR (2002) The future of the teaching profession, *Management in Education*, 15(3), 17–22.

*LDR* (2004) Growing leaders, *LDR Magazine for School Leaders*, 11, March, 16.

Lincoln, Y. & Guba, E. (1986) But is it rigorous? Trustworthiness and authenticity in naturalistic evaluation, in: D. D. Williams (Ed.) *Naturalistic evaluation* (San Francisco, CA, Jossey-Bass), 73–84.

McCall, M. W. (1998) *High flyers: developing the next generation of leaders* (Boston, MA, Harvard Business School Press).

Muijs, D. & Harris, A. (2003) Teacher leadership: improvement through empowerment? An overview of the literature, *Educational Management and Administration*, 31(4), 437–448.

O'Connor, M. (2004) Succession planning: a key strategy in nursing leadership education, *Nurse Leader*, October, 21–25.

Quinn, C. L., Haggard, C. S. & Ford, B. A. (2006) Preparing new teachers for leadership roles: a model in four phases, *School Leadership and Management*, 26(10), 55–68.

Rhodes, C. P. & Brundrett, M. (2005) Leadership succession in schools: a cause for concern, *Management in Education*, 19(5), 15–18.

Rhodes, C. P. & Brundrett, M. (2006) The identification, development, succession and retention of leadership talent in contextually different primary schools: a case study located within the English West Midlands, *School Leadership and Management*, 26(3), 269–287.

Rothwell, W. J. (2005) *Effective succession planning: ensuring leadership continuity and building talent from within* (3rd edn) (New York, American Management Association).

Shaw, M. (2006, January 13) New signs of crisis in leadership recruitment, *Times Educational Supplement*, p. 2.

Thomson, P., Blackmore, J., Sachs, J. & Tregenza, K. (2003) High stakes principalship—sleepless nights, heart attacks and sudden death accountabilities: reading media representations of the United States principal shortage, *Australian Journal of Education*, 47(2), 118–132.

Wallace, M. (2002) Modelling distributed leadership and management effectiveness: primary senior management teams in England and Wales, *School Effectiveness and School Improvement*, 13(2), 163–186.

Williams, T. R. (2003) Ontario's principal scarcity: yesterday's abdicated responsibility—today's unrecognised challenge, *Australian Journal of Education*, 47(2), 159–171.

Wolfe, R. (1996) *Systematic succession planning: building leadership from within* (Menlo Park, CA, Crisp Publications).

# 8   *Every Child Matters*: 'tinkering' or 'reforming'

An analysis of the development of the Children Act (2004) from an educational perspective

*Jeremy Roche and Stanley A. Tucker*

## Uncomfortable reading

The story behind the development of the Children Act (2004) makes uncomfortable reading for politicians, children's service managers, practitioners and academics alike. For the momentum behind the Act, i.e. the *Every Child Matters* agenda (Department for Education and Skills [DfES], 2003), was born out of the tragic circumstances surrounding the death of Victoria Climbié (Department of Health [DoH], 2003) and numerous other child abuse inquiries. This article is concerned not only to highlight the serious shortcomings of previous attempts to safeguard children, but also to focus on key messages for practice for those directly involved in education of the young.

Some legislation should rightly be accorded major status in terms of the impact it has on the lives of children and young people; the Education Act (1944) is an example of that kind of legislation. An initial interrogation of the Children Act (2004), in terms of the structural and procedural reforms proposed, tends to suggest that it is also likely to be highly influential in shaping the development of services. One of the primary intentions here is to come to a clearer view as to whether the legislation concerned should be viewed as mere 'tinkering' with that already in existence or if it has the potential to provide a strong and robust platform for significant reform of the safeguarding children agenda. The question is also explored as to what kind of impact both *Every Child Matters* and the Children Act is likely to have on educational policies, practices and structures in the longer term?

In reviewing the political drivers for change in respect of safeguarding children work it can be argued that emphasis is now being placed on the need for radical reform. Challenges to established structures and processes and the introduction of new working arrangements are predicated on a perspective of professional 'failure' to keep children safe, a mistrust of the quality of practice and the inability and inflexibility of structures, services and institutions to respond to the needs of children at risk of abuse, neglect or even death. The Climbié inquiry left political and professional worlds reeling. For Lord Laming, who led the Climbié inquiry, the outcomes were 'deeply disturbing':

Victoria's case was altogether different. Victoria was not hidden away. It is deeply disturbing that during the days and months following her initial contact with Ealing Housing Department's Homelessness Person's Unit, Victoria was known to no less that two further housing authorities, four social services departments, two child protection teams of the Metropolitan Police Service, a specialist centre managed by the NSPCC, and she was admitted to two different hospitals because of suspected deliberate harm. . . .

(DoH, 2003, p. 3)

The outcomes of the Soham inquiry into the deaths of Jessica Chatman and Holly Wells also revealed a high level of systems failure. A direct quote from that inquiry (cited in Parton, 2005, p. 134) illustrates the point only too well:

The inquiry did find errors, omissions, failures and shortcomings which are deeply shocking. Taken together, these were so extensive that one cannot be confident that it was Huntley alone who 'slipped through the net'.

A key issue raised concerned itself with how a person like Huntley, who had come to the attention of the police before, was able to work in a school. In June 2005 the DfES issued new guidance on safeguarding children (DfES, 2005) predicated on the assessment that current checks on staff working in schools were insufficient to protect children. Not only are teachers and teaching assistants covered by the guidance, but so are caretakers, caterers and volunteers.

A presumption underpinned both inquiries that improved communication, more effective inter-agency working and a significant revamping of the ways information is stored and transmitted would eventually lead to better outcomes for children and young people. For government the need for change was marked out by the fact that:

Children have varying needs which change over time. Judgements on how best to intervene when there are concerns about harm to a child will often and unavoidably entail an element of risk—at the extreme, of leaving a child for too long in a dangerous situation or of removing a child unnecessarily from their family. The way to proceed in the face of uncertainty is through competent professional judgements based on a sound assessment of the child's needs, the parents' capacity to respond to those needs—including the capacity to keep the child safe from significant harm—and the wider family circumstances.

(Her Majesty's Government, 2006, p. 3)

Implicit in the statement is the idea that it is impossible to eliminate all risk in this area of work. The notion is also presented that risks have to be balanced against possible negative outcomes and this will involve a variety of 'judgement calls' on the part of a range of professionals. But look also at the kind of assessment process that is advocated. Clearly, a range of factors has to be considered before any course of action is decided upon. Later in the document the case is made that a wide range of agencies should be involved in that assessment process by bringing together individuals with complementary professional skills and expertise. The onus of responsibility for the safeguarding of children is transformed as it is argued that 'all agencies and professionals' have a direct responsibility to 'be alert to potential indicators of abuse', minimize the opportunities of children and young people being exposed to risk, share and assist in the analysis of information to support effective assessment and 'safeguard and promote the child's welfare' (Her Majesty's Government, 2006, pp. 31–34).

At one level the drivers for change proposed here are clear and unequivocal. Concerns exist about the nature of fragmented services, a failure to effectively 'join up' provision in ways that will work for all children and families, and there is ongoing debate about the unnecessary segmentation of the roles and responsibilities of those working with the young (Horner & Krawczyk, 2006). Yet, as Parton (2005) also noted, the introduction of *Every Child Matters* and the legislation to support its implementation should be viewed as a staging post for a government that is on a significant journey of reform for child-related policy and practice.

## A different agenda?

The ideas presented here are powerful, but at the same time they have the ability to disable professional activity, especially when those involved lack appropriate levels of training, expertise, knowledge or confidence to intervene. The notion of the multi-professional response is questionable unless all those working with children and young people feel that they have a real contribution to make to the safeguarding of children that is afforded status and equal value by all those involved (Tucker *et al.*, 2002). Above all, there is a need to move away from seeing protection and prevention as opposite sides of a coin—'hard' and 'soft' activities that are artificially divided by intervention indicators, risk assessment criteria and socially constructed categories of what it means to be 'neglected', 'at risk' or 'abused'. The language of safeguarding children can quickly become dense, impenetrable and shrouded in mystery when it is owned by a few, driven by assumptions and probabilities and dressed up in the language of biological inheritance, family pathology and class-based stereotypes.

The safeguarding agenda advocated argues the case for moving away from a narrowly conceived child protection agenda that is primarily preoccupied with investigation, detection, 'removal' and punishment, an agenda where the business of safeguarding children is seen to rest almost exclusively with the police and social work personnel. The development of a more preventative and educationally based focus on safeguarding work potentially brings with it the opportunity to change working relationships and practices. Accordingly, the task of safeguarding children becomes the responsibility of everyone and not 'someone else'. This approach has been further reinforced through *Working together to safeguard children* (Her Majesty's Government, 2006, pp. 11–12), in which explicit guidance is offered on the roles and functions to be carried out by all those working with the young. Common themes emerging include the need for effective and appropriate joint interdisciplinary training as well as a requirement for 'refresher training'. The importance of having 'policies in place and promoting the welfare of children is emphasised'. The need to create a 'culture of listening' is advocated and 'whistle blowing' is championed if any agency is failing to meet its responsibilities in this area.

One theme lurking here, however, is an immanent distrust of those who work with children and young people (Roche & Tucker, 2003). The project of minimizing the risks to which children and young people might be exposed has led to the proscribing of particular kinds of relationship. For example, the Sexual Offences (Amendment) Act 2000 introduced the offence of 'the abuse of a position of trust' in relation to children and young people under the age of 18; persons working with 'looked after' children and in schools were covered by this legislation.

However, it is not just a question of reconfiguring acceptable relationships and forms of communication, it is also a matter of recognizing that there is a common core of skills and knowledge that all those who work with children and young people in a range of settings require. Part of the problem has been that too many professionals have not had these skills and knowledge, with the result that errors of professional judgement have been made. Yet, the agenda within *Working together to safeguard children* (Her Majesty's Government, 2006, pp. 38–40) goes further. Specific roles and responsibilities are assigned to particular areas of professional practice. In the case of schools and further education institutions attention is given to matters concerned with both protection and prevention. For example, Personal, Social and Health Education (PSHE) is seen as offering important curriculum opportunities to assist young people: in managing risks; to understand and 'judge' the appropriateness of physical contact; to resist bullying and abuse. Staff within schools are seen to have a vital role to play in 'helping identify welfare concerns, and indicators of possible abuse and neglect, at an early stage. . . . Contributing to the assessment of a child's needs and where appropriate ongoing action to meet those needs'. It is also argued that educators have a role to play in putting 'arrangements' in place to combat drug and alcohol misuse, implement 'school security' and respond to the 'health needs of children with medical conditions'. Yet this is not uncontroversial. Under section 175 of the Education Act (2002) schools and local authorities were already under a legal duty to promote and safeguard the welfare of pupils. Schools should have a designated member of staff dealing with child protection matters and who would liaise with social services and other agencies. Smellie (2006) noted that schools are now required to report any misconduct to the relevant authorities. Under the Education (Prohibition from Teaching or Working with Children) Regulations (2003) the school is required to report to the Children's Safeguarding Operations Unit when a person is dismissed for misconduct or when they resign in circumstances where they might have been dismissed.

What is apparent from reviewing government documents such as *Working together to safeguard children* is that an attempt is made to more clearly define how different agencies, and the professionals working within them, should respond to the safeguarding children agenda. Increasing significance is now being placed on common roles and responsibilities, as well as the specific functions that can be related to particular areas of occupational activity. It seems reasonable to argue that significant changes in both policy and practice will be required of those working within schools with children and young people. The potential scope of that change is considered in the next section of the article, with specific reference to multidisciplinary working, the role of extended schools and workforce reform. We now turn to an exploration of multidisciplinary working.

## Multidisciplinary approaches

> Professionals will be encouraged to work in multi-disciplinary teams based in and around schools and Children's Centres. They will provide a rapid response to the concerns of frontline teachers, childcare workers and others in universal services.
>
> (DfES, 2003, p. 9)

The election of a Labour government in 1997 brought with it a policy mandate for all services working with children and young people to develop more effective and efficient multidisciplinary approaches to work. An early manifestation of this policy driver could be seen in relation to the development of early years provision. The mandatory introduction of Early Years Development and Childcare Partnerships (EYDCP) in every local authority area clearly signalled central government's intentions to construct multidisciplinary working relationships across the public, private and voluntary sectors that would encompass education, social care and health. Crucially, the local education authority was given the lead role in bringing together relevant agencies 'to draw up an annual local plan, linked together into the government's targets for early education places for 3- and 4-year-olds and the expansion of childcare' (Pugh, 2001, p. 15). This policy has continued apace and can again be seen directly reflected in the quote from Lord Laming provided above. As with the EYDCP policy, it is also interesting to note the central role of education (this time particularly focused on 'extended schools' and Children's Centres) in the delivery of 'multidisciplinary' practice.

At one level the policy agenda here is relatively clear and easy to understand. A desire is expressed to move away from seeing service delivery in compartmentalized and bureaucratic terms to a position where the needs of communities, families and individuals are viewed as paramount. Bagley *et al.* (2004, p. 596) took this point further in emphasizing the government's intention to bring about 'vertical' and 'horizontal' 'integration' of both national and local services intended to create 'new partnerships'. More radical approaches may also mean the pooling of budgets, 'combining resources' and 'working in partnership across organizational boundaries'.

Within such an approach a refocusing and potential restructuring of the teaching role appears possible and even likely. The interdisciplinary agenda for safeguarding children (and the assumptions that underpin it) comes alive when the concept of an 'integrated approach' is reviewed from the perspective of those working within schools across all age ranges. Traditional protection functions remain—looking for indications of abuse, reporting suspicions of abuse, etc. However, other functions that will increase the level of multidisciplinary involvement are also explicitly articulated—sharing and analysing information, being centrally involved in common assessment processes, 'regularly reviewing outcomes for the child against specific plans' (Her Majesty's Government, 2006, p. 4). In addition, a demand is also placed on all schools to designate a senior staff member 'to take lead responsibility for dealing with child protection issues, providing advice and support to other staff, liasing with the authority, and working with other organisations as necessary' (Her Majesty's Government, 2006, p. 39).

Within such a perspective the educationalist based in school is seen as a central player when it comes to developing services for socially excluded children and families and those who are considered to be 'at risk'. Their contribution to multidisciplinary work is viewed as vital, for it is argued that 'health, education and social services' all have an important role to play in 'improving and safe-guarding the well-being of "vulnerable children" and their families' (Abbott *et al.*, 2005, p. 230). Yet at the same time it is important to note that there are difficulties attached to moving this working agenda forward in a meaningful way. As Willan *et al.* (2004) noted, there have been difficulties in promoting the vision of multidisciplinary working across organizations and they also consider a report from the Audit Commission (2003) that points towards poor and ineffective leadership within this area at a senior level. Abbott *et al.* (2005, p. 230) go further in their criticisms, arguing that there is a 'dearth of evidence to support the notion that multi-agency working in practice brings about benefits for children and families'. Yet it remains the case that such a form of professional practice is high on the government's agenda and has in fact contributed to one key area of reform in the shape of the 'extended school'.

## Extended schools

The development of extended schools has to be seen as part of the wider intentions of government, through the *Every Child Matters* agenda, to roll out multidisciplinary and integrated provision to support children's educational and health development and social care. The role and function of the extended school model is summarized in terms of its intention to provide 'a range of services and activities beyond the school day to help meet the needs of its pupils, their families and the wider community' (DfES, 2002, p. 5). In addition, the provision of 'wraparound' childcare is seen as a an important function for extended schools in order to promote, for example: social inclusion; 'respond to inter-linked problems of persistent late arrivals, poor attendance, and under-performance'; provide a 'single point of access for an integrated range of family services'; offer the opportunity for parents and carers to return to work or access appropriate training (Department for Education and Skills & Department for Work and Pensions, 2002, pp. 3–4).

In support of this particular development, the Education Act (2002) enables school governors 'to enter into agreements with other partners to provide services on school premises', extend local community use, consult with LEAs and other 'stakeholders' about the development of such facilities and protect the 'main duty to educate pupils'.

Clearly, the connection can be made with this kind of work and the five principles of *Every Child Matters*. 'Enjoying and achieving', 'staying safe' and 'being healthy' lie at the heart of much of the work proposed for extended schools. However, in reality there is a danger that the agenda for reform will amount to little more than 'adult education plus', the letting of schoolrooms to community groups and visits from various social care and health agencies. For the approach to work, structural and legal changes have to be coupled with a different, philosophically driven, view of the school and the roles, relationships and responsibilities of those working within it.

According to research conducted by Wilkin *et al.* (2003) specific 'arenas' for the development of extended schools appear to be emerging. Of the 160 schools reviewed, some were using the extended school model to enhance curriculum provision and opportunities while others were focusing on developing community learning and leisure facilities, early years 'wraparound' care, provision to support families and carers and more specialist offerings aimed at providing information technology, business and sport and cultural opportunities. The evaluation of the 'pathfinder' extended schools project conducted by Cummings *et al.* (2003, p. 1) revealed that:

> there is no single model of 'the extended school' and there is considerable variation between projects depending on factors including community need, geography and access to funding streams. . . . The 'full-service' school in which services are located on the school site is less common, though many schools are working towards this.

The challenge to those working in schools to deliver effective extended schools is considerable. Perhaps the greatest challenge lies in the area of changing the culture of some schools. As Smith (2005) argued, collaborative, multidisciplinary work will challenge the 'isolated' position of many schools; 'where schools have had to work with other agencies their relative size, statutory nature and high degree of control over what happens within their walls have often made them difficult partners'. Clearly, issues are likely to arise concerning the control of both personnel and resources that are not directly in the control of the school. For some heads the issue of supervision and control of all staff working on school premises is extremely important:

Certainly there has been a tendency for heads in a number of schools to insist on the new cadre of workers, assistants and mentors being responsible to them rather than some outside agency.

(Smith, 2005, p. 13)

At the same time, those occupying teaching roles may find new demands and expectations being placed on them. The safeguarding agenda pursued through extended schools is one concerned with prevention and inclusion—the improved integration of children and families in communities through the creation of extended education, leisure, care and health opportunities. In all this it is likely that teachers will find themselves undertaking different forms of work. As the 'lead professional' they may find themselves working closely with families, especially when it comes to brokering their access to services that are based on school premises. As curriculum opportunities are extended and adult learning is fostered teaching staff may find themselves working with children, young people and their families. Increased support from teaching staff will also be required for those acting in learning mentor roles or as classroom assistants or in other 'paraprofessional' roles (Cajkler *et al.*, 2006). Such forms of work require a significant degree of workforce reform. This issue is explored in the next section.

## Workforce reform

The demand to change the roles, responsibilities and relationships performed by teaching staff outlined within this paper have been influenced, at least in part, by a government-inspired policy agenda to significantly reform the education and training of those working with children, young people and their families. At the heart of that agenda lies recognition that professional groups will require new skills, knowledge and competencies to work more effectively across occupational/ professional boundaries. For, as Abbott and Hevey (2001, p. 180) pointed out, the development of new and innovatory ways of working will 'require something more than benign co-operation across existing professions'. Indeed, they go on to argue that the development of a new children's workforce requires a flexibility in approach and a sharing of 'values' and 'attitudes' that had been advocated much earlier in the Rumbold Report (DES, 1990).

Within the context of the *Every Child Matters* agenda it is argued that all those working with the young will require 'knowledge and skills' in six broad areas of expertise—this is referred to as the *Common core of skills and knowledge for the children's workforce* (DfES, 2005). The areas of expertise include: the development of effective communication skills; an understanding of child development; promoting children's welfare and safeguarding them; 'supporting transitions'; 'multi-agency working'; the 'sharing of information'. Early work in the development of this framework reflected the fact that a 'common core' was likely to produce more flexible working patterns, improved communication between professionals groups and encourage the interchange of skills and expertise through multidisciplinary practice (see Tucker *et al.*, 2002). Advocates of the 'common core' specifically argue that the roles and responsibilities outlined within the *Every Child Matters* framework require individuals and groups to develop such a range of skills and knowledge in order to increase their ability to work across professional boundaries.

In addition to the promotion of a 'common core' of skills and knowledge emphasis is also now being placed on the development and implementation of an *Integrated workforce strategy* (CWDC, 2006) to meet the local demands, expectations and priorities of *Every Child Matters*. As part of such a strategy schools may be actively encouraged to develop their staff training plans to meet the demand of, for example, becoming an extended school. Such plans may also need to reflect the support requirements of those moving into schools to develop a 'full-service' model. The important point to note about such a strategy is that it is intended to meet local needs and provide a high degree of flexibility. At the time of writing the introduction of such strategies nationally are at an early stage of development.

## 'Tinkering' or 'reforming'

The article has attempted to review the implementation of *Every Child Matters* from an educational perspective. One of the key intentions has been to provide a brief overview of the factors that have influenced the introduction of this particular change agenda, an agenda heavily influenced by a consistent failure to properly safeguard and protect children and young people and thereby promote their welfare. Specific attention has also been given to how the policy framework is likely to evolve from the point of those working in schools. Specific areas concerned with multidisciplinary work, the development of extended schools and workforce reform have been reviewed to demonstrate the scope and complexity of the proposed reforms.

The impact of *Every Child Matters* certainly appears to be influential in terms of the way it is transforming structures and processes at both the national and local levels. *Every Child Matters* has provided government with a framework for shaping practice, particularly as it relates to multidisciplinary working and the expectations of teachers and their managers within schools to support both preventative and protection elements of safeguarding work. Emphasis is placed on extending the current focus of the work of school personnel whilst providing them with 'core' skills and knowledge to improve the quality and outcomes of safeguarding activities.

Yet, at the same time the emergence of this new agenda carries with it a range of problems and challenges that will need to be proactively managed. Take for example the requirement for schools under OfSTED inspection arrangements to report the way they are meeting the 'five outcomes'. The arena for considering the delivery of the ECM agenda is transformed from what might be described as an aspirational framework to one where evidence is sought in relation to specific targets against each outcome. For example, OfSTED inspectors in reviewing the target for 'staying safe' will evaluate:

- the behaviour of learners;
- the attendance of learners;
- the extent to which learners adopt safe practices and a healthy lifestyle;
- the extent to which provision contributes to the learners' capacity to stay safe and healthy (www.ali.gov.uk/GoodPractice/Products/Inspection+toolkit/A+Z+of+inspection).

At the same time the agenda is far-reaching in that it covers the behaviour of children and young people both in and out of school. 'Staying safe' includes children being 'safe from crime and anti-social behaviour' (OfSTED, 2005, p. 3). Perhaps what we are witnessing here is a fundamental shift in responsibility for the care and education of the young, where schools are judged against learner behaviours both in the specific institution and wider community.

The signs are then that this particular agenda for change is beginning to have a major influence on policy, structure, process and practice. An education and training agenda is emerging that is likely to impact on the initial and continuing professional development agenda of senior managers, teachers and support staff within schools. New working relationships will emerge that require a reworking of previous roles and responsibilities. In order to meet the demands of ECM there will need to be consideration given to improved systems of record keeping, to demonstrate proactive engagement with a preventative agenda, and an auditable demonstration of how the school managed particular incidents or problems. One outstanding question that might arise in meeting the 'five outcomes' is how the school can more effectively engage with the wider community in order to promote and safeguard the well-being of its learners? This feels like radical reform, rather than an exercise in tinkering.

# References

Abbott, D., Watson, D. & Townsley, R. (2005) The proof of the pudding: what difference does multi-agency working make to families with disabled children with complex health needs?, *Child and Family Social Work*, 10, 229–238.

Abbott, L. & Hevey, D. (2001) Training to work in the early years: developing the climbing frame, in: G. Pugh (Ed.) *Contemporary issues in the early years, working collaboratively for children* (London, Paul Chapman), 179–193.

Audit Commission (2003) *Corporate governance: improvement and trust in local public services* (London, HMSO).

Bagley, C., Ackerley, C. L. & Rattray, J. (2004) Social exclusion, Sure Start and organizational social capital: evaluating inter-disciplinary multi-agency working in an education and health work programme, *Journal of Education Policy*, 19(5), 595–607.

Cajkler, W., Tennant, G., Cooper, P. W., Sage, R., Taylor, C., Tucker, S. A. & Tiknaz, Y. (2006) *A systematic literature review on the perceptions of ways in which support staff work to support pupils' social and academic engagement in primary schools (1988–2003)*, Research Evidence in Education Library (London, University of London Institute of Education).

Children's Workforce Development Council (2006) *Integrated qualifications framework* (Leeds, CWDC).

Cummings, C., Todd, L. & Dyson, A. (2003) *Extended schools pathfinder evaluation: issues for schools and local education authorities*, Research Brief no. RBX18-03 (London, DfES).

Department for Education and Science (1990) *Starting with quality report of the committee into the Quality of Education offered to 3–4 and 4-years olds, chaired by Mrs Angela Rumbold, CBE, MP* (London, HMSO).

Department for Education and Skills (2002) *Extended schools providing opportunities and services for all* (Nottingham, DfES Publications).

Department for Education and Skills (2003) *Every child matters* (London, DfES).

Department for Education and Skills (2005) *Common core of skills and knowledge for the children's workforce* (Nottingham, DfES Publications).

Department for Education and Skills & Department for Work and Pensions (2002) *Childcare in extended schools* (Nottingham, DfES Publications).

Department of Health (2003) *The Victoria Climbie inquiry report by Lord Laming* (London, HMSO).

Her Majesty's Government (2006) *Working together to safeguard children. A guide to inter-agency working to safeguard and promote the welfare of children* (London, HM Government).

Horner, N. & Krawczyk, S. (2006) *Social work in education and children's services* (Exeter, Learning Matters).

Office for Standards in Education (2005) *Every child matters—framework for the inspection of children's services* (London, OfSTED). Available online at: www.ofsted.gov.uk (accessed 1 December 2006).

Parton, N. (2005) *Safeguarding children in a late modern society* (Basingstoke, Palgrave/Macmillan).

Pugh, G. (2001) *Contemporary issues in the early years, working collaboratively for children* (London, Paul Chapman).

Roche, J. & Tucker, S. (2003) Extending the social inclusion debate: an exploration of the family lives of young carers and young people with me, *Childhood*, 10(4), 439–456.

Smellie, D. (2006) School staff as police officers, *Education Law Journal*, 7, 10–19.

Smith, M. K. (2005) Extended schools—some issues for informal and community education, in: *The encyclopaedia of informal education*. Available online at: www.Infed. org/schooling/extended-schools/htm (accessed 12 December 2006).

Tucker, S., Strange, C., O'Hagan, C. & Moules, T. (2002) Conceptualising, processing and developing: the construction of an interdisciplinary framework for working with children, young people and communities, *Journal of Vocational Education and Training*, 52(2), 305–320.

Willan, J., Parker-Rees, R. & Savage, J. (2004) *Early childhood studies* (Exeter, Learning Matters).

Wilkin, A., Kinder, K., White, R., Atkinson, M. & Doherty, P. (2003) *Towards the development of extended schools* (London, National Foundation for Educational Research).

# Part III

# The primary curriculum

Maths, Science, IT and
Technology Education

# 9 Craft Design Technology in the primary school

Let's keep it primary

*Iain Milloy*

## What's in a name?

The obvious answer must be that it depends on the name! Take 'Craft Design Technology'. Among teachers this title conjures up a wide range of impressions . . . and prejudices. Now link 'CDT' with primary education – particularly across the Infant years – and you will certainly provoke from primary teachers some interesting responses.

Many teachers will state that they do not know what CDT really means. They will point out, however, that CDT 'sounds' very secondary . . . very male-orientated; that it must be a highly specialist subject that requires extensive, 'hi-tech' resources.

Some teachers will welcome the practical nature of CDT with its emphasis upon learning through direct experience. Yet, they have considerable reservations about their competence to manage the 'teaching' requirements of CDT. Furthermore, they may feel wary of committing themselves and their children to a 'subject' that appears to lack a clear structure and well-marked routes of progression.

Not surprisingly, there are teachers who have been encouraging CDT-style activities with their children, but who have been completely unaware that they were 'doing' CDT!

The most immediate response to these comments must be that many teachers have difficulty in reconciling their impressions of CDT with everyday experience of primary education.

So where does this semantic investigation lead? Two basic conclusions emerge:

(a) the title 'CDT' must be recognised as a very heavily-charged term that can cause a great deal of confusion and prejudice among teachers – to the disadvantage of children;
(b) there is an urgent need to offer primary teachers a 'working definition' of CDT–style activities as a necessary prelude to promoting primary CDT.

## What is CDT?

Most teachers would initially assume that CDT is a subject, or an amalgam of subjects based, for instance, upon craft and science. The essence of CDT, however, does not lie in any specific combination of subjects. CDT is an approach to learning. It represents a commitment to the value for children of learning through genuine problem-solving experience.

CDT in action reflects the general characteristics of any problem-solving activity, eg a realistic situation in which children recognise a need and identify a problem, the application of a range of problem-solving strategies set within a 'team context', and the evaluation of a 'solution'. Yet, CDT introduces a distinctive element into this experience for the children through the intensely practical and 'immediate' nature of the problem and possible solutions: children use simple materials, tools and equipment to produce their solutions. The moving force behind CDT is, however, the conviction that, when sensitively guided by the teacher, problem-solving engages children in highly relevant learning experieces: experiences that have an enabling influence upon the intellectual, practical, personal and social development of children.

There can be little doubt that the principles underlying CDT are in full sympathy with the major aims and objectives of primary education. Yet, the move from principles into practice is not so straightforward. The basic challenge at primary level lies in the promotion of a genuinely primary orientation to CDT-style activities.

This challenge breaks down into at least five basic requirements:

(a)  Primary CDT must evolve from a foundation of 'good' primary practice. It cannot, and must not, take root as a secondary transplant. If it is a valid form of problem-solving experience at primary level, it must have direct relevance across the full primary age and ability range – and, in addition, carry no taint of male bias. Consequently, the development of primary CDT should not be allowed to be dominated and moulded by impressions of secondary practice. (This does not deny the urgent need for thorough liaison between primary and secondary CDT.)
(b)  CDT-style activities must be manageable for the 'generalist' teacher.
(c)  The activities themselves must be capable of accomodation within the general-purpose classroom.
(d)  CDT-style activities must not be dependent upon specialist or 'hi-tech' resources.
(e)  Appropriate INSET provision must be made to help teachers develop greater awareness, confidence and competence in respect of CDT.

These requirements raise complex issues, but this article, however, focuses upon some of those connected with the first four points.

First of all, back to semantics! The term, 'Craft Design Technology', is not particulary teacher friendly. It lacks primary appeal. This dissatisfaction with 'CDT' is not new. Other titles have been proposed. Probably the most effective alternative is quite simply, 'Designing and Making.'

As a title, 'Designing and Making' has distinct merits:

•  It 'sounds' primary. It has no secondary or specialist overtones. It avoids any obvious pressure for 'hi-tech' activities. It is reasonably gender-neutral.

- The leading word, 'Designing', stresses the thinking or problem-solving character of the experience for children. Moreover, it links the 'Making' directly with problem-solving as the means of expressing the solution.
- 'Making' underlines the practical, physical nature of this activity. The simplicity of the term, 'Making', is particularly fortunate since it relates very easily to the resources, activities and general scenario in primary classrooms, from Nursery and Reception through to Top Junior.

From this point onwards, 'Designing and Making' will be used in preference to 'CDT'.

How does this view of Designing and Making fit in with the realities of teaching?

> 'We go to be talked to by unbelievably enthusiastic and terribly articulate specialists, freed from classroom concerns, and let loose on a giant ego-trip. By the experts, for the experts, with little relevance when you attempt to translate their stimulating ideas into the classroom and integrate them with everything else you're trying to do.'[1]

With classroom reality clearly in mind, two basic guidelines can be recommended for the promotion of Designing and Making:

(a) it cannot be justifiably forced by unimaginative planning or rigid timetabling into a weekly 'slot'; and
(b) it must be set in a context that gives children the opportunity to involve themselves in real problem-solving.

This perspective reinforces the earlier claim that Designing and Making should not stand as a subject, but should be applied as an approach to learning – an approach that can in principle be integrated with most, if not all major aspects of the planned curriculum. In practice, however, projects and topics prove the most fertile and appropriate context for Designing and Making.

## Why topics and projects?

Many teachers would offer the following types of comment in support of the general educational value of topics and projects:

- Topics and projects are a means of promoting more realistic and integrated learning experiences for children. They usually involve a direct, 'practical' base of experience for children set within a multi-disciplinary approach to an overall theme.
- The typically broad 'umbrella' themes for topics and projects readily encourage children to contribute their personal interests and insights to the development of themes. This motivational element considerably strengthens the impact of the work upon children's experience and learning.

In terms of Designing and Making, the topic and project setting offers four advantages:

1.  The outline themes devised by the teacher usually offer a rich source of starting points for problem-solving through Designing and Making. Of equal importance, however, is the manner in which children's interest and contributions to those themes can readily expose starting points. As a result, the teacher is not continually faced with the need to contrive pre-set problems for Designing and Making. The children-teacher dialogue helps the teacher to avoid the dangers of teacher-imposition and contrivance – dangers that could effectively trivialise Designing and Making.
2.  Topics and projects usually involve a strong element of individual and small-group activities. This small-group focus is particularly suited to Designing and Making. It creates a 'team setting' in which problem-solving can develop. A team not only provides a source of inspiration and feasible proposals. It can also undertake real responsibility for the direction and quality of the Designing and Making. In this sense, individual responsibilities can evolve against a background of co-operation and mutual support.

    The small-group base greatly facilitates the organisation and management of Designing and Making within a classroom. Under this system, teachers can easily organise Designing and Making as one of the several small-group activities that evolve during the topic or project. (Designing and Making is not restricted to one particular group for the duration of a topic. As the work progresses, new groups will form. Typically these groups will consist of a maximum of six to eight children at any one time.) This tactic shifts the focus of resourcing Designing and Making from the potentially overwhelming demands of an entire class to the much more modest and realisable requirements of a small group. Thus, the small-group organisation typical of topic and project work assists Designing and Making to become a realistic proposition for the classteacher.
3.  The organisation of topics and projects is generally quite liberal and flexible in the use of time. This is particularly significant for Designing and Making since problem-solving activities do not readily lend themselves to strict, pre-set allocations of time. In contrast, they require time to be used by the teacher as an 'adjustable' resource to support the continuity of the children's work. In this respect, topics and projects form a very appropriate setting for Designing and Making.
4.  Topics and projects form part of the programmes of work devised by the majority of class-teachers. Therefore, in terms of current practice, the curriculum setting for Designing and Making is already very familiar and well established. The promotion of Designing and Making does not require teachers to introduce a new subject into their schemes of work. What is sought is a subtle shift of emphasis in the nature of the children's experience[2] – a move towards a more child-centred approach, the development of problem-solving and the recognition of the educational value of practical activity. Hopefully, the fact that the introduction of Designing and Making

is a matter of integration and consolidation of 'good' practice could contribute to its more widespread adoption by primary teachers.

## Making a start

If topics and projects form the appropriate setting for primary Designing and Making, how can a teacher actually 'start' Designing and Making? There are four preliminary points:

1.  It would be wrong to assume that every topic and project should necessarily contain a Designing and Making element. In fact, when one reflects upon the range of planned curricular inputs relevant to topics or projects, one is faced with the obvious need for careful selection and management of inputs in the interests of a well-balanced programme for children throughout their primary years.
2.  It is vital to view Designing and Making as a process of problem-solving – not craft! The experience for children of Designing and Making from the initial awareness of a need, through to the production of a refined solution is arguably more important than the product itself.
3.  Real problem-solving cannot be conveniently packaged within work-cards or design briefs. Logically there needs to be a problem-context in which children recognise a need before problem-solving can proceed. Typically, work cards and design briefs lead to a highly simplistic and mechanical experience of problem-solving in which both the problem and the solution has been pre-determined.
4.  It is important for the teacher to clarify her/his intentions underlying the introduction of Designing and Making. It is not sufficient to launch into this type of work in the hope of vague outcomes! This in turn implies that any planning decisions taken by the teacher must be based firmly upon a knowledge of the children concerned, and her/his general aims and objectives over the school year.

There seem to be three distinctive types of teacher-approach to initiating Designing and Making:

(a) The teacher plans in outline a topic or project. From her/his knowledge of the class and the particular topic theme, she/he devises a specific Designing and Making assignment for the topic. For instance, for the general topic of 'Transport', the teacher may decide to set as the assignment 'Design and make a model land vehicle that is powered by a rubber band.' Since the Designing and Making activity is based upon a clearly stated assignment, the teacher can thoroughly research and resource the activity. This feeling of being in control of the activity makes this approach very acceptable with teachers who are 'new' to Designing and Making.

    Beneath this apparent convenience, organisation and control lies the danger of an over-prescriptive view of what problem(s) a given theme will present to children. This approach runs the risk of trivialising the experience of problem-solving for children since it tends to ignore the context for problem-solving and present a semi-formed solution. For this reason, this article includes little reference to topic or project themes and related Designing and Making 'problems'.

(b) As experience and confidence develop, teachers recognise the limited scope for children's problem-solving inherent in the previous approach. Similarly, they appreciate more clearly the range and diversity of problems that topics and projects can generate. Therefore, when planning a topic they tend to forecast a number of problems that could be expected to emerge without narrow prescription or contrivance. This forecast offers a pool of probabilities that helps the teacher to prepare for a potential range of resourcing and organisation requirements. As the topic unfolds, she/he is then able to support a variety of Designing and Making proposals from the children.

For example, in a project on 'Shops', one predictable focus of interest might be the packaging of goods. Another focus of interest could be advertising and the promotion of products. During the topic, some children may elect to design and make carrier bags and cartons for products of their choice. Other children may decide to design and make promotional packaging and wrapping material, adverts or display 'gimmicks'. In this case, the teacher would be prepared for these and similiar choices as a result of her/his forcast.

This approach is clearly more sophisticated than the former. Its particular merit is that it encourages a more genuine and comprehensive experience of problem-solving for children.

(c) The third approach is not so much a matter of planning as an attitude on the part of the teacher. In this case, the teacher may have certain preconceptions about the range of Designing and Making opportunities that a certain theme will present. However, she/he carefully avoids predetermining the nature and outcomes of any Designing and Making. It is a 'wait and see' situation where the teacher tries to capitalise upon the children's responses to the theme.

For instance, in a Maths project on 'Time', some children became very involved in practical 'timing' experiments. They decided to make their own timers for a specific purpose. The teacher did not set or contrive this problem, nor could she forecast that this particular need would arise. It was really a question of the teacher meeting the children's request.

Similarly, work in a school garden 'patch' led to some unsuspected Designing and Making. A Reception class had been planting seedlings. After a time, the plot looked decidedly disorganised and many seedlings were in danger of being trampled. Some of the children noticed this. They also pointed out that they were no longer sure of where the rows of seedlings were, or who had planted each row. They wanted some form of marker system. This need led very naturally to the children investigating the problem, and designing and making their own markers for use in the school garden.

The important feature of these three approaches is not simply their differences, but the progression they represent in a teacher's confidence and understanding. There seems little point in describing and recommending a theoretically ideal approach if it requires an unrealistic level of initial teacher confidence and experience. The preceding descriptions may act as route markers for teachers to work out their own tactics. The most influential factor in this process is not a teacher's 'technical' knowledge or expertise. It is a teacher's appreciation of what constitutes problem-solving, and her/his confidence and ability to encourage children in this type of experience.

This comment relates directly to the very common observation from primary teachers that, because they tend to lack a 'technical' background, they feel unable to help children in Designing and Making. In answer to this, I have consistently placed the teacher firmly in the role of managing learning through problem-solving. Teacher-success in Designing and Making does not depend upon technical expertise so much as upon those fundamental professional qualities that apply across the curriculum.

There is a certain amount of craft and technological experience that teachers will come to need to support Designing and Making. Obviously, a measure of teacher intervention and 'teaching' is required. But very often teachers over-estimate this particular requirement. For instance, many teachers express deep concern about teaching craft techniques. Provided the teacher is not trying to force upon primary children secondary techniques, tools and materials, then the craft element is far less demanding than one might initially assume.[3] The same observation holds true for technology since at primary level the focus is upon practical experience and using 'common sense' to make things work.[4] Certainly, experience shows that INSET courses can usually provide this 'technical' input with relative ease.

Many teachers also feel that Designing and Making can only be started after a foundation of thorough craft teaching and techniques has been established. Obviously, craft techniques do need some teaching input if children are to apply them effectively and safely. However, technique teaching is best provided when children appreciate the need for a particular technique. Therefore, in Designing and Making techniques tend to be taught as the need arises through the children's work – not in isolation. This needs' approach is highly realistic when one remembers that at any one point the teacher is concerned with a maximum of 6–8 designers and makers in a group setting.

## Resources

Resources was mentioned vaguely during the description of possible approaches to initiating Designing and Making. As with 'craft teaching', the issue of 'resources' is extremely important but capable of producing a false impression of Designing and Making.

Teachers tend to assume that resources for Designing and Making must involve predominantly tools, craft materials and science or technology equipment.

Similarly, they assume that these resources must be rather 'specialist' – at the very least, not usually found in primary school.

This impression is quite false. The commonly available range of primary resources like 'found' materials, basic tools and science equipment can support the vast majority of Designing and Making activities. But before giving any details of particular resources, certain more general comments need to be made.

There are two very important resourcing issues that tend to be overlooked and can subsequently hold back the development of Designing and Making throughout a school:

- Designing and Making requires a considerable range of reference-type resources to initiate and support investigation, research and planning. Whether at Reception or Upper Junior level, children need appropriate resources to make informed decisions throughout their problem-solving. Therefore, specific provision must be made for this aspect of resources. A general outline of resources is presented in the Appendix.
- As emphasised above, Designing and Making involves resource-based learning. Consequently, children must be able to access independently the vast majority of the relevant resources. This implies that the school's resources should be organised and managed with this need in mind. Resourcing for Designing and Making cannot be viewed simply as the development of a wide range of resources. It requires a school policy and system to facilitate 'open access' by children to resources not held within classrooms. It also calls for the creation of a highly portable or mobile resource facility that can be used conveniently within each classroom.

A mobile or portable storage system for basic tools, materials and equipment is vital if Designing and Making is to be accommodated efficiently within each classroom. Many schools base their facility around a light-weight, purpose-built carrying case or trolley. Trolleys have the additional advantage of extra carrying capacity for materials and equipment. In addition to mobility of basic constructional resources, trolleys and carrying cases ensure that resources can be organised, presented and cared for in a professional manner. This not only aids the efficient management of resources, but also has an influence upon children's attitudes to the work.

Some schools complement the trolley or carrying case system with a set of very light-weight drop-over tops that instantly convert a table or desk into an attractive activity-area for Designing and Making. As with the constructional resources, these tops can be easily moved from classroom to classroom.

## Classroom management and organisation

It is a statement of the obvious but Designing and Making activities will often require thoughtful management and organisation of the classroom. Basically, the need for a specific organisation occurs when a Designing and Making group has progressed from initial research and planning to the point when it wants to construct prototypes of solutions and, subsequently, a finalised version of the solution.

At this point the group needs an area that will support a range of 'research and development' and constructional activities. For instance, children may want to construct with card, 'found' objects or wood. They may decide to set up Lego models to test out designs. They may need to experiment with, for example, lighting circuits. In other words, the group needs an activity-area that remains relatively undisturbed by the ebb and flow of classroom life.

One immediate answer might be to let the children work outside the classroom. Apart from general safety considerations, that tactic is educationally unsound. For instance, it segregates Designing and Making from the apparently mainstream classroom activities. It prevents other children in the class from sharing the experiences of a Designing and Making group. It makes sensitive teacher guidance extremely difficult. Finally, it may even discourage or prevent some teachers from attempting to involve Designing and Making in their schemes of work. Despite individual differences, teachers' solutions to this accommodation challenge share the following characteristics:

- The Designing and Making activity-area is set up in a part of the classroom that is outside the major thoroughfares used by children. (It would be unwise, however, to confine Designing and Making within a corner since a corner position can pose problems for longrange teacher supervision.)
- The activity-area is formed from ordinary classroom desks or tables – equipped ideally with drop-over tops.
- The area is kept clear of 'obstacles', eg sandwich boxes, sports bags, musical instrument cases, etc.
- There is a high level of natural and artificial lighting in the area.
- The area allows children easy access to resources, eg trolley or carrying case, craft materials or reference-type materials.
- It has display facilities that the children can use as an 'open' folder for the work under development. This feature – involving real, not exhibition work – can be particularly influential since it provides a direct means of sharing information and experience throughout the class.

When one considers the portable or mobile resource facility that underpins this approach, then the temporary re-organisation of a classroom proves very simple and convenient.

## Conclusions

The review of classroom management and organisation marks a convenient 'breaking-off' point for this discussion. So what have I tried to achieve?

I set out to sketch in broad outline one model for a curricular starting point for primary Designing and Making, and raised some immediate, practical issues that influence any attempt to introduce Designing and Making. I have not looked much beyond the opening move of a Designing and Making initiative within a school. For instance, there has been insufficient space to explore issues of more long-term consequence such as:

- progression and continuity within Designing and Making, across the nursery-primary phase and onwards throughout the secondary phase.
- sex stereotyping and bias in Designing and Making.
- professional development needs of teachers in relation to Designing and Making.

I have, in particular, discouraged the packaging of Designing and Making in terms of topic or project themes and 'instant' Designing and Making assignments.

I have, however, presented, one very important and optimistic message: that Designing and Making is very much in sympathy with the aims and objectives of good primary practice, and can be highly relevant in the general education of primary children.

The implication in this message is that it is the particular responsibility of primary teachers, headteachers and advisers to ensure that Designing and Making is firmly and consistently rooted in 'good' primary practice. Undoubtedly, much of the spirit of Designing and Making already exists and flourishes in primary classrooms. The development of Designing and Making requires a sensitive extension and expansion of this 'good' practice. This is a pioneering challenge. Designing and Making offers an exciting dimension to the primary curriculum. We need the conviction and confidence to realise that potential.

## References

1  Sandford P. (1986), 'The hills were alive', TES. 4.7.
2  Williams P. H. M. (1985), *Teaching Craft Design and Technology 5–13*. Croom Helm.
3  Williams P. and Jinks D. (1985), *Design and Technology 5–12*. (Ch 7). Falmer Press.
4  DES (1985), *The Curriculum from 5–16*. HMSO para 87.

## Appendix: Resources for designing and making

The following lists present an outline guide to the range of resources required for Designing and Making. No information has been given concerning recommended suppliers since LEAs usually have their own specific arrangements in this respect.

### *Reference-type resources*

| Books | Magazines | Leaflets | Brochures | |
|-------|-----------|----------|-----------|---|
| Posters | Pictures | Slides | Filmstrips | Videos |

Cassettes/Recordings of Radio Programmes

Toys             Mechanical Artefacts

Constructional/Technology Kits, eg Lego, Capsela, Meccano, Fischer-technik
Natural and 'found' objects

## Constructional resources

'Found' Materials:

| | | |
|---|---|---|
| Matchboxes | Cardboard Boxes and Tubes | Plastic Bottles and Containers |
| Soft Drink Cans | '45' Records | Coffee-jar lids |
| Cardboard discs | Rubber Bands | String |
| Wire Coathangers | Wood Shavings and Sawdust | |
| Beads | Wool | Fabrics |
| PVC Tubing (narrow diameter) | Balloons | |

## Wood

Softwood off-cuts – planed all-round and in a variety of cross-sectional dimensions up to 25 mm × 10 mm. The most useful size is 10 × 10 mm.
Dowel, eg diameters 3 mm and 4.5 mm
Balsa
Jelutong is an ideal wood for young children. It is worth buying one of the special 'primary' packs that a number of the major suppliers offer. These packs are particularly useful since their contents have been adjusted to suit the general requirements of primary Designing and Making. For further information about wood, especially Jelutong, please contact your local CDT Adviser.

## Plastics

For most activities, 'found' plastics materials will prove very suitable.

## Metal

There is often a need for short strips of thin aluminium (18 or 20 gauge). For safety reasons, tinplate should not be used.

## Card

The value of card as a constructional material is easily overlooked because it seems so 'ordinary'. It has, however, many advantages for young children. Therefore, it is worth developing stocks of different thickness, colour and quality of card.

### Adhesives

PVA glue and Balsa Cement
Pritt

### Fasteners

| | | | |
|---|---|---|---|
| Sellotape | Masking Tape | Paper Clips | Paper Fasteners |
| Drawing Pins | Stapler | Blue-Tak | |

To a very limited extent, panel pins, screws, nuts, bolts and washers.

### Finishes

The general range of 'finishes' used in Art and Craft activities will be very relevant for Designing and Making.

### Tools

Safety Rules
Scissors and Craft Knives
Junior Hacksaws or Mini Hacksaws (with spare blades)
Hammers (Warrington 6 oz)
Hand Drill and Twist Drill Set
Small Screwdriver (75 mm)
Electrical Screwdriver
Wire Stripper
Centre Punch
Hole Punch
Clamp-on Vices
Bench-hooks (primary sizes)
Drop-over Table or Desk Tops
Glasspaper (various grades)

Reminder: Tools housed in a carrying case or trolley.

### 'Technology' resources

Technology/Constructional Kits – see reference-type resources for details.
Electrical Components – general primary science resources such as insulated connecting wire; crocodile clips; batteries; bulbs; bulb holders; switches; electric motors; bells; buzzers.
Mechanical Components – wheels from broken toys; cardboard, plastic or wooden discs; gear wheels and pulleys; propellers; rubber bands.

# 10 Who is a scientist?

## Children's drawings reveal all

*Catherine J. Tuckey*

## Introduction

The stereotypical image of the scientist is a balding, middle-aged man in a white coat surrounded by bunsen burners or doing unspeakable things to rats. Chambers[1] demonstrated that among Canadian children this stereotype can develop very early. In his study children as young as seven drew pictures displaying many of the 'indicators' of the standard image of the scientist including lab coat, spectacles, facial hair and/or baldness, symbols of research and knowledge and so on. Hadden and Johnstone[2] also found that primary school children (in this case in Scotland) had well developed ideas about scientists, including the idea that scientists are men. Among several hundred children questioned, not one described a scientist as female. Such strongly held ideas about appropriate gender roles may be expected to subvert attempts to encourage females to take up science as a career, or to study it at an advanced level in school. The aim of this study was to assess current ideas about scientists among Scottish primary school children.

## Method

The study was carried out as part of an evaluation of a hands-on science centre, Satrosphere, in Aberdeen. I visited schools participating in the study, told the children I would be going with them when they went to Satrosphere, and then asked them to draw a picture of a scientist, and to explain orally, or by means of a caption, what the scientist is doing. In all, 135 primary school children (61 female and 74 male), aged between eight and 11, from six schools throughout the Grampian Region, took part in the exercise. The method was an adaptation of Chambers 'draw-a-scientist' test; it differs in that in this study the children were asked to supply an explanation of the drawing. This is likely to give better insight into children's ideas than drawings alone. The drawings were analysed and placed into a number of discrete categories. Categorisation was on the basis of the action that the scientist is performing rather than on physical characteristics. To minimise the effect of personal bias two further judges independently assigned pictures to categories and any disagreement between the judges resulted in the pictures being excluded from further analysis.

**(i) The alchemist or mad scientist**

The pupil (boy, aged 9) provided the caption 'The Mad Scientist. My man is making a potion to make the Earth quick!'

**(ii) The pure scientist**

This pupil (girl, aged 8) explained that the scientist is digging up dinosaur bones.

**(iii) The technologist**

In this picture the scientist is 'inventing a new kind of washing-up liquid' (girl, aged 10).

**(iv) The school scientist**

The caption supplied was 'The girl is finding out about the planet Saturn and its moons' (girl, aged 10).

**(v) Inappropriate drawing**

In this case the pupil (boy, aged 8) was unable to give any account of what the 'scientist' is doing.

*Figure 10.1* Children's drawings of scientists exemplifying categories

## Results

Disagreement between judges arose on 14 occasions and so the total number of drawings analysed was reduced to 121. The categories to which pupils' drawings were assigned were as follows: a. 'Alchemists' or 'mad scientists' inventing secret formulas, invisible potions or plotting to destroy the world; b. 'Technologists' inventing machines, new consumer products, medicines etc; c. 'Pure scientists' digging up dinosaur bones, looking at fossils, looking down microscopes or through telescopes, or doing experiments; d. 'School scientists' showing the child her/himself engaged in some scientific activity; and e. 'Inappropriate' drawings showing people doing things unconnected with science

Table 10.1 The number of drawing of female and male scientist in each category, and the distribution of drawing by age and gender of pupil (numbers of children, percentages in parentheses)*

| Age of pupil | Alchemist/mad scientist | | | Technologist | | | Pure scientist | | | School scientist | | | Inappropriate | | | Total | | |
|---|---|---|---|---|---|---|---|---|---|---|---|---|---|---|---|---|---|---|
| | Female | Male | | Female | Male | | Female | Male | | Female | Male | | Female | Male | | Female | Male | |
| | all F | by F | by M | all F | by F | by M | all F | by F | by M | all F | by F | by M | all F | by F | by M | | | |
| 8 | 0 | 1 | 9 | 0 | 0 | 1 | 0 | 0 | 1 | 3 | 0 | 0 | 5 | 1 | 5 | 8 | 2 | 16 |
| 9 | 2 | 1 | 3 | 0 | 2 | 1 | 4 | 2 | 1 | 1 | 0 | 1 | 2 | 0 | 2 | 9 | 5 | 8 |
| 10 | 3 | 5 | 11 | 3 | 2 | 3 | 4 | 1 | 7 | 4 | 0 | 1 | 2 | 2 | 2 | 16 | 10 | 24 |
| 11 | 0 | 0 | 9 | 0 | 0 | 1 | 4 | 0 | 6 | 0 | 0 | 0 | 0 | 0 | 3 | 4 | 0 | 19 |
| Total | 5 | 7 | 32 | 3 | 4 | 6 | 12 | 3 | 15 | 8 | 0 | 2 | 9 | 3 | 12 | 37 | 17 | 67 |
| | (4) | (6) | (26.5) | (2.5) | (3) | (5) | (10) | (2.5) | (12) | (7) | (0) | (2) | (7.5) | (2.5) | (10) | (31) | (14) | (55) |

*All drawings of female scientists are by female students. Male scientists drawn either by male pupils or female pupils.

such as playing football or walking the dog. Figure 10.1 shows some examples of children's drawings.

The distribution of children's drawings by age and gender is shown in Table 10.1. No particular trend emerges with age, although the proportion of children drawing 'inappropriate' scientists is greatest among the 8 year olds, indicating that at this age the concept of 'scientist' may be hazy. The largest single grouping was of alchemists/mad scientists (44 of the 121 drawings, 36 per cent). These were the most stereotyped of the drawings showing many of Chambers' indicators. Only five of these drawings depicted females. A greater proportion of pure scientists was depicted as female (12 out of 30 drawings, 40 per cent), and girls were more likely to draw themselves doing science at school than were boys (eight of the 10 drawings of school scientists were by girls). The three categories, pure scientist, technologist, and school scientist, may be thought of as representing 'realistic' images of science (in contrast to the alchemists or mad scientists). A little under half of these realistic images depicted females (23 out of 53 drawings, 43 per cent).

## Discussion

As was found by Chambers only girls drew female scientists. However, in Chambers' study only 28 women scientists were drawn by a sample of 4,807 children, of whom girls made up 49 per cent of the total. In this study 37 of the 54 drawings by girls were of female scientists (69 per cent). It is interesting to compare the results of the present study with Hadden and Johnstone's work with Scottish primary school pupils in which no child described a scientist as being female. This may indicate that a genuine shift in children's perceptions of scientists has occurred over the past 10 years or so.

It remains unclear, however, why girls are more likely to depict scientists in roles such as digging up dinosaur bones and looking down microscopes than are boys who tended to draw very mad-looking scientists plotting to destroy the world. Such a difference in the way girls and boys view science was also found in Chambers' study. It is possibly a reflection of gender differences in choice of reading matter and television programmes.

## Summary

Children hold a wide range of ideas about what science is, but boys tend to have very stereotyped ideas about scientists, exclusively depicting them as male and often seeing in science something weird or magical – this is the antithesis of what science claims to be, and yet it is easy to see how the ideas can become fused or confused. Girls in this study did not see science as an exclusively male preserve and are more likely to view science in a 'realistic' way than are boys. In interviews with the teachers of these children (all women) awareness of the need to avoid gender stereotyping was expressed. This study shows that among their girl pupils at least, their attempts are beginning to bear fruit.

## Acknowledgements

I would like to thank the staff and pupils of the six schools who kindly agreed to take part in the study.

## References

1 Chambers, D. W. (1983) 'Stereotypic Images of the Scientist: The Draw a Scientist Test', *Science Education*, 67, 255–65.
2 Hadden, R. A. and Johnstone, A. H. (1983) 'Primary School Children's Attitudes to Science: The Years of Formation', *European Journal of Science Education*, 5, 397–407.

# 11 Maths from a tube of Smarties

*Carol Aubrey*

## Introduction

Since the introduction of the National Curriculum debate concerning the role of primary teachers' subject knowledge has intensified. Alexander, Rose and Woodhead[1] stated:

> 'The resistance to subjects at the primary stage is no longer tenable. The subject is a necessary feature of the modern curriculum. It requires appropriate kinds of knowledge on the part of the teacher.'
>
> (Summary, para 3.2)

The follow-up to this report (OFSTED[2]) concluded:

> 'improvement of teacher's subject knowledge was widely acknowledged as of central importance if primary schools were to make the looked-for progress with teaching the National Curriculum.'
>
> (para 32, p16)

The National Curriculum Council[3], too, recommended a number of changes including the greater use of single subject teaching and of subject teachers, the provision of further guidance and training with respect to teaching methods and subject knowledge and the revision of initial teacher training which, currently, did not ensure mastery of subject knowledge across the full range of the National Curriculum or focus sharply enough on teaching skills. Most recently the call has come from a DFE Circular[4] for the strengthening of subject knowledge and practical teaching skills through courses which equip initial teacher education students to teach effectively and which are the foundation for further professional development. The need to strengthen the subject knowledge of class teachers and initial teacher education students is a recurrent theme. But what is meant by subject knowledge?

It appears that throughout these documents, references to subject knowledge concern:

(i)   the subject expertise of the curriculum leader, however defined, and its deployment within the school context, through semi-specialist or specialist teacher or the teacher as consultant;

(ii)  subject knowledge for teaching National Curriculum subjects.

What is subject knowledge? How and when is it acquired? Before one can consider how teachers' subject knowledge changes and develops these questions must be addressed.

The assumption that subject knowledge in itself is essential to teaching is incontrovertible. The nature and course of the development of teachers' subject knowledge, however, has been little examined in this country. Although it is accepted that subject knowledge is central to the activity of teaching, recent research in this country has tended to have focused more on classroom organisation and teaching strategies than on the nature and development of teachers' subject knowledge (see the report of Alexander, Rose and Woodhead[1]).

Whilst there can be little argument that teachers need to know what they are teaching, there may be less agreement about what is needed to be known about a subject, or how much, in order to teach it. Clearly teachers need to know more about their subject than the specific topics in the curriculum they teach. Schulman[5], for instance, suggested three categories of subject knowledge: subject content knowledge, pedagogical subject knowledge and curricular knowledge. Subject content knowledge involves knowledge of the substance of the field, the major concepts and procedures, and the relationships between these. It also involves the syntax of the field, or knowledge of the discourse of the subject and the major 'tools', or methods of enquiry for establishing truth in the field or undertaking new work within it. Furthermore the particular experiences received in learning the subject will influence the views which are held with respect to the nature of the subject and its activities, as well as dispositions towards the subject and the self in relation to the subject. In other words, learning a subject is more than the acquisition of knowledge and facts, it involves engaging in the ideas and procedures of the subject and applying these, ideally, with the ultimate goal of better understanding the everyday world.

It will be clear already from this discussion that beyond content knowledge lies the consideration of content knowledge for teaching, or pedagogical content knowledge. Within this category lie the topics most commonly taught in one's subject area, the most compelling ways of representing these to young children, the illustrations, examples and explanations. Also involved is an appreciation of what young children find difficult to learn about the subject, their common errors and misconceptions. As Shulman noted it is here that research on teaching and learning most closely interrelate. Our understanding of children's emergent subject knowledge is most pertinent to the consideration of the teaching of subject content we plan.

It is difficult to consider ways of representing specific ideas or concepts in a subject area without recourse to the consideration of particular curriculum materials which exemplify that content. Knowledge about alternative teaching materials, texts, apparatus, software programs available is essential to the preparation of topics for teaching and constitutes the third category of content knowledge, curricular knowledge. It is through the introduction of such resources by the teacher, designed to represent ideas and procedures, that children acquire understanding and mastery of specific content. The extent to which subject content knowledge, pedagogical content knowledge and curricular knowledge are practically or conceptually distinct is beyond the scope of this article to consider. Suffice it to say, at this point, that whilst there is clearly considerable overlap amongst these three categories they are useful distinctions to make when considering the current debate about the nature of teachers' subject knowledge. It is also clear that the focus for the debate, whether related to experienced teachers or to students in initial teacher education, has been pedagogical subject knowledge. Implicit, however, is a devaluing of subject content knowledge at all stages of professional development.

It is evident that teachers' substantive knowledge of their subject, its nature and discourse, will influence the quality of their teaching and children's opportunities to learn. Ball[6] has provided a powerful illustration of the way subject knowledge informs the moment-by-moment decisions made by teachers in classroom contexts. The example comes from a lesson which involved teaching 6 year olds to identify geometric shapes. One child points to a blue square and says that it is a rectangle. Another child tilts the square and says that now it is a diamond. Ball invites the reader to consider how s/he would respond, and whether the response of either child would be considered insightful or incorrect. Then she points out that any interpretation of the situation will be shaped by two factors: knowledge about children of a particular age and understanding of the mathematics involved.

> Can a square be correctly labelled a rectangle or a diamond? Is a diamond a mathematical term? What is the effect of changing the orientation of a geometric shape? How does one answer such questions in mathematics? Are these issues things that first graders (6 year olds) can or need to understand? Would exploring the hierarchical relationship between rectangles and squares be confusing to the rest of the class?

This example nicely illustrates the importance of subject content knowledge in teaching. It also indicates that subject knowledge cannot be simply reduced to the question of whether or not you can define a rectangle. Knowledge of mathematics is enmeshed within assumptions about what constitutes good mathematics teaching: how pupils learn mathematics at a particular age, conceptions about teaching and ways of translating this into classroom practice, as well as meeting the requirements of the school mathematics curriculum. The teacher's own knowledge of mathematics is critical to the effective teaching of mathematics though, in practice, this can be examined only within the context of its operation in conjunction with knowledge of learning and teaching and classroom contexts.

With this introductory background in mind, my aims are

- to examine what is included in knowing subject matter for teaching,
- to consider some of the origins and outcomes of teachers' subject matter for learning in order to begin some proper debate about teachers' subject matter preparation in initial, and post-experience training.

This is done through the detailed examination of one introductory data handling lesson and an interview with an experienced, or 'expert' teacher. The data are taken from an on-going project centred at the University of Durham which is investigating teachers' subject knowledge, in particular, in terms of its influence on the content and processes of mathematics teaching in reception classes. Each section is followed by a discussion and some general concluding comments are made.

## Maths from a tube of Smarties

It is October as a small group of four year old reception children and their teacher prepare for a mathematics lesson. The only props are a tube of Smarties (small coloured chocolate sweets) and a large sheet of white paper.

> This is all sorts (says their teacher to the observer). It's almost, well, it's pictorial representation, counting, it's a multitude of things. It's shape. It's logic in a way.

The effect on this teacher of having an observer present was to cause her to make explicit her agenda or dynamic mental plan, containing the goals and actions of the lesson. First of all there is letter recognition.

> Right. A tube of Smarties. Can you see . . . Smarties written here? What does it start with? ('S', responds a child). Smarties begins with an 's' (repeats the teacher). Can you find an 's' on the alphabet tree?

A child is sent to find both the letter and to count the number of objects on the alphabet label. It is noted at this point that Sarah's name begins with the same letter. The number of letters in Smarties can be counted, too, so the group finds out that there are eight letters in Smarties. Choral counting allows the scaffolding of those in the group who are less assured in this activity.

On to the shape of the Smarties tube as the teacher continues by classifying and describing 2-D and 3-D shapes. Starting from what is already known about 2-D and 3-D shapes the teacher holds up the Smarties tube.

> Anyone know what shape this is? (Round) Yes, round. Can we think of any other thing we can say. It's round, there (she points to the end of the tube) and round there (points to the other end). Do you know what that shape is on the bottom? Yes, it is round but there is a posh name for it and that's a circle. One there and one there.

Moving on to the 3-D shape, the teacher searches for a verbal analogy or parallel representation.

> This . . . all of the box, all of the packaging . . . is not a cuboid, but it's a cylinder! Say it . . . (children chorus, Cylinder) . . . and cylinders will roll. Right you find me a cylinder in this room.

'Cylinder', by this time, has been repeated a number of times as the children hunt through the solid mathematical shapes and through the junk modelling box for other examples of cylinders. At the same time they are reminded of what the cylinder is not. (It is not a cuboid.) Each child's example is greeted with 'here's another one . . . a cylinder, and another one . . . .' and so on, as the term 'cylinder' is repeated and linked each time to the appropriate 3-D shape. Next comes comparing and ordering once the cylinders have been stood on end and lined up. 'Which is the tallest cylinder?'. This time the term is linked to the language of measurement as children discuss the various cylinders in terms of 'tallest' and 'shortest'.

> 'Can we put them in order of size, do you think? There's the tallest. Which comes next . . . and next . . . What shape are they? Well, let's put the cylinders out of the way and get on with the Smarties.

The teacher prepares for the next section of the lesson by pouring the Smarties onto the sheet of paper. Not to miss a learning opportunity she reminds the children that all of the Smarties are on the paper and that the tube had been full to the top. Another challenge is on the way. 'I wonder how many different colours there are?' muses the teacher, providing the next goal. Various predictions are made: 8, 15, 13.

> Shall we try and sort the Smarties into colours?

Each child is asked which colour s/he will sort: red, pink, orange, blue and brown. This leaves purple and yellow for the teacher to sort. It is now time to comment on the results. How many does each child have? There are five red, five orange, eight blue, five pink, four brown, three yellow and three purple. On to the language of number with the question 'who has most?'. Tony has eight Smarties but someone else shouts, 'Me!'. By way of correction through the provision of additional scaffolding, the teacher goes round the group repeating, 'how many did you have?'. To the response of the child who made the error she repeats 'you had **five**' and to the child who had most, 'how many did you have, Tony?'. Tony counts again to eight and the teacher repeats her original question, 'who had most?'. 'Me', says Tony. 'So blue had the most', concludes the teacher. The next goal is recording with the Smarties. The teacher draws a straight line on the paper as a baseline and, since this is new learning, she demonstrates.

I've got three yellow, like that, and I've got three purple and I'm going to put them on like that.

She lines up the Smarties perpendicular to the baseline. Her 'talk aloud' strategy means that children have simultaneously a verbal and a concrete representation. 'You haven't got many', observes one child. Again, incorporating the child's response the teacher replies.

No, I haven't got many. I've only got three of each. How many have I got altogether. (Six, replies one child.)

The group counts aloud to check his answer. In this simple combination of two small sets to make a total set the idea of addition has arisen quite naturally. The activity continues as the teacher supports each child to place his/her Smarties in columns.

Now then, Tony, can you put yours there in a long straight line. How many were there?

It is suggested that Tony finds the number eight on a nearby chart. Then the rest of the group is invited, one by one to place their Smarties in a line and to count them again. At all points the teacher's verbal representation is linked to the child's physical action, thus, reinforcing it. Time now to comment on the results. Again different verbal representations are offered which, at the same time, pave the way for an introduction to the purpose for the next stage of the lesson.

Oh this is a lovely pattern . . . a lovely picture of all the Smarties. I want to put a picture up on the wall of these Smarties.

The teacher is easing the group forwards. Her comments link the children's actions to the recording of the Smarties and, at the same time, prepare the ground for drawing them. One child has realised this, 'I don't know how to draw Smarties', he says. 'I do', says another.

Let's pretend we don't want to stick the Smarties up on the wall because we want to eat them, don't we? How could we put up a picture on the wall, of these Smarties?

We could draw them. (The same child repeats his earlier comment.)

We could draw them, yes (repeats the teacher).

They collect felt tipped pens of compatible colours. Again the teacher demonstrates using 'talk aloud' strategies to accompany her actions.

So I would have to draw round all those . . . This is blue. How many do I have to draw for blue? Can you remember?

The teacher cross-references to an earlier section of the lesson as the column of Smarties is carefully moved aside to allow a one-to-one correspondence between each sweet and the teacher's representation of it. She moves each sweet, counts, draws and then replaces the Smarties. The pictorial representation is complete and the sweets can be put back in the tube.

Now we can eat them after dinner, can't we, because we've got a picture haven't we? Right, we'll put them back in this . . . (. . . **Cylinder!**). It was a cylinder (confirms the teacher).

(To the researcher she explains) I thought I might do. I might photocopy this and then they can actually record. I thought I might try to do it again with another group and compare the tubes.

Time now to review one stage of the lesson and set the goal for the next.

Now this is a copy of what I did except it hasn't got the colours on . . . what the Smarties were like. So if I put on the bottom here (she marks a colour code, for each column) you can then go off and colour them in.

The teacher 'talks aloud', prompting and coaching individual children.

So all of that row will be . . . orange. That's it. All of that row will be . . . pink . . .

We did some chromatography on Smarties on Friday and we put the water on them and got the colours out. They are all over there. (She tells the researcher about a previous lesson.)

Sarah needs to be checked and supported. 'What is after pink, Sarah?'. 'Red'. 'Red', repeats the teacher. The children also question the teacher. 'What's after blue?'. 'It's on the bottom, pet . . . brown. Do you remember how we put them out in rows?'. She prompts another child. 'Now colour them and count them while you colour them in'. As children finish, she links the completed charts back to the original tube of Smarties.

Now these are our Smarties to eat after dinner.

Time now, for the final summary.

Now that's what this tube of Smarties, or cylinder of Smarties looked like, isn't it? That's the picture of what we've got inside here, isn't it?

For the observer, she has another comment.

> Here you've got colouring, you've got pencil control. It's 's', so there's all that language built in. There's shape, there's number. There's pictorial representation, which is abstracting . . . so much involved here.

As Leinhardt, Putnam, Stein and Baxter[7] have shown, the function of the **agenda** is to provide a map or chart for the lesson. It outlines the lesson sections and the strategy for explaining the mathematical topic to be taught. The teacher makes this explicit to the researcher at a number of points of the lesson. The curriculum **script**[8] provides the structure for lesson content and is, thus, relatively stable. It is built up through amassed experience of teaching the topic to different groups of children and, as shown in this lesson, is composed of goals and sets of actions, explanations and representations which support learning. Furthermore Leinhardt, Putnam, Stein and Baxter[7] have suggested that since teachers' agendas and scripts reflect subject matter content they provide rich sources for the examination of teacher knowledge. But the lesson is not yet finished and the teacher has to set the target for a further activity.

> I'm going to do Smarties with another group this afternoon. I wonder when we open another cylinder of Smarties, or a tube of Smarties if we'll find that it's got eight blue and five green and five orange and five red and four brown and three yellow and three purple? Do you think they will make the same pattern? Do you think in the factory they put the same number of colours in the tube?

The teacher reminds the children of an aim she set early in the lesson but the children now know considerably more than how many different colours there are in a tube of Smarties. One child comments, 'I've done blue, green, orange, pink, red, brown, yellow, purple'. This provides the teacher with the opportunity to offer yet another challenge.

> How many Smarties were in the tube altogether, William?

William solemnly counts the pictorial representation of his Smarties with no support. There are 38 (see Figure 11.1). He clearly realises this is the same as counting the Smarties which have been put back in the tube. 'Oh, that's a big number', is the reply.

> Thirty-eight Smarties. Well done. Right, I'm going to put these pictures on my desk with the Smarties that we'll eat after dinner.

## Discussion

Throughout the lesson the teacher cross-references different lesson segments as well as different areas of mathematics, number, shape and space and data handling.

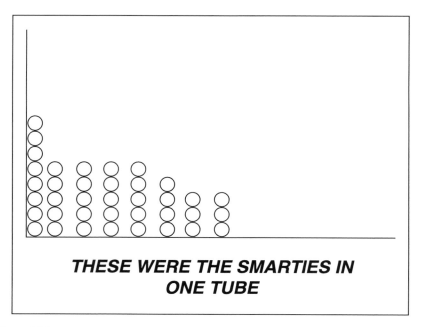

THESE WERE THE SMARTIES IN
ONE TUBE

*Figure 11.1*

In each segment goals and purposes are clearly identified, relevant existing knowledge and skills are checked and accessed, before being deployed within the lesson. Links are made between the old and familiar and the new as more elements are added. Verbal demonstrations are provided which thread through the key actions, thus, verbal and physical moves are linked. Parallel verbal representations serve to draw attention to key points.

There is surprisingly little of what Edwards and Mercer[9] have described as 'cued elicitation', where teachers attempt to elicit from children through question-answer-feedback sequences what has been pre-determined by the lesson aim, motivated by a perceived need for knowledge to appear to 'emerge' spontaneously from children. The teacher stated goals clearly, informed children how to carry out unfamiliar procedures and provided scaffolded support where necessary, for instance, in response to children's errors and in carrying out tasks beyond children's independent means. Schon[10] has talked about professional performance as 'knowing-in-action' which may or may not be accessible to the professional concerned. This teacher is well able to make explicit and to communicate to the researcher the basis for the actions she takes. The exemplar lesson represents a teaching performance of considerable expertise. It illustrates in a powerful way the complexity of subject knowledge as well as the level of skill that is required to combine this with knowledge of learning and teaching and classroom contexts in order to bring about meaningful understanding.

# The teacher interview

The detailed consideration of on-going classroom processes provided some access to this teacher's subject knowledge when combined with pedagogy and reflected in her practice. The interview offered the opportunity to gain further background information about her own previous learning experiences, about some of the formal sources of her subject knowledge as well as an indication of her conceptions of learning and teaching. In terms of her pre-college experiences, she had always liked mathematics and puzzles. At home mathematics was valued. She had passed the eleven plus and gained a GCE ordinary level pass in mathematics. She noted she had passed examinations in mathematics but she was aware that this did not necessarily indicate that at this stage she had gained meaningful understanding of the operations she was able to carry out.

Her college experience had been positive. The mathematics tutor had taken her through the stages of conceptual development experienced by young children, concepts of place value, equivalence and transformation, analysis of number (natural numbers, integers, rational numbers and real numbers) as well as number operations (addition, subtraction, multiplication and division). She remembered, in particular one specific textbook used at college.

> She (the college tutor) made us work through Skemp" from cover to cover and do every single exercise. We talked it through as we did it . . . Number lines with negative and positive numbers, for instance. She had us moving and shifting and telling us why . . . explaining things . . . She explained every-thing we'd learned already and for which we had already passed exams . . .

In terms of teaching advice, this tutor had been very practical. Advice was given concerning the organisation of group work, for instance. From this tutor she had learned that she could not teach everybody at the same level at the same time. Her style of working intensively with one group at a time, whilst other children were engaged in an activity which demanded less support was first suggested by this tutor. She still organised her teaching with small groups of five children, 'sometimes with only three less able children'.

Work could be organised in mixed ability groups.

> You can work with children at different levels and present things within that framework which stretch your more able . . . you've got to think through what you are going to do, want from it and know you are going to have William in your group and what can I add to this for him . . . or for Sarah . . .

Tuesday and Friday were 'maths days': Tuesday was a 'computational, skills sort of day' involving recording and Friday was usually a maths games day. Games 'which was Cockcroft[12] really' had a crucial part to play in teaching and could constitute the main learning tool. Games she regarded as her most valuable equipment.

Most of the mathematics content was, as she described it, 'in her head'. Planning was largely 'thinking time' whether she was at home in the bath or ironing, and what was written down was minimal. Where did it come from? It started off with commercial schemes.

> I have been through Ginn, SPMG and Peak. I have found fault with them all. Nevertheless, you need them for a variety of reasons: when you are inexperienced or supply teaching. Schools need continuity and some teachers do need them . . . need their structure . . . the ideas and the sequence . . . but I just know it now.

In terms of what was considered important for the reception class curriculum to include, she believed, all children should have a chance to learn. Number was very important, language of mathematics, symbols and number and then certain operations on those numbers, in other words, number work led eventually to addition, subtraction, multiplication and division. Shape was important, and pattern, sequencing, ordering and measurement, to an extent, but she thought a lot of measurement was learned out of school. This was the only explicit reference made to informal knowledge gained in out-of-school contexts.

Whilst she regarded the National Curriculum as a wonderful checklist, she wondered whether teachers had taken on board AT 1, using and applying mathematics, perhaps, because assessment made it difficult to measure. Her own way of introducing investigations was through regular, fortnightly whole class discussion. Resources were then made available in the classroom for children's independent exploration. She felt that Plowden and the notion of learning by discovery had been misinterpreted.

> . . . children and their needs are first and then you have got to match and that's where the message that you didn't teach the children (came from) . . . that children must discover for themselves.

> You have got to teach children something just for them to go on to discover. Teach them how to learn, teach them the facts and methods, as well as how to do things . . . Plowden[13] was misread. Learning is like an apprenticeship, isn't it? You know we are further on in life so we pass on what we've learned by showing, speaking, explaining, talking, getting some things back, you know, and this is exchange.

The conception of learning and teaching expressed here has much in common with the style of adult–child interactions termed by Wood, Bruner and Ross[14] as 'scaffolding'. This was used to describe the verbal strategies used by mothers to support the early stages of their young children's learning which faded as independent mastery was established. Here the adult takes a leading role in modelling strategies to be used, providing coaching and feedback for children's early independent efforts and gradually fading this as children become more active and self-instructional in their strategies. More recently such self-instructional strategies have been incorporated in teaching interventions designed to increase children's active role in learning[15].

The importance to this approach of accessing existing knowledge structures to which new knowledge can be related is evident. The difficulty experienced by teachers in **measuring** the development of knowledge, however, was powerfully captured by this teacher. With respect to recording what children had learned, she found the notion of progress was very misleading.

> (It) infers linear movement . . . going forward . . . but all you note is change, forward and back . . . you could be noting regression. There are a lot of things reception children know . . . like roots of the plant . . . that you can't see, that they don't tell you about but, nevertheless, it is being absorbed, being learned . . . You need a strong rooting system before any leaves are going to shoot on the top. I might do something and get absolutely nothing, perhaps, nothing back, but something's been absorbed . . . you look and you are looking for the wrong thing . . . it's demoralising . . . you write something one night in a notebook about a child and in 24 hours it can be different.

As Brophy[16] noted, the development of knowledge is a dynamic process that features construction and deconstruction in response to experience and situational demands. How this can be best represented in National Curriculum terms is yet to be adequately determined.

## Conclusion

Clearly this teacher's own experiences of learning mathematical subject content through primary and secondary school had been positive and she was aware she had been relatively successful in terms of external examinations passes. Whether or not she had had meaningful, conceptual understanding of mathematics is uncertain. In discussing her college experiences, however, she **did** recognise and draw the distinction between procedural knowledge required for examination success and the deeper conceptual understanding which her college tutor had attempted to instil in her students. Ball and McDiamid[17] have noted that whether or not pre-college experience has a greater influence on subject matter learning than formal college studies remains an open question. Whatever its source, Wilson, Shulman and Richert[18] have argued that conceptual understanding is prerequisite to effective subject teaching. Teachers must understand subject content in terms of substantive and syntactic structures, as suggested in the introduction. They must understand the relationship amongst ideas within a particular content area as well as the relationship amongst ideas in different content areas. In the exemplar lesson described the 'unity of mathematics' was emphasised as data handling was interwoven skilfully with number and shape and space.

In contrast to this teacher's college experience, there is some research evidence to suggest that undergraduate students, in general, and not solely students in teacher education, can meet the requirements of the formal assessment system, without necessarily developing conceptual understanding. A longitudinal study[19] of prospective undergraduates in teacher education for elementary and secondary mathematics showed they had difficulty in remembering ideas and procedures and many were unable to demonstrate conceptual understanding of the mathematical operations they were able to carry out successfully. Whilst mathematics undergraduates produced more correct answers for division involving fractions, zero and algebraic equations than undergraduate elementary school teachers they, too, frequently struggled in making sense of division of fractions, making mathematical connections to the real world and in offering explanations which went beyond the mere recycling of known rules.

In terms of conceptions of teaching this teacher was able to consider her own work in the context of changing ideology. She noted the misinterpretations of the Plowden Report and the flaws inherent in conceptions of learning by discovery. She also recognised the college mathematics teaching she received in the mid 1960s was, perhaps, atypical. She was aware of some of the major recommendations of the Cockcroft Report and was able to offer some view of teachers' continuing neglect of mathematical applications. Particularly interesting was her conception of children's learning. Children must actively construct their own mathematical knowledge. Both her observed practice with its careful introductions with explicit goals, guided practice and modelling, assessment and coaching and review and her own description of this as an 'apprenticeship' are entirely compatible with models of scaffolded teaching. Both lesson observation and the interview showed that this teacher engaged in on-going critical reflection on and revision of her own practice, as well as a debate about wider educational purposes and classroom practices. Less clear is how the spirit of critical enquiry was first fostered.

Development of the mathematics content, structure and sequence in her teaching had been supported by existing curriculum material in the early stages though it is not entirely apparent from this interview the nature and extent of her original use of published infant schemes. The work of Skemp had been a major influence on her practice. Ball and Feiman-Nemser[20] described the development of a young teacher's conceptual understanding from working through an elementary mathematics topic in a textbook, though caution was sounded with respect to the use of such sources, which are liable to distort or misrepresent subject knowledge. Stodolosky[21] carried out an analysis of US elementary textbooks indicating that mathematical ideas, if figuring at all, tended to be portrayed as linear and introduced in a step-by-step fashion with undue emphasis on calculation. They provided an inaccurate or, at best, inadequate view of subject knowledge. Aubrey[22] in a small study of British reception class practice showed that teachers seemed to lack awareness of the rich, informal mathematical knowledge children brought into school and relied instead on the rational analysis of subject knowledge provided by infant mathematics schemes, the content and sequence of which, similarly, bore little relationship to young children's early constructions and representation of mathematics.

Furthermore teachers, themselves, as products of primary and secondary schooling often display the same gaps and misconceptions in subject knowledge as the pupils they teach.

The intention of this article has been, first to illustrate the richness and complexity of one 'expert' teacher's mathematical subject knowledge. It should be emphasised here that 'expert' is not the same as 'experienced'! Length of service is not necessarily an indication of the level of expertise achieved. Her interview sheds some light on the changes in and development of her own subject knowledge and some of the influences on the pedagogical content knowledge deployed in her practice. The sources of teacher subject knowledge, however, are subtle and complex and by no means yet clearly understood. This teacher's account of her practice reveals the continuing influence of her college education interacting with her developing understanding of young children's learning, as well as the critical reflection on personal practice, available curriculum materials and changing educational orthodoxy.

Clearly we need to know far more about changes and development in subject knowledge at all stages of professional development before we can make assertions about the inadequacy of initial teacher education or take far-reaching decisions which affect the existing means of increasing teachers' subject knowledge as part of their initial or continuing professional development. Teachers learn much of their subject knowledge as well as dispositions towards particular subjects in their 13 years of compulsory education long before they enter their relatively short period of undergraduate study.

Documenting the development of and changes in teachers' subject knowledge has barely started in the UK. A period of unprecedented change in school and college curriculum organisation may not provide the best context in which to investigate teacher preparation or to bring about improvements in professional practice, but a project at the University of Durham is slowly building up a bank of reception class mathematics practice[22]. Accumulated case studies of individual teachers, experienced and novice, may be one way to help increase our understanding of the course and development of teacher' subject knowledge.

## Acknowledgements

ESRC who supported the project, the Research Associate and 'Expert' Teacher who prefer to remain anonymous, as well as the school and children involved.

## References

1. Alexander, R., Rose, J. and Woodhead, C. (1992) *Curriculum Organisation and Classroom Practice in Primary Schools – A Discussion Paper.* HMSO: London.
2. OFSTED (1993) *Curriculum Organisation and Classroom Practice in Primary Schools.* A follow-up report. DFE Publications Centre: London.
3. National Curriculum Council (1993) *The National Curriculum at Key Stages 1 and 2.* NCC: York.

4. DFE (1993) *The Initial Training of Primary School Teachers.* Circular 14/93. London, Sanctuary Buildings.

5. Shulman, L. (1986) 'Those who understand: Knowledge growth in teaching', *Educational Researcher*, 15, 2, 4–14.

6. Ball, D. L. (1991) 'Research on Teaching Mathematics: Making subject matter knowledge part of the equation', in Brophy J. (ed) *Advances in Research on Teaching.* Vol. 2. JAI Press: Greenwich, CT 1–49.

7. Leinhardt, G., Putnam, R., Stein, M. K. and Baxter, J. (1991) 'Where Subject Knowledge Matters', in Brophy, J. (ed) *Advances in Research on Teaching.* Vol. 2. JAI Press: Greenwich, CT. 87–113.

8. Putnam, R. T. (1987) 'Structuring and adjusting content for students: A study of live and simulated tutoring of addition', *American Educational Research Journal*, 24, 1, 13–28.

9. Edwards, D. and Mercer, N. (1987) *Common Knowledge: The development of understanding in Classrooms.* Methuen: London.

10. Schon, D. (1983) *The Reflective Practitioner: How Professionals Think in Action.* Basic Books: New York.

11. Skemp, R. R. (1964) *Understanding Mathematics.* Book 1. University of London Press: London.

12. Cockcroft, W. M. (1982) *Mathematics counts: The Report of the Commission of Inquiry into the Teaching of Mathematics in Schools*, under the chairmanship of Dr W. H. Cockcroft. HMSO: London.

13. DES (1967) *Children and their Primary Schools. Vol. 1. The Plowden Report.* HMSO: London.

14. Wood, D. J., Bruner, J. S. and Ross, G. (1976) 'The Role of Tutoring in Problem-solving', *Journal of Child Psychology and Psychiatry*, 17, 2, 89–100.

15. Wang, M. C. and Palincsar, A. S. (1989) 'Teaching Students to Assume an Active Role in their Learning', in Reynolds, M. C. (ed) *Knowledge Base of the Beginning Teacher*, Pergamon Press: Oxford.

16. Brophy, J. (ed) (1991) *Advances in Research on Teaching.* Vol. 2. JAI Press: Greenwich, CT.

17. Ball, D. L. and McDiarmid, G. W. (1990) 'The subject matter preparation of teachers', in Houston, W. R. (ed) *Handbook of Research on Teacher Education.* Macmillan: New York. 437–449.

18. Wilson, S. M., Shulman, L. S. and Rickert, A. E. (1987) '150 Different Ways of Knowing: Representations of Knowledge in Teaching', in Calderhead, J. (ed) *Exploring Teacher Thinking.* Cassell: London. 104–124.

19. Ball, D. L. and Feiman-Nemser, S. (1988) 'Using Textbooks and Teachers' Guides: A dilemma for beginning teachers and teacher educators', *Curriculum Inquiry*, 18, 401–23.

20. Ball, D. L. (1990) 'The mathematical understandings that prospective teachers bring to teacher education', *Elementary School Journal*, 90, 449–66.

21. Stodolsky, S. (1988) *The Subject Matters: Classroom Activity in Math and Social Studies.* University of Chicago Press: Chicago.

22. Aubrey, C. (1994) 'An Investigation of Children's Knowledge of Mathematics at School Entry and the Knowledge their Teachers Hold about Teaching and Learning Mathematics, about Young Learners and Mathematical Subject Knowledge', *British Educational Research Journal*, 20, 1, 105–20.

23. Aubrey, C. (1993) 'An Investigation of the Mathematical Competences which Young Children Bring into School', *British Educational Research Journal*, 19, 1, 19–37.
24. Aubrey, C. (1995) 'Teacher and Pupil Interactions and the Processes of Mathematical Instruction in Four Reception Classrooms over Children's First Year in School', *British Educational Research Council*, 21, (in press).

# 12 Planning to use ICT in schools?

*Peter Twining*

## Introduction

Anyone involved in education in the 'developed' nations cannot have failed to notice the massive drives that are taking place to introduce information communications technologies (ICT) into schools in recent years. In the UK this is most clearly highlighted by the Government's targets for ICT in education up to 2002.

These include:

- serving teachers to be confident and competent to teach using ICT;
- all schools, libraries, colleges and universities connected to the NGfL [National Grid for Learning] enabling perhaps some 75% of teachers and 50% of pupils to have their own email addresses;
- most school leavers to have a good understanding of ICT;
- making Britain a world leader in the field of digital learning;
- DfEE [Department for Education & Employment] communications with the education service to be mainly electronic.

(DfEE 1999 p3) Text in square brackets added

These targets clearly put pressure on the UK education system to radically enhance their use of ICT, with a specific focus on computers and related communications technologies. The Government has also provided support to help meet these targets, in the form of 'a coordinated programme of investment totalling over £1.6 billion up to 2002 which underpins the delivery of the Government's targets for ICT in education and lifelong learning' (DfEE 1999 p3).

This pressure to make greater use of ICT to enhance learning is based on a range of different rationales. Some of these relate to preparing children for the world of work and trying to establish an economic advantage in the global market as we move from the 'Industrial Age' to the 'Information Age' (see Trilling and Hood 1999) for a convincing argument that this change is taking place). Other rationales for the increased use of ICT in schools are based on evidence that ICT can enhance learning, if used in certain ways (eg Davis, Desforges *et al.* 1997; Stevenson, Anderson et al. 1997; Moseley, Higgins *et al.* 1999; Schacter 1999; Scrimshaw 1997; Trilling and Hood 1999).

| | March 1998 | April 1999 | April 2000 |
|---|---|---|---|
| Proportion of schools connected to the internet | 17% | 62% | 86% |
| Average number of pupils per computer | 18 | 13.4 | 12.6 |
| Average expenditure per pupil on ICT for teaching and learning | £11 | £27 | £30 |

*Figure 12.1* Evidence of increasing investment in ICT in Primary Schools (DfEE 1998; DfEE 2000)

| | March 1998 | April 1999 | April 2000 |
|---|---|---|---|
| Proportion of schools connected to the internet | 83% | 93% | 98% |
| Average number of pupils per computer | 9 | 8.4 | 7.9 |
| Average expenditure per pupil on ICT for teaching and learning | £38 | £45 | £47 |

*Figure 12.2* Evidence of increasing investment in ICT in Secondary Schools (DfEE 1998; DfEE 2000)

There is evidence that there has been some change in UK schools since the Stevenson report (Stevenson, Anderson *et al.* 1997 Summary) noted that 'the state of ICT in our schools is primitive and not improving'. Thus, for example, Figures 12.1 and 12.2 indicate that the level of resourcing for ICT in English schools did improve between 1998[1] and 2000.

However, there is a substantial amount of evidence to suggest that computers have not made much impact on the educational practice in most schools, despite the massive investments identified above. The quotations below illustrate this point:

> We became increasingly aware of the constraints under which schools and teachers are working. All the teachers involved in the project, including those who were identified as intensive ICT users, could find only limited time when pupils could use computers to improve their literacy or numeracy (typically about half an hour a week each). Further-more, although the amount of ICT equipment in schools increased during the life of the project, much computer use in primary classrooms was planned as an addition to the curriculum rather than as a key teaching strategy. This was reflected in the low use of ICT for direct instruction generally and by the average provision of one or two computers in a typical primary classroom.
>
> (Moseley, Higgins *et al.* 1999 p23)

The growing importance of IT and increasing recognition of its potential impact on the organisation of learning and the role of the teacher has had very little impact on the organisation of primary classrooms. . . much of the equipment was relatively old, of varying make, of low specification, and rarely used, so that out of almost 1000 records of curriculum activity, just twelve recorded the use of IT.

(Galton, Hargreaves *et al.* 1999 p46)

. . . research has shown that at present many teachers do not yet use ICT in their teaching at all.

(Preston, Cox *et al.* 2000 p1)

. . . generally the quality of work in information technology is lower than in other subjects

(OFSTED 1999 Para 23, Primary)

This lack of impact of substantial investments in ICT in schools may be due to a large number of factors. However, it is clear that in order to maximise the likelihood of such investments leading to learning enhancements, and hence representing good value for money, you need to have a clear ICT development plan (BECTa 1999). Such a plan should identify:

- your starting point (ICT audit)
- your end point (vision in terms of aims and broad learning objectives)
- specific details identifying how you are going to get from your starting point to your end point (an implementation plan)
- specific and easily identifiable criteria so you know when you have reached your end point (an evaluation plan)

A good deal has been written about developing an ICT plan (see for example North 1991; NCET and NAACE 1997; Harrison 1998; BECTa 1999). However, thinking about the objectives for ICT use and the impact that such use (if successfully implemented) will have remain complex and confused. Furthermore, the relationship between objectives and the organisation of resources is not always clear. In order to help unravel these issues I have developed the Computer Practice Framework (CPF). This presents three key dimensions for thinking about computer use in schools. The CPF is presented here in the form of three questions, one for each dimension of the framework:

- What are your main objectives for using ICT?
- What impact do you want ICT use to have on learning in your school?
- How much time do you want to your children to spend using computers?

These three questions are explained and explored in order to provide you with a framework for thinking about your vision for computer use in your school. Advice is then provided on how to use this framework to help you to refine your school's development plan.

# What are your objectives for using ICT? (*Focus*)

ICT initiatives in schools are most successful when they are based on the technology meeting pre-determined objectives. In other words, the objective should exist prior to the decision to use the technology, which is introduced as a solution to an identified 'problem', 'rather than introducing the technology and afterwards seeking 'problems to solve'.' (BECTa 1999 p11.)

The Focus dimension of the Computer Practice Frame-work identifies three possible objectives, or foci, for using computers to support learning in schools:

> *IT*: this is where your objective is to help the children to develop their ICT[2] skills, knowledge and understanding. The emphasis here is on using a computer in order to extend the children's knowledge, understanding or skill in computer use itself. The technology is the focus of the learning.

> *Learning Tool*: this is where your objective is to use computers as a tool to help children learn where the focus of their learning is not on the technoogy. This learning may fall into three distinct areas:

>> *Curriculum* – Using computers as tools to help children to develop skills, knowledge and understanding in a curriculum area other than ICT. For example, you may use software (eg a database, spreadsheet or graph generating program) to facilitate the process of analysing data in Science, where your focus is on exploring an hypothesis rather than on learning how to operate the software (ie the focus is on Science). Similarly, using the computer to enable children to access the curriculum would fall into this category. An example of this would be providing a child who finds reading challenging with access to information in a multimedia format (eg audio, images, video, animations) rather than asking them to use predominantly text based information sources. An important aspect of *curriculum* is the use of computers in order to overcome social or economic inequity. For example, by enhancing access to computers for children who do not have such access outside school, in order to help reduce the 'information divide'.

>> *Mathetic* – Using computers as tools to develop children's ability to learn and enhance their approaches to learning. One example of this would be if you explicitly teach children to teach each other how to use particular programs. Teaching children about how to formulate good questions, search for and evaluate evidence, and communicate their findings would be another example.

>> *Affective* – Using computers as tools to support and enhance the affective aspects of children's learning. Using a computer in order to build children's self esteem (for example by allowing a child who may be perceived as 'less able' to teach other children how to use a new program) or as a means of motivating a child would both fall into the 'Affective' category.

*Other* – this is where your objective is to use the computer for any reason that does not fit within *IT* or *Learning Tool* above. Reasons for using computers that fall within this category may be focussed on practical aspects of the learning situation or the larger context in which the computer use is taking place. Some clearly identifiable aspects of Other include:

*Reward* – Using computers as a holding or filler activity or as a reward for children would fall into this category. An example of this would be allowing children who have finished other work to 'go on the computer'.

*Marketing* – Using computers as a mechanism for presenting the school in a good light or in order to be seen to be using them. This would include using computers in order to impress visitors to the school, such as OFSTED inspectors or prospective parents. It would also include using computers in response to external pressure, such as central directives or criticisms in inspection reports.

Clearly all three foci will apply to some degree. However, establishing the balance of the three should help to clarify the most suitable ways in which to organise your computer resources. Figure 12.3 provides a brief overview of a number of common organisational models for computer resourcing. Figure 12.4 maps each of these organisational models onto the different foci or objectives for computer use in schools, based on evidence from the literature and experience of computers in schools.

## What impact do you want computers to have on the curriculum? (*Mode*)

BECTa (1999) identified that ICT is most effectively implemented in institutions where staff involved in supporting the plan 'understand fully the implications of

| Model | Description |
| --- | --- |
| Computer lab | A room with sufficient computers for the whole class to use them at one time, even if they have to work in pairs/threes. Ideally there should be a large monitor or data projector. |
| Computer clusters | Three or more machines grouped together in a shared area, but not sufficient for the whole class to use at once. |
| Classroom computer | One or two computers 'inside' the classroom. |
| Notebooks | Portable computers, capable of running the same software as desktop machines. Mains and/or battery powered. Short battery life (Max 3 hours). |
| Sub-notebooks | Hand held computers with integral keyboards that cannot run the same software as a standard desktop machine, but which tend to include 'office' software such as word processors, spreadsheets, etc. Long battery life (10 hours to several months depending on particular device). |

*Figure 12.3* Overview of common models of computer resourcing

| Resourcing model | Focus | | |
|---|---|---|---|
| | **IT** | **Learning tool** | **Other** |
| **Computer lab** | Easy to demonstrate to the whole class, followed by immediate individual practice | Good for ILS (if one computer per child or adequate supervision available) but otherwise access problems minimise its value as a learning tool. | Very visible show of investment in ICT (Marketing) |
| **Computer clusters** | Not as good as lab that caters for whole class, but better than individual machine. Good for encouraging peer support. | Tends to be more accessible than computer lab, but supervision and scheduling are issues. | Less visible than computer lab (Marketing) More readily accessible than computer lab (Reward) |
| **Classroom computer** | Not enough children involved to justify teacher time | Difficult to manage as only 1/2/3 children can use it at once. | Readily available for children who have finished other work (Reward) |
| **Notebooks** | Difficult to demonstrate to more than a couple of children at once. The more you have the better. | 'Easy' to locate them where they are needed to support learning. Issues relating to battery life. If children within your classes are organised into groups then 5 notebooks are usually adequate to allow a whole group to use them at once. | Notebooks seen as 'progressive' but are not highly visible (Marketing). Good for supporting staff development (if staff encouraged to take them home) |
| **Sub-notebooks** | Non-standard software. Difficult to demonstrate due to screen size/ quality. | Good for text entry and editing. Very portable. Child sized. Long battery life. | Relatively cheap way to provide large numbers of machines balanced against low visibility and non-standard software. |

*Figure 12.4* Summary of resourcing models supporting different objectives

implementing an ICT programme and the curriculum and resource requirements.' (p10) One aspect of this is understanding the impact of your vision for ICT use in terms of the degree of change it represents.

Introducing computers into schools inevitably involves change. The greater the degree of change the more difficult, costly and time consuming the process will be. Cuban (1988) identified two different categories of change, which he described as first and second order.

'First-order changes, then, try to make what already exists more efficient and more effective, without disturbing the basic organizational features, without substantially altering the ways in which adults and children perform their roles. . . Second-order changes seek to alter the fundamental ways in which organizations are put together. . . Second-order changes introduce new goals, structures, and roles that transform familiar ways of doing things into new ways of solving persistent problems.

(Cuban 1988 p342)

Maddux (1994) identified two different categories of computer applications, which map onto Cuban's categories of change. Maddux termed these as Type I and Type II: Type I applications 'make it easier, quicker, or otherwise more efficient to continue to teach in traditional ways.' (p131), whilst Type II applications 'make new and better methods of teaching and learning available to us – ways that would not be available without technology.' (p131).

Maddux (1994) identified that Type I applications were easier to implement than Type II applications because they do not require significant modification of current practices. This supported Cuban's claim that 'first-order changes succeeded while second-order change were either adapted to fit what existed or sloughed off, allowing the system to remain essentially untouched.' (Cuban 1988 p343).

This useful distinction between uses of ICT that support current practice and those that alter it is unpacked further within the *Mode* dimension of the Computer Practice Framework. It identifies three different ways in which ICT can impact on 'the curriculum' with schools, where 'the curriculum' is used in the broad sense of the term, which includes both content and process, and extends beyond the explicit curriculum (e.g. within England is not restricted to the National Curriculum). The three different modes of computer use within the CPF are:

*Support* – where the computer is being used to enable you to do something more effectively and/or efficiently but without changing the content of what is taught. The process may be automated but is otherwise essentially unchanged. Examples of this would include: using 'drill and practice' software to reinforce basic maths or English skills (eg number bonds, spelling); using a word processor to type up best copies of work for display; or using a graph generating program to draw a bar chart (where the time saved was not used to extend the range or depth of the data analysis).

*Extension* – where the computer is being used to do something which changes the curriculum within the classroom. i.e. the teacher (or her children) are doing something that they would not have done if it were not for computers. The content and/or process are different – but these changes *could* have been achieved without a computer. Examples of this would include: using a word processor to allow you to repeatedly re-draft your work, and hence to focus on each phases of the writing process in turn (eg

| Mode | Curriculum | | |
|------|---------|---|---------|
| | **Content** | | **Process** |
| | (What they learn – knowledge, skills) | | (How they learn it) |
| **Support** | Same | and | Automated but otherwise essentially unchanged |
| **Extend** | Different – but *does not require* a computer | and/or | Different – but does not require a computer |
| **Transform** | Different – and requires a computer | and/or | Different – and requires a computer |

*Figure 12.5* Summary of key distinctions between the three modes of computer use within the Computer Practice Framework (CPF)

compose, revise, edit, format); using data analysis software to enable you to analyse substantial amounts of information and/or to compare a range of different forms of data analysis (eg graphical representations) to see which is the best in order to answer your original question; explicitly teaching children to teach each other.

*Transformation* – where the computer is transforming the curriculum, i.e. the teacher (or her children) are doing something that they *could not* have done if it were not for computers. Examples of this would include: using the Internet to find information and communicate with people who would otherwise not have been accessible; creating multimedia presentations; creating music or art compositions using techniques only available through new technology.

*Support* corresponds to Maddux's Type I application and represents a first-order change. *Transformation* corresponds to Maddux's Type II application and represents second-order change. Extension provides a bridge between these two extremes.

Figure 12.6 provide a summary of the key dimensions of practice that are often associated with moves towards using technology to extend and transform practice (adapted from Trilling and Hood 1999).

## How much time do we want our children to spend using ICT? (Quantity)

It is clear that the quantity of ICT use on its own tells us very little about the extent to which children's learning will be enhanced (Maddux 1993). None the less, having a clear picture of how much time you think children should be using ICT does help to inform your ICT development plan in a number of ways.

The quantity of ICT use interacts with the *Focus* of that use. There is a clear relationship between the amount of time that children spend using a particular

| 'Traditional' learning practice | 'Transformed' learning practice |
|---|---|
| Teacher as director | Teacher as facilitator, guide, consultant |
| Teacher as knowledge source | Teacher as co-learner |
| Curriculum directed learning | Student directed learning |
| Time-slotted, rigidly scheduled learning | Open, flexible, on-demand learning |
| Primarily fact-based | Primarily project- & problem-based |
| Theoretical, abstract | Principles and Surveys |
| Real-world, concrete | Actions and reflections |
| Drill & Practice | Inquiry and design |
| Rules and procedures | Discovery and invention |
| Competitive | Collaborative |
| Classroom focused | Community focused |
| Prescribed results | Open-ended results |
| Conform to norm | Creative diversity |
| Computers as subject of study | Computers as tool for all learning |
| Static media presentations | Dynamic multimedia interactions |
| Classroom bounded communication | World-wide bounded communication |
| Tested/assessed by norms | Performance assessed by experts, mentors, peers and self |

*Figure 12.6* A comparison of 'Traditional' and 'Transformed' learning practices (adapted from Trilling and Hood (1999) p11)

application and the proportion of that time spent learning how to use the technology. In order for children to use ICT as a learning tool they must first learn how to use it. Thus, if your main *Focus* for using ICT is *Learning Tool* then the quantity of ICT use will need to be higher than if your *Focus is IT*.

There is also a relationship between the quantity of use and the *Mode* dimension. In essence the quantity of use you want children to have gives an indication of the level of resourcing required, once you have decided on the organisation model that you are going to adopt. This is because there is a direct correlation between the level of investment in ICT equipment[3] and the amount of time that children potentially can spend using ICT in school. As you move from *Support* (first order change) through *Extension to Transformation* (second order change) the level of change and hence the level of investment required increases significantly (see Figure 12.7). This is due to the increasing complexity of the proposed change. Thus, if you only wish children to use computers for a relatively small amount of time, and hence only wish to invest relatively small amounts of money in ICT, you are unlikely to be able to operate effectively at the *Transformation* end of the *Mode* dimension.

Maddux (1994 p131) suggests that the goals achievable by Type I applications (i.e. where the *Mode is Support*) are trivial and do not justify the expense of the technology. BECTa (1999) seems to support the view that investments in ICT should go beyond *Support* when they argue for the educational benefits of 'connectedness' and 'networked learning', and state that 'In schools, the technical heart of the National Grid for Learning is the networked computer linked to the Internet.' (p31) and that 'Connection to wider networks is now a fundamental part of ICT.' (p32). This suggests that the greater the quantity of computer use that you wish children to have, and hence the greater the level of investment you plan to make, the greater the need to move from using ICT for *Support* and towards *Transformation* in order to justify that expenditure.

## Using the Computer Practice Framework to help you develop your ICT development plan

The first two questions, which are based on the *Focus* and *Mode* dimensions within the framework, should help you to clarify your thinking about your vision for ICT use within your school. The third question, which is based on the *Quantity* dimension within the frame-work, provides one mechanism for starting to think about the extent to which your vision fits within the practical constraints of your context.

The first two dimensions within the framework build upon each other. If your *Focus* is *not Learning Tool* then the *Mode* dimension does not apply. This is because the Mode relates specifically to the impact of computer use on the curriculum (excluding ICT as a subject). Thus when thinking about your vision for ICT in your school, you should start by thinking about your objectives for using computers *(Focus)*. This should help you to identify the ideal organisational model for your ICT resources, which may well be a hybrid based on more than one of the models presented in Figures 12.3 and 12.4.

If your *Focus* for computer use includes a significant element relating to using computers to support learning in other subjects then you should consider the impact that you wish computers to have on the curriculum (*Mode*). Otherwise you can ignore this dimension, as it will not apply to you.

Having done this you should have a clear vision of why you want to use computers and the impact that you wish them to have on the curriculum in broad terms. You should also have a vision of how to organise your resources in order to meet these overarching aims and objectives.

The third dimension within the framework helps to provide a bridge between your vision and your current position, by helping you to see the extent to which your vision matches the level of resourcing that you have available to you (as illustrated in Figure 12.7). Thus it feeds into your implementation plan, which identifies specific actions that you need to take in order to move towards your overall goal.

## Conclusion

Schools are under increasing pressure to make use of ICT in their teaching. Whilst there is evidence that the levels of ICT resourcing in schools have improved, there

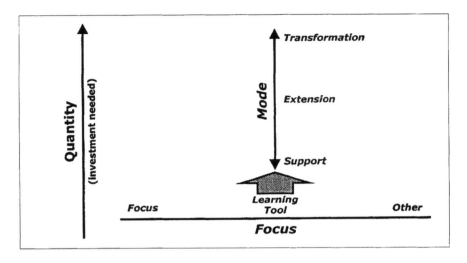

*Figure 12.7* A diagrammatic representation of the relationship between Focus and Mode, with Quantity superimposed

is also a significant body of evidence to suggest that ICT is having very little impact on educational practice in most schools.

One approach to enhancing the impact of investments in ICT in education is to ensure that such investments are based on clearly articulated development plans. Such plans should identify explicit visions of why we want to use ICT and the impact that we want it to have, as well as how we are going to implement those visions in the light of the constraints operating in our individual school contexts. However, developing such visions and thinking about how to implement them is difficult.

The Computer Practice Framework (CPF), which was presented here in the form of three questions, aims to help you clarify your vision for ICT in terms of the overall objectives for using ICT and the impact that we want it to have on the curriculum. This was linked with the implementation plan through the discussion of the *Quantity* dimension and the provision of guidance on the suitability of different models of resource organisation to support different objectives for using ICT.

The discussion of the *Mode* dimension raised issues about the relative difficulty and value of using ICT in ways that supported, extended or transformed the curriculum. It was argued that investing in ICT was only justified if that investment extended or transformed the curriculum. However, it was pointed out that this involves second order change, which is notoriously difficult:

> For those who seek fundamental, second-order changes that will sweep away current structures and start anew, as was done in the mid-19th century, *basic social and political changes would need to occur outside of schools.*
>
> (Cuban 1988 p344)

The evidence presented here suggests that such basic social and political changes are taking place outside schools. The UK government is investing heavily in ICT in education, with a major emphasis on the National Grid for Learning (NGfL). This use of Internet technologies fits most clearly into the *Transformation* category on the *Mode* dimension. One of the rationales underpinning this major government drive is a perceived shift in society from an 'industrial age' to an 'information age', which is described so persuasively by Trilling and Hood (1999). Perhaps we are at a turning point in educational history. Perhaps the time is now right for us to plan for ICT to extend and transform learning and teaching.

## Notes

1. Data from March 1998 'gives the picture of provision before the Government introduced its implementation strategy and accompanying funding programmes. The data will form the baseline for monitoring and evaluating Grid development and the challenges the Government has set itself.' (DfEE 1998 pl).
2. The term ICT is used here to refer to the National Curriculum subject. The revised version of the National Curriculum in England and Wales (DfEE and QCA 1999) has blurred the valuable distinction between the notion of learning about the technology (IT) and using the technology to support learning (ICT) so clearly described by the QCA (1998 Teacher's guide p19).
3. It is important to bear in mind that it is estimated that the original purchases price of a computer represents only 20% of its total cost (BECTa 1999 p18).

## References

BECTa (1999). *Connecting Schools, Networking People 2000: ICT planning, purchasing and good practice for the National Grid for Learning*. Coventry, BECTa.

Cuban, L. (1988). 'A Fundamental Puzzle of School Reform.' *Phi Delta Kappan* 69(5): 341–344.

Davis, N., C. Desforges, *et al.* (1997). Can quality in learning be enhanced through the use of IT? *Using Information Technology effectively in Teaching and Learning: Studies in Pre-Service and In-Service Teacher Education.* B. Somekh and N. Davis. London, Routledge: 14–27.

DfEE (1998). Survey of Information and Communications Technology in schools 1998. Norwich, DfEE.

DfEE (1999). Survey of Information and Communications Technology in schools 1999. Norwich, DfEE.

DfEE (2000). Information and Communications Technology in Schools, England: 2000, DfEE.

DfEE and QCA (1999). The National Curriculum: Handbook for primary teachers in England Key stages 1 and 2. London, DfEE & QCA.

Galton, M., L. Hargreaves, *et al.* (1999). *Inside the Primary Classroom: 20 years on.* London, Routledge.

Harrison, M. (1998). *Co-ordinating information & communications technology across the primary school: a book for the primary IT co-ordinator.* London, Falmer Press.

Maddux, C. (1994). 'Editorial: Integration is the Only Option We Have.' *Journal of Information Technology for Teacher Education* 3(2): 129–133.

Maddux, C. D. (1993). Past and Future Stages in Educational Computing Research. *Approaches to research on teacher education and technology.* H. C. Waxman and G. W.

Bright. Virginia, Association for the Advancement of Computing in Education. 1: 11–22.

Moseley, D., S. Higgins, *et al.* (1999). *Ways forward with ICT: Effective pedagogy using Information and Communications Technology for Literacy and Numeracy in Primary Schools.* Newcastle, University of Newcastle.

NCET and NAACE (1997). *Implementing IT: Resource Pack.* Coventry, NCET & NAACE.

North, R. (1991). 'Managing the integration of information technology across the curriculum of the secondary school.' *Computers Educ.* 16(1): 13–16.

OFSTED (1999). *Annual report of Her Majesties Chief Inspector of Schools 1998/99.* London, HMSO.

Preston, C., M. Cox, *et al.* (2000). *Teachers As Innovators: An evaluation of the motivation of teachers to use information and communications technologies.* London, MirandaNet.

QCA and DfEE (1998). *Information Technology: A scheme of work for Key Stages 1 and 2.* London, Qualification and Curriculum Authority (QCA).

Schacter, J. (1999). The Impact of Education Technology on Student Achievement: What the most current research has to say. Santa Monica, Milken Exchange on Education Technology.

Scrimshaw, P. (1997). Education Departments' Superhighways Initiative (EDSI): Synoptic Report. Milton Keynes, The Open University.

Stevenson, D., I. Anderson, *et al.* (1997). Information and Communications Technology in UK Schools – An independent Enquiry. London, Independent ICT in School Commission.

Trilling, B. and P. Hood (1999). 'Learning, Technology, and Educational Reform in the Knowledge Age or 'We're Wired, Webbed, and Windowed, Now What?'.' *Educational Technology* May–June 1999: 5–18.

# 13 'Science is not my thing'

## Primary teachers' concerns about challenging gifted pupils

*David Coates*

## Introduction

In recent years there has been much interest expressed in the identification and teaching of highly able pupils in English schools. Research findings in England (DfES, 2002), however, indicated that children with high ability do not always attain highly. In the U.S.A., Archambault *et al.* (1993) found that instruction in the regular classroom was generally not tailored to meet the unique needs of gifted pupils. Within the context of primary science education underachievement is often linked to lack of appropriate challenge (OFSTED, 1996, 2001).

In 1993, the U.S. Education Department released a report which estimated that less than 20% of gifted students were appropriately challenged in schools (PAGE, 2001). Providing effective challenge to allow able children to achieve their potential is therefore a problematic area for many schools. In 1998, an unpublished OFSTED report, submitted to the House of Commons Education and Employment Select Committee, identified it as a key issue in 20% of primary schools and a significant number of secondary schools in England. In the following year, the Select Committee's report 'Highly Able Children' established that many teachers were unsure about how to provide challenge for able pupils. By 2002, the proportion of primary schools in which gifted pupils made unsatisfactory progress had fallen to one in eight, but they were only making good progress in less than half of schools (OFSTED, 2002). It has been argued that the consequences of not developing children's scientific capability can have a potential influence at both a personal level and in relation to national competitiveness.

This research was undertaken in an above-average-sized primary school in Oxfordshire. The purpose of the research was to identify what teachers thought were the factors which limited their capability to challenge gifted children in science lessons. Professional development in gifted education needs to address not only 'the how to' but also the 'why' of interventions. Diezmann and Watters (2000) suggested that many challenges exist to engage teachers in being more reflective about teaching of gifted children.

## Challenge and gifted scientists

*Excellence and enjoyment: learning and teaching in the primary years* (DfES, 2004) sets out the following key principles for learning and teaching for all children. Teachers are expected to:

- set high expectations and give every learner confidence they can succeed,
- establish what learners already know and build on it, and
- structure and pace the learning experiences to make it challenging and enjoyable.

As this document discussed all primary-aged children, the principles need to be utilised so that the needs of gifted children are met in science alongside all other subjects.

The National Curriculum (DfEE/QCA, 1999), interestingly, required teachers to provide effective learning opportunities for all pupils. It stated that:

> Science stimulates and excites pupils' curiosity about phenomena and events in the world around them. Because science links direct practical experience with ideas, it can engage learners at many levels. Scientific method is about developing and evaluating explanations through experimental evidence and modelling. This is a spur to critical and creative thought. Through science, pupils understand how major scientific ideas contribute to technological change—impacting on industry, business and medicine and improving the quality of life.
>
> (DfEE/QCA, p. 76)

Recent studies in America have identified materials, with a similar emphasis to the English National Curriculum, that are most appropriate for challenging gifted children in primary schools (Johnson *et al.*, 1995). These include a balance between process and content, an emphasis on original student investigations, concept development and interdisciplinary applications. If this vision of science is realised then it will be an exciting and challenging subject for all primary children. Parke (1992) argued that the challenge for a primary teacher is to plan for a working environment in which all pupils, including the most able, can fully develop their capability and interests within the confines of a normal mixed-ability class. Montgomery, in her evidence to the Education and Employment Committee (1999), suggested that teachers should change their teaching for able children in particular from a 'competence based' to a 'cognitive based' curriculum:

> This would ensure children developed 'cognitive skills' such as thinking, planning, organisation, problem solving and creativity, and reflecting upon and monitoring their learning.
>
> (Education and Employment Committee, 1999, p. xiii)

Science has the potential to provide an ideal framework for developing these cognitive skills as it should be a practical subject where children can be involved in all aspects of investigations. Montgomery (1996, p. 63) draws a valuable comparison between product-based and process-based curricula. She contends that 'content models emphasise the importance of learning skills within a predetermined domain', and that 'in these systems, a large amount of rote learning (learning material by heart) is seen'. The potential superficiality of such learning is highlighted. Process models cannot operate without a content base but the explicit teaching of investigatory and problem-solving skills is predominant within this process model. At the heart of the process-based approach is enrichment and extension of the curriculum, where the 'syllabus can be addressed in greater depth for the highly able' (Education Select Committee, 1999, p. liv).

Recent advice to teachers has suggested that the curriculum for all children should be more cognitively based. The teacher's guide update to the Science Scheme of Work (QCA/DfEE, 2000) gave guidance on different types of thinking skills and which topics would benefit by their inclusion:

> By using thinking skills children can focus on knowing how as well as knowing what—on learning how to learn. Many aspects of science contribute to the development of thinking skills.
>
> (QCA/DfEE, 2000, p. 8)

Although this document deals with making science education more challenging for all children, similar activities in the classroom could be adapted to include aspects of enrichment and/or extension so that the gifted children are challenged by the work. Winebrenner (2001) suggested that if teachers improve the challenge for gifted children, they significantly improve learning experiences for all students in normal classes. A challenging curriculum, where there is high achievement, is perceived by gifted children as one where they work hard and they get good results. The curriculum is slightly beyond their grasp and requires significant effort to master it (Davis & Rimm, 1998). This could equally be applied to all learners (below average, average, or above average).

Challenge for gifted children could be achieved through 'appropriate teaching and expectations of pupils . . . and through the curriculum' (Education Select Committee, 1999, p. liv.) As George (1997) indicated, all children, including the most able, need to be challenged by their science work in order to achieve their full potential. Porter (1999) defined gifted young children as 'those who have the capacity to learn at a pace and level of complexity that is significantly advanced of their age peers . . .' (p. 33). Maker (1982) suggested that gifted pupils differ from their classmates in three ways: the pace at which they learn, the depth of their understanding, and the interest they hold. A curriculum that challenges and meets the needs these children in the normal classroom should address and accommodate these characteristics. For gifted children there should be an even greater emphasis on the 'How?' to increase the complexity of their work, and the use of higher-order thinking skills (Bloom, 1956). Science teaching should be differentiated, to allow for the needs of gifted and talented pupils, by 'task, inputs and outputs, for example through a range of learning outcomes' (QCA/DfEE, 2001, p. 2). The specific characteristics of gifted children in relation to science could therefore form the basis of a challenging science curriculum. These characteristics may include some or all of the following (Coates & Wilson, 2001, 2003):

- a natural curiosity about the world and the way things work,
- an enjoyment of hypothesising,
- an ability to express scientific knowledge and understanding logically and coherently,
- scientific vocabulary used accurately and appropriately,
- an ability to transfer knowledge and understanding from one situation to another,
- an ability to spot and describe patterns in results,
- innovation in experimental design and/or in the collecting and recording of data.

## Methodology

This research lies firmly within the qualitative paradigm as it aims to understand experiences as nearly as possible 'as its participants feel it or live it' (Sherman & Webb, 1988, p. 7 in Blaxter *et al.*, 1996). The research was set in the natural settings of the teachers' own schools. The school was in a small town in Oxfordshire and there were approximately 325 pupils between 5 and 11 years of age in the school, together with a nursery class which catered for 50 children. Excluding the nursery, there were 13 full-time teachers including the headteacher. The school served a mixed catchment area made up of private and local authority housing.

A semi-structured interview schedule was devised to obtain data from all of the teachers in the school. This type of format was devised because it would provide the opportunity to develop further questions to clarify ideas and points raised. Questions were carefully selected and trialled and then modified before being used with the interviewees. A case study approach has been used in this research as Hitchcock and Hughes (1995) stated this methodology should focus on a particular actor or groups of actors and their perceptions. The concern was with the rich and vivid description of events within the case. As Denscombe (1998) asserts, the study tried to capture the 'complex reality under scrutiny' (p. 39).

## Discussion

The concerns which the teachers indicated limited their ability to challenge gifted children in science lessons could be placed into four main categories:

- their own science knowledge and understanding,
- performing science investigations,

- organisation of science teaching to allow for extension and differentiation,
- boredom of gifted and talented children.

This was not a surprising list as The National Curriculum in England (DfEE/ QCA, 1999) has equal emphasis on knowledge and understanding, and scientific skills in the Programmes of Study. These two aspects are complimentary and not discrete, which means that skills are taught through contexts set out in the knowledge and understanding sections of the curriculum. This has clear implications for classroom management and organisation where pupils are involved in practical activities. This is further complicated when there is a recognition that gifted children have different needs if they are not to become demotivated by the work.

### Teachers' subject knowledge and understanding

Effective teachers of gifted children need to have a good knowledge and understanding of their subject (Maker & Nielson, 1995) and also need to be confident when applying this knowledge in the classroom (Education Select Committee, 1999). This is not simply to convey factual information to children but to have the confidence

> to ask questions which will lead children to reveal and reflect on their ideas, so they can avoid 'blind alleys', so that they can provide relevant sources of information and other resources, so that they can identify progress and the next steps that will take it further.
>
> (Harlen, 1997, p. 335)

Alexander *et al.* (1992) argued that effective teaching depends on the successful combination of knowledge, understanding and skills. When these are combined together they should 'provide pupils with maximum opportunity to learn' (Silcock, 1993, p. 13). The majority of teachers saw their lack of science knowledge and understanding as the most challenging factor for them when addressing the needs of gifted children. Teacher 1 went so far as to indicate that:

> Science is not my thing at all. I didn't enjoy it at school. I found it difficult. I find the literacy and the numeracy and other things a lot easier. But I would think that is very often true of primary school teachers who are not scientists . . . It is not their main subject. I mean after O-level I did not do any more science. I mean not that I wanted to.

Teacher 2 went even further and stated:

> I feel a complete failure as a scientist at school.

Most teachers therefore saw science as a 'hard' subject. These ideas, however, are not unique to England. One of the problems, in Australia, associated with teaching science in primary (elementary) schools was that 'the teaching profession seems to self-select people for elementary teaching who tend to fear science rather than those who love it' (Appleton & Kindt, 1999, p. 11).

This opinion, however, contrasted with a small minority of teachers. Teacher 3 indicated:

> I think science has just got a label, because it is science and I think teachers veer round it because it's science and it's supposedly difficult and complicated. I think if teachers got stuck in they would actually see that it is actually not that difficult, really exciting.

She and Teacher 4, who had similar opinions, had both studied science in their teacher-training courses and were in the early stages of their teaching careers. This could explain why they seemed to be an exception. Most teachers did, however, indicate that to teach science in the primary school effectively and to challenge gifted pupils a good knowledge was essential. This was illustrated by Teacher 5 who went on to say:

> The fact that not all teachers are scientists means that there are a lot of big, steep learning curves. For them to be able to challenge the more able, then they've got to understand what they want them to do themselves, before they [the children] can do that.

This positive attitude was demonstrated by Teacher 6 when she indicated what she thought was the best way forward for primary teachers, who wanted to challenge gifted pupils:

> I enjoy science. I hope that comes across. I am very willing to go and find things out.

As knowledge and understanding increased, confidence to challenge gifted pupils would also improve. Teacher 7's comments illustrated this when she stated:

> With the increased confidence and knowledge then the teachers have the ability to push forward and challenge their children better.

This supports evidence from HMI (1992) who reviewed education of able pupils and identified a variety of factors associated with these pupils achieving a high standard of work. One of the factors was the teachers' deep understanding of their subjects.

Adequate knowledge and understanding was viewed by most of the sample of teachers to be a factor which influenced their interest in science. This is summarised by Teacher 5 who said:

> I think it is a lack of understanding of science, perhaps. I think teachers are keen to teach science well but I think with the lack of knowledge comes a lack of enthusiasm, because they are unsure of their own facts.

Teachers who are enthusiastic about science, however, are more likely to recognise the need to challenge gifted pupils (QCA/DfEE, 2001). The majority view of the teachers does contrast with two colleagues from the sample. Teacher 8 indicated:

> with increased confidence and knowledge teachers would become more enthusiastic and this will be transferred to the children.

Teacher 9 developed this idea further and stated:

> I felt that although I was not initially a science person, that I had not had a great background in science (I had some GCSE's). But because of the enthusiasm of the children . . . it made me enthusiastic and so I became more and more interested in how I could stretch the children.

Inadequate scientific knowledge and understanding also affected the way the science was taught because, as Teacher 7 indicated, insufficient knowledge 'makes me less able to let them challenge themselves and become independent.' This view is supported by Carré (1998) who found that many primary teachers do not have a science background and are concerned about knowing the 'right answers'. Symington (1980) found that teachers who lacked confidence to teach science tended to use teaching strategies which allowed them to maintain control of the classroom knowledge flow, but which were not appropriate ways of engaging pupils in science. This would mean not giving children the freedom to explore for themselves and possibly arriving at answers that the teacher does not know or understand. Teacher 5 went on to explain this:

> They (the teachers) won't let children go because they're not sure they can control it at the end of it. And they need to be in control. So the more understanding they have the more they are able to say 'go ahead and try it' and know that they will be able to help with the outcomes.

If science teaching is to be effective, gifted children need to be allowed to develop independence (Maker, 1982; HMI, 1992) rather than being directed all of the time. These independent study interests should then be followed up by both teacher and pupils (Clark & Callow, 1998). This could be achieved by: greater flexibility in the timing of activities (Clark & Callow, 1998), children being given help to develop their study skills and receiving rewards for their scholastic achievements (Gallagher, 1985).

### Performing science investigations

Allebone (1998) identified one of the characteristics of able children as their ability to use higher-order thinking skills (HOTS) at an earlier age. Lewis and Smith (1993, p. 136) considered the difficulty of defining higher-order thinking and offered the following definition:

> Higher order thinking occurs when a person takes new information and information stored in memory and interrelates and/or rearranges and extends this information to achieve a purpose or find possible answers in perplexing situations.

Thinking skills can be divided into two levels: higher-order and lower-order (Bloom, 1956; Fisher, 1995). The teaching of these basic *and* higher-order skills should be closely interwoven in the classroom (Lewis & Smith, 1993). Gifted children should, however, spend more time on higher-level activities (Davis & Rimm, 1998). Science investigations can provide ample opportunities for higher-level thinking.

The scientific method, scientific thinking, and critical thinking have been terms used at various times to describe science skills. The Commission on Science Education of the American Association for the Advancement of Science, and the Science—A Process Approach (SAPA) grouped process skills into two types—basic and integrated (Padilla, 1990). These processes form a hierarchy so that the effective use of the integrated processes requires utilisation of the basic processes (Lewis & Smith, 1993). The basic processes provided the data or experiences that the problem-solver needed to manipulate and integrate in order to solve a problem. A science investigation is a specific type of problem-solving defined as a task for which pupils cannot immediately see an answer or recall a routine method for finding it (Gott & Duggan, 1995). The hierarchy suggests a difference between lower-order and higher-order thinking skills. The basic (simpler) process skills include observing and classifying, whereas integrated (higher-order) processes include interpreting data, controlling variables, formulating hypotheses, and experimenting. Investigative science can therefore provide ample opportunities for the use of HOTS where there is a concentration on procedural and thinking skills (Coates & Eyre, 1999). However, the greatest variation, in science, was found in experimental and investigative work with gifted and talented pupils being insufficiently challenged in some schools (OFSTED's Annual Report for 1997/98). This picture did not improve in subsequent years because in 2001 OFSTED again found that 'high achieving pupils are still often given insufficiently challenging investigative work' (p. 3).

Developing science investigations for gifted pupils was understood by teachers to be 'one that is most difficult to do in the classroom . . . for children to get a sense of having achieved something' (Teacher 9). Gifted children were seen to need greater independence 'to be given the freedom to explore and set up their own parameters' (Teacher 10). This can be viewed as a problem for teachers in two ways. Firstly, there was perceived pressure to cover the content knowledge of the National Curriculum. Teachers 'have the curriculum to cover so you have to gear them (gifted children) away from what they would like to do' (Teacher 11). This would lead to content-based teaching (Luxford, 1997), which she described as the focus of most primary science lessons, where the teacher only dealt with lower-order thinking.

Secondly, the fear that gifted and talented pupils will take their investigations beyond the teachers' understanding. This is illustrated by Teacher 7 who stated:

> I find that when there are topics that are more open to investigation I find that they are more difficult because I don't know what is going to come from the children, I don't know what avenue it is going to take, because it is open.

Gifted children do still need to be taught the higher-order processes associated with science investigations, for example, planning, questioning, and interpreting results. Without this teaching, gifted children, like other children, will not have the confidence to explore for themselves. Teacher 9 drew a parallel with herself when she stated:

> Perhaps I feel myself the more investigation I do the more confident I become and the more willing to have a go and put something forward and it is the same for the children. As their confidence grows and as we do more investigation they (gifted children) are more willing to put themselves forward and put forward an idea of let's try this and let's try that. So I think confidence is a huge thing really, both for the children and for the teacher.

### Organisation of science teaching to allow for extension and differentiation

The main issue here was the need to organise science at distinct levels for different abilities in the class allowing all children the maximum opportunity to learn. Bennett (1988) suggests that this was most likely to occur where tasks are well-matched to ability as learning is something children do, not something that is done to them (Silcock, 1993). Research in America would indicate, however, that teachers are more inclined to make adjustments for struggling learners than for advanced ones (PAGE, 2001). This was reflected in the information from the teachers in this research. They were unsure about extension activities and the next steps to take to challenge gifted pupils. Again lack of teacher confidence affected this aspect of science as Teacher 2 indicated:

> I am a bit of a control freak . . . you have got to have the confidence to let control go a bit. Then it is not knowing where it might lead and whether you are going to be able to cope.

This was supported by Teacher 8 who went on to say:

> I think I have got to be braver about the activities I set up, and letting them (scientifically gifted children) have a go with them.

The challenge for primary teachers in the context of differentiation and extension of science is matching activities to ability. QCA/DfEE (2001) recommended that extension should be provided through breadth rather than teaching aspects of science that pupils would be covering in later years. Gifted children were perceived to bring a different dimension, and the challenge was to extend thinking and reasoning, to provide something that will 'stretch them'. As Teacher 2 indicated:

> I find it more difficult to plan for the able child, in that because there are certain objectives that the children have got to learn once they have learnt those and they are established in their minds. Then I find the next stage on quite difficult to look at . . . it is actually what next should they be learning to advance their skills.

The teachers in the study indicated that the major problem for them was to have a suitable bank of sufficiently challenging materials to differentiation for both ends of ability. This would mean having to find out what the children know already, and then planning challenging activities for three separate ability groups, which would take all of pupils' learning further to challenging everyone in the class. This was seen to be a key issue for large classes where the teacher had to work on her own. Teacher 4, however, was more positive when she stressed:

> I think you can differentiate activities to make them harder, more challenging for the more able children or less challenging for the less able . . . I don't think differentiation is a problem.

This may again be a reflection of her confidence and interest in science as this was specialist subject during her teacher training.

Printed resources were also limited in the support they gave to teachers as Teacher 11 said:

> I would like more help with identifying, the children firstly and where I should take things on further, because lots of the stuff that you have, lots of the stuff that you read is starting points.

Developing questioning skills for a wide ability was seen as a demanding part of differentiation when teaching science. This was emphasised by Teacher 10 who stated:

> I think what I need is to be given pointers of areas about when you have done the practical work, what sort of questions you should be asking for the more able.

The lack of time given to science caused organisational problems. This meant that teachers felt limited in the time they could talk to gifted children and allow them to plan for themselves and develop their science through extension activities. In their research, Archambault *et al.* (1993) found that competing demands on teachers' time made it difficult for them to adapt activities to meet the needs of gifted children. Science was taught in approximately one hour sessions in the school but this needed to be adapted sometimes as Teacher 1 stressed,

> If you want to do something really good you have got to have a whole morning.

### Boredom of gifted and talented children

The teachers saw the need to make the work exciting and stimulating for children or they could become bored with the science lesson. They were seen to have knowledge beyond the rest of the class and 'often knew the answers'. This became an issue at times when the class were taught all together at the beginning and end of sessions where they had to sit and 'feel this (the work) is too easy for them'. This has implications for gifted pupils as lack of interest and motivation could lead to behavioural problems.

Again the issue of the teachers' own knowledge came into play. This was summarised by Teacher 6 who said:

> My knowledge has to be secure and I have to know what the next stage in the process is really to get them interested, because if it is more of the same thing they know that straight away. Especially more able children . . .

Gifted children need as much support and encouragement to succeed as other children (Freeman, 1995). According to Gagné (1991), environmental and motivational catalysts transform innate ability into academic performance. Eyre (1997) has summed up these ideas in a model of provision that indicates how achievement might be maximised:

> achievement = ability + opportunity + motivation

Eyre *et al.* (2002) found that teachers believed it was important for gifted children to be challenged to the point where they might risk failure. The teachers in this research went on to develop this idea, which are summarised by Teacher 7's comments:

> You do not push them so far that it becomes hard and it becomes off-putting for them. You want to hit the right spot, I suppose don't you. But you do want it to be exciting. The children want to do it. They want to question. They want to find out for themselves. It is finding out for themselves, and being excited by it . . . that makes science challenging.

## Conclusions

The skills needed by teachers of gifted children in science include strong content knowledge (Van Tassel-Baska, 1998). This was a key concern for the primary teachers because the recurring theme that came through this research was the disquiet they had about their own subject knowledge and understanding, and how this affected all aspects of their science teaching to gifted pupils. This is not a new issue, as HMI in England reported that the most severe obstacle to improving science teaching for all pupils in primary school was teachers' lack of scientific knowledge (Department of Education and Science (DES), 1978). Nor is it an issue unique to England, as primary teachers in Australia were found to have poor background knowledge in science and to lack confidence in teaching science (Australian Science, Technology and Engineering Council, 1997).

What teachers know about a subject does, however, have a crucial influence on how they teach. Teachers need first to understand the concepts before they can provide appropriate analogies or representations to help children towards more adult understanding (Carré, 1998). Those who are effective teachers of science are flexible in their classroom management, and have the capacity to question pupils' understanding through metacognition and assessment techniques (Van Tassel-Baska, 1998). The more teachers know about science, therefore, the more they will be able to provide a framework to help children think in a scientific way.

If we wish to improve teaching and focus on pupils' learning, then teachers need help in teaching for understanding (Cohen *et al.*, 1993). Purposeful change by teachers in their science teaching to increase challenge has the potential to generate improvements in students' perceptions of classwork. Rogers (1999) has synthesised research, in America, regarding gifted education and has found that gifted pupils are significantly more likely to retain science content accurately when taught 2–3 times faster than 'normal' class pace. They are more likely to forget or mislearn science content when they must drill and review it more than 2–3 times. Through careful attention to aspects of challenge, having high expectations (Lee-Corbin & Denicolo, 1998) and incorporating Rogers' findings teachers can improve the extent to which pupils perceive school science as providing them with productive learning challenges. One of the challenges for primary teachers, if they are to achieve this, is to create a learning environment in which gifted pupils can fully develop their abilities and interests without losing their sense of membership as part of the class (Parke, 1992).

Increasing teachers' own understanding is therefore a key factor in improving the quality of teaching and learning in science. Without this, they will not be able to meet the needs of gifted pupils. What holds teachers' understanding back is not ability to grasp ideas but opportunities to discuss and develop them (Harlen, 1997). In-service training would provide the opportunities for teachers to do this. The National Research Council in the U.S. recommended that 'teacher education be viewed as a career-long process that allows teachers of science . . . to acquire and regularly update the content knowledge and pedagogical tools needed to teach in ways that enhance student learning and achievement' (NARST, 2001, p. 1). Research on staff development as well as effective teaching demonstrates the need to provide systematic follow-up procedures to ensure teacher action (Joyce & Showers, 1995, cited in Van Tassel-Baska, 1998). There is therefore a need for staff development to meet the needs of scientifically gifted pupils, which incorporates training in gifted education. This would allow primary teachers to develop the potential of all of the pupils in their classes by engaging, enthusing, challenging supporting, and reward their effort and achievement (DfES, 2004).

# References

Allebone, B. (1998) Providing for able children in the primary classroom, *Education 3–13*, 22, 64–69.

Alexander, R., Rose, J. & Woodhead, C. (1992) *Curriculum organisation and classroom practice in primary schools* (London, HMSO).

Appleton, K. & Kindt, I. (1999) How do beginning elementary teachers cope with science: development of pedagogical content knowledge in science. Available online at: http://www.educ.sfu.narstsite/conference/appletonkindt/appletonkindt.html

Archambault, F., Westberg, K., Brown, S., Hallmark, B., Zhang, W. & Emmons, C. (1993) Classroom practices used with gifted third and fourth grade students, *Journal for the Education of the Gifted*, 16(2), 13–28.

Australian Science, Technology and Engineering Council (1997) *Foundations for Australia's future: science and technology in primary schools Canberra, Australia* (Canberra, Australian Government Publishing Services).

Bennett, N. (1988) The effective primary school teacher: the search for a theory of pedagogy, *Teaching and Teacher Education*, 4(1), 19–30.

Blaxter, L., Hughes, C. & Tight, M. (1996) *How to research* (Buckingham, Open University Press).

Bloom, B. (Ed.) (1956) *Taxonomy of educational objectives*, Volume 1 (Harlow, Longman).

Board of Studies (1991) Science and Technology K-6. Syllabus and Support Document. New South Wales Education Department.

Carré, C. (1998) Invitations to think in primary science lessons, in: R. Burden & M. Williams (Eds) *Thinking through the curriculum* (London, Routledge).

Clark, C. & Callow, R. (1998) *Educating able children. Resource issues and process for teachers* (London, David Fulton Publishers).

Coates, D. & Eyre, D. (1999) Can encouraging the use of higher order thinking skills in science help young able children to achieve more highly? In: 4th Summer Conference for Teacher Education in Primary Science. 'The Challenge of Change'. University of Durham, UK.

Coates, D. & Wilson, H. (2001) Science, in: D. Eyre & L. McClure (Eds) *Curriculum provision for the gifted and talented in the primary school* (London, David Fulton Publishers).

Coates, D. & Wilson, H. (2003) *Challenges in primary science* (London, David Fulton Publishers).

Cohen, D., McLaughlin, M. & Talbert, J. (1993) *Teaching for understanding* (San Francisco, CA, Jossey-Bass).

Davis, G. A. & Rimm, S. B. (1998) *Education of the gifted and talented* (Boston, Allyn and Bacon).

Denscombe, M. (1998) *The good research guide for small-scale social research projects* (Buckingham, Open University Press).

Department of Education and Science (DES) (1978) *Primary education in England: a survey by HM inspectors of schools* (London, HMSO).

DfEE/QCA (1999) *The National Curriculum. Handbook for primary teachers in England Key stages 1 and 2* (London, HMSO).

DfES (2002) *School achieving success.* Available online at: www.dfes.gov.uk/achievingsuccess (accessed November 2004).

DfES (2004) *Excellence and enjoyment: learning and teaching in the primary school.* Available online at: www.standards.dfes.gov.uk/seu/coreprinciples1/core-principles.doc

Diezmann, C. M. & Watters, J. J. (2000) An enrichment philosophy and strategy for empowering young gifted children to become autonomous learners in science, *Gifted and Talented International*, 15, 6–18.

Education Select Committee (1999) *Highly able children* (London, HMSO).

Eyre, D. (1997) *Able children in ordinary schools* (London, David Fulton Publishing).

Eyre, D., Coates, D., Fitzpatrick, M., Higgins, C., McClure, L., Wilson, H. & Chamberlin, R. (2002) Effective teaching of able pupils in the primary school: the findings of the Oxfordshire effective teachers of able pupils project, *Gifted Education International*, 16, 158–169.

Fisher, R. (1995) *Teaching children to learn* (Cheltenham, Stanley Thorne).

Freeman, J. (1995) *Actualising talent* (London, Cassell).

Gagné, F. (1991) Towards a differentiated model of giftedness and talent, in: G. A. Davis & S. B. Rimm, *Education of the gifted and talented* (4th edition) (London, Allyn and Bacon).

Gallagher, J. J. (1985) *Teaching the gifted child* (Newton, Allyn and Bacon).

George, D. (1997) *Gifted education: identification and provision* (London, David Fulton Publishing).

Gott, R. & Duggan, S. (1995) *Investigative work in the science curriculum* (Buckingham, Open University Press).

Harlen, W. (1997) Primary teachers' understanding in science and its impact in the classroom, *Research in Science Education*, 27(3), 323–337.

Hitchcock, G. & Hughes, D. (1995) *Research and the teacher: a qualitative introduction to school based research* (London, Routledge).

HMI (1992) *The teaching of very able children in maintained schools* (London, HMSO).

Johnson, D., Boyce, L. & Van Tassel-Baska, J. (1995) Evaluating curriculum materials in science, *Gifted Child Quarterly*, 89(1), 35–43.

Joyce, D. & Showers, B. (1995) *Standard achievement through staff development: fundamentals of school renewal* (2nd edition) (White Plains, NY, Longman Publishers).

Lee-Corbin, H. & Denicolo, L. (1998) *Recognising and supporting able children in primary schools* (London, David Fulton).

Lewis, A. & Smith, D. (1993) Defining higher order thinking, *Theory Into Practice*, 32(3), 131–137.

Luxford, H. (1997) Where do I go from here? An approach to planning in primary science, *Educating Able Children*, Spring 1997, 1, 3–9.

Maker, J. (1982) *Curriculum development for the gifted* (Rockville, Aspen Systems Corporation).

Maker, C. J. & Nielson, A. B. (1995) *Teaching models in education of the gifted* (Austin, pro-ed).

Montgomery, D. (1996) *Educating the able* (London, Cassell).

National Association for Research in Science Teaching (NARST) (2001) NARST News, available at: http://www.sci.sdsu.edu/CRMSE/NARST_News44_Abell.html 2002

OFSTED (1996) *Subjects and standards. Issues for school development arising from Ofsted inspection findings 1994–95 Key Stages 1 and 2* (London, HMSO).

OFSTED (1999) *The Annual Report of HMCI 1997/1998* (London, HMSO).

OFSTED (2001) *The Annual Report of HMCI 1999/2000* (London, HMSO).

OFSTED (2002) *The Annual Report of HMCI 2000/2001* (London, HMSO).

Padilla, M. J. (1990) Research Matters—to Science Teacher. No. 9004. Available online at: http://www.narst.org/research/skills.htm

Parke, B. N. (1992) Challenging gifted students in the regular classroom, ERIC Digest#E513. Available online at: http://www.ed.gov./databases/ERIC_Digests/ed352774.html

Pennsylvania Association for Gifted Education (PAGE) (2001) Inclusion. Available online at: http://www.penngifted.org/bulletin/inclusion.html

Porter, L. (1999) *Gifted young children. A guide for teachers and parents* (Buckingham, Open University Press).

QCA/DFEE (2000) *A scheme of work for Key Stages 1 and 2. Science teacher's guide update* (Sudbury, QCA).

QCA/DFEE (2001) *Meeting the needs of gifted and talented pupils in science. a guide to successful practice* (London, QCA).

Rogers, K. B. (1999) Research synthesis regarding gifted education provision. Available online at: http://www.nswagtc.org.au/info/articles/RogersResearchSynthesis.html

Sherman, R. & Webb, R. (Eds) (1988) *Qualitative research in education: forms and methods* (London, The Falmer Press).

Silcock, P. (1993) Can we teach effective teaching?, *Educational Review*, 45(1), 13–19.

Symington, D. (1980) Elementary school teachers' knowledge of science and its effect on choice between alternative verbal behaviours, *Research in Science Education*, 10, 69–76.

Van Tassel-Baska, J. (1998) *Planning science programs for high-ability learners.* Available online at: http://ericec.org/digests/e546.html

Winebrenner, S. (2001) *Teaching gifted kids in the regular classroom* (New York, Free Spirit).

# Part IV

# The primary curriculum

English, Humanities and the Arts

# 14 Getting the message

*James Britton*

Listening to somebody talking to me, I look *through* the noises he makes in order to discover, if I can, what he has on his mind. The words are, as it were, transparent, and what I see is something beyond them; or, to put it another way, the text dissolves as I listen to it and I am left with a meaning, a *message*. Much of my reading works in a similar fashion.

There is research evidence to demonstrate that this is no fanciful description of what goes on. Bilingual speakers were given to read aloud a passage which was written in a number of the languages they spoke (For example, 'His horse, followed de deux bassets, faisait la terre resonner under its even tread'). They grasped the meaning without any difficulty but consistently misread the original text by translating words from the one language to the other, and *were not aware that they had done so.*[1] Again, in the work of another experimenter, subjects were asked to identify sentences either excerpted or adapted from a paragraph they had read less than a minute earlier; they were unable to detect quite substantial changes in wording which left the meaning unchanged, but had no difficulty in recognising quite minimal alterations in form that resulted in changes in meaning (as for example, 'There he met an archaeologist, Howard Carter, who persuaded him to . . .' and 'There he met an archeologist, Howard Carter, and persuaded him to . . .'). The researcher, Jacqueline Sachs, comments: 'The findings are consistent with a theory of comprehension which contends that the meaning of a sentence is derived from the original string of words by an active interpretative process. That original sentence which is perceived is rapidly forgotten, and the memory then is for the information contained in the sentence'.[2] This 'active interpretative process' by which text is transformed into message is, in essence, the learning process. And it is worth looking at a little more closely.

When I listen, as part of a conversation, I take to the task a complex set of expectations and a considerable body of knowledge. As a speaker of English, I have a knowledge of word meanings and of the rules by which, in English, words are combined into sentences. I have a vast fund of knowledge about the world, and hence a set of expectations regarding the kinds of things that might enter into a conversation about homing pigeons, let us say, or horoscopes perhaps, or hardy annuals or homosexuality — or a great number of other topics. From this wide field of knowledge, *relevant* areas must be 'activated', 'lit up' as it were, by my general sense of what this particular speaker has presently on his mind — a sense that builds up as I respond to any or every clue the situation offers.

Included in this prior knowledge is my knowledge of the speaker and of the situation in which we find ourselves together — the objects in the environment, the events taking place. And all this, in the linguists' terms, is the *context* of the utterance — described by John Lyons as 'the knowledge shared by hearer and speaker of all that has gone before'[3] To the psychologist, it constitutes the *frame of reference*, the prior understanding to which we relate what we see and hear and so construct our own interpretation of the meaning intended by the speaker.

The context, as we have already implied, is not static: it builds up as we talk, taking into itself all that is relevant from the words spoken and whatever else is happening in the situation. We might in fact claim that the meaning we take from an utterance lies in the difference between our initial 'context' (our expectations on entry) and our final 'context'.

Let us turn from considering the context and look at the process of interpreting. What is it we construe? Where do we find meaning? First, of course, in the utterance itself, both the words spoken and the manner in which they are spoken, the tempo, pitch, volume, the emotional overtones. But also in the rest of the speaker's behaviour: his facial expressions and gestures, his bodily position and movements. And, beyond that, in the situation itself; if, for example, there are other people present, their unspoken* responses become a part of what we construe; or if relevant objects are present (say biological specimens in a biology lesson), we shall take into account what they do and what happens to them.

That we are able to pay attention to so much and in such variety has been explained by claiming that we operate at two levels of awareness. We are *subsidiarily* aware of word meanings and syntax – the linguistic code that is English — and of the relevant aspects of our knowledge of the world and the speaker; we are subsidiarily aware of the words he speaks and all other aspects if his behaviour; and of the situation in which it is all taking place. What we are *focally* aware of is the emerging message, what the speaker appears to have on his mind. This awareness is focal in the sense that it directs and focusses the use we make of all that is given to us through our subsidiary awareness. We owe this explanation to Michael Polanyi,[4] who illustrates his point by a simple analogy from everyday experience. Imagine you have dropped some small object — a stud, a brooch – and it has rolled under the furniture so that you can't reach it. You fetch a stick and probe beneath the furniture to recover it. You must focus your attention, Polanyi says, on the *far end* of the stick. You have only the near end to manipulate, so you must be aware of that, but only subsidiarily. If you focus your attention on the near end you will become clumsy and probably fail to find the object. It is your focus on the far end, remote and out of sight, which must guide and direct the movements of your muscles. In much the same way as we use a tool such as a stick, we use our language: our focus of attention is kept on what it we want to achieve — grasping the speaker's message or finding words to make our own meanings clear to another: and our awareness of the language by which we achieve this purpose is kept subsidiary.

Experiment has shown that we can identify individual printed letters at a, rate of three to four letters per second, which would be equivalent to a reading rate of from 30 to 42 words per minute.[5] Since we read normally at a rate of something like 300 words per minute, our awareness of a text, when it is effectively controlled by a focal awareness of the emergent meaning, must be in fact a process of picking up minimal verbal cues, far less than the sum-total of visual information available. The more information we take to the page from context (in the broad sense in which we have defined it above), the better directed is our focal awareness of an emergent meaning, and hence the less we require in the way of visual information from the page. In listening to a speaker, the more information we take from context, and the more we glean from non-linguistic sources (gesture, situation etc.), the less we shall rely upon the actual words spoken (How often we have known, at the moment of his speaking, exactly what a speaker was going to say!) Tolstoi illustrates this point when, in Anna Karenina, he has the lovers, Kitty and Levin, communicate in a very unusual manner. Levin speaks first:

> 'I have long wished to ask you something'.
> 'Please do'.
> 'This,' he said, and wrote the initial letters: W Y A: I c n b, d y m t o n.

These letters meant: 'When you answered 'It can not be', did you mean then or never?' It seemed impossible she would be able to understand the complicated sentence.

> 'I understand' she said, blushing.
> 'What word is that?' he asked, pointing to the n which stood for 'never'.
> 'The word is 'never', she said, 'but that is not true'. He quickly erased what he had written handed her the chalk, and rose. She wrote i c n a o t.
> His face brightened suddenly: he had understood. It meant: 'I could not answer otherwise then'.
> She wrote the initial letters: s t g m f a f w h. This meant: 'So that you might forget and forgive what happened'.
> He seized the chalk with tense, trembling fingers, broke it, and wrote the initial letters of the following: 'I have nothing to forget and forgive. I never ceased loving you'.
> 'I understand', she whispered.[6]

Tolstoi concludes the episode by having Levin propose marriage in like manner — and he is accepted!

Our ordinary experience as eavesdroppers (if we are willing to admit to it), say in a railway carriage or a restaurant, should teach us how much in understanding speech we rely upon general expectations, broad dimensions of our knowledge of the world. Once we have correctly deduced from our observations how the speakers are related – whether they are husband and wife, father and daughter, lovers or casual acquaintances – we *hear* so much more of what is said! 'Catching the drift' is a good expression to use here because it aptly suggests the way particulars become meaningful when global features of the context are established and we can then shuttle, as it were, between the particulars as they occur and the embracing context. This aspect of the way we attend to an utterance may be typical of the way in general we 'pay attention': to quote Bruner,[7] 'If one were to sum up the past decade of work on attention in a few words it is that attention is a feature extracting routine in which there is a steady movement back and forth between selected features and wholes. Neisser has characterised the process as analysis-by-synthesis, a process of positing wholes (topics) to which parts or features or properties may be related and from which new wholes may be constructed!. The posited 'whole' in our case is the emergent message, our questing conception of what is on the speaker's mind: the 'new whole' we construct is our interpretation of what he said.

Daniel Jones, in the late twenties, was interested in this relationship between the whole and the particulars of an utterance. In his phonetics laboratory in Gower Street he played to a group of students a mechanically distorted record of a conversation between two people. They could not make head or tail of it. He sent half the group away and played the record through again, with a similar result. He then had the other half back, told them this was a conversation between a fitter and a customer in a tailor's shop, and replayed the record: they were able to make out quite a lot of the conversation. This general expectation had vastly reduced the possibilities of meaning they had to scan in constructing the sense of the sounds they heard.

We have said a good deal to suggest that spoken utterance is deeply embedded in other ways we have of making sense of experience. Until recent years, linguists who studied the way infants learned to speak were primarily interested in analysing the grammatical structures of their early utterances and noting the successive stages by which they arrived at the grammar of the language as we know it. Much that was of interest and importance was learned from this work, for it is the grammatical structure of languages that makes them the most highly specialised system of human communication. Recent years, however, have seen a change of emphasis. It has been recognised that observers who arrive on the scene only when a child is able to talk have missed a great deal of interesting earlier behaviour — behaviour in which he exchanges understandings with his parents and begins to discover meaning in the world around him. Today, psycholinguists in many parts of the world are providing evidence of the way an infant's earliest uses of speech evolve from, and depend upon, ways of handling meaning that do not employ language.

Thus, Bruner's observations of the behaviour of young babies with their mothers form part of a fascinating new chapter in language study. He suggests that shared looking and listening and shared activity, mother and baby, are key processes in the infant's first attempts to make sense of the 'meaningless flux' that surrounds him. Between mother and child patterns of action are set up: to the child, these emerge, as it were, from the flux and become recognizable as they are repeated. As the mother follows the child's direction of gaze, and the infant's comes to follow the mother's, objects become established. Expressive gestures and sounds and (from the mother) speech, accompany the actions and accentuate their patterns. Some of the patterns are, as Bruner says, 'in earnest' — that is to say are concerned with 'mothering', with feeding habits for example — but most of them are play. It is a characteristic role of the mother in these joint sequences to mark the completion, the climax — a hug at the end of peek-a-bo, perhaps, or a 'Good boy!' when the child successfully negotiates a mouthful of food.

The role of speech or speech-like noises in these sequences is strictly supplementary to the meaning already attached to the joint activity. Bruner suggests that conventional speech sounds, as spoken by the mother, are arrived at by the baby in gradual steps. He describes, for example, a mother and child who have established a routine of giving and receiving. When she gives the object — ball or rattle or whatever — to the child, the mother says, 'Look' or 'There you are', and she says 'Thank you' when she receives it from the child. After a while, the baby begins to add his noises to the exchange, but they are his own sounds, not recognisable words. Then at 9 months and 2 weeks, Bruner records, the baby says, 'Kew' when the mother takes the object he has offered; a month later, he says 'Kew' whenever he offers her something; and two months after that he says 'Look' when handing to her and 'Kew' when receiving from her.[8]

Bruner makes the important point that the routines devised by mother and child introduce and ring the changes upon basic elements in human interaction. Thus, there is an action, a doer or agent, sometimes the object of the action, the recipient, and sometimes an instrument with which it is carried out. All these features, Bruner points out, are relationships encoded in the grammar of languages. Gordon Wells in Bristol uses similar categories in his analysis of the speech and speech contexts of young children,[9] and Roger Brown's latest work[10] surveys a number of language acquisition studies which support the same notion. What is evident from these and other studies is that precursors of many of the features of adult grammar are to be found in children's earliest utterances and in their pre-speech cooperative behaviour. It is not enough to explain that in the course of his evolution man has come to perceive and act in ways derived from the structure of the language he uses: we have also to put forward the alternative hypothesis that the structure of language has developed to reflect the nature of man's cognitive processes, the ways in which he attends to and interprets experience. Or, in Bruner's words, 'language is a specialised and conventionalised extension of human co-operative action.[11]

Much has been said about the importance of the language a child experiences at home in infancy as a basis for his later social and intellectual development. It has been suggested that the give-and-take, the rough-and-tumble of language as it is unselfconsciously used for work and play in the home constitutes a better learning situation than would anything more deliberate. That the home, in other words, provides a language workshop, an environment of language-in-use — often interrupted, often fragmentary. It seems likely that such experiences are more productive than any focus upon language — or any attempt to give language instruction in the home — could be.[12] What we now have to do is to extend that notion and see the early co-operative activities of the infant as productive of meanings which are essential for his entry into language, and which constitute a mode of inter-communication which will support and enrich verbal interchange at all stages.

The early activities we have described are widely successful over a great variety of homes because they are eagerly undertaken, and they are eagerly undertaken because they yield such high dividends in terms of the understanding and mastery of the environment. What we have to do in school, from 3 to 13 and beyond, is to maintain as far as we can the directness of that means-end tie-up.

## Note

\*    As of course, their spoken responses; but in that case they become in turn speakers and the whole process we are describing re-applies.

## References

1. Paul A. Kolers, 'Three stages of Reading' in Frank Smith (Ed), *Psycholinguistics and Reading* (Holt, Rinehart & Winston, 1973), pp 4708.
2. Jacqueline Sachs, 'Recognition memory for syntactic and semantic aspects of connected discourse' in *Perception and Psychophysics*, 1967 (2), p 422.
3.  John Lyons, *Structural Semantics* (Blackwell, 1963), p 84.
4. Michael Polanyi, *Personal Knowledge* (Routledge and Kegan Paul, 1958), p 92.
5. Paul A. Kolers, *Op. cit.*, p 31.
6. Leo Tolstoi, *Anna Karenina*, Part 4, Ch. 13. (See L.S. Vygotsky, *Thought and Language*, MIT Press, 1962, p 138.
7. Jerome S. Bruner, 'The Ontogenesis of Speech Acts', in *Journal of Child Language*, Vol. 2 No. 1, 1975, p 5.
8. Jerome S. Bruner, *Op. cit.*, pp 20–21.
9. Gordon Wells, *Language Development in Pre-School Children*. Second Annual Report, University of Bristol School of Education 1974.
10. Roger Brown, *A First Language: The Early Stages* (Allen and Unwin, 1973) pp 168–201.
11. Jerome S. Bruner, *Op. cit.*, p 3.
12. Courtney B. Cazden, *Child Language and Education* (Holt, Rinehart and Winston, 1972) p 128.

# 15 Teaching young children about the past

*Joan Blyth*

In the last issue of *Education 3–13*,[1] Colin Richards, in his editorial, wrote of the concern of H.M.I. to strengthen academic content in the primary school curriculum.[2] He emphasised the awareness of the 'neglect of these central concerns in many classes, especially in relation to science, craft, history and geography'. This article attempts to focus on this 'neglect' in the teaching and learning of historical material among young children aged five to seven. At this stage of school life 'historical material' means any people, events and ideas concerned with a period before 'now' for the children. This could be 'yesterday' or palaeolithic man. In the words of David Attenborough 'all living things are influenced by messages from the past'.[3] So are young children, whether consciously or unconsciously, and to them the past is important to help them to understand themselves in time, and to help them to relate more sympathetically to other people, especially their parents and grandparents. These ideas are supported by Margaret Donaldson who believes that other people's past helps the self-centred child to 'decentre'.[4] This article has two main purposes, in the first place, to look at present practice, its underlying assumptions and what happens in the classroom, and secondly to suggest some possible approaches to replace or improve upon them.

## Present practice

### (1) Underlying assumptions

Three assumptions appear to influence teachers of young children in relation to historical material. One is that their training at college supplies them with the philosophy and tools of their trade for a lifetime. This training is child-centred rather than subject-centred, it favours the child progressing at his own pace and not undertaking new learning tasks until he is 'ready', in the teacher's view, or wants to (in his own view), and it accepts that intellectually the young child is easily satisfied. Therefore the day's programme concentrates on language and number, art work and physical education. Any reference to the past is incidental, unprepared and decided on by the individual teacher. Story-time, at the end of the day, when we are all tired, is one of the few opportunities to introduce historical material and this is not likely to be a programme with any purposive historical content at all. A skilled teacher may also use the past in role-playing and dramatic work. Assuming that young teachers start their careers with such clear guide-lines it is not surprising that publishers do not produce suitable books, pictures, games and resources. The Gittins Report warned of the dangers of the non-specialist trying to use historical material with younger children.[5] The Environmental Studies 5–13 Project found difficulty in supplying their pilot schools with material about the past and saw a need for support from an historian or archivist in the preparation of material.[6]

Another, almost unspoken, assumption is that young children will actually be damaged emotionally and intellectually by the 'pressure' of the 'academic approach'. Children should not have to listen too long to the teacher and be imprisoned by a planned and structured programme of work, beyond language and number. This assumption is conveyed to the children who believe that hard thinking will damage their brains for future schooling. At the end of a period of work in a first school with six-year olds, one of my brightest pupils said that she had enjoyed the work on the past but feared that she had 'used up her brain' and would not have enough left for her junior and secondary schooling! This second assumption is closely related to the third, which is that history is too difficult for young children to understand. This may partly arise from the old-fashioned view that History is all facts and dates, and the young teacher may have exhausting memories of preparing for 'O' and 'A' Level History papers.

This third assumption, that the nature of History is 'facts', dies hard and this to some extent may be the fault of specialist historians in relation to younger pupils. Yet historians would agree that all facts can never be known and that 'hunches', in the words of Professor Jerome Bruner,[7] or sensible guesses, are most important tools for the historian. Another difficulty about teaching for the past is the language used by historians to describe events and people of the past. This seems unnecessarily difficult when young children cannot even use everyday language correctly and the learning of two different vocabularies appears an additional burden. In addition, concepts, especially those of chronology and time, are even more obvious problems. On the other hand Gustav Jahoda thinks that at five years old 'the ordering of events into earlier and later begins to emerge' and that the child of five can understand the words "yesterday, to-day and to-morrow"'.[8] A more recent view supporting this is that of John West who writes 'Recent practice by inspired and skilful infant teachers should persuade us that even 7 years of age is unnecessarily late to begin to develop young children's awareness of the meaning of "Long, long ago" and "Once upon a time"'.[9] Thus it is the responsibility of historians to interpret their discipline and its nature anew to teachers of young children, to broaden its scope and relate it more obviously to the 'here and now' of children's understanding.

*(2) Classroom practice*

These three assumptions are established, strongly felt and are part of the 'raison d'être' of the teacher of young children. They lead in most classrooms to unplanned introductions of historical material as it comes into story-time as myth or truth, or on national historic occasions such as a coronation, the Queen's Jubilee, a royal marriage or a school centenary when ready-made teaching resources are cheap and easily accessible. Such material may also be discussed incidentally during 'News' if some children have watched an historical T.V. programme, or discussed more thoroughly a weekly T.V. programme watched in school and supported by a good pamphlet (e.g. *How We Used to Live* – social life in the nineteenth century). The weaknesses of this 'hit and miss' approach are many. There is often confusion in children's minds between myth and truth, and teachers in different years repeat the content taught if a careful watch is not kept on schemes of work. Children do not gain any historical continuity if all stories are 'one-off', and unless they undertake some activity of their own, the work is just 'listening to teacher' and the material may not be related to the children.

Yet there are some outstanding enthusiasts in using the past with young children and the freedom allowed traditionally to primary teachers has borne much fruit in these cases. In three cases known to me, the teachers were in positions of authority in school and so influenced the whole school. In two cases the teachers provided their colleagues with correct and scholarly historical information which involved them personally in much hard work. In one of these cases the school's centenary (1876–1976) was used as a big historical project for every class in the school and each class contributed to the display, and made its own 'Book of Learning 1876–1976'. In the other case the head teacher used local historical sources to help his colleagues to teach the local history of the town, and the children wrote stories and poems and made models using this material for detailed information.[10] In a third case, in a small all-age village school, the head teacher based all the children's work for a period of time on the model of a lake village or at another time on a frieze of Roman Britain.[11]

Other able teachers have used historical artefacts of the nineteenth and early twentieth centuries for discussion of historical evidence and sequencing of material.[12] The history of a town has been pieced together by young children asking older people to answer a simple questionnaire and bringing these older friends into the classroom.[13] Certain museums pay particular attention to working with young children and using the genuine artefacts from the museum to teach about the past. At the Bethnal Green Museum of Childhood Imogen Stewart helps young children to use her collections of dolls' houses from 1673 and dolls from 1750 and she feels strongly that 'things should not be avoided because children do not understand them', that is, in the first place.

Views as to classroom practice vary. On the whole Government Reports have not been pessimistic about what is being done in this area and what it is possible to do. The Hadow (1933) and Plowden (1967) Reports have not been very concerned to discuss historical material in the five to seven age range but the Primary Education Handbook of 1959[14] believes that true stories should be mingled with fantasy stories and should not be separated in the child's mind. But it did suggest the teaching of family history and the use of artefacts, if children and teachers could be given help with the work. Although finally not favourable to the use of historical material in this age-range, the Gittins Report emphasised the need for discussion about the past between teacher and child. This is supported by Joan Tough's work on the importance of talking with children and also by the Russian psychologist L.S. Vygotsky when he writes 'verbal intercourse with adults thus becomes a powerful factor in the development of the child's concepts'.[15] Last year's Primary School Survey makes no particular reference to the five to seven age-range but generally thinks that History is taught 'superficially' in four-fifths of schools, giving children little idea of change and evidence, and that there is 'lack of planning in the work'. On the other hand teachers of young children who have worked out original and stimulating approaches are enthusiastic in their talking and writing, and together with some research workers, believe that more successful work could be done with historical material than is at present the case.

## Possible approaches

The teachers mentioned earlier in this article are dedicated people who probably spend too much of their leisure time preparing historical material for their classes! This part of the article is concerned to help the less dedicated, or those dedicated to other areas of the curriculum, to give their classes a satisfactory diet of the past. For these teachers it is hoped to start them thinking about the historical content of their work (i.e. what of the past should they teach?), the possible teaching techniques to help children to overcome the problems of understanding the past (i.e. methodology) and finally the resources more readily available to provide activity for children.

### (1) What 'past' to teach

The essential thinking behind the appropriate scheme of work is dependent upon the organisation of the school, the interests and knowledge of the teacher and the local environment. During these early years all schemes should be flexible and historical material may not be used in all terms. But there should be some scheme linked with work to be done in later years and so avoiding unintentional repetition. Teaching the past has been found most satisfactory in vertically grouped schools as the seven year olds can help the younger children, especially in discussion. In order to understand the difficult concept of time Gustav Jahoda has suggested working backwards,[16] from 'now' to 'then'. An example of this could be starting with the children themselves in the present and in their own locality and broadening out in the second year to 'Children in Victorian Times'. Throughout the two years, either told or read, the building up in word books of historical vocabulary (e.g. the meaning of 'century', 'monarch', 'coach', 'battle') and all the time constant reference to simple time-lines on the walls of the classroom. During one term, stories from the past could be introduced during three or four separated weeks grouped according to topic (e.g. 'soldiers in ancient times', 'famous queens', 'children of the past'). With this background, a possible scheme might evolve. (See Figure 15.1).

|  | Term 1 | Term 2 | Term 3 |
|---|---|---|---|
| Year 1 Aged 5–6 | Myths through stories. | Stories of the past grouped in topics ------ role playing. | Study of artefacts brought by teacher and later the class. |
| Year 2 Aged 6–7 | Family history. | Local history of own village, town, area. | Local visits and a patch of national past related to their own locality. |

*Figure 15.1*

This scheme may seem rather parochial except for the extension allowed by the stories, yet it provides time for discussion and activity related to the child's own knowledge, lays a foundation for a development of local and national themes in later schooling and keeps the child's thought on change and evidence rather than facts. It also has a unity, as family history, artefacts, local history and visits can obviously and easily be linked.

### *(2) How to teach it*

Techniques of teaching such a scheme are more difficult when children are only just learning to read and write. The obvious technique is that of discussion which requires good class control and great patience, both from teachers and children. This may be difficult for inexperienced teachers. In my work with six-year olds I used three approaches. They were the use of artefacts, a museum visit and family history.[17] The children and I each brought an 'old object' to school, we felt them, named them and then tried to put them in order of oldness from various pieces of evidence. We could have developed this further to collect them into categories of objects such as books, toys and jewellery in order to develop concepts further. This links with Gustav Jahoda's remark about 'ordering of events' beginning at the age of five, quoted earlier in this article. This technique requires 'hunches' on the part of the children, supported by knowledge of likely chronology on the part of the teacher. Many of the objects brought by the children were too close to each other in time to distinguish age-sequence but the wedding-dress of my great-grandmother (1857) was certainly agreed by all to be 'very, very old' especially compared with toys brought by two of the boys (Christmas 1975). With such young children I should have gained more help from parents, or better still, pro-vided obviously different artefacts borrowed from the Schools Museum Service. These borrowed objects would have had the advantage of being genuine evidence as well as being more varied (e.g. Stone Age axe-head, Saxon brooch, Victorian sewing box, Second World War gas-masks, etc.) Yet the six-year olds had confi-dence to make guesses and consider evidence.

My second approach, which was the most successful, was a visit to the city museum, situated in a genuine Tudor building. This involved preparation for the visit, the visit and the follow-up. These three parts took place on three consecutive mornings. To my surprise a 1611 Speed Map, wall-size, became the real teaching medium. Town walls, gates, churches, the castle, sea and land seemed obvious to all the children and we found the Tudor house we were to visit on the map. I provided a simplified rough sketch-map for each child to complete and this also proved easy. This bears out Dr. Tough's advice that children should be introduced to maps and diagrams as early as possible.[18] The visit to the museum rather overpowered the children who had never been before and they saw a plethora of 'old objects', including feeling the actual stones of the medieval town wall. On our return to school, the next day, we discussed what 'old objects' each had seen and why they seemed old. We also tried to put them in order of age, as we had done with their own artefacts, but this proved difficult, especially in the absence of the actual objects. Yet they realised that walls, buildings and fireplaces were 'old', as well as smaller objects.

The third approach was that of family history starting from my own life and family, and developing into their lives and families. Intense interest was shown in my life and family and much discussion evolved which I tape-recorded. Recollection was their stumbling-block when it came to making up their 'life-lines' as nothing of importance seemed to have happened to them! The contrast between my thirty-five years and their six staggered them! Constructing their 'family plans' on the model of mine proved easier, and as with mine, we worked from right (recent time) to left (earlier time) of the page. The horizontal 'family tree has been found easier for young children to understand than the usual vertical one. Many years ago Sir Fred Clarke wrote that the word 'grandfather' had more meaning in teaching historical time than dates.[19] In the same way 'Tales of a Grandfather' by Sir Walter Scott may still inspire teachers of stories of the past. During this work on families I found that the children understood family relationships very well and were good at giving evidence for what they said. Time and age concepts were more difficult to grasp but even these were developing at the end of the nine weeks in which I taught them. All the children, for example, seemed more conscious of what person or object was 'older' or 'younger' than another. Although I did not use role-playing and drama to any extent owing to lack of space, this could be a most stimulating and normal technique for young children, especially after a true story has been told from true historical scores giving adequate detail for miming and role-playing. If done well this can stimulate imaginative historical thinking.[20]

### (3) Help for the teacher

In these days of economy, resources for new forms of teaching are inadequate and many excellent young and experienced teachers are doubtful about implementing new ideas without good and accessible support which will not mean working into the night once more. Artefacts from museums and homes are fairly easy to collect and quickly presented displays can be made of these, with labels made by the children where possible. Children, however young, can lend a hand in mounting a display. Old maps and photographs of the locality may be bought cheaply from the local museum and/or Record Office. Many parents and older friends and relatives constitute useful oral evidence and can be tape-recorded. Local buildings, even the school itself, are resources. Pictures of all sorts, posters and postcards from museums and art galleries, and slides made from books may all be used individually, in groups or as a class. John West, who is researching into these techniques, writes 'it seems evident that *powers of observation* are high at 6–8 years'.[21] He uses period pictures to accompany artefacts; a nineteenth-century fan could be used with a picture of nineteenth-century ladies using fans at a ball. This practice is supported by the 1933 Hadow Report which believes that the child of six can 'read' a picture to the extent of knowing what is happening in it; he may need more help from the teacher with an historical picture. T.V. programmes with pamphlets are usually excellent but cannot be built into a scheme of work as they are not always repeated, especially at convenient times. Many more suitable books, very well illustrated, are badly needed. In the 1960's Longmans published a series for five to seven year olds called 'Little Books' and one set was concerned with historical topics. These are small books to hold, using bold type face and are well-illustrated. A. & C. Black have published a series called 'People Around Us' and the first two books,[22] accompanied by photographs, a book of mastercopies for duplicated sheets and a teacher's guide may now be bought. Above all, in these early days teachers talking with children is one of the best resources.

Having looked at what is happening in schools to-day and suggested possible approaches to introduce more structured and academically rigorous work using historical material, it is important to emphasise that all this work is strengthening the basic teaching of language and number, at the same time as developing expressive activities. Above all the new context for the teacher to master is minimal. Just as all children do not master language and number without considerable effort, and some never do, so the same will happen with this new area of the curriculum. Because an area of work is difficult it should not be avoided. In the words of one psychologist 'there is a gap between what (children) can do and what they actually do do'.[23]

# References

1. Richards, C. 'A different shade of green', *Education 3–13*, 7:1, Spring, 1979.
2. *Primary Education in England: a survey by H.M. Inspectors of Schools*, 1978.
3. *'Life on Earth'* B.B.C. Spring, 1979.
4. Donaldson, M. *Children's Minds*. Penguin, 1978.
5. *Report of the Central Advisory Council for Education (Wales). Primary Education in Wales.* H.M.S.O., 1967.
6. *Environmental Studies 5–13: the Use of Historical Resources*, Schools Council Working Paper No. 48, Evans/Methuen, 1973.
7. Bruner, J.S. *The Process of Education*. Vintage, 1963.
8. Jahoda, G. 'Children's Concept of Time and History', *Educational Review*, Vol.15, No.2, 1963, p.90 and p.101.

9. West, J. 'Young children's awareness of the past'. *Trends,* Spring 1978, p.9.

10. Newton, E.E. 'An Evertonian Spilling-Over'. *Teaching History,* Vol.1, No.4. November, 1970.

11. Marshall, S. *An Experiment in Education,* C.U.P. 1970.

12. West, M. 'History and the Younger Child' *Teaching History,* Vol.1, No.4. November 1970.

13. Le Fevre, M. 'Introducing History to Young Children' *Teaching History,* Vol.1, No.2. November 1969.

14. *Primary Education: suggestions for the consideration of teachers and others concerned with the work of Primary Schools.* H.M.S.O. 1959.

15. Vygotsky, L.S. *Thought and Language.* M.I.T. Press and John Wiley, 1962, p.69.

16. Jahoda. Ibid.

17. Blyth, J.E. 'Young Children and the Past' *Teaching History.* June, 1978, Number 21. See diagram 'The Line of Old Objects'.

18. Tough, J. *Listening to Children Talking.* Ward Lock, 1976, p.79. See diagrams 'Mrs. Blyth's Life-Line' and 'Mrs. Blyth's Family Plan'.

19. Clark, F. *Foundations of History Teaching.* Oxford, 1929.

20. Fines, J. and Verrier, R. *The Drama of History.* Bingley, 1974.

21. West, J. Ibid., p.11.

22. Wagstaff, S. *Two Victorian Families* and *Kolo's family.* A. & C. Black, 1978.

23. Bryant, P.E. 'What the Young Child has to Learn about Logic' *Constraints on Learning,* ed. R.A. Hinde and J.S. Hinde. Academic Press, 1973.

## Further reading

Donaldson, M. *Children's Minds.* Penguin, 1978. *Environmental Studies 5-13: the Use of Historical Resources.* Schools Council Working Paper No.48, Evans/Methuen, 1973.

Marshall, S. *Experiment in Education,* C.U.P. 1970. Martin, N., Williams, P., Wilding, J., Hemmings, S., Medway, P. *Understanding Children Talking.* Penguin Education, 1976.

Pluckrose, H. *Let's Use the Locality.* Mills and Boon, 1971.

# 16 The quality of writing 7–13

*Andrew Wilkinson*

## Introduction

We know a good deal about how children acquire and develop language in the pre-school period, and there is a fair measure of agreement about the stages of their growing competence with its forms.

After that, however, little is known. Take writing, for instance, what exactly are the differences between the writings of children of (say) seven, ten and thirteen. We all have our intuitions; teachers might say 'quite good for an 8 year old' or 'you'd expect better than that at 12' – thus indicating that they possess expectations based on experience. But, as far as we have been able to discover, the characteristics of the writing on which they base their judgments have never really been examined. This is what the Crediton Project set out to do. A team of researchers from the University School of Education at Exeter worked with teachers at their schools in Crediton, Devon.[1]

## Obtaining the compositions

In studying the competence of a writer to use language it is no use taking one example only. We are all aware of how we vary from situation to situation in our speech and writing. Skilled teachers have a broadly based 'model of discourse' – that is to say they see to it that each pupil carries out a variety of tasks so that the different aspects of linguistic competence are required and developed. A common but uninformed view of primary teaching is that it emphasises 'creative writing' to the exclusion of other forms of writing. A common view of secondary schools, for which there is some evidence is that they stress factual writing (particularly in the examination dominated years) and require very little personal writing. Clearly in both cases the 'model of discourse' is far too narrowly based.

Within the limits of our resources it was not possible to take all the written work of the pupils we wished to study. Instead we had to select tasks which would be representative of pupils' abilities. The Assessment of Performance Unit, facing a similar problem, decided to choose tasks on four dimensions; narrative/descriptive or reflective/analytical; control by writer or tester (treatment fairly free or closely prescribed): first or second-hand subject matter; literary or functional.

This resulted in 7 tasks for 11 year olds, and 8 for 15 year olds. We selected tasks on the basis of function and reader. It seems sensible to choose tasks which would lead both to personal and to discursive writing, and to postulate readers in the school situation and known directly to the children. After various trials we chose four such tasks which also included the APU dimensions except that they all required first-hand subject matter.

The tasks – four compositions – two personal, two discursive – were as follows. One was a piece of autobiography – 'The happiest or saddest day of my life'. This is a well-tried title used by Schonell, notable for its success. For the adolescents the title was modified to 'The best/worst experience I ever had'. The reader was assumed to be the class's normal teacher. Another composition was a fictional story, the pupil selects a picture from three, and the instruction is 'Write a story for which your picture is one of the illustrations'. The writers knew that the results would be seen by their peers either on the class noticeboard or in a class anthology, both normal devices in the schools used. The third composition was an argument on the topic 'Would it work if children came to school when they liked, and could do what they liked there?' with the peer group as readership. The fourth composition was an explanation. The intention was that the writer could speak with authority. The task was to explain how to play a game. (Once again a Schonell topic). The reader was anyone who wished to learn the game.

The design of the project was simple. We took groups of pupils at seven, ten and thirteen and elicited from all of them the four compositions just described. No sophisticated matching procedures were used to select the pupils. We took a secondary school and one of its primary feeder schools in a community of considerable stability; the children in the one school often had brothers and sisters in the other. Within these schools we needed good average groups which were fairly compatible and relied on the professional knowledge of the teachers to provide these. We were thus able to compare like with like.

To meet possible criticisms that the written tasks were imposed and 'unnatural' we tried to make them such as normally occur in English lessons, linking them as closely as possible with the direct experience of the pupils. Our collaborating teachers required the compositions as part of normal classroom work over a period of three months. This we felt would minimise the possible Hawthorne effect in the sample (a difference brought about by the sheer fact that the subjects know they are involved in a research project) and the negative effect of 'examination backwash' on the children's understanding of the tasks themselves.

## Assessing the composition

Once we had obtained the compositions our task was to assess them, and here a major problem presented itself. The method of assessment chosen is related to one's belief about one's role as a teacher of language. If one seeks to develop only the 'skills' of writing then one chooses a marking scheme focusing on these. But if one believes one is concerned foremost with the growth of individuals for whom language is a means to that end, then one's scheme of assessment is conceived fundamentally to perceive that growth ('skills' and all) and to further it. This was our belief; and thus we sought such a scheme. Commonly used 'marking' schemes are at once far too narrow and far too vague. Certainly none of the schemes would come anywhere near describing the development we had in mind.

We were thus thrown back on what originality we could muster. If we were concerned with writer as a developing being we felt we must be as comprehensive as possible and look at the quality of thought, of the feeling, and of the moral stance manifested in the writing, as well as at the style. Matters such as punctuation, spelling, grammatical correctness are of course important, but these are commonly marked anyway. We wanted to look at other ways of assessment.

## Model of assessment

Hence four models were devised to serve as systems of analysis – in the fields of cognition, affect, morals and style. The complete models are printed in Wilkinson et al., 1980. In summary they are as follows:

Cognition. The basis of this model is a movement from an undifferentiated world organised by mind from a world of instances, to a world related by generalities and abstractions.

Affective. Development is seen as being in three movements – one towards a greater awareness of self, a second towards a greater awareness of neighbour as self, a third towards an inter-engagement of reality and imagination.

Moral. 'Anomy' or lawlessness gives way to 'heteronomy' or rule by fear of punishment, which in turn gives way to 'socionomy' or rule by a sense of reciprocity with others, which finally leads to the emergence of 'autonomy' or self-rule.

Stylistic. Development is seen as choices in relation to a norm of the simple literal affirmative sentence, which characterizes children's early writing. Features, such as structure, cohesion, verbal competence, syntax, reader awareness, appropriateness, undergo modification.

These models are not intended as examination instruments but to enable us to pay due regard to the varieties of activity going on in the process of writing. In one sense they are assessment instruments, but only in the sense that assessment is an essential part of education – we need to make assessments of development to help further development. On the other hand they should not be regarded as day to day marking schemes, since they have in total about 100 items. However it was the teachers working with us on the project who pressed for publication in full, since they felt their own levels of awareness had been greatly heightened by detailed application of them – an awareness which became part of their impressionistic judgement of further written work. Certain LEAs have recently been organising intensive workshops with these considerations in mind.

It is not possible here to include the full models and demonstrate their application. However simplified models are set out below which will serve to give some idea of the general dimensions.

**THE ASSESSMENT OF WRITING**

Simplified models based on Wilkinson, A., Barnsley, G., Hanna, P. and Swan, M., *Assessing Language Development* (OUP, 1980)

| COGNITIVE Overall Detail | Describing Simple facts, statements | Interpreting Explanations and deductions | Generalising Summaries, conclusions classifications | Speculating Substantial hypotheses, arguments, conclusions |
|---|---|---|---|---|
| AFFECTIVE | Self Self Self Self | Becoming aware – motives, context, image – of Self<br>Becoming aware of neighbour as self – of Others<br>Becoming aware of, celebrating, physical, social Environment<br>Coming to terms with the human condition – 'Reality' | | |

| MORAL Attitudes determined by – | Physical characteristics or results | Rewards and punishments | Social approval | Conventional norms, laws | Motives | Abstract concepts |
|---|---|---|---|---|---|---|
| STYLISTIC | Organisation Cohesion Syntax Lexis Reader Appropriateness | Fragmentary, becomes more and more complete<br>Separate items (e.g. sentences) become cohesive<br>Simple, complex, best suited for purpose<br>General, unqualified uses become exact, chosen<br>Growing sense of reader's needs<br>Movement into more acceptable/efficient mode | | | | |

*Figure 16.1*

## Assessment of autobiography

Let us look at the work of a seven year old writer in these terms

Peter:

I got up from bed and in front of me was loads of parcels I opending them, And there was a England football kit. A ball a pair of football boots I was ever so happy. Then I went down stairs and thier was a huge dinner on the table then I rember it was my birthday I had a nother supise as well my anty came round for tea and she gave me three pounds and we had a tea party. I was ever so good that night so my mum let me stay up and watch match of the day then I went to bed that was the happest day of my life.

As far as the cognitive category is concerned this writing is *descriptive*. It records a series of *facts* and *events* linked chronologically. In the affective category it is egocentric and a statement about the satisfaction of the needs of the *self*. *Others* have no existence except as servicing agencies to the writer – Mum as a universal provider, aunty as a bearer of three pounds on one's birthday. There is, not surprisingly, little reference to the physical environment, and the attitude towards 'reality' is that it is completely under one's control – as long as one is 'good'. In the moral category in fact the thinking is quite low level – that *virtue is rewarded* and vice punished. That this is not universally true needs no argument, but the assumption is a convenient one fostered by parents and teachers in the furtherance of efficient child-rearing and management.

In stylistic terms the *organisation* is complete, but elementary – almost entirely chronological. *Cohesion* is attained by simple connectives – *and, but, as well, so*. The syntax is predominantly simple sentences in form if not in appearance. *Lexis* is general; adjectives and adverbs for instance have a specifying function and there are scarcely any of these. We are seeing a stage of word use here which has two features. One feature is that the words are multipurpose – a few words can be used to do a large number of jobs (the principle of Ogden and Richards's *Basic English*). Take the verbs, for example: nearly all of them are forms of *be, have, got, go* – overwhelmingly the most common verbs in the language. At this age these multi-purpose verbs do not therefore carry particular shades of meaning. The other feature is that words used at this stage tend to have single connotations derived from the context in which they were learned; they haven't been encountered in the contexts with different connotations – e.g. dinner as an evening as well as a mid-day meal. As far as the *reader* is concerned there is an attempt to interest him, though the list of events is a little monotonous there are the deliberate devices of 'rembering' and 'supise'. These are devices from literature, showing movement towards *'appropriateness'* in written form, though the opening is very like speech.

If we apply the same criteria to another writer's work on the same theme we see some differences. Pauline is a year or so older than Peter (though we are not saying that the differences are necessarily due to age):

Pauline:
I had just moved into a new house. I had no friends my sister was only about 4 years old I looked for some friends but I couldn't find any. Then I heard a noise someone was bouncing on a matrue then I looked over the wall and there I found somebody I said who are you? what is your name? she said the same to me it was my old friend I knew in play school (she is in this school now) she is called nicola Thorn. We played skipping until it was time for me to go in. I had my tea and I watched television and I went to bed I said to myself I think that was the happiest day in my life. Nicola has been one of my Greatest friends right from that day. And she sometimes breaks but with me but she soon comes running to me when she is my friend again.

Cognitively, Pauline gives us a descriptive narrative, but the most notable dif-ference between her work and Peter's is that she *interprets* and *explains* – her opening isolation, for instance, is accounted for. In her last sentence she is moving towards a *generalisation* about friendship of the order of 'friendship can withstand shocks'. She is less egocentric than Peter in the sense that Nicola is a part of her happiness: it lies in an interaction not merely an assertion of *self* – she can also look on herself externally, 'I said to myself . . .'. Awareness of the *other* is shown in the large amount of information we receive about her. There is no active relationship with the *environment;* but the sense of *reality* is more mature than Peter's, not all one long focus of adoration. People are lonely, quarrel, a happy state is not permanent, and no connection is made between this and *moral* deservings.

The *organisation* is interesting in that it is moving from chronology to narrative. Chronology gives us the relentlessness and undifferentiated march of events, almost entirely ordinary. Narrative selects and presents by interrupting and disrupting the ordinary. There is a chronology in Pauline's account. Had Peter been writing it, it would have begun at the noise, and finished with tv and bed. But Pauline inserts before it a retrospect so as to convey the necessary background; after it she brings us up to the present. Both these devices, and others, arise from a careful consideration of the needs of the *reader*, though there are features of the writing (asides, for instance) more usually felt to be appropriate in speech. *Within* the chronological story Pauline skilfully withholds a piece of information – the name of her friend – ('someone', etc.) in order to build a climax. Effectively she is disrupting the time sequence in the sense that both name and person would have 'occurred together' in the incident. The *lexis* is more differentiating – with a greater variety of verbs for instance – *moved, heard, bouncing, played skipping*, in addition to the basics. In *syntax* there is a greater variety of sentence though none complicated.

A third piece – by an eleven year old girl – well demonstrates other features.

Jill:
  The best day of my life was at Barry Island. We were all staying at butilands holiday camp. It was the last day, we woke up to the sounds of the sea crashing against the rocks. My sister and me got up early and got dressed went into the kitchen and took some money and went out. We left a note for mum and dad to say gone to get the paper and to go along the sea front. We did not wake my brother up. When we got out it was a lovely day with the sun shining and a cool breeze. We went out of the camp site and down on to the sand. We took our sandles of and went in to the sea it was cold but refreshing. Then we played hit but it was not very good with just two of us. Then we wrote names in the sand. Then got the paper and came back when we got back everyone was up and we had breakfast then dad said Debras the greatest is she. He had seen what my sister wrote in the sand. Then we all went out and saw a realy funny fight no one got hurt then we went and bought some presents and things and went on to the beach. Had our lunch in a restruant. Went back and packed our bags. Then went to the station. we did not want to go, we walked through the fair to the station. Got on the train which was crowed it was very hot. when we got back home we had tea unpcked wtached t.v. then we went to bed. When we got in bed my sister and we talked about the day.

**Describing** is the principle cognitive operation – an immense amount of information is given with explanation (e.g., the note) where necessary. In the affective area there are two new features. One is an awareness of the *other* in terms which realise his unique personality. Nicola Thorn was as it were a dependent of the writer with no real distinguishing features: but here 'dad' is brought alive as a personality in his own right, just in the single phrase he speaks: we know what sort of person he is. The other is an awareness of the *environment*. Jill certainly illustrates it. *The moral* dimension is not explicit; the assumption is of a world in which responsibility to others is a norm.

Stylistic features are interesting. *Organisationally* a narrative is embedded within a chronology. 'My sister and me' . . . as far as 'He had seen what my sister wrote in the sand' is clearly a shaped whole, held by the device of withholding the information about what Debbie had written in the sand. In time, what she wrote and her writing it were simultaneous: here they are separated. The rest of the composition is conscientious reporting. The *syntax* is fairly simple – except that Jill demonstrates an ability to curtail it by leaving out subjects. Certain items of *lexis* are literary ('sun shining and a cool breeze'). It seems that children may need to attain to the conventional before gaining the individual. Otherwise, however, there is a great deal of very basic vocabulary (notice the verbs). There is still a strong element of oral language but there is a striving after written *appropriateness*. In the kernal story the *reader* is very skilfully handled; less so elsewhere.

The writing of a thirteen year old is likely to display characteristics not found earlier as well as others that were foreshadowed. This is a piece by Nina:

> It was just like any other Tuesday. Normal breakfast, normal lessons, little did I know that this was going to be one of the saddest days of my life.
>
> I got off the bus as normal, walked up the hill, opened the gate, walked down the steps, pressed on the latch. Then, it was different.
>
> My Mum opened the door, her eyes were red her cheeks puffed out, she'd obviously been crying. Bewildered, I asked 'What's happened?' Thoughts flashed through my mind, who's hurt, Dad, Nana, Papa?
>
> I was led into the sitting room, Mum held me and said,
>
> 'There's no other way I can break this to you, Papa died this morning'.
>
> The words were like a bombshell. I cried.
>
> 'Come and see Nana' Mum said 'She's been very brave'.
>
> I walked to the other room and flung my arms around my Grandmother. Tears fell like raindrops, until all my emotions were drained.
>
> 'How?' I asked.
>
> 'He was just sitting on the bed, getting his breath when he collapsed, and he was probably dead before he fell'.
>
> Dead, dead, dead, dead, the word ran through my mind, Papa is dead.
>
> Memories flashed back, when he used to push me in my small pram when I was young. His teasing, his twinkling eyes when he laughed.
>
> I cant cry anymore, all I can do is remember, it hurts though.
>
> The words 'Papa died this morning', kept on in my head for days. I couldn't stop them, it was like a disease, my whole body longed for him to be back. I hoped it was just a nightmare.
>
> I couldn't accept the fact that he was gone.
>
> I expect I will have to soon though.
>
> I long for the day when I can think about him without it hurting too much.
>
> I'll just put on a brave face, its all I can do.

This is not of course offered as a piece of abstract writing; in the *cognitive* category it is descriptive and interpretative: Nor does the writer raise any moral questions of the kind, *why him*, implying considerations of 'justice'. Rather is she concerned to cope with her own complex emotions. It is the responses in the *affective* category that are most significant.

Nina's grandfather dies, and she feels his loss very deeply. She draws a contrast between the events of a normal day and those after she gets the news of her grandfather's death. She tells of her grief not only through direct expression but also by reporting her words and actions: she is bewildered, is compassionate with her grandmother, and recognizes they must live for a time with despair, waiting for the hurt to lessen. It would appear that she has a well-developed understanding of the progress of grief. She shows skill in her selection of action and dialogue to heighten the reader's awareness of the feelings involved. She also shows an understanding of the effect of emotional shock: 'Dead, dead, dead, dead, the word ran through my mind, Papa is dead'; 'memories flashed back'. Here she appears to be going back over the cause of the shock, trying to sort it out, to come to terms with it. Nina compares her experience to a nightmare, even wishing it were so that she could wake up and know that it did not happen in reality. In all she expresses a highly developed sense of the nature of the emotion within herself, an awareness of that of others, and a general disposition to be compassionate, an awareness of the way emotion works in such a situation – the recall of past incidents for example.

The *stylistics* aspect of the writing are interesting. The predominant *organisation* is chronological but interspersed with reflection and flashback. There is a 'prospect' in the first paragraph which gives a 'hint of foreboding'. The last eight paragraphs are essentially reflective. *Cohesion* is less by specific grammatical devices, more by the semantic connection between each section. The use of *syntax* shows control, not only an ability to vary it with the meaning, but the ability to use incomplete grammatical forms for effect ('Dead, dead . . .', 'His teasing, his twinkling eyes when he laughed').

The most important development to be noted is predominantly in the area of lexis, the movement from general unqualified language with little emotional content, to emotionally charged words and phrases, similes, metaphors. There is an attempt to find metaphorical equivalents for the emotion in order to cope with it: 'like a bombshell', 'like raindrops', 'like a disease', 'just a nightmare'. The language may seem conventional, but we must beware of thinking that, necessarily, the emotion is not genuine. Unique expression for unique emotion is a hard won achievement. In the work of great writers we often find a working through conventional to individual language. Thus poets so diverse as Pope and Blake both set themselves an apprenticeship in which they modelled themselves on other writers.

## Assessment of argument

The feature of the kinds of writing we have looked at above are such as to show up particularly when analysed on the affective and moral models, but less so on the cognitive model. In argumentative writing the reverse is likely to be the case.

The subject, it will be remembered, was 'If children could come to school when they wanted to and could do what they liked there would it be a good thing'. The responses of some young children were on the level of assertion. Robert for instance is operating on the pleasure principle:

> No school on Friday and Thursday and Tuezday and Monday but Weday come for fut ball.

Slightly less elementary pieces gave a reason or so for the position taken, as with Dan:

> I think that we ought to be allowed to come school when we like and we wouldnt get so cold in the mornings.

Seven year olds are however capable of a logical organisation as in Kate's piece, though this was exceptional in our sample.

> I think school should stay like it is. Because if we did not come to school we would not have anafe education to get a job then we would get no money and we would become tramps the we would diey but if we went to school we would get some education and we could go to college then we could get a very good job and get lots of money. So I think school is very good.

She is not restricted to her particular school in arguing her case. She is able to raise a hypothesis in the first sentence, looks first at the consequences of not attending, and finally comes to a conclusion supporting her position. She is able at a certain level to classify and conclude, and we would see her work moving towards the **generalising** class.

Kate has dispensed with the narrative line. But it is such a powerful way of organising experiences that children older than Kate hold on to it even when it is inappropriate. Witness Sandra:

> To say I would like to do is come to school because of you can learn things out if I did not come to school I think that my mum and dad would say you are going to school if you like or do not like it.
> Sometime I feel like I do not what to come to school to work I just feel like sitting at home but mum and dad said get to school sandra you are not staing at home to day sandra you are getting to school now sandra go on.
> I think some times that we are better at School and that home.
> Mum says sandra in a way you are much butter being at school.
> But mum can I just today can I stay home, no sandra, please Just to day no no sandra. When you come home you can go to bed do I have to go to bed yes Sandra.

> When I got home I did have to go to bed but I thot that I was best to go to
> School because I learn more at School and what I will at home like are mum's
> and dad's can not give us exmahams so . . .

Sandra's is not a logical argument, but fundamentally a piece of description. It is
a dialogue, which proceeds by statement and counter statement between parent
and child, a far cry from arguing a point of view. The piece is lively and amusing,
and for this reason many teachers would accept it and praise Sandra, whilst
perhaps drawing attention to the problems of presentation. To do this would be
to have an inadequate 'model of discourse', to think that 'good English' is in
some sense one thing. In fact narrative is not the same as argument, autobiography
as explanation, and so on. Differing aspects of competence are required for
differing functions. In fact Sandra is avoiding the issue, fundamentally the problem
of logical thinking on paper. And yet one of the important ways we learn to think
is through writing. Problems can be held in attention, considered, selections tried
out in the very act of writing them down. Direct teaching can introduce the
thinking modes. Thus clearly Sandra could understand and use the way Kate (3
years younger) organises her piece if it were explained to her.

Space permits of only one further example. We may take here a piece from the
middle range of 13 year olds. These writers, like Colin, for example, tended to see
something of the complexity of the issues, recognising that there are two parts to
the logic – the question of optional attendances and the student choice of
activities:

> No. there would be so many difficulties inherent in this idea that it would be
> a non-starter. A few of the problems would be (1) A fluctuating demand for
> teachers (everyone might come one day and but a few another day).
> (2) Some children not realizing the importance of education would never
> come (3) How literaly is the above question taken (could children go to
> school at midnight if the late film isn't any good?) (4) Some children would
> attend school for 4 or 5 hours every day, they would be at a very different
> level of understanding in the subjects than the people who seldom came and
> it would therefore be impracticable to put them in the same class, and as only
> 20 people might want to do RE it would be impracticle to split the class into
> the necessary 4 or 5 levels. (5) In a school of 1600 it would not be possible
> to let children do exactly what they want (only 4 or 5 people might be
> interested in falconry). (6) The planning of the curriculum would be a
> nightmare. (7) The school lunch system would be useless as the lunches
> might be left one week and over subscribed the next. These seven points
> show just how ludicrous that sugestion really was.

He starts with an overall evaluation which he proceeds to justify. Each of the listed
items is a relevant difficulty, leading to the conclusion. Each item gives a reason
for the impracticability concerned. He is at the level of *generalising*. He is
beginning to classify, but has not built up a classificatory system – e.g. by discerning

the various issues in the topic and discussing them in turn. He has however clearly outgrown the need to organise this type of material chronologically.

The cognitive model has more detailed dimensions which we cannot use here, and we have not demonstrated the higher reaches of thinking which was found in a few thirteen year olds. But perhaps enough has been said to illustrate the general thrust of the model and the kinds of insights it gives into childrens' writing.

## Conclusions

In this article we have been able to look at a few compositions – of two types only – autobiography and argument – in the light of the Crediton model. Nevertheless by using a simplified version of the model we hope we have been able to demonstrate some of the applications of it. We feel that the general implications of the project are as follows:

(1) Since teachers of language are not just concerned with the child as a spelling and punctuation producing machine, but as a growing being, and since language is one of the chief means by which such growth takes place, then it follows that the way teachers view writing must be influenced by this.

(2) It is possible to discern a developmental process in children's writing, by examining the thought, emotion, moral stance, and style. This process is not to be compared to climbing the steps of a ladder, so that one attains a stage once and for all; rather is it more like the waves breaking on a beach, advancing and retreating in particular areas. Thus no one piece of writing can be seen as representing the 'stage' of a particular writer. Assessment is made by means of the teacher's knowledge of other work and of the child.

(3) Assessment is seen here essentially as a teaching not as a testing device. One must perceive growing points in order to further them. The assessment instruments of the Crediton Project are not intended as day-to-day marking schemes. Rather is it hoped that they may become assimilated into the internalised criteria which teachers are using when they carry out 'impression marking'. A simplified scheme such as the one in the present paper will not be found too onerous to use as a means to this end.

It should be emphasised that the models have been based on the work of about 150 children in rural Devon, and are making no claims about 'universal' development. Nevertheless over the past two years work has gone on, not only in various LEAs in the UK, but also in Australia and Canada. The indications are that children elsewhere may not be very different.

## References

1. Wilkinson, A., Barnsley, G., Hanna, P. and Swan, M. (1980) *Assessing Language Development*, Oxford University Press.

# 17 The arts in the primary school
## Snapshots of practice

*Michael O'Hara*

## Introduction

The unexamined rhetoric for change associated with the National Curriculum is relatively seductive to the concerned lay person. There is now a new language around which talks of strengthening standards, common goals, attainment targets, transferability, student profiles, assessment, parental rights, opting out, and teacher appraisal. It all appears to offer a new deal to the educational consumers, but it is teachers who must deliver the new programmes, and it is they and the schools who will be responsible for creating the sorts of circumstances in which the requirements of the National Curriculum will be met. The pressures are substantial, so it is no great surprise that in many contexts the curriculum is being pruned and pared to ensure that maximum attention is devoted to satisfying those curriculum requirements perceived as urgent, important and immediate.

In such circumstances something has to give. The uncertainty and insecurity associated with an imposed curriculum can hinder creativity, stifle initiative and lead to a narrow view of the purposes of education. In any event, who wants to be adventurous at a time of change when the ground rules are not very clear and the goal posts keep shifting? The perception is growing that the line of least resistance is to play safe, keep one's eye firmly on the attainment targets and surgically work towards their attainment. Those aspects of the curriculum, which previously had been perceived as 'not crucial', now run the risk of being relegated to an even more minor role or indeed of disappearing entirely.

This is perhaps particularly true in the case of drama, because although its place is acknowledged in the attainment targets for English, there is substantial anecdotal evidence about to suggest that it is seen by some primary teachers as even more peripheral to the language curriculum than it was in pre-National Curriculum days. Furthermore the separation of drama from music and art which arose out of the requirements of the National Curriculum has not only had the effect of further pigeon holing the creative arts, but it also may have frustrated, at least to some extent, the possibilities of generically planning for the arts in schools.

To get a feeling for the extent to which there was any substance to these perceptions, a number of primary schools were visited and teachers interviewed. Clearly what was discovered cannot realistically be generalised from, but insights gained do provide at least some snapshots of current practice. The initial concern was to discover what was happening in the areas of drama and the arts and the level of commitment to these areas which teachers had. The picture uncovered was generally not very encouraging.

## Practices in schools: Teachers talking

At the very beginning of the investigation, and in a large primary school, an offer of assistance in designing an arts and drama curriculum was politely refused by those teachers perceived by the headteacher as the curriculum leaders in the areas. The teachers apologised for their reluctance 'to get involved in anything else'. 'We are snowed under', was the claim, 'in trying to keeps our heads above water handling the basic areas in the National Curriculum'. One teacher was disarmingly honest:

> 'Quite frankly I never do much drama. I don't know much about it and anytime I've tried it, it's been chaotic. The odd time I might let them act out a poem mostly because they pester me . . . we have an art session on Friday afternoons and every second week, I have a music class which is generally a singing class . . . I don't have any scheme as such . . . I select some topic or song from the school's suggestions for the year group . . . and as far as art is concerned, once they start work I find it's a bit of a break.'

Such attitudes reflect the findings of The Gulbenkian Report[1] which pointed up the lack of adequate provision for the arts in schools. Similar concerns have also been implied in recent HMI reports, and more recently the same problem has been identified by the NCC Arts in Schools Project.[2] Indeed the latter has given important new perspectives on curriculum development in the arts and has provided a general framework for schools to consider in developing their own arts policies. It also provided a staff development workpack for in-service workshops in schools and for use in initial teacher training. The project is rich in the kinds of 'practical support' suggestions perceived as being so important for teachers. But none of the teachers spoken to in the context of this research had heard of the project. Nor indeed were any of them aware of recent publications from the DES which reiterated the crucial role of drama in the curriculum through providing illustrations of good practice. This was particularly surprising because the recommendations of these publications had all been realistically focused through the requirements of the National Curriculum.

Drama, it was discovered, was certainly very far down the list of teachers' priorities. Some immediately declared that they just didn't do any drama. Very few schools had anything which even approximated to specialist facilities for the area, and in those schools where individual teachers took special drama sessions, the school hall, which also served as a canteen and a gymnasium, was used. Most of the teachers spoken to 'felt' that drama was important and 'very useful' for the children, but explanations for its 'usefulness' rarely exceeded 'it brings them out of themselves'. Certainly some teachers were using this medium as a 'method' in their classes, mostly in the form of dramatisation and generally in an effort to make the experience of some content more interesting. But none of the teachers spoken to talked with any real conviction or enthusiasm of the wider curriculum possibilities in systematically using dramatic method to help children develop an empathy with characters, moods, situations, and contexts through doing and experiencing. It was, indeed, only in the infant classes that music, mime and movement was used as an extension and supplement to learning activities for the very young, although it was rather disappointing to see the very limited range of music and sound used by teachers in this type of creative activity. Too much slavish reliance was placed on drama and movement radio broadcasts. Programmes were too often used as ends in themselves rather than as springboards to extended work both in drama and in the wider curriculum. The use of drama as a way into speech work was generally not explored to any extent, nor was there any real evidence of attempts at exploring its effectiveness in the development of oral communication skills. The integration of activities and processes in music, movement, dance, physical education, art and storytelling using the dramatic medium showed little sign of having been built into the curriculum, and it was depressing to note how work of this type, and indeed learning through any kind of dramatic play, appeared to evaporate as children move up through the primary school. 'Playtime ends in P3', claimed one teacher.

There was, surprisingly, lots of support for the kinds of drama associated with the school play, festival work and school assembly. The public and presentational aspects of drama were seen as important to give as many children as possible experience of performing in public (an extension of the 'bringing them out of themselves' syndrome), and it was claimed that activities of this kind provided a welcome break in the routines of the school. Some teachers testified to dramatic input sometimes giving life to otherwise boring assemblies, while others saw formal school performances as providing opportunities for the school to show off a 'public face'. But drama as a learning medium was not extensively used by teachers. Timetabled space for drama didn't exist at all except in one of the schools visited, and when pressed about curriculum planning in this area, teachers largely confessed to ignorance, lack of knowledge or just disinterest, although, in the words of one teacher, 'a few practical suggestions wouldn't be turned down.'

When discussions with teachers shifted to the other main arts areas of art and music (drama, art and music were seen by teachers as constituting the creative arts in the primary curriculum), there was a sense in which they felt more secure. 'You know where you are with art and music' was the comment of several teachers, but when asked to amplify, it became apparent that the confidence which they felt came from the fact that these areas were just better established in the curriculum and were at least perceived as having better defined roles. Art in particular was spoken of as 'very important' for all primary children. A rhetoric about the crucial role of creative expression in the educative process was used by nearly all the teachers interviewed, but when interviewees were invited to expand on the function of art in the curriculum, and on what children were expected to learn through participating in art activities, teachers' responses were limited to speaking about objectives in particular activities. Art-based activities, however, were used in all the work of the primary curriculum as was expected, even though teachers had difficulty in talking about the role of art both as a subject and as a learning medium. Comments of the type reported by Ross,[3] and suggestive of the extreme difficulty in even finding a language to talk of creative learning encounters, were quite common. But when the teachers spoke of music, it was noticeable that the language of creative expression seemed to disappear. Except for two schools which had teachers with specialist qualifications in music, teachers viewed music in a rather skills-oriented way. It was seen as important for the children to sing, have some knowledge of notation and, perhaps, learn to play the recorder. Participation in the school choir was encouraged for the 'singers', and peripatetic music teachers regularly visited all the schools to give 'instrument' lessons to children who had the appropriate skills. Listening to music was not a popular activity, nor was music extensively used to heighten the experience of other subjects. Strangely enough, no obvious efforts appear to have been made to take account of 'where the children were'. Children's own rich musical background in street games and songs, folk and pop music, their natural propensity to respond to time-beat, rhythm and climax, and their known interest in sound stories and music making, were not used as springboards for curriculum initiatives. Indeed, in both art and music, the organisation, focusing and structuring of curriculum experiences was a very ad hoc practice indeed, and was acknowledged by several teachers to constitute no more than dipping into the recommendations of prescribed curricula. The relationship *between* the arts was, as can be imagined, not explored to any extent at all.

## Remembering school and college experiences

Teachers acknowledged the possibility that their general lack of interest and commitment to the arts could stem from their own uninspiring experiences as pupils and as trainee teachers. Memories of participation in arts-based activities at school were blurred, but yet rather pleasant, for all of the teachers spoken to. Reflecting on their primary school years, many remembered the 'Friday afternoon art classes', the Christmas and Easter presentations, the singing classes and the recorder sessions, but even at that early stage, teachers confessed to perceiving these activities largely as rewards for application in the 'academic' areas. Drama, art and music were 'curriculum frills'. Secondary school experiences were similarly recollected in a fragmented way. All pupils had art and music at least once a fortnight for the first three years (drama was generally not remembered as a subject study), and the associated activities were not dissimilar to those remembered in the primary school. After that, from years four to six, the arts became the domain of the 'talented' who took the subjects to GCSE and A Level. Because of the minimal attention paid to arts-type subjects, some of the teachers spoken to claimed it was little wonder that many pupils failed to develop an interest or feeling for the arts, and how easy it was for children to buy into a perception that the arts were for the minority.

In the teacher training institutions, where some contact with the arts was obligatory, the encounters were recollected as 'rag-bags' of tips for teachers. There was certainly an experiential element in courses but because this was not connected into any real conceptual map of understandings in the arts, nor into basic ways of designing the arts curriculum, nor indeed into investigations about the relationships between the arts, teachers quickly perceived a peripheral set of curriculum concerns. All teachers remembered what was called 'speech and drama' sessions, but the lasting memory of these was the speech activities used to help them ostensibly become effective classroom communicators. 'We all enjoyed these', claimed one teacher, 'but only because they were such a laugh . . . definitely not to be taken seriously . . . they were called the cuckoo classes.' Drama workshops were certainly not remembered as beginning from 'where the students were' and activities were seen by some as 'unrealistic' and by others as 'positively embarrassing'. Although it wasn't every teacher's memory, some lamented that they weren't even shown how to dramatise stories or poems . . . 'instead we had to be trees or clockwork soldiers or we were dashing through wind blown cornfields being chased by giants . . . no wonder I'm not interested or know anything about it.'

On teaching practice, teachers confessed the hidden agenda was that

'. . . art was OK because after the kids started to work you just walked around looking interested . . .'

'never attempt music unless you can sing, play something or know something . . .'

'drama was to be avoided like the plague . . . you are particularly exposed in drama . . . it never worked out like "the odd bit of crack" you got in the college sessions . . . and there was sure to be discipline problems at best and chaos at worst.'

There was a lot of evidence to suggest that the obligatory nature of the arts, in the training courses followed by interviewees, had only a minimal impact on recipients' knowledge of the arts, and because they had very little experience and knowledge, teachers admitted to having no real motivation to induct children into these areas. 'In any event', claimed one teacher, rather cynically, 'and if we are brutally honest about it, . . . the arts are not important to headteachers or boards of governors . . . except, of course, as little show pieces which on public occasions can mislead the public into thinking that a broadly balanced curriculum is in operation.'

The majority of teachers claimed that their attitudes to the arts in education were indeed a reflection of those attitudes held by the schools in which they worked '. . . but even more so now that the National Curriculum has a gun at headteachers' heads.' Even those teachers with a commitment to the arts also associated themselves with this view. They spoke of the 'conservative nature of schools', their 'natural resistance to change', and how the structure of most schools is about 'prioritising the curriculum' with literacy and numeracy as 'the flag ships'. Drama and the arts are more and more being seen as specialisations, they lamented, and only talented, enthusiastic and skilful practitioners are perceived as being able to successfully manage these areas.

It must be remembered, many teachers claimed, that lack of support for the arts is also to be found among the majority of parents. They will generally attend concerts and shows and visit displays of children's work to 'support' the school, but parents 'would never dream of complaining about the lack of the arts'. 'Perhaps, it is just like some teachers', the claim continued, '. . . they see the arts only as a break from "real school work."' Some teachers expressed the view that calls for adequately catering for the arts, and the identification of supporting networks, are not 'getting through', particularly when the rallying cries for accountability, vocationally based education and the raising of standards are heard everywhere '. . . and are irresistible in a social world where there is high unemployment and fierce competition for fewer and fewer jobs . . . and indeed, where young school leavers can no longer hope for a job for life'.

## Towards a policy for in-service support and teacher education in the arts

If schools, for whatever reason, have been remiss in adequately catering for drama and the arts, their difficulties arguably could be compounded by the new requirements under the National Curriculum that all children must be exposed to literature, drama, dance, the visual arts and music up to age 14. To fulfil this requirement, attitudes will have to change quite drastically and a very substantial programme of support and development will be required. A great irony, however, is that some recent research[4] points to teachers feeling most confident in teaching maths and English, and least confident in science, technology and music. The claim is further made that something must be done to help teachers acquire the knowledge to give them confidence in handling these areas. There can be little argument with this, but the brief must be extended to include more of the arts than music. There is substantial evidence to suggest that teachers lack confidence in the creative arts in general, and to address this problem would require not only a knowledge update, but also practical experience in the arts. Even if the teachers spoken to in this research represent only a fraction of the attitudes held about the arts in the profession, there still seems to be an urgent need to provide the sort of in-service and/or staff development programmes which will support busy classroom practitioners in their attempts to fulfil the requirements of the National Curriculum in these areas.

The nature and structure of such provision does, however, need to be carefully considered because awareness of the role of the arts in education must arguably be associated with, and internalised through, practical experience in the arts for the interactions to make sense. A staff development and school-based curriculum development programme already exists, and with the minimum of expense (relatively speaking) could be initiated almost immediately. The *NCC Arts (5–16) Project Pack* for teachers is now readily available, and it represents a timely and imaginative attempt at proposing an organic way of planning for the arts in school. This programme, through its rationale and structure, aims towards providing the sorts of insights, understandings and perspectives on the functions and roles of the arts in education so necessary as a basis of understanding for practising teachers. But such school-based work needs a substantial measure of practical and experiential support, not only to complement the staff development pack of activities, but also to provide the sort of remediation or reconstruction of experience that this research suggests is necessary. Running concurrently, therefore, with school-based staff development sessions led by curriculum leaders, must be provision for the experience of the arts in well resourced contexts. Practically speaking, it may only be possible for teachers to experience one of the arts because of the pressures of time and resources, but even this would go a long way towards providing that experiential dimension so necessary as a supplement to just thinking about the arts. Even a short programme over one term with a group of schools combining to follow the *Arts (5–16) Project Pack* would be some sort of support for teachers. It is also possible that a group of schools working together might find it easier (through the pooling of resources) to arrange for the in-service experience of the arts referred to as a necessary supplement to the school-based work. Such initiatives are both crucial and urgent, not only for the arts to survive in schools, but also to satisfy the demands of the National Curriculum.

To effect real change, however, in curriculum practices in a more positive and effective way, it will also be important to look at the quality of pre-service training courses. Many of the teachers spoken to in this research agreed that the design of all arts pre-service courses should begin from the premise that students have no experience in the arts at all and are therefore meeting an entirely new area. Recent research reported in the NCC *Arts (5–16) Schools Project* could be a help in this regard. It has pointed the way towards the recognition of the shared concerns of the arts in education and has highlighted many of the common processes, practices and functions of the arts. This initial mapping of the role of the arts could provide a sound base from which arts teacher educators could construct the pedagogies that would consider the contributions of the individual art areas to the development of the person. Training institutions have a responsibility not only to help students develop their background knowledge and experience of the arts, but the knowledge perceived as being important must, arguably, develop through experiencing the arts. It is essential that students are helped to respond to the different arts areas, and it is the recognition that such help is needed which should influence the design of courses. Without being helped to respond to the arts themselves, it will be difficult, if not impossible, for teachers to create the sorts of circumstances in which children will be able to respond.

The challenge for arts educators in pre-service education, then, is first of all to seek out the ways in which the arbitrary divisions between the concerns and aspirations of the different arts areas can be broken down and reconstructed to find a common core. Such an attempt is implied by the *NCC Arts (5–16) Project Pack*[2] for teachers which examines the crucial questions in arts education which need to be addressed in very practical contexts. Among the questions posed are: what are the arts? . . . what is distinctive about the arts? . . . what are the differences between the arts disciplines? . . . what are the common roles of the arts in education? . . . what are the specific roles of the different arts disciplines in education? . . . what range of arts provision is necessary in the school curriculum? . . . what should be included in arts courses? . . . how should pupils' progress and attainment in the arts be assessed?

Attention to these questions would point up the problematic curriculum design issues in creative arts teaching, including the thorny notions of sequence, progression and evaluation. The basic aim, however, would be to produce teachers who will be knowledgeable in the arts areas and who, as indicated in *The Arts in the Primary School: Reforming Teacher Education*[5] will have a clear grasp of the educational role of the arts and an understanding of how children learn through the arts; will be confident in encouraging creative work across the range of the arts; will be able to recognise and evaluate the creative and artistic quality in children's work; will be able to apply their particular expertise in support of non-specialist colleagues; will be able to assist in the development of an arts policy for a school; and will be able to play an active role in staff development and the design and management of the arts curriculum.

A basic course led by aims of this kind and focused by the sort of content identified by the Arts (5–16) Project would then lead onto the experience of, and studies in, the main arts areas. It clearly would not be possible for students to have contact with all the areas which might be identified as the arts, so specialisation would be likely. It would be important, however, for any specialisation to get its flavour and direction from the proposed core. Alternatively, of course, if the arts teams in particular institutions could subscribe to a basic philosophy for the arts of the type rehearsed above, then these core concerns could be reflected through the design of each of the individual arts areas, which would then, in turn, treat the core issues through their own medium, language and processes. But whatever the design of the course, students' competencies, skills and knowledge of the arts should be assessed with the same rigour as any other area of the teacher training curriculum. Students should further be required to be seen teaching arts lessons during their teaching practices.

Such a change in existing training practices would go a long way towards ensuring that when they do get teaching appointments, and regardless of the practices in the arts in those schools to which they are appointed, teachers may have been sufficiently enthused for the arts that their teaching will be honed with the humanising effect that comes from contact with these areas. It is also to be expected that through their having experienced the arts, having developed skills in the arts, and having recognised the fundamental nature of all the arts areas and their importance in the educative process, practices in some schools may very gradually change. In the particular case of drama, which has now to a large extent been submerged into the concerns and practices of the English curriculum, teachers must also be prepared (in initial training) to see how children can be provided with opportunities 'to develop dramatic concepts, knowledge, imagination, skills and attitudes', and how these can be woven into children's general experience of the curriculum.[6] Furthermore, through the curriculum planning of the school, student teachers must be taught to be aware of what drama can contribute year by year.[6]

These things cannot happen without a very serious review of training programmes. Courses must be structured from the premise that student teachers have to a large extent a very fragmentary knowledge of the arts, little or no experience of the arts, no real motivation to acquire skills in the arts, nor indeed any great desire to become more knowledgeable and aware of the role of the arts in education. Training institutions, then, must develop the course patterns which can provide the kinds of sanely conceived experiential programmes capable of equipping teachers with the necessary skills, attitudes and insights to turn the aspirations of the arts in education into programmes of curriculum action in their schools or, at the very least, in their own classrooms.

In the meantime, however, let's get on with providing the staff development and in-service support so badly needed by practising teachers in case they begin to doubt the commitment of the providing agencies to delivering the arts dimension of the National Curriculum.

## References

1 Calouste Gulbenkian Foundation (1982) *The Arts in Schools: Principles, Practice and Provision.*
2 *NCC Arts (5–16) Project Pack* (1990). Oliver & Boyd: London.
3 Ross, M. (1972) 'Cooling the Arts Curriculum', *Times Educational Supplement*, 2991, 22 September.
4 Wragg, E.C., Bennett, S.N. and Carre, C.G. (1989) 'Primary Teachers and the National Curriculum', *Research Papers in Education*, 4, 3, 17–45.
5 Calouste Gulbenkian Foundation (1989) The *Arts in the Primary School. Reforming Teacher Education.*
6 DES (1989) *Drama from 5–16* (Curriculum Matters 17). HMSO: London.

# 18 Giants, good and bad

## Story and drama at the heart of the curriculum at Key Stage 1

*Joe Winston*

### The appeal of giants for children

Folk tales and fairy tales create for children an imaginative world which is alluring in its promise of fantasy, adventure and wish fulfilment. It is a world where giants proliferate but theorists disagree over their symbolic function within the tales. Bruno Bettelheim[1] argues that, for children, they may represent adults in general:

> 'we . . . appear to them as selfish giants who wish to keep to ourselves all the wonderful things which give us power'
>
> (p 27)

Bringing an orthodox Freudian perspective to his analysis, he reads more specific meanings into tales such as *Jack and the Beanstalk;* here he sees the giant as 'the father who blocks the boy's oedipal desires', a figure upon which 'the oedipal boy projects his frustrations and anxieties' (ibid, p 114). The child *needs* to kill the giant at a symbolic level to grow up into a secure adult; the particular importance of fairy tales for Bettelheim is their unique ability to fulfil that psychological need. For Jack Zipes[2], on the other hand, giants are figures of socio-political rather than psychological importance. Basing his theories on the cultural evolution of folk tales, he sees the real and original significance of the tales in what he terms their 'liberating magic'. 'Folk tales and other fantastic literature', he writes, 'can be used to suggest ways to *realise* greater pleasure and freedom in society'. In this context, giants represent the tyranny and injustice of brute force and political repression which can nonetheless be destroyed through communal and individual demonstrations of bravery, wit and decisive action.

Zipes' thesis focuses on meanings in the tales as derived from the oral tradition of the peasant communities to whom they originally belonged; Bettelheim's context is the psychology of young children. In both cases, however, giants are seen as metaphors of aggressive power and violence which need to be overcome. And, whatever our opinions of these theories, there is no escaping the fact that young children are small and relatively powerless figures in a world controlled and dominated by people much bigger than themselves; that the fear of being bullied, physically overwhelmed and hurt by these people is a real one; and that traditional tales such as *Jack the Giant Killer* and *Jack and the Beanstalk* can be seen as providing fictional frameworks for these fears to be purged.

There is another type of giant, however, one who has appeared in more recent children's literature written in the fairy tale tradition. Such creations as Oscar Wilde's Selfish Giant and Ted Hughes' Iron Man are altogether more vulnerable and more sympathetic. They are figures of strength and aggression, lonely and unhappy, who are finally redeemed through their contact with children. More sophisticated creations than their counterparts in earlier tales, they carry a different message of empowerment for children. They intimate that there is no need to kill the giant; if you tame it with love and friendship, then it will use its strength and power to protect and look after you. Within this tradition, though with a further shift of emphasis, is the short picture story book *Giant* by Juliet and Charles Snape. Here the giant is indeed strong and powerful but lacks the aggression of the traditional giant. Most significant of all, this giant is female.

## Topic 1: *GIANT*

The narrative of *Giant* owes its dynamic as much to its pictures as to its words. The story begins with a young girl, Lea, looking out of her window at the mountain beyond the village where she lives. The villagers call the mountain 'Giant' and, in the next illustration, we see the fields where the animals graze, the fruit trees, the woods and the stream which provide the villagers with many of their needs. The children, too, like to play on the mountain and the third picture illustrates them happily playing by the stream. Looking closely at this picture, however, we notice the damage done to the trees and spot the litter and rubbish scattered over the ground and dumped in the water. The next picture very clearly establishes the personification of the mountain as a woman and, what is more, as a woman very sad at the way her care for the villagers is not being returned. That night, she decides to leave them and when the villagers awake next morning, she is gone. At first they panic but soon decide that they don't really need her and that they can create their own mountain by filling with rubbish the hole she has left. Only Lea and her friend, Felix, show any sorrow for her loss and Lea expresses pity for the sad figure of Giant who now stands alone in the sea, with nowhere to go. The villagers build their mountain of rubbish but nothing will grow on it and, when it starts to smell, they decide to set it on fire. The flames and smoke are soon out of control, however, and the villagers flee in terror. Lea runs to the beach and implores Giant to return and help them. This she does by blowing away the smoke and by lifting up the sea bed and pouring the waves over the flames. The final picture shows Giant at rest once more alongside the village and we are assured that the villagers have learned their lesson and will never take their mountain for granted again.

The story of *Giant*, through its symbolism and its content, puts forward some very potent arguments:

• Giant symbolises mother earth. Like a good mother, she is a generous provider. But she cannot tolerate mistreatment and neglect forever.

- The welfare of the earth and the welfare of humanity are inextricably interlinked.
- The earth will continue to provide for humanity only if humanity ceases to abuse the earth.
- Our hope for the future lies with our children (inasmuch as it is Lea who most appreciates Giant and persuades her to return)
- Our hope for the future is dependent upon our elevating the status of the traditional female values of care and mutual support (as embodied in the mother/daughter relationship between Giant and Lea and in the values they embody).

The story of *Giant* could readily and superficially be incorporated within an environmental topic as a straightforward cautionary tale about the dangers of pollution, which the teacher might read and briefly discuss with her class. But having appreciated the potential of the story to convey the understandings and values listed above, the challenge identified by this particular teacher was how to construct a curriculum framework which was *consciously driven by these values as much as it was determined by the content of the National Curriculum*. The way the tasks were framed in six weekly units within the topic web (Figure 18.1) show her strategy for achieving this over-riding aim across the curriculum. Tasks in the first two weeks encouraged children to get to know the mountain's physical attributes but also its aesthetic beauty and its qualities as a generous provider. The next two weeks concentrated on the villagers' neglect and misuse of her while the final two weeks focused on the themes of motherhood, the community and the values of caring and appreciation. Individual tasks within these units were framed to build up not only knowledge but, to coin a phrase, 'knowledge with attitude'. So, for example, in Week 3, Task 2, children were encouraged to compare their understanding of the old mountain (Giant) with the new one made of rubbish. They were asked to do this not only in *physical* terms (life-giving/sterile) but also in *aesthetic* terms (ugly/beautiful) and *moral* terms (good/bad). This task had meaning for the children because they had 'made' both mountains themselves (cf tasks in Weeks 1 and 3) and had gotten to know them in qualitatively human terms. Using drama, the teacher was able to deepen this empathy by locking into the story's powerful symbolism and by enabling the children to symbolically engage in direct conversation with the characters in the story, in particular, with Giant herself. In the words of Booth and Haine,[3] it was a way to 'externalise the interior world of the reader and allow us to bring the text into a closer relationship with him'. Thus, if the personification of Giant, the story's central metaphor, was the hub at the centre of the topic wheel, the dynamic which helped set this wheel moving was drama.

## Topic 1: *GIANT* – the use of drama

Margaret Donaldson[4] wrote some years ago of young children's ability to understand and perform tasks which are 'humanly comprehensible', which are not 'abstracted from all basic human purposes and feelings and endeavours.'

## Week 6: CARE AND APPRECIATION: MOTHERHOOD

1. What is special about mothers? What is special about my mummy? (Writing) [English: AT 3] who else cares for me? How can we return the love and care that is given to us?
2. Drama Session 6.
3. Dig up the rubbish - examine what has happened to it. Predict first. [Science: AT 2, 2d]

## Week 5: CARE AND APPRECIATION: THE COMMUNITY

1. Compare our own village with the village in the story. Where is my village? County/country. My address. Who helps us in our village? [Geography: AT 2, 1a, b, c, e]
2. Paint a picture of somewhere I have been outside my village – (hill? mountain?) [Geography: AT 2, 1d; Art: AT 1,1c]
3. How can we help look after our village/school?
4. What services are needed for our village/school? [Geography: AT 4, 2c]

## Week 4: INVESTIGATING WASTE

1. What should the villagers do with their waste materials? How much do the children know about what happens to their rubbish? Show through labelled diagrams. [Geography: AT 2, 1b]
2. Collect litter at the end of a playtime and categorise. Bring in rubbish to categorise. [Science: AT 3, 1 and 2a]
3. What will happen to our different categories of waste over time? Bury some, burn some. How will it change? [Science: AT 2, 2b, 2d]
4. Drama Session 5.
5. Talk about how the earth sustains us, giving life – what can we give in return?

(Centre diagram)
STORY
GIANT
DRAMA

## Week 1: GETTING TO KNOW GIANT

1. Drama Session 1.
2. Make GIANT as person (3D sculpture). [Art: AT 1, 1b]
3. Make GIANT as mountain (2D display – collage style). Introduce words like footpath, river, stream. [Geography: AT 1, 2b; Art: AT 1, 1a]
4. Work on sets, grouping animals and trees in fields. [Maths: AT 5, 1a]
5. Make a map of the mountain. [Geography AT: 1, 2a]

## Week 2: HOW GIANT PROVIDES FOR US

1. Discuss what we need to grow things in class. Grow cress and observe daily. [Science: AT 2, 2a]
2. Discuss what lives in the soil. Create a wormery. Observe daily. Children feed and care for African snails. [Science: AT 2, 2a]
3. Write: what grows in my garden? [English: AT 2]
4. Observe and draw examples of rocks and stones. Explore differences between rocks and soil. [Geography: AT 1, 2a; Art: AT 1,1b]
5. Discuss seasonal changes and draw how the mountain might look in [GIANT] ] Spring, Summer, Autumn, Winter. [Geography: AT 1, 2a; Art: AT 1, 1c] Look at the different ways Cézanne painted Mt. St. Victoire. [Art: AT2, 1c]
6. Ta,Identify the forms in which water occurs on the mountain – rain, fog, clouds, ponds, rivers, frost and snow. [Geography: AT 3, 2b]
7. Drama Session 2.

## Week 3: POLLUTING THE MOUNTAIN

1. How have the villagers changed the mountain? Buildings, roads, land for farming/leisure, water and air pollution. [Geography: AT 5, 2b]
2. Build a new Giant/mountain of litter. Will it support life? [Science: AT 2, 2a] Compare the old mountain with the new one. What is good/ bad; ugly/beautiful; life-giving/sterile? [Science: AT 2, 1a, 1b, 2d; Geography: AT 5, 1a, 1b]
3. Drama Session 3.
4. Invent and write a story about our new giant and its dastardly behaviour. [English: AT 3]
5. Design anti litter posters. [English: AT 3; Art: AT 1, 1c]
6. Drama Session 4.

*Figure 18.1*

(p 24) *Giant* is a perfect example of an abstract idea made comprehensible to young children through story and, most importantly, through the use of personification to humanise the argument. 'In the veins of 3 year olds', she writes, 'the blood still runs warm'. In the blood of 5 and 6 year olds, too. Drama was used in this topic to tap into and channel the flow of that warmth. Below I describe how it opened the topic, an important session which was intended to immerse the children within the narrative, to engage their imaginations and feelings so that the issues in the story might begin to matter to them. I then go on to summarise the form drama took throughout the rest of the six weeks. These lessons did not necessarily occur in the hall in a regular weekly slot; they were taught in the classroom if necessary, as and when the teacher judged the time to be right.

### Session 1

This session took place in the hall. The children had already listened once to the story.

We began by sitting together and looking in detail at the opening illustrations of the book which show (a) the farming activities and (b) the children at play by the stream. We focused our discussion on the human activities we could see illustrated on the page.

As the children had never done drama of this kind before, we made a simple contract. The children all agreed that they could *pretend*; pretend to be *someone* different and *somewhere* different. In this case, they would be children from the village in the story and they agreed to let me join in as the farmer. Finally, using one of Gavin Bolton's strategies, I introduced the chair as a control mechanism; whenever they saw me sit in it, they would know I was being Mr Winston, that we were no longer pretending and that they were to stop what they were doing and come and sit quietly in front of me so that we could discuss what had been happening.

Having established that they were pretending to be visiting the farm illustrated in the book, I opened the drama in role, welcoming the children to my farm, thanking them for agreeing to help me and asking them which jobs they wanted to do. Picking fruit, feeding the pigs, collecting the eggs, mending the barn, an array of jobs were shared out and children were soon busily engaged while I toured from group to group, asking questions and offering advice. After several minutes of dramatic play, I called the children together, thanked them for their hard work and split them into pairs so that they could share what they had been doing with their friends.

Still in role as the farmer, I invited them to explore the mountain, so long as they agreed to avoid places of danger. We discussed what these were and they set off in small groups. After a few minutes of this, I called them back together and asked them to sit in a circle. I apologised for interrupting their play but told them I was upset. I then fetched a large bin-bag and emptied it in the centre of the circle; plastic bottles, food cartons and other items of (specially selected) litter fell in a heap on the floor. I informed the children that I had found and collected this rubbish from various parts of the farm while they were playing. Would they help me search for and collect any more? I handed out imaginary binbags, pointed out some imaginary rubbish and we discussed which items of rubbish were too dangerous to touch. Soon children were returning with binliners full, telling me what they had found and where they had found it. Still in role, we discussed why people might have dumped it; I was quick to emphasise that I knew none of the children were responsible. Many ideas were shared as to why such dumping was bad and potentially dangerous before I asked them how I might get rid of all this rubbish. One of the children, a boy, suggested that I might phone for a bin lorry and agreed to ask his parents who the bin lorry worked for and where it would take the rubbish. Once again I thanked them for their help.

We ended the session by looking at the pictures again. I asked the children if they could see, in the illustrations, where they had been working and exploring and any of the rubbish they had collected or had decided was too dangerous to collect. The book was left in the reading corner of the classroom and the teacher noticed a number of the children looking carefully at it over the next few days. The boy did ask his parents about the bin lorry and was quick to tell me what he had found out the next time I was in the class; he also told me that he was anxious to have a look at the barn he had helped mend, to check that it hadn't fallen down.

This initial session established two important contexts which the teacher was able to utilise throughout the topic:

- the children identified with the village children, as characterised by Lea and Felix; quite simply, the teacher was able to say *we* instead of *they* whenever she discussed the villagers' relationship with Giant,
- the children saw themselves as *responsible agents*, whose task it was to identify with and protect the interests of Giant.

### Summary of further sessions

These sessions mainly took place in the classroom.

- In Week 2, the teacher explained that the farmer was still having trouble with people dumping their rubbish on the mountain. The children agreed to try and dissuade anyone they saw with rubbish from doing so. She then entered in role with the full binbag and the children were as good as their word.
- In a session in the hall in Week 3, the children, in groups of three, developed and refined mountain shapes. Slowly and silently these mountains had to move from the village to the sea. The teacher asked the children to invest their movements with feelings of sadness and loneliness.
- Again in Week 3, the teacher asked the children how Lea might have tried to persuade Giant to return before the litter mountain had been built. After some discussion, she then took on the role of Giant. Later, the children helped her write down some of the conditions Giant had mentioned. They

then took these to the mayor and his council (played by the teacher and a group of children) and tried to persuade them to agree to them.

- In Week 4 the children redrafted and expanded Giant's conditions into a series of promises which they would adhere to if she returned. These ranged from promising not to rip branches off the trees, to putting signs up directing people to a proper rubbish tip, to remembering to say thank you to her at least once a day. A small group of children took on the role of Giant and grouped around the 3D Giant the class had made. The rest of the class took and memorised a promise each. They grouped in a semi-circle in front of Giant and each spoke their promise in turn. After listening to all the promises, Giant had a brief, private discussion with herself and decided to return.
- In Week 6, the teacher took on the role of Lea in later life, now grown up and a mother herself. Children questioned her on her memories and feelings about the events of the story and about whether the children had kept their promise to look after Giant.

## Conclusion and evaluation

The teacher saw this project as a great success and in this conclusion, I quote her words directly.

> 'The subject of children having responsibility for their own actions and influence over other people's actions really struck a chord with the children. The effect was lasting as children still remember it, almost a year later, as a "brilliant project".'

Particularly interesting are her comments on the long-term effects of the children's learning in the area of values and attitudes:

> 'Having taken on an extremely difficult class, I had found it very difficult to get them working cooperatively in groups and this project marked the turning point. Children who had previously, quite literally, been deliberately tipping out and untidying resources began to develop a sense of pride in putting things away and tidying the classroom efficiently. This sense of responsibility has continued to grow; now children will, quite independently, tidy and put things in their proper place. This attitude would probably have developed over a period of time but *Giant* definitely sped up the process.
>
> The *Giant* project emphasised the fact that children can think for themselves and each other, that they can know what is right, that adults don't always have the answer. This attitude is essential if you want to 'target teach' groups and not be constantly interrupted by questions about needs that can be met by others in the classroom. *Giant* addressed in a very powerful way that they were important and responsible members of our group. Within a

safe and caring theme, they were able to talk about and accept these responsibilities, willingly and without fear.'

## Topic 2: *Jack and the Beanstalk*

This topic was also framed around a story but it had a qualitatively different effect on the work in science, maths and geography; for, although it provided the imaginative stimulus to create the environment of the beanstalk and the study of minibeasts (albeit giant minibeasts!), the values of the story had no influence on the choice or ordering of the content in these areas (Appendix 2). However, like all stories, *Jack and the Beanstalk* does convey certain implicit values, although we might argue about what these values are and what children might be learning from them. Children may well admire Jack's qualities of courage, initiative, charm and determination; they may also see in him a role model who lies, disobeys, steals and kills, all for financial gain. From Zipes' perspective, Jack can be seen as a figure who is winning back his rightful inheritance from an ogre who robbed and killed his father. In this light, Jack's disobedience, deception, thieving and killing are being presented as justifiable due to the poverty he and his mother are having to endure because of the wrongs he has suffered. Bettelheim1, on the other hand, interprets this tale through a Freudian analysis of its symbolism; it is about a struggle to reach maturity, whose meaning is understood by the child at a subconscious level. It therefore becomes redundant to analyse its moral ambiguities in a literal way. What matters is the psychological reassurance it provides to children: 'the reassurance . . . that they can eventually get the better of the giant – ie they can grow up to be like the giant and acquire the same powers' (p 28).

It might be tempting for a teacher either to ignore these theoretical implications as pure bunkum and treat the tale as 'only a story', or to leave the moral maze of this particular fairy story on a high bookshelf and choose the *BFG* as an altogether safer option. Our own responses to these considerations were as follows:

- that the story is a great story and part of every child's cultural entitlement; and that the figures of Jack and the Ogre are, in the words of Jones and Buttrey, 'examples of the archetypal symbol. They live in the mind and their suggestive power increases as experience grows'[5] (p 13),
- that Jack is a very attractive figure for young children but also morally ambiguous for them inasmuch as he is disobedient, deceitful and a thief; and that children ought to have the opportunity to explore and think about these ambiguities,
- that the Ogre in the story is an embodiment of pure evil, and as such his demise is reassuring and empowering for young children; but that there are learning opportunities in portraying him as a violent bully, in allowing children to confront him in his defeat and tell him why they think his behaviour is unacceptable.

# Topic 2: *Jack and the Beanstalk* – the use of story and drama

The topic web (Figure 18.2) shows how the work in English and PSME was very closely connected with the children's experience and understanding of the story. The principal intentions were:

- to expose the children to different versions of the story so that they could recognise and talk about their similarities and differences and their own personal preferences,
- to include a long, episodic telling (as opposed to reading) of the story as part of this exposure,
- to use drama to give the children ownership of the story and to encourage exploration of the moral issues embodied in the characters of Jack and the Ogre,

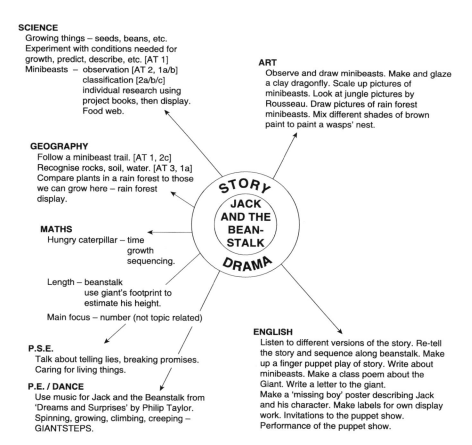

**SCIENCE**
Growing things – seeds, beans, etc. Experiment with conditions needed for growth, predict, describe, etc. [AT 1]
Minibeasts – observation [AT 2, 1a/b]
classification [2a/b/c]
individual research using project books, then display.
Food web.

**ART**
Observe and draw minibeasts. Make and glaze a clay dragonfly. Scale up pictures of minibeasts. Look at jungle pictures by Rousseau. Draw pictures of rain forest minibeasts. Mix different shades of brown paint to paint a wasps' nest.

**GEOGRAPHY**
Follow a minibeast trail. [AT 1, 2c]
Recognise rocks, soil, water. [AT 3, 1a]
Compare plants in a rain forest to those we can grow here – rain forest display.

**MATHS**
Hungry caterpillar – time
growth
sequencing.

Length – beanstalk
use giant's footprint to estimate his height.

Main focus – number (not topic related)

STORY
JACK AND THE BEAN-STALK
DRAMA

**P.S.E.**
Talk about telling lies, breaking promises. Caring for living things.

**P.E. / DANCE**
Use music for Jack and the Beanstalk from 'Dreams and Surprises' by Philip Taylor. Spinning, growing, climbing, creeping – GIANTSTEPS.

**ENGLISH**
Listen to different versions of the story. Re-tell the story and sequence along beanstalk. Make up a finger puppet play of story. Write about minibeasts. Make a class poem about the Giant. Write a letter to the giant.
Make a 'missing boy' poster describing Jack and his character. Make labels for own display work. Invitations to the puppet show. Performance of the puppet show.

*Figure 18.2*

- to use all these experiences to encourage children to write their own versions of the story,
- to create a finger-puppet theatre in the home corner to encourage children to perform these versions.

Kevin Crossley-Holland's book was used as the inspiration and reference point for the teacher's oral telling of the tale. She completed one episode with Jack climbing the beanstalk for the third time. For the subsequent episodes, drama took over.

The *dramatic convention* I used for this work was a combination of drama and story-telling. This has become an increasingly popular theatrical convention over recent years and I found it to be a simple, clear and highly successful technique for creating classroom drama. Quite simply, it allows for narration to be combined with the portrayal of character. At the beginning of each session I introduced children to the very basic costume I would be using to denote the various characters we might meet; a black shawl and walking stick for the old woman at the top of the beanstalk, for example; a blue shawl for the giant's wife; a baseball cap for one of Jack's friends. They understood that whenever I wore one of these I would become that character. If I removed the costume, I could narrate in the third person, thus being able to move the story on as and when I judged it appropriate. So, for example, after the children had been talking to the old lady at the top of the beanstalk, I could remove the black shawl and say, 'The children thanked the old lady and made their way to the ogre's castle'. With that, we could set off on a walk around the classroom, 'Until they reached it and stopped in front of the enormous door'; whereupon we would stop, I would put on the cap which meant I was now Jack's friend and ask, 'Does anyone feel brave enough to knock on the door?' and the drama would continue.

For the children to find entrance into this story drama, I decided to use a strategy described by Booth and Haine[3]:

> 'the teacher can add characters not found in the story and expand minor characters so that they become central to the implications of the action of the story. (By character addition and expansion, the teacher can change the outcome of the story and the story drama.)
>
> (p 44)

Given our desire for the children to explore the story from within, to question and perhaps advise Jack and also to defeat the Ogre themselves, this seemed an ideal strategy. Consequently, I cast the children as friends of Jack from his village and began the drama by narrating the discovery by Jack's mother that he had gone missing for the third time. Taking on the role of the mother I asked the children if any of them knew where he might be. When some of them suggested he might have gone up the beanstalk I replied that I didn't believe that as he had promised me faithfully he would never climb it again. But Jack was a boy who broke his promises, they told me; one little girl said that he had promised to buy her an ice-cream and never did. They all agreed that breaking promises, especially to one's mother, was wrong and they volunteered to go up the beanstalk and bring him back home. Before they did this, I made them promise not to let him steal any more money from the ogre; it was too dangerous and, besides, we didn't need any more money. This they all did in unison, up the beanstalk they went and their adventure began.

The drama lasted for three 50-minute sessions spread over a fortnight. Below I give a summary of its progress.

### Session 1

The children met the old woman at the top of the beanstalk who informed them that the ogre beat his wife every time Jack stole something from him. The children made a second promise not to steal any money if she told them the way to the ogre's castle. Once there, the wife opened and peered through a crack in the door. I played her as a timid, frightened woman and told them Jack had been there but that I had chased him because I was frightened of what the ogre would do to me if he managed to steal anything else. I then mimed shutting the door in their faces. The children, however, spotted an open window, decided that Jack had climbed through it and quietly did the same, making their way along the castle's corridors and into the ogre's kitchen.

### Session 2

The children explored the kitchen, looking for places to hide should the ogre come. While they were doing this, I took on the character of Jack for the first time and narrated my appearance out of the spout of a giant kettle. The children had talked in detail since the previous drama session deciding what sort of a boy Jack was; he was naughty and a bit of a rogue but definitely a lot of fun, so this was how I played him. A long discussion ensued. The children began by trying to persuade Jack to leave straightaway; but soon some of them were saying that maybe he should steal the money as it was probably his father's. 'But mightn't some of it belong to the ogre's wife?' asked one little girl. I wouldn't be dissuaded, however, and interrupted the discussion, changing character and announcing the arrival of the ogre. Everyone hid and remained silent while I shouted and stamped and ate and counted my money. When the ogre finally fell asleep, I stopped the drama and asked a little girl to take on the role of Jack. We set up a version of the game 'Keeper of the Keys' to see if Jack would take the money or not. He did. Talking out of role, the girl was quite clear in her own mind that Jack shouldn't have taken the money; but she was equally convinced that he would have done.

### Session 3

I organised a game similar to 'Control Tower' (see Brandes[6], p 39) to see if the children could manage to creep out of the kitchen without waking the ogre. This they did, only to meet his wife in the corridor. My shriek of surprise and dismay

awoke the ogre and I told them all to hide while I persuaded him to let me make
him some hot chocolate so he could get back to sleep. My intervention worked,
keeping the children from being discovered and, very possibly, eaten. I narrated
us out of the castle where I took on the role of Jack's friend, asking the children
if we shouldn't do something to help the ogre's wife, seeing as she had helped us.
They agreed and we talked of how we might do this. One little girl eventually
suggested that we should tie up the ogre while he slept and then make him
promise to change his ways. This we staged through another game, a version of
'grandmother's footsteps'. I chose four children who had to attempt to sneak up
on the ogre from behind and touch him all at once. If I turned round suddenly
and saw them move, they would fail; if they were successful, then the ogre would
be tied up. They succeeded in their first attempt and I screamed and yelled and
struggled in vain to their great amusement and satisfaction. The children then
began telling the ogre that he was horrible and why he was horrible. One girl said
he should try to imagine what it must feel like to be his wife. Another asked him
why he couldn't change his ways and become a friendly giant? The lesson ended
with the ogre still tied to the chair and the children were asked to think up
possible endings to their version of the story.

## Evaluating the contribution of the drama

1.  There was no doubting the effect of the theatrical elements and the children's
    dramatic involvement in bringing the story alive. In Figure 18.3 I include a
    sample of work written by Cara, who, until this point, had been a very reluc-
    tant writer. The sample is a small extract from 20 pages of story which, as the
    extract shows, gets much of its substance and imaginative power from the
    drama she lived through. When I spoke to her about this work, she told me
    proudly how she had spent most of a weekend writing it and how it had taken
    her sister a whole hour to read it! Gordon Wells[7] has written about the
    importance of children *owning* the stories they write:

    > 'Ownership is vital if the child is to make a real commitment of time and
    > effort to the task of learning the craft of writing.'
    >
    > (p 202)

    By energising the imagination, by creatively embedding the thinking of
    children within the story, drama can provide such ownership.
2.  The drama enabled the children to engage in moral discussions with the main
    characters in the story; with Jack they spoke about disobedience, stealing and
    selfishness; with the ogre about bullying and violence. As with *Giant*, such
    discussions could continue within this imaginative context outside the drama.
    For example, after the first drama session, the teacher wanted the children to
    consider the character of Jack, his good points and his bad points. She began
    by asking them why they had agreed to go and look for him; 'because he's
    our friend' was the general response. 'Why is Jack your friend?' she enquired
    and they provided her with a long list of his qualities: he plays good games,

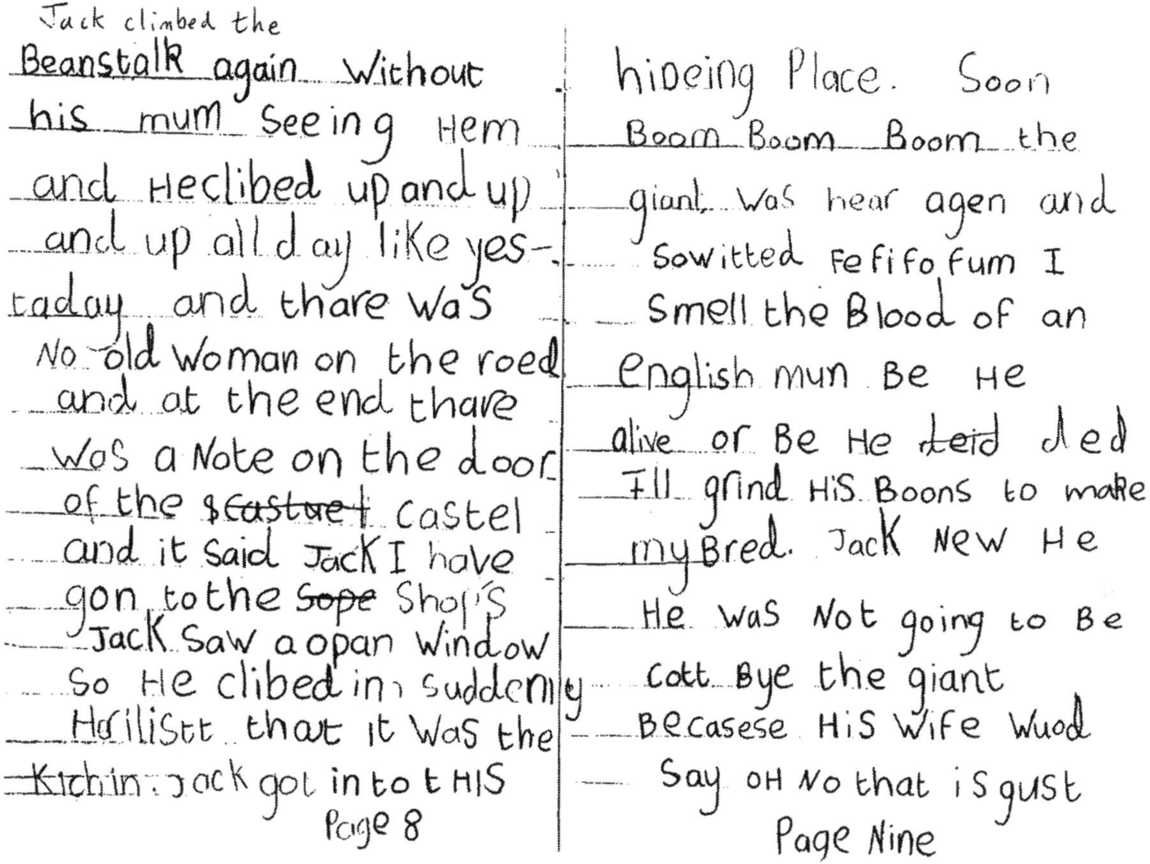

Jack climbed the
Beanstalk again Without
his mum seeing Hem
and Heclibed up and up
and up all day like yes-
taday and thare waS
No old woman on the road
and at the end thare
was a Note on the door
of the castet castel
and it said Jack I have
gon to the sope shop's
Jack Saw a opan window
So He clibed in suddenly
Halliset that it was the
Kitchin Jack got in to tHis
Page 8

hideing Place. Soon
Boom Boom Boom the
giant was hear agen and
Sowitted Fefifo fum I
Smell the Blood of an
english mun Be He
alive or Be He ded ded
I'll gfind HiS Boons to make
my Bred. Jack New He
He was Not going to Be
Catt Bye the giant
Becasese HiS wife wud
Say oH No that iS gust
Page Nine

*Figure 18.3*

he's friendly, he's brave, he looks after you when you've fallen over, he's rich, he's strong. Some of these ideas came from the drama but all were consistent with the Jack of the story. Similarly, when asked if there were any things about Jack that were not so good, the children could be highly specific; he breaks promises to his mummy; he didn't buy me an ice-cream; he doesn't always tell his mummy where he's going; he told lies to the ogre's wife; he takes back things that don't belong to him, like the golden hen.

3. The children's puppet performance showed great knowledge of and attention to the details of the story, many of which were borrowed from the drama we created. Their direct exposure to someone playing the people from the story influenced their own characterisation, the way the different characters spoke and, most importantly, the vocabulary they used. All of the groups used the same mix of story-telling and theatre that I had used with them.

## Conclusion

In their report *Primary Schools: Some Aspects of Good Practice,*[8] HMI devoted a whole section to drama and emphasised the 'highly motivating practical and imaginative experiences' it could provide for children. Just six years later, in the light of the government's revisions of the National Curriculum English regulations, it is astonishing to consider that Drama has practically no statutory place whatsoever in the primary school curriculum. In the face of this, the recent publication from NATE, *Move Back the Desks,*[9] is a welcome reminder of the power and place of drama in children's learning. The lessons described in the publication stretch over Key Stages 2 and 3; I trust that the accounts of how drama was used in these two topics will help remind or persuade some teachers that it still has an important place in Key Stage 1.

## Sources

Snape, J. and C. (1989) *Giant.* Walker Books: London.
Crossley-Holland, K. (1987) *British Folk Tales.* Orchard: London.

## References

1 Bettelheim, B. (1976) *The Uses of Enchantment.* Penguin. 27.
2 Zipes, J. (1979) *Breaking the Magic Spell.* Heinemann.
3 Booth, D. and Haine, G. (1982) 'Story Drama', *2D*, 1, 2.
4 Donaldson, M. (1978) *Children's Minds.* Fontana.
5 Jones, A. and Buttrey, J. (1970) *Children and Stories.* Basil Blackwell.
6 Brandes, D. and Phillips, H. (1977) *Gamesters' Handbook.* Hutchinson.
7 Wells, G. (1986) *The Meaning Makers.* Hodder and Stoughton.
8 HMI (1987) *Primary Schools: Some Aspects of Good Practice.* HMSO.
9 NATE (1993) *Move Back the Desks: Using Drama to Develop English and Cross-curricular Themes.*

# 19 Growing towards citizenship

## Humanities in the revised primary national curriculum

*Alan Blyth*

It appears that drastic action is now thought necessary, at least for two years, in order to drive up standards in the EMITS subjects (English, mathematics, information technology and science) in the primary curriculum. As for the rest, despite official assurances that schools will need to 'have regard' to all of them, they are not to be closely inspected either in general terms or with emphasis on individual Levels, however vague. So in practice there is a danger that there will be cut-throat competition between the minor foundation subjects, at both local and national level, especially – and shamefully – in places where the prior mastery of language and number is least likely.

The purpose of this article is to show that, irrespective of the public support which it may command, Humanities is essential to that other goal of primary education often enunciated by Dr Nicholas Tate, now Chief Executive of QCA, namely *preparation for citizenship*.

The term 'Humanities' is usually taken to comprise history and geography, though it can well extend into the social sciences too, and sometimes into the sphere of religious education in its contemporary forms. It has largely replaced the older social studies, which was often thought to exclude those two more established subjects, and environmental studies, which (as still in Scotland) includes the natural sciences. In the 1970s a Schools Council Project *Place, Time and Society 8–13* (Blyth et al, 1976) had considered the relation between the Humanities subjects, and some published series of pupil materials have continued to exemplify similar approaches. But Humanities, as at present conceived, was first and formatively defined by Campbell and Little (1989), and more recently by Kimber et al (1995), in symposia which show the contributions of individual subjects or aspects of subjects rather than Humanities as a totality. Almost inevitably, the treatment of primary Humanities in the National Curriculum has been similar, with links within and beyond Humanities usually confined to spasmodic suggestions. Subsequently (eg Blyth, 1990; 1994), I attempted to go a little further in suggesting how the *perspectives* developed by different academic disciplines can be brought together within the broad framework of Humanities. That is the framework on which the present discussion will be based.

## The present situation

Much of the structure of the revised, 1995, curriculum assumes that the emphasis in Humanities should be on what children should know, rather than on how children learn. On that assumption, the 1995 programmes are reasonable and have been relatively well received. In geography, the expansion of experience from the home locality to contrasted localities and then to distant places, combined with an increasing grasp of geographical skills and themes, presents most children with a sequence which they are able to follow from Level to Level with some success. In history, the process features incorporated in the key elements certainly represent some recognition of cognitive growth across levels, as does the programme of study for Key Stage 1. But the chopping up of the programme at Key Stage 2 into a somewhat arbitrary set of units largely drawn from British history and open to any order of presentation, is not so obviously attuned to children's learning. This programme could give the impression that these content areas comprise the information which adults consider most appropriate for children aged 7 to 11: even perhaps that they were assigned to Key Stage 2 after the programmes for Key Stages 3 and 4 had been decided. To substitute for the present programmes an alternative fully based on how children learn, and suited to the essential contribution of Humanities to education for citizenship, it is necessary to consider not only the content of Humanities, which figures so prominently in the present dispensation, but also the approach in the classroom, which does not.

## Content

For Key Stage 1, any changes in content would do well to build on what is at present prescribed. Indeed, the case for this content could be strengthened by recognising that it is not merely accessible to young children long before compulsory school age, but also necessary to the development of their personal identities.

To a large extent, Humanities begins, like charity, at home. In Europe there is indeed a tradition of *Heimatskunde* or study of the children's immediate habitat and its geography, history, and also botany and social organisation and much else. There is some evidence that exploration of this very local environment, long before Year 1, is one of the ways in which the capacity to stimulate multiple intelligences and to learn is itself fostered. If, as often happens, children move, or rather are moved, from one habitat to another at a very early age, the learning of their new surroundings itself becomes one important way of adapting and thus preserving their identity. If that does not take place effectively, this can in one sense deprive them of a stake in society. It would be an exaggeration to say that this is direct education for citizenship, but it is the essential seedbed in which such education can be cultivated; a first step towards that basic curricular equation whereby children study their society and learn its expectations, while society studies its children and learns their needs.

Key Stage 1 geography lays much (though not exclusive) stress on the local physical and built environment and on mapping and wayfinding within it. Key

Stage 1 history is also substantially concerned with what is immediate in children's experience: their homes, their surroundings, their families, the cultural traditions prevalent in their community and those which they may have brought with them from elsewhere. Even in a highly mobile world, there are some children who can find their families' tombstones in a nearby graveyard: for others, their nearest relatives may be a day's journey away, or even in another continent. In any particular school there can be a need for sensitivity in looking at all the children's habitats at Key Stage 1, but still it is important to attempt that, in addition to which there is a time-saving element where the Humanities are studied as a whole and in relation to language development.

Meanwhile some attention is, and should be, paid to the excitement of other cultures distant in place and time, since the curriculum for these younger children needs to avoid the stigma of parochialism which might otherwise adhere to their *Heimatskunde*. So, at Key Stage 1 there should be flexible content, much of it local, but including exciting, significant, comprehensible and genuine examples of people in other cultures, such as Amundsen's polar journeys, alongside other tested and avowedly imaginary stories and what might rather pompously be called an introduction to the skills of social understanding.

It is this pattern which needs to be extended more widely and systematically into Key Stage 2, and especially into Years 5 and 6: Key Stage 2b as it might be called. For it now becomes possible for children to begin to sort out their expanding experience by looking at it from the different perspectives of history, geography, and also elementary economics and what might be regarded as sociography rather than sociology. Carefully-chosen examples of people in places, past and present, can now be introduced in order to widen horizons. In this new curriculum with its cutbacks in time, each would need to take a sufficient block of time to make possible some demanding study, even if it had to be followed by a gap before Humanities again qualified for its ration. The present historical prescriptions for Ancient Greece and non-European civilisations, together with examples of distant places in geography for which the Geographical Association and some aid agencies have provided well-devised materials, could be adapted as examples where Humanities can be combined. So, valuably, could European and American places familiar to teachers and children from holiday experiences, with maybe a sampling of a foreign language in use. And it is here that the Internet, where available, can so immensely enrich the available repertoire, extending even (though at present in a very few cases) to interactive conferencing with adults and schools across the world.

Among these examples the home country must however have a definite place, as part of the wider environment in which children live. This is not to be jingoistic or even ethnocentric. Education must be candid and comprehensive about human affairs, but it cannot claim the right to edit the past or to sanitise the present, or to create either in its own image. In any case, were that to be tried in any context other than a total prison, some less desirable version of Humanities would percolate through by other means: TV, the Internet, adult conversation. Think of Northern Ireland. However, there is a strong argument for allowing each individual school to choose, for the very few Key Stage 2 examples which time permits, themes or units or topics (pardon the memory) which are particularly suitable to that school. Some teachers may be enthusiastic about rocks and landscapes and orienteering, or philately, or castles, or railways; some about stories of the Civil War, some about the archaeology of the Bronze Age or of the Industrial Revolution. Some may want to involve children with local industry and commerce, as has been successfully done in recent years, or to involve them in mock decision-making about planning and the environment in their own locality.

But there is another, vital, consideration. The choice cannot be made only because of a teacher's prior enthusiasms, or those of the children. To do that would be to revert to the worst of the pre-1988 primary curriculum. There must also be some 'breadth and balance' in teachers' choices: not only between what have come to be called 'subject-led units' but also between principles resembling the 'themes and dimensions' of the original National Curriculum. It is important, for example, to balance us with them, near with far, now with then, the familiar with the unfamiliar, and also to involve gender, multi-cultural, environmental and legal concerns which raise matters of conflict which go beyond the bounds of Humanities and confront teachers and children alike with uncomfortable realities, which they will meet in any case simply by dint of living where they do. So any one unit has to be of a multi-purpose nature. If devising such units seems to lay too great a burden of responsibility on individual teachers and raises the spectre of triviality, then there could be a nationally-approved databank from which to choose, somewhat as in Scotland.

Increasingly, these few examples could be set in the necessary frameworks of centuries and periods, continents and oceans, so that children become able to understand globes and maps and time lines and gradually to build up a world picture which would become clothed with more substance at Key Stage 3 and later. Meanwhile they – or at least some of them – should, as they move through Key Stage 2 into 3, come to know for themselves, and see the purpose of knowing, more general concepts such as Tudors, France, Europe and, more systematically, nation, the economy, justice, democracy and (for there is such a thing) society; and, of course, citizenship itself. For all these require the kind of 'systems thinking' of which most younger children are not yet capable. But it is on the fostering of this kind of understanding that the emphasis at Key Stage 2 must be placed. To try any more complete coverage would be to leave most children floundering in a sea of partial knowledge in which they would hope to swim by parroting a few half-understood notions which they think the teacher would like them to be able to reproduce.

## Approach

As one official document indicates (NCC, 1990), preparation for a common democratic citizenship requires not only the learning of concepts and skills necessary to understand society, but also the practice of democracy itself. This in turn involves a major value-question: in what ways are children regarded and treated as persons?

It is evident that in this respect the experiences of individual children, and teachers, in a school will vary greatly. The relative security of some children's homes, by no means correlated with affluence, will contrast with the relative insecurity of others. And the richness of experience of some will differ from the poverty of experience of others. Attention nowadays is often focused on these differing 'baselines' in an attempt to define value-added in measures of attainment in the EMITS subjects. It is equally, if not more, important to take account of the impact of such differences on the schools' socialising processes themselves. For one essential aspect of democratic citizenship, and of the evolution of a common culture in our society, must be the capacity to understand and tolerate such differences. This in turn requires deciding how to learn from one another's experiences and to face up to the need for fairness and some kind of equalisation of esteem and opportunity within a school class and community. By Year 6 some limited practice of democratic citizenship is already possible, and perhaps essential. To some extent this practice is bound up with ability, with status linked with attainment in the EMITS subjects, and even more so with other kinds of status, of which boys' football is probably the dominant one.

Here the teacher can and should exemplify what democratic citizenship is about. The management of this kind of socialisation presents a great challenge, which in any one situation is more subtle than can be suggested by sociological generalisations or management principles, still less by an umbrella term such as 'interactive teaching'. In a school serving a fairly homogeneous community which shares the school's basic values, it is probably easier than in one which does not, or – more difficult – when one part of the community does and another does not. Yet if a teacher is herself or himself a principled person, firm enough to establish with the children a set of agreed rules about how discussion should be conducted, and able to value every contribution while knowing how to handle the silly or disruptive comment, that provides a starting-point. Next, children will begin to learn by really listening to what the others are saying; to feel confident in sharing their experiences with each other and with the teacher; and to learn how to present and defend a point of view, rather than playing safe by repeating what they think the teacher wants them to say. For then they will know that their point of view will be weighed for its value rather than being ridiculed because of who expressed it. In this way they gradually come to exercise *critical thinking skills*, certainly across the curriculum, but especially in Humanities. An approach of this kind, combined with the re-structuring of content previously outlined, indicates the kind of primary Humanities which can best contribute to developing democratic citizenship.

This is only one part of the necessary approach to democratic citizenship. The other is to foster those critical thinking skills necessary to prevent domination of opinion by any influence: government, media, community leaders, neighbours, other children, multinational corporations or whatever – including teachers. The sort of discussion just referred to is a valuable context in which this kind of questioning can be developed. It requires the teacher to lead, not by imposing views (though it should eventually become evident that he or she does hold firm views) but by raising stimulating questions. These must steer between platitude and abstruseness. The simplest ones are: who? where? when? how? why?: more searching questions can follow. The very accessibility of so many sources of information today makes it all the more important to use them critically: who compiled this CD-ROM, and why? What sort of information do we want to download from the Internet, and why? What should we ask of our partners in conferencing, and why? Why did they give those particular answers? Such questions need to be blended into discussions: not only in Humanities, but especially there.

Of course, there is a danger that such questions may widen divisions within a class. They could also encourage wild speculation, or experiments in challenging adults for the sake of challenging. But that is a risk which must be taken, as part of the process of leading towards responsible democratic citizenship.

This issue draws attention to a third and still more important 'approach' question to which I have already alluded. As Dr Tate often emphasises, democratic citizenship also involves more than procedural tolerance; holding the ring. In any class, children will exemplify a range of values, sometimes conflicting, some more firmly held than others. The question is: how far should a teacher feel under obligation to weld some of these into a common culture giving a sense of identity to the class, the school, the community, the region or the nation? Or should they foster a series of subcultures with overlapping values? My own belief, reminiscent of J. S. Mill, but from a liberal Christian standpoint, is that teachers as a profession should represent a value-system neither confined to, nor entirely rejecting, what is perceived as their democratic heritage, with toleration as a central feature; toleration which is more than procedural but also personally felt. Within this professional orbit, individual teachers should be free to deviate, partly in accordance with their own beliefs, and partly because of what they consider to be the needs of their particular class; but not in such a way as to influence them unduly because that would violate the fundamental requirement of toleration. But, here again, no teachers will be in a position to work out their own value-position fully without some understanding of Humanities.

## Prospect

It may appear at first sight that these suggestions for content and approach, combined as they would need to be with suitable provision for progression, differentiation and assessment, make laughably great demands on teachers. That objection is not a trivial one, especially now when the emphasis is on *reducing* the input teachers are to make in primary Humanities and the proportionate reduction of provision for Humanities that will ensue, where it has not already taken place, in initial teacher education and in INSET. However, a closer examination of the demands on *content* will show that much *less* would be expected, and moreover that what is expected would draw much more on teachers' own enthusiasms than on the requirements of an externally-imposed programme. At the same time, teachers would be following guidelines (again rather as in Scotland) which would prevent them from overlooking the essential purposes of primary Humanities.

This range of available information could be supplemented in another way, for there are 'units' such as the ones based on local industries, for which the detailed knowledge would come more effectively from other adults than from teachers. Much the same applies to older people talking about family history, or travellers giving lively detail about distant places: judicious incorporation of adults other than teachers into the primary classroom is itself a form of democratic citizenship, because it counters the impression of a teacher as a unique source of knowledge. In addition, the recent explosion of IT makes detailed *information* much more accessible than ever before. What remains necessary is that *teachers* should have acquired and mastered the framework of understanding towards which children are being guided. For example, they do need to know in outline when and why the Romans came to Britain; why the Rhine is important; what is meant by cost/benefit analysis; and other such relevant broad-brush elements in Humanities. This framework, though largely built up during secondary and higher education, does require to be systematised during teacher education. In addition, teachers would need to know about how they themselves can question what they find and experience; how children learn; and why certain kinds of content and approach make for democratic citizenship. This should be part of basic professional equipment, and should not be so difficult as the acquisition of knowledge of the minutiae prescribed as content by a committee of others.

Even so, it is obviously unrealistic to suggest that any beginner teacher would be able to embark fully on such a programme of Humanities. Realistically, they would need first to establish their own competence and confidence and credentials as EMITS teachers. Then they would be able to develop expertise also in the Humanities area, and to advise colleagues about policy. They could also, usefully, work with RE which is concerned with many of the same issues, notably those related to values and cultures, even if RE is not always seen as itself part of Humanities. Indeed, RE coordinators are often administratively linked with Humanities and, with their statutory position guaranteed, could be useful allies in the current battle for survival. For although the EMITS subjects, especially English and IT, with their obvious links with Humanities, might appear to offer a safer haven in the current storms, they might mount a takeover bid for the whole Humanities area, using historical and geographical material for their own purposes without reference to the purposes of the Humanities perspectives themselves.

The appeal of the approach suggested here is that those teachers who do develop this kind of expertise would be working with the grain of children's learning and of their own enthusiasms. It may not be easy for a management expert, or an accountant, to appreciate that satisfaction of that kind matters. But I believe that a teacher would know better what I mean.

It might still be contended that the advantages claimed here for including this kind of content and approach to Humanities can be equally well met by other elements in the primary curriculum. Alternatively, that claim might be admitted, but its validity in *primary* education questioned on the grounds that older children can understand these things better, after they have been well grounded in the 'basics'. Reasoning of that kind flies in the face both of what children experience, and of how they learn. They do not stack up information acquired in isolated blocks, like winter fuel, during primary education, ready for use later. Nor do they wait for a signal from the National Curriculum before taking note of their social world. No doubt much more thought and attention need to be devoted to the issues that have been raised in this article (see, for example, the contributions to Ahier and Ross (1995)). But I hope I have shown that if anybody asks whether the content of primary Humanities, and a sensitive approach to it, are necessary to children's growth towards democratic citizenship, the answer has to be Yes.

## Note

This article is developed from a memorandum submitted to the Qualifications and Curriculum Authority in November 1997.

## Acknowledgement

I am grateful to Joan Blyth for her comments on the draft of this article.

## References

Ahier, J. and Ross, A. (eds) (1995) *The Social Subjects within the Curriculum: Children's Social Learning in the National Curriculum*. Falmer Press: London.

Blyth, A. et al (1976) *Place, Time and Society, 8-13: Curriculum Development in History, Geography and Social Science*. Collins/ESL Bristol, for the Schools Council: London and Bristol.

Blyth, A. (1990) *Making the Grade for Primary Humanities*. Open University Press: Buckingham.

Blyth, A. (1994) 'History and geography in the primary curriculum', in Jill Bourne, *Thinking Through Primary Practice*. Routledge, for the Open University: London.

Campbell, J. and Little, V. (1989) (Eds) *Humanities in the Primary School*. Falmer Press: London.

Kimber, D. et al (1995) *Humanities in Primary Education*. David Fulton: London.

National Curriculum Council (1990) *Education for Citizenship, Curriculum Guidance 8*. NCC: York.

# 20 Picking a path through the phonics minefield

*Henrietta Dombey*

## Introduction: Why the fuss?

Learning to read means learning to get sense from the marks on the page. With an alphabetic writing system such as ours, it is tempting to equate the whole process with phonics learning: learning to match the written letters on the page to the spoken sounds they represent. So, when public anxiety about children's reading scores reaches a panic level – an increasingly frequent occurrence as we move to ever greater dependence on the written word – any 'expert' purveying a simple phonic nostrum is likely to get a good hearing. In 1955 Rudolph Flesch took the US by storm with *Why Johnny Can't Read and What You Can Do About It*, which stayed in the best seller lists for 30 weeks and was serialised in countless newspapers (Flesch, 1955). Last year Diane McGuinness published *Why Children Can't Read and What We Can Do About It*, which hit a similar spot and led to a host of articles in newspapers and appearances on radio talk shows on both sides of the Atlantic (McGuinness, 1998). We also have our own Ruth Miskin, whose insistence on a simple phonic approach has led her to refuse to commit her school to the National Literacy Strategy. All purvey a straightforward 'commonsense' approach (although McGuinness dresses this up with some rather tendentious linguistics). This starts from the premise that learning to read is a matter of learning to match individual phonemes (speech sounds) to individual graphemes (letters or letter combinations such as 'th' or 'ea').

There are three problems with this approach. The first is that the spelling system of English – English orthography – is more complex than this commonsense conception recognises; the second is that what appears to be simple and straightforward to proficient readers of English can seem very different to young children operating on a different logic; the third is that there is much more to learning to read than learning phonics. I will look at these problems in turn. After that I will set out an approach supported by much recent research that is gaining increasing support in primary classrooms: whole to part phonics. Then I will examine how phonics is treated in the Literacy Hour materials.

## English orthography

The spelling system of English is often thought of as chaotic: it is certainly complex. This is in part because we have a long history of literacy in this country, involving more changes in how words are pronounced than changes in spelling. We have also been voracious in our appetite for new words from other languages, incorporating new spelling patterns with these new words. And sometimes our erroneous ideas about the origins of particular words have led to strange spellings. So the spelling system of English is much less regular than those of languages with a shorter history of literacy and less contact with other languages.

But even if we were starting our spelling system from scratch, we would have problems. English has probably the widest range of pronunciation of all current languages using an alphabetic writing system, and so cannot be represented by one phonically regular set of spellings. The Englishes of Australia, Canada, India, the Caribbean, Scotland, England and the United States all sound too different to make that possible. And within each of these there are accent differences following geographical and social patterns. In the UK, words such as 'world' or 'tunnel' are pronounced in very different ways in different parts of the country. Words which are *homophones* (pairs of words pronounced in the same way) in one accent may differ significantly in another. Try 'court' and 'caught' in Glasgow, 'moan' and 'mown' in East Anglia, or 'world' and 'weld' in any accent outside London. To make English spelling an accurate representation of the spoken language, we would have to make it variable, with different spelling patterns for Glasgow, Norwich and London, to say nothing of the Bronx and Brisbane.

Even if we were to make the politically dangerous decision to confine our new regular spelling to the Received Pronunciation of England, our troubles would not be over, since English is inherently more problematic than many other languages, because of the complexity of its sound system. This poses real challenges for the Roman alphabet.

Spoken English has 40 to 44 phonemes, the exact number depending on your accent. Words made up of these phonemes are represented by the 26 letters of the extended Roman alphabet. (Other languages using the Roman alphabet tend to do without 'y', 'w' and 'x'.) So, without substantial further extension of this alphabet, we cannot have a system in which one letter stands for one phoneme. Some of the problems relate to the consonants: for example the letters 'c' and 'g' represent two different phonemes each, as shown in words such as 'cage' and 'grace'. But the problem of our vowels is greater.

English is a vowel-rich language. As against the straightforward five vowels of Spanish, each one of which is represented by a separate letter, in all British accents of English we have some 12 single phoneme vowels, supplemented by some eight diphthongs, or vowel combinations, as in the 'ow' sound of 'now'. The 'y' and the 'w' of our alphabet help by pairing up with vowel letters to represent a number of these diphthongs, as in 'say' and 'low,' but that still leaves too few letters standing for too many vowel sounds. And the vowel sounds themselves are far from stable. And then there is the 'schwa'. There is no English term for this very English phoneme which occurs in the unstressed syllables of very many words in most accents of English.

In most British accents, you can hear it in the first syllable of 'delay' and the last syllable of 'London'. It's also in the middle syllable of 'terrible', the first syllable of 'parental', the last syllable of 'station', the first syllable of 'unload'. These six different spellings of this one vowel sound do not exhaust all the possibilities. Over the centuries since the spelling of these words was fixed, a pronunciation change has been at work here. These unstressed vowels have merged, surrendering their distinct phonemic identities, while holding onto their distinct spellings. In addition, some one-syllable words such as 'the' and 'to' use the schwa sound when they are unstressed, but on the rare occasions when they are stressed, revert to their original vowel identities. Try saying 'We're going to St Ives' and then 'We're going *to* St Ives'.

Many other single-syllable words deviate from the phonetic ideal of using one letter to stand for one vowel. We can get some idea of the extent of this complexity when we look at the various vowel sounds represented by the letter 'a' in such common and regular words as 'cat', 'car', 'call' and 'cake'. In these words, whatever your accent, this one vowel letter represents four distinct vowel phonemes. Yet these spellings are not unusual, irregular, or difficult for those experienced in making sense of written English. We know how to pronounce the 'a' by looking at the letters that follow it. Words ending in 'ar', like 'far' and 'tar' all have the same sound value for the letter 'a': they all rhyme. The same is true for words ending in 'at' and 'ake', and for nearly all words ending in 'all'. This is not unusual. Many English spelling patterns are dependent on *groups* of letters standing for *groups* of phonemes. As they do in the words examined above, these groups frequently take the form of the back part of a syllable – omitting only the initial consonant sounds, and thus consisting of the vowel sounds at the heart of the syllable and the consonant sounds that follow. The spelling of such straightforward words as 'cure' and 'prance', which pose problems for rule systems based on single grapheme to single phoneme correspondences, can be seen as regular when the back part of the syllable is treated as one unit in this way. The importance of this grouping in English orthography has been recognised by a number of linguists from the 1960s on. See for example, Hockett (1967) and Halle and Vergnaud (1980).

In recent studies of early reading, this unit just below the level of the syllable has been termed the 'rime' (Goswami and Bryant, 1990). The initial part of the syllable, formed of one or more consonants, is termed the 'onset', so 'prod', 'pram' and 'prance' share an onset, while 'prance', 'dance' and 'chance' share a rime.

When orthography is seen as operating at the level of onset and rime, rather than the individual phoneme, accent variation also poses fewer problems since, in any given accent, words such as 'grass' and 'class' sharing a rime in their spelling, tend to also rhyme in their pronunciation.

# A simple way in for young children?

Treating phonics as a set of one-to-one relationships will not help children to recognise words as common as 'he, 'they' or 'is'. Even with such apparently straightforward words as 'but', 'ran' or 'top', it does not seem the best way into word recognition. A traditional phonic approach implies that young children can mentally break up the words they hear into their constituent phonemes, and assemble the words they read from sequences of phonemes. But phonological awareness – awareness of speech as a sequence of sounds – does not come naturally to children. In languages represented by a non-alphabetic writing system, such as Chinese, even literate adults find it difficult, if not impossible, to identify the phonemes making up a simple word. Non-literate people and young children tend to be unaware even that language is made up of words: they are much more concerned with what utterances mean than with how they sound (Morais et al, 1979). Even where word play is encouraged, learning to think of utterances as composed of word units, and of words as composed of sound units, takes young children a long time (Ehri 1975). Those who have played 'I spy' with 4 year olds are aware of their bizarre misconceptions about 'beginning sounds'. The final and medial phonemes of simple cvc words are much harder for young children to identify.

Indeed, far from being a route into reading, phonics appears to be largely learnt *through* reading. Peter Bryant (1993), one of the foremost researchers into children's development of phonic knowledge, writes that 'children begin to break words up into constituent phonemes as a result of learning to read' (Bryan, 1993, p 93). He cites a large body of experimental evidence on pre-literate children's explicit judgements about phonemes, showing that 'by and large they are quite incapable of making distinctions which are transparently clear to any literate adult' (Bryant, 1993 p 85). This is a recurrent theme in research studies on this topic, and a far cry from the view of traditional phonics that learning to read all starts with 'c' 'a' 't'.

It is true that with energy, determination and time, charismatic teachers can teach children the lessons of traditional or synthetic phonics – to recognise individual letters, relate these to phonemes and assemble these phonemes into words. We can see the evidence of this in some of the Literacy Hour videos, where children are translating 'robot talk' – that is words split into their individual phonemes – into recognisable language. We can also see it in the videos of children at Ruth Miskin's school in East London, produced for OFSTED, where squirming nursery school children are shown matching letters to phonemes

But this kind of synthetic phonics does not easily equip children to deal with words with more complex spelling patterns. And, as numerous research findings over the last 20 years have shown, it goes against the grain of children's developing phonological awareness. Other approaches that work with what we know of children's phonological learning, and with the pattern of English orthography, appear to offer a more productive way forward (Goswami, 1999).

## Phonics is not enough

Phonics on its own will not produce fluent reading. Although arguably the most important, phonics is only one among a number of cueing systems – systems which contribute to word identification. The other systems also matter. Cattell's pioneering work at the end of the last century showed that in a given time educated adults recognise a greater number of letters when these are shown in words rather than randomly, and a greater number still when these are shown in connected sentences (Cattell, 1886). Our very perception is directed and made more efficient by our knowledge of language.

This knowledge is partly syntactic: where a word is unclear, the rest of the sentence can nearly always provide a strong indication of the word class involved and the particular form it should take – such as a verb in the present tense with a third-person singular ending. Semantics also has a role to play: the meaning of the larger context and the surrounding text can help to identify the particular word. As a mother, keen to help her daughter to read despite her own literacy problems, said, pointing to the word 'gnome': 'We puzzled it out and knew it had to be "goblin".' It is our knowledge of syntax and semantics that helps us with problem words such as 'lead', 'house' and 'live' that can be pronounced in more than one way and have more than one meaning and grammatical status. More frequently this knowledge helps us to identify words more rapidly than we could manage if they appeared in a random sequence. The positioning of a word on a page – or on the cover of a book, or a sign in the street – can also give important clues. And particularly in texts written for young children, as well as enlarging the meaning of the text in significant ways, pictures can also provide support for word identification, rather as armbands support the novice swimmer.

Becoming a fluent and accurate reader means learning to make effective and efficient use of all these cueing systems – the grapho-phonic, the syntactic, the semantic, the bibliographic and the pictorial. It also means learning to put the information together harmoniously, to 'orchestrate' it, to use the term favoured by Bussis et al in their intensive study of 26 beginner readers in 13 different schools in the US (Bussis et al, 1985). As they found, to read fluently, children need to use their developing construction of sense from the text they are reading, both as an aid to word identification and as a corrective when the process has gone awry. This view is supported by their finding that young readers, when presented with a book at the edge of their reading competence, read the second half with greater fluency and accuracy than they do the first. Phonics plays a crucial part in reading, but on its own is not enough for readers of any age to identify ambiguous words or words with unusual spelling patterns, or the very many irregularly spelled English words.

## Beyond word identification

Learning to read is much more than fluent, accurate word identification. Learning to read means learning to make sense of written texts, to relate them to your own first-hand experience and to other texts you have heard and read, and to mull over and reflect on them. Learning to make sense of written text is a recursive matter. It cannot really be separated into a neat sequence where, say, learning to construct literal meaning precedes evaluation. It is hard to say when the business of learning to construct literal meaning is fully achieved: it develops over many years, as learners encounter increasingly complex texts involving increasingly complex subject matter and language. Nor does it make sense to deny young children the opportunity to engage in the 'higher order skills' of evaluation and criticism. Three and four year olds can and do react to the texts that engage their interest with penetrating questions and acute predictions. 'Why they not helping her?' asks three-year-old Anna of her mother, recoiling self-righteously from the laziness of the Little Red Hen's companions. When the frog's bosom friend, the minnow, lies gasping on the river bank, four-year-old Lee, from a much less bookish home, but with a rich school experience of vividly rendered narratives, observes with practised tentativeness: 'But the frog might push him back.'

These children cannot yet read. Their phonological awareness is as yet relatively underdeveloped. But they are engaged in some important and deeply satisfying meaning making. They are learning that the printed word can deal in important issues such as fairness, friendship, life and death. They are learning the language through which such meanings are realised – explicit language, very different from the largely context-bound language of conversation. And they are also learning that through their active participation they can give stories greater meaning and personal significance.

## Whole to part phonics

Over recent years, contrasting with the synthetic approach of traditional phonics, which proceeds from parts to wholes, another approach to phonics has developed – an analytic approach, based on analysis of known words and the use of analogical reasoning to relate these to unknown words. This approach is based principally on a large body of research into the development of children's phonological awareness, coupled with work on children's capacity to draw analogies. While much important research has been carried out in the UK, principally by Peter Bryant and Usha Goswami, the term 'Whole to Part Phonics' was coined by a researcher in the US, Margaret Moustafa (Moustafa, 1997).

Work by Ehri and Treiman in the US, as well as those cited above, has shown us that children's awareness of language as a sequence of sounds cannot be taken for granted: it follows a developmental pattern (Ehri 1975; Treiman 1985). It can certainly be accelerated by teaching, but this is likely to be more effective if the pattern of development is respected.

As stated above, young children have to learn that language is made up of words. They learn with relative ease that nouns such as 'dog' or 'cat' are words. Verbs are a bit harder. And it is quite some time before young children are confident that 'the' and 'and' are also words (Ferreiro & Teberosky 1979). Repeated experience of written text read aloud can accelerate this learning, when the reader points to each word as she reads it. So experience of whole texts leads to recognition of its parts – individual words – and enables children to match spoken to written words.

Paradoxically, syllables pose fewer problems. There is a physicality about these units that enables young children to clap them out with relative ease. However, the key finding of the last 20 years has been that young children find the units just below the level of the syllable, that is the units of onset and rime, much more accessible than the individual phonemes of which they are composed. They can hear that 'cat' has an 'at' bit in it much more easily than the 't' on the end or the 'a' in the middle (Treiman 1985; Goswami and Bryant 1990). And Goswami's work shows us that they are capable of using this knowledge through a process of analogical reasoning to identify new words on the basis of their similarity with words they already know (Goswami, 1992). Thus knowledge of 'cat' can help them identify 'hat'.

But while it is clearly advisable to draw children's attention to these patterns in spoken words and to the letters that represent them, as Bryant points out, children can begin to learn to read before they have acquired the stock of phonic knowledge necessary for decoding new words. Indeed, children are only in a position to spot onsets and rimes and draw analogies if they already have a repertoire of words which they can recognise with confidence. Thus, just as familiarity with whole texts lays the foundation for matching spoken to written words, so familiarity with a number of whole words lays the foundation for attention to their patterning and the way they are composed.

Frith's work (1985) gives us a very useful conceptual framework for phonics learning and teaching. Motivated by a desire to identify different types of dyslexia, and supported by a number of research studies, Frith sees word recognition as proceeding in three overlapping phases. The first is the *logographic* phase, in which children learn to recognise words as whole entities, making idiosyncratic use of features such as size and colour in the early stages, then moving on to overall shape and the presence of particular letters. At the beginning of this phase, which usually starts at around three, children learn to recognise their names and such important words in their environment as the McDonald's sign. Towards the end of this phase, usually some time during the first year of school, as their repertoire increases, they begin to notice aspects such as the initial letters.

They are thus poised to move on to the second, the *analytic* phase, when their knowledge of alphabet letters and their awareness of onset and rime become centrally important, and learning by analogy can come into play. They are now in a position to inspect unknown words and relate them to words they already know. Of course, some of the words they come across have still to be learnt largely on the logographic principle, as they are either not regular, or they exhibit patterns too complex for their current state of knowledge. But as children move through this phase, they should be able to work out more and more of the new words they encounter, as they draw analogies with those they already know.

They are then in a position to enter the third phase, the *orthographic* phase, in which they identify new words from their spellings, virtually immediately. On topics that are familiar to them, children in this phase can tackle unfamiliar text on the run. They no longer process new words bit by bit: instead they draw on a complex repertory of spelling patterns to identify them rapidly. This is the phase we skilled readers operate in for most of the time – at least until we encounter an unusual word or a name that challenges our knowledge of spelling patterns. The goal of phonics teaching is to bring children to this stage while also enabling them to develop a powerful grasp of the other reading lessons.

## What teaching promotes whole to part phonics learning?

Children's first encounters with print need to be meaning-centred. The surroundings of their everyday lives provide a ready source of 'environmental print', from the marmite jar to the route indicator on the bus. But books provide much more: a greater semantic reward, an initiation into the language of the written word and exposure to the left-to-right, top-to-bottom conventions of print in English. It is therefore not surprising that children who are read to extensively learn to read more rapidly and effectively than those who are not (Durkin, 1966; Clark, 1976; Wells, 1981).

To progress through Frith's phases of word recognition, children need to start by learning a repertoire of words recognised on sight – the only means of word recognition available to them. Some of these words will be the irregular but vital words such as 'you', 'I', 'one' and 'two'. It is useful if others are regular three-letter words, exhibiting the most straightforward grapho-phonic relationships, which will later provide material for analysis into onset and rime. These should also be words of genuine interest to children, 'hop' rather than 'hip'.

As well as a vocabulary of such words, a sound foundation for phonics learning also requires phonological awareness, developed to a point where children can identify onsets and rimes, and produce strings of words that share these. Much can be and is done in nursery and reception classes through nursery rhymes and nonsense word play. Such play with the sound of language, including the invention of nonsense words, appears to help children to 'hear' the units of onset and rime in words. This is an essential precondition to matching these to their spelling patterns. Alphabet friezes and 'I spy' games can help to establish the simplest connections between one-phoneme onsets and letters of the alphabet.

The other essential element in this foundation for phonics learning is the knowledge and confidence to draw analogies. Initially, most children need to be shown how to do this: the words 'it's like' can be a powerful teaching tool here, showing children patterns and similarities in many spheres. But this capacity for analogical reasoning is particularly valuable in the early stages of reading. Goswami has shown that even 4 year olds can be taught this process of active cognitive engagement, and that it brings great benefits in terms of their search for pattern and predictability in the relationship between spoken and written words (Goswami, 1992).

Nursery and reception teachers can do much to promote phonics learning. But the most productive approaches will not involve 'sounding out' unfamiliar words phoneme by phoneme in a mechanical process that seldom results in the target word. Instead, they will be enjoying stories, delighting in the sounds of language and actively searching for patterns.

As well as continuing to develop their awareness of rhyme and alliteration, children moving into the analytic phase are helped by activities with movable letters, involving the manipulation of one-letter onsets before a constant simple rime, changing 'hop' to 'top' and 'cop' and back again. Then they can highlight such 'word families' in familiar poems and songs. They can also make collections of related words gathered from their reading, and play card games involving collecting words with a shared onset or rime. 'Useful' words can be displayed for reference on the classroom wall in 'families' – 'he', 'she', 'we' and 'me'. Asking children to look for little words in big words can also be very productive.

One of the chief spurs to impel children into and through this phase is developmental spelling. It seems easier for young children to spell words recognisably than it is for them to recognise even the most straightforward spellings. If they are encouraged to use developmental spelling, that is to 'have a go' at unknown words, this assists their ability to decode new words. During all these activities it is important to encourage the active use of appropriate metalanguage 'rhyme', 'onset, 'letter', 'syllable'. And asking a child who has identified an apparently 'new' word 'How did you know it said that?' can both promote a useful reflectiveness and self-awareness in the individual and demonstrate to others how they too can go about this business.

Clearly, it makes sense to present children entering this phase with 'simple' words – 'cat' and 'dog', not 'catch' and 'frog'. Once these are fairly well established, complications can follow, involving digraphs ('th' etc) and consonant blends ('bl' etc) in both onset and rime, and also rimes where the following consonant changes the value of the vowel before it ('all' 'or' etc). However, it does not seem necessary or desirable to teach to a set list, in a fixed order. Children encouraged to think for themselves will catch on to the central principle – that words you know already can help you with those you don't. 'That's like my name!' says 5-year-old Jack pointing to 'back'. The teacher's main role is to draw children's attention to the patterns, admit the exceptions such as 'snow' and 'cow' and help children search for regularity. Towards the end of this phase, when children are capable of recognising an increasing number of new words through analogy, children's awareness of the full phonemic structure of words can be developed, in words exhibiting one-to-one phonemic-to-grapheme regularity – so children can be made aware of *all* the separate phonemes in words such as 'ground' or 'stream'. But, because they operate on more complex spelling principles, with words such as 'care', 'little' and 'should', analysis down to this level is less helpful, even though their spellings are all regular. It is of no use at all with words such as 'once' or 'two'.

When children make the transition into the orthographic phase, recognising nearly all new words effortlessly, and able, at last, to focus entirely on the meaning of what they are reading, little more needs to be done. They have learnt the important phonic lessons: the basic patterns that shape our spelling system and the active use of analogy that enables us to tackle words we have not seen before.

Now it's a matter of looking at the structure of complex words at prefixes and suffixes, and of studying word roots and origins. Here, increasing familiarity with unusual spelling patterns in their reading can help them spell such words in their writing. Making personal word collections and specialist dictionaries can heighten awareness of structure. There will still be one or two words in their reading – names, particularly – that pose problems. But this is now a small proportion.

However, smooth transition through these phases, essential though it is, should not be equated with learning to read. Phonics learning should always be embedded in experience of text as the search for meaning. This will not only teach children many other vital reading lessons, but also, in impelling children to read more, will give them a much greater opportunity of putting their phonic lessons into practice. The teacher's challenge, where phonics is concerned, is to find the texts that engage real interest and include appropriate word patterns, and to ensure that the attention to individual words enriches the whole instead of obscuring it. It is also necessary to have a very clear idea of whereabouts in which phase each child is, and how s/he might move on.

For, unlike learning to understand text, phonics learning is essentially linear. Children cannot enter the orthographic phase without having gone through the logographic and analytic phases. Children in the successive phases operate according to different principles and need different kinds of help. This linearity does not seem to extend down to the detailed level proposed by many traditional phonics proponents. But success in one phase is a necessary precondition of entry to the next.

Children who are taught phonics in this way experience phonics as fun, and as power. Instead of passively following rules, they are actively searching for patterns and analogies. As well as learning how to recognise words efficiently and effectively, they are learning cognitive autonomy, learning that they have the power to extend their own knowledge.

## Phonics in the Literacy Hour

So how does the Literacy Hour match up to all this? Firstly, there is no simplistic equation between phonics and reading. Children are to work at sentence and text level, as well as developing systematic strategies for word recognition. However, the positioning of word level work in the left-hand column with text level on the far right, suggests that phonics has primacy and should come first.

As to its relationship to research findings, the document that presented the National Literacy Strategy claims that this detailed framework is 'based on the evidence of inspection and research' (Literacy Task Force, 1997, p 17). But there are no precise references to back this claim, either in this document or in the Framework for Teaching (Standards and Effectiveness Unit, 1998a). However, the influences of some research can be detected. It is recognised that children's awareness of phonemes cannot be taken for granted, that it has to be taught, and that in simple CVC words, young children find initial phonemes easiest, final phonemes harder and medial phonemes harder still. And the very first item in the long list of word level work in Reception concerns the recognition of rhyming patterns. By the end reception children are also to be taught to discriminate onset from rime in speech – and spelling. In the first term of Year 1, rhyme also features at the beginning and end of the phonics section. But all references to onset and rime have disappeared in the 'summary of specific phonics and spelling work' that appears in List 3 at the back of the ring-binder. And there are no further references beyond the first term of Year 1.

What we have instead is a focus on individual phonemes, and initial and final consonant clusters. By the end of reception children are expected to discriminate, write and read 'final sounds in simple words' and by the end of their first term in Year 1, to do the same with 'middle (short vowel) sounds'. By this point they should 'blend' phonemes to read CVC words in rhyming and non-rhyming sets. Essentially this is a traditional programme of synthetic phonics, with a sprinkling of undeveloped references to onset and rime. There is no clear dynamic, no recognition of children's powers of analogy, no recognition of Frith's phases. Children in reception are expected to operate in ways essentially similar to those in Year 2, albeit on simpler material. There is no clear relation between the lists of words to be recognised on sight and the phonics learning proceeding at the same time. Nor is there much encouragement for autonomy: although children are to explore and play with rhyming patterns in the first term of Year 1, the vast bulk of the phonics work laid down is closely specified and to be taught through highly didactic instruction.

The Teachers' Notes on Phonics in the Literacy Training Pack (Standards and Effectiveness Unit, 1998b) give further causes for concern. There are some sensible practical recommendations, such as eschewing elaborate displays and worksheets that ask children to trace dotted lines. Useful positive recommendations include making interactive use of magnetic letters and rhyming texts that catch the children's interest. But there is no coherent argument to support these practical ideas and no attempt to develop a coherent understanding of the dynamics of phonics learning. This is seen as 'a body of knowledge' to be 'introduced to children in a logical and interesting manner'.

Unfortunately, the knowledge seems flawed and the logic takes little account of what we know of the psychological progression of children's learning in this area. Taking the knowledge first, what is presented consists of a set of 71 rules governing grapheme – phoneme relationships. These rules fail to account for such straightforward words as 'cure' and 'dance'. They certainly do not attempt to explain all our spelling patterns. While not absolutely reliable, onset and rime are more inclusive, allowing words like 'sense' and 'should' as well as 'pure' and 'chance' to appear as regular and accessible. As to the logic, it really does seem perverse to fly in the face of what we now know about the patterning of children's learning in this area. Children are capable of learning whole words *before* they can manage the complex business of analysing the visual components of written words and matching these to the sound components of spoken words. Rimes are simply easier to perceive than the individual phonemes of which they are composed. It is not surprising that, when asked to extend the word family 'fog', 'dog', etc, children in a class on the demonstration video in the Literacy Training Pack (op cit) quietly insist on treating the rime 'og' as a single unit, rather than following their teacher's instruction to pick each letter in turn.

In all the materials the emphasis is on teaching children rules, not helping them to perceive patterns and make active use of analogical reasoning. The video does have a short interview with Usha Goswami, who speaks lucidly about the importance of analogy. But like the references to onset and rime, this is presented as a kind of fashionable garnish, not an integral part of a coherent approach.

Our hope has to be that, like the children in the video, teachers will adapt the instructions in ways that make sense to them. Provided they equip their children with a reliable strategy for tackling unknown words, they should not be fearful of being penalised by OFSTED. At the University of Brighton we have consistently tried to approach this area in the light of research evidence. This has led us to adopt a whole to part approach, in conflict with the Teacher Training Agency's (TTA) syllabus for primary English (DfEE, 1997) which takes a fixedly synthetic line. This did not prove a difficulty in our recent OFSTED reading inspection, where students' understanding of the stages of development in learning to read was highly commended, as was their knowledge and practical understanding of developing children's phonological awareness.

To move forward with confidence teachers need real understanding. Quick-fix training sessions, which do not look at the underlying dynamics of phonic learning, are no substitute. In an investigation commissioned by the TTA into the knowledge underpinning effective literacy teaching in primary school, Poulson et al found that in addition to a thorough knowledge of books for the age group, what characterised successful literacy teachers was not the knowledge about the language that the TTA expected, but 'situated knowledge' developed in the classroom, and substantial in-service courses focusing on processes of literacy learning and teaching (Poulson et al, 1997). Disappointment with the findings seems to have delayed publication by the TTA.

It is certainly true that in the 1970's and 1980's a number of primary school teachers neglected to teach phonics. Frank Smith and others at this time presented a seductive picture of reading as an entirely top-down business and learning to read as a matter of implicit learning alone (Smith, 1971, 1978). While this provided an exhilarating alternative to the pedestrian approaches of 'look and say' and synthetic phonics, it represented only partially both the act of reading and process of learning to read. Rumelhart's work has shown us that reading is a highly complex process – both bottom-up and top-down – in which we work up from letter patterns and down from large expectations of meaning (Rumelhart, 1976). Studies have shown that instruction *does* make a difference (Bradley and Bryant, 1983; Lundberg et al, 1988; Cunningham, 1990).

Phonics is an essential element in literacy learning, and for the vast majority of children it needs to be taught. But phonics on its own will not teach a child to read. And phonics programmes are not all equally effective. The research of the last 20 years has made it possible for us to teach phonics in a way that respects the pattern of children's development and engages them in exciting intellectual activity. We need to give all primary teachers the knowledge, confidence and understanding to put all this into practice, rather than impose on them a lock-step approach that goes against the grain. We have now arrived at a point where we can make a principled synthesis between whole-text approaches, whole-word approaches and analytic phonics. Frith (1985) has given us the framework in which to make this synthesis. Goswami (1992 and 1999) has shown us how powerful children's learning can be when our teaching is adapted to its dynamics and to the patterning of English orthography. Given time to develop this understanding and to integrate it into the larger picture of children's literacy learning, primary teachers, with their imaginative inventiveness, could considerably enhance the effectiveness of their teaching of reading. But a set of authoritarian directives, based on a limited view of English orthography and a distorted view of children's learning, is unlikely to accomplish this end.

## Note

1. A fuller account of whole to part phonics is presented in Whole to Part Phonics by Henrietta Domber, Margaret Moustafa and the Staff of CLPE, published by the Centre for Language in Primary Education (0171 401 3382).

## References

Bradley, L. and Bryant, P. (1983) 'Categorising Sounds and Learning to Read: A Causal Connection', *Nature*, 301, 419–21.

Bryant, P. (1993) 'Phonological Aspects of Learning to Read', in R. Beard (Ed) *Teaching Literacy, Balancing Perspectives*. Hodder and Stoughton: London.

Bussis, A. Chittenden, E. Amarel, M. and Klausner, E. (1985) *Inquiry into Meaning: An investigation of Learning to Read*. Lawrence Erlbaum Associates: Hillsdale NJ.

Cattell, J. (1986) 'The Time it Takes to See and Name Objects', *Mind*, 11, 63–65.

Clark, M. (1976) *Young Fluent Readers: What Can They Teach Us?* Heinemann: London.

Cunningham, A.E. (1990) 'Explicit Versus Implicit Instruction in Phonemic Awareness', *Journal of Experimental Child Psychology*, 50, 429–49.

Department for Education and Employment (1997) *Initial Teacher Training: National Curriculum for Primary English*, Annex B of *Requirements for Courses of Initial Teacher Training*, Circular No 10/97. DfEE: London.

Durkin, D. (1966) *Children who Read Early: Two Longitudinal Studies*. Teachers' College Press: New York.

Ehri, L.C. (1975) 'Word Consciousness in Readers and Pre-Readers', *Journal of Educational Psychology*, 67, 204–12.

Ferreiro, E. and Teberosky, A. (1979) *Literacy Before Schooling*. Heinemann: Exeter NH.

Flesch, R. (1955) *Why Johnny Can't Read and What You Can Do About It*. Harper and Brothers: New York.

Frith, U. (1985) 'Developmental Dyslexia', in Patterson, K.E. et al (Eds) *Surface Dyslexia*. Lawrence Erlbaum Associates: Hove.

Goswami, U. (1992) *Analogical Reasoning in Children*. Lawrence Erlbaum Associates: Hove.

Goswami, U. (1999) 'Phonological Development and Reading by Analogy: Epilinguistic and Metalinguistic Issues,' in Oakhill, J. and Beard, R. (Eds) *Reading Development and the Teaching of Reading: A Psychological Perspective*. Cambridge University Press.

Goswami, U. and Bryant, P. (1990) *Phonological Skills and Learning to Read*. Lawrence Erlbaum: Norwood, New Jersey.

Halle, M. and Vergnaud, J-R (1980) 'Three Dimensional Phonology', *Journal of Linguistic Research*, 1, 83–105.

Hockett, C.F. (1967) 'Where the Tongue Slips There Slip I', in *To Honour Roman Jacobson: Essays on the Occasion of his 70th Birthday*. Mouton Press: The Hague.

Literacy Task Force (1997) *The Implementation of the National Literacy Strategy*. DfEE: London.

Lundberg, I., Frost, J and Petersen, O-P (1988) 'Effects of an Intensive Programme for Stimulating Phonological Awareness, *Reading Research Quarterly*, 23, 263–84.

McGuinness, D. (1998) *Why Children Can't Read and What We Can Do About It*. Penguin: London.

Morais, J., Cary, L., Alegria, J. and Bertelson, P. (1979) 'Does Awareness of Speech as a Sequence of Phones Arise Spontaneously?', *Cognition*, 7, 323–31.

Moustafa, M. (1997) *Beyond Traditional Phonics: Research Discoveries and Reading Instruction*. Heinemann: Portsmouth NH.

Poulson, L., Wray, D. and Medwell, J. (1997) 'Subject Knowledge and Practice in Primary Literacy Teaching', Paper presented at the annual conference of the British Educational Research Association, York.

Rumelhart, D. (1976) 'Toward an Interactive Model of Reading', *Technical Report No 56*, San Diego Center for Human Information Processing, University of California at San Diego.

Smith, F. (1971) *Understanding Reading: A Psycholinguistic Analysis of Reading and Learning to Read*. Holt, Rinehart and Winston: New York.

Smith, F. (1978) *Reading*. Cambridge University Press: Cambridge.

Standards and Effectiveness Unit (1998a) *The National Literacy Strategy: Framework for Teaching*. Department for Education and Employment.

Standards and Effectiveness Unit (1998b) *The National Literacy Strategy: Literacy Training Pack*. Department for Education and Employment.

Treiman, R. (1985) 'Onsets and Rimes as Units of Spoken Syllables: Evidence from Children', *Journal of Experimental Child Psychology*, 39, 161–81.

Wells, C.G (1981) 'Some Antecedents of Early Educational Attainment', *British Journal of Educational Psychology*, 2, 2, 180–200.

# 21 Arts education in the 21st century – frill or fundamental?

*Andy Mortimer*

In planning a journey forward these authors necessarily need to look back, to take stock of where arts education has come from, if nothing else, to prevent repeating the mistakes of the past. This is the starting point for Francis Prendiville's article on 'Teacher in Role', which makes a strong plea for the return of feelings, values and different ways of understanding into the current curriculum. He uses the key phrase 'to contextualise learning' and suggests an important way to do this through the teaching of drama. Not surprisingly, this is also a central concept within Rod Taylor's article on visual arts and one which I shall return to in this editorial.

Prendiville, like other authors, suggests not only that the strategies and methods that he outlines are underpinned by a clear philosophy and understanding of the role of the arts in education, but that they are accessible to *all* teachers, regardless of their previous experience or training or the curriculum constraints imposed upon them.

David Harmer's up-beat article 'Poetry in the Primary School' continues this message with the proposal that the Literacy Strategy could be seen as a useful developmental tool for improving the teaching of, and interest in, poetry in the classroom. As well as examples of his own approaches to teaching poetry, he also provides a useful list of resources which will enable teachers to consolidate learning and language skills amongst their pupils.

Rod Taylor, in his article on content and meaning in art and design education, calls for a radical re-appraisal of how art is taught in schools. He welcomes the apparent shift in emphasis contained in the new National Curriculum 2000 document to allow pupils 'to communicate what they see, feel and think' (DfEE/QCA, 1999, p.18). His explanation of the 'Universal Themes' model places the arts, once again, back into the core of social and cultural education, no longer a recreational frill on the edge of significant learning (another theme I shall return to later). It is hoped that the introduction of 'Citizenship' into the National Curriculum in 2002 does not overlook the important role that the arts can play in developing a child's social awareness and inclusivity. Every school should read Rod Taylor's and Francis Prendiville's articles before they plan their 'Citizenship' policy or schemes of work.

Similarly, a school might be well advised to review its ICT programme in the light of Kevin Hamel's article.

Hamel examines shortcomings in educational planning for ICT in the music curriculum, but highlights useful research, information and projects aimed to help Key Stage 1 and 2 teachers to develop their practice. He goes on to outline the use of PCs and the Internet as exciting new tools with great potential for teaching and learning in music. Specific examples of how to do this are explained and supported by a list of some key resources in the article's references.

Prendiville, in his article on drama, quotes from the National Advisory Committee on Creative and Cultural Education report, *All Our Futures*: 'Education throughout the world faces unprecedented challenges: economic, technological, social and personal' (NACCCE, 1999, p.9). This is not a surprising view given the earlier warnings of research like the 'Global 2000 Report' commissioned by the American government in 1977 (CEQ and DoS, 1982).

However, despite the 30 years which politicians and policy makers worldwide have had to consider the problems we will face in the twenty-first century, their piecemeal economic, social and political solutions have tended to ignore both the role of education (there was no significant reference to it in the 'Global 2000 Report') and they fail to define what might constitute an appropriate educational programme to address those problems.

Urgent consideration needs now to be given to these issues, to the evidence from both educational and other research and to methods available to meet these challenges. As the NACCCE report goes on to state:

> 'New approaches are needed based on broader conceptions of young people's abilities, of how to promote their motivation and self-esteem, and of the skills and aptitudes they need. Creative and cultural education are fundamental for meeting these objectives.'
>
> (ibid, p.9)

The articles contained in this edition of the journal could be seen to start from this agenda and offer some exciting ideas for new approaches.

If these articles are to help move the practice of arts teaching forward, it is not inappropriate for this extended editorial to outline some general principles which might inform that practice and to examine some of the recent research and other case studies that provide important evidence to support the key role that arts education must play in the new century. Some coherence needs to be established across the curriculum to ensure its relevance for the future, to see it as supporting holistic education, rather than a patchwork of temporary band-aids to solve individual problems. Throughout the last decades of the twentieth century, it has been political expediency and partisan views which have predominated and led to *ad hoc* changes described optimistically as 'reforms'. Increasingly this has resulted in the marginalisation of the arts. It is time that arts education was considered a fundamental rather than a frill because, as Victor Papanek wrote in his book *Design for the Real World:*

'Design is composing an epic poem, executing a mural, painting a masterpiece, writing a concerto. But design is also cleaning and reorganising a desk drawer, pulling an impacted tooth, baking an apple pie, choosing sides for a back-lot baseball game, and educating a child. Design is the conscious effort to impose meaningful order.'

I believe that the arts curriculum offers the most significant opportunity for children to rehearse this 'underlying matrix of life' (Papanek, 1974, p.17).

I intend to examine arts education through two specific hypotheses:

1. *The arts are a way of developing*, inter alia, *life skills and attitudes which are transferable across the curriculum.*
2. *The arts are a way of contextualising other learning.*

Clearly, these two aspects are closely related, almost opposite sides of the same coin, but an understanding of their significance appears continually to escape attention despite the seminal work of arts educators like Dewey (1934), Read (1945), Eisner (1972), Gardner (1973), and many others over the last 70 years. More recently, David Hargreaves argued:

'there is widespread agreement amongst teachers, researchers and educators that it is vital to educate children in the arts: the arts provide unique opportunities for the development of personal qualities such as natural creative expression, social and moral values and self-esteem. Paradoxically, there is also general agreement that this is not being done adequately: that the arts are grossly neglected in relation to other areas of the curriculum such as reading, mathematics or science.'

(Hargreaves, 1989, p.vii)

He supports this view with reference to several HMI curriculum surveys, the Gulbenkian Report 'The Arts in Schools' and other research evidence, but I believe that it is, once again, worth re-stating some arguments for the '*vitalness*' of the arts.

## 1. The arts and life skills

Cohen and Cohen, in their book *Special Educational Needs in the Ordinary School* (Cohen, 1986), detailed those key skills and attitudes which, from their research, all schools hope to develop in all their pupils. They included dexterity, agility, tool/material control, interaction, non-verbal reasoning, observing, investigating, problem-solving, judging, selecting, perseverance, initiative, imagination, concentration. Their list obviously also mentions other skills explicitly related to arts education, like aesthetic awareness and artistic expression. However, I have selected those which can immediately be seen as *life* skills, that are transferable to *all* areas of the curriculum and to the world beyond school. One need only consider the needs of the historian or scientist to recognise the significance of most of these skills. (I am continually reminded of Einstein's dictum that 'In Science imagination is more important than knowledge'.)

What is important, of course, is that these skills and attitudes are precisely those which are central to the arts and which all arts activities in schools foster. Think of any visual arts, any drama, any music, any dance, any creative writing in the classroom and the teacher's learning objectives are certain to include many, if not most, of the words in Cohen's list. The problem for many arts educators and teachers, however, has been that a focus on the design process and the transferable learning that might accrue from it is seen, in some way, to threaten the integrity of the activity as a 'pure' arts learning event. As a result of this attitude, teaching then tends to over-emphasise the significance of the end product and deny the wider relevance of the process or *usefulness* of the arts. I believe that this is fallacious. J.Z. Young, formerly Emeritus Professor of Anatomy at University College, London, concluded from his research into the functioning of the human brain that:

> 'To say that religion or art or music are *useful* seems to me not in the least to devalue them but on the contrary it improves our estimation of their value. I believe that these "spiritual" and creative activities are even more important, in the literal, practical sense, than the more mundane ones that are the concern of politics, business and industry.'
>
> (Young, 1978, p.38)

New evidence from the Crafts Council's investigation into 'Learning Through Making' would also suggest that these creative skills are essentially the ones needed to enhance the quality of outcome in commerce, business and manufacturing industries (Eggleston, 1998).

Too narrow aims for arts education, related only to the specifics of art production, can result in its marginalisation by relegating the activity to mere recreation or therapy, or lead to a mechanistic orthodoxy. (See, for example, the restrictive focus on detailed observation and formal qualities contained in the examples of children's landscape paintings illustrated as models in 'Exemplification of Standards in Art at Key Stage 3', SCAA, 1996, pp.8–9, and compare these with the more imaginative and worthwhile process-based approach illustrated in 'Expectations in Arts at Key Stages 1 and 2', SCAA, 1997a, p.36). For an excellent critical analysis of the National Curriculum for Art which expands this point, see Atkinson, 1999.

Interestingly, further, more recent evidence from research by the National Foundation for Educational Research would indicate that, despite a narrow set of objectives:

> 'the effects of the arts were seen to be much broader than the aims set out for arts subjects in the National Curriculum . . . teachers referred to pupils' personal development and self-awareness especially fostering self-esteem,

self-confidence and developing the whole person . . . This was mentioned more often than all the direct art form knowledge and technical skills . . . put together. The second most frequently cited category was the perceived capacity of the arts to improve performance on other areas of the curriculum through the transfer of skills and knowledge acquired in the arts.'

(NFER, 1998, p.2)

Although there is not scope within this brief paper to examine reasons for this in any depth, from my observations of children working in the arts, one significant possibility is that the arts allow children opportunities to take risks within a 'safe' learning environment. The arts allow for Holt's famous concept of 'going wrong without feeling a sense of failure' (Holt, 1964). They allow children to grasp the notion of diversity and to realise and feel secure in the knowledge that, as in many aspects of life, there is no right or wrong answer. This might be because 'Art is a game where the rules are made up as the game is in progress, where the exact meaning of words or images is known only in the context of each new statement or articulation' (Wittgenstein, 1953).

An understanding, therefore, of the processes involved in making art, can provide us with a basic security in our actions. The contemporary British artist, Andy Goldsworthy, summed it up when he said, 'I can only accept uncertainty because I know what I am doing. When you don't know what you are doing, you have to be so certain about it' (Goldsworthy, 1996, p.22).

Once children have this grasp on the process, then the tensions, joys and endless possibilities of the arts can engage, stimulate and challenge them, as in this example of a written review of her collage work by a 9-year-old pupil:

'I used the parts I picked because they were all interesting shapes but as I looked and thought about it, I noticed they all went into four groups . . . metal . . . wood . . . animal . . . stone. Wood turns into charcoal when it is burnt and the stone wears away to sand on the beach. Animals turn into bone remains. The metal rusted. I liked the colours of the rusty burgundy the most . . . My title changed as I was working. [At first] it was like an old and rusty dreamcatcher – but its shape and pieces were more like life-cycles and changes.'

(quoted in Mortimer, 1999)

Recognising the broader benefits of the arts in education in this way does not threaten the specific art form aims or objectives; rather, it enriches them. I believe that this can be represented in the diagrammatic form shown in Figure 21.1.

## 2. The arts and the contextualising of other learning

In 1998, I was invited to teach on an arts course for elementary teachers at Central Connecticut State University. The course had been set up as an arts awareness programme for the generalist primary teacher at a time when several

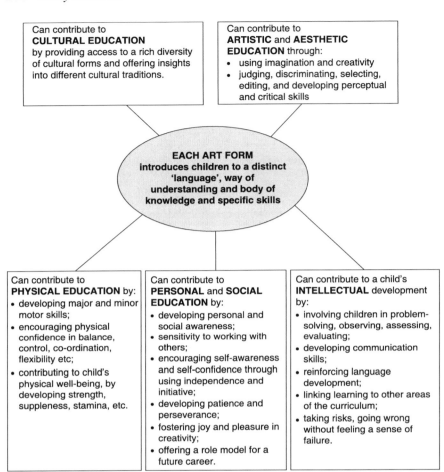

Can contribute to
**CULTURAL EDUCATION**
by providing access to a rich diversity
of cultural forms and offering insights
into different cultural traditions.

Can contribute to
**ARTISTIC** and **AESTHETIC**
**EDUCATION** through:
• using imagination and creativity
• judging, discriminating, selecting,
  editing, and developing perceptual
  and critical skills

**EACH ART FORM**
introduces children to a distinct
'language', way of
understanding and body of
knowledge and specific skills

Can contribute to
**PHYSICAL EDUCATION** by:
• developing major and minor
  motor skills;
• encouraging physical
  confidence in balance,
  control, co-ordination,
  flexibility etc;
• contributing to child's
  physical well-being, by
  developing strength,
  suppleness, stamina, etc.

Can contribute to
**PERSONAL** and **SOCIAL**
**EDUCATION** by:
• developing personal and
  social awareness;
• sensitivity to working with
  others;
• encouraging self-awareness
  and self-confidence through
  using independence and
  initiative;
• developing patience and
  perseverance;
• fostering joy and pleasure in
  creativity;
• offering a role model for a
  future career.

Can contribute to a child's
**INTELLECTUAL** development
by:
• involving children in problem-
  solving, observing, assessing,
  evaluating;
• developing communication
  skills;
• reinforcing language
  development;
• linking learning to other areas
  of the curriculum;
• taking risks, going wrong
  without feeling a sense of
  failure.

*Figure 21.1* What are the benefits of the arts in education?

school districts in Connecticut and other States were developing what they called
'HOT' (Higher Order Thinking) programmes for their students. Concerned
about declining levels of literacy and numeracy, educators found that recent
research by neuroscientists into the workings of the brain indicated that, by
increasing the arts curriculum of a school, children were helped to contextualise
and reinforce learning especially from language and mathematics lessons.

'A survey of studies suggest that music plays a significant role in enhancing a
wide range of academic and social skills. For one, it activates procedural
(body) memory and, therefore, is learning that lasts. In addition . . . arts
education facilitates language development, enhances creativity, boosts

reading readiness, helps social development, assists general intellectual achievement and fosters positive attitudes toward school.'

(Jensen, 1998, p.38)

Furthermore, there was evidence to prove that 'by learning and practising art, the human brain actually rewires itself to make more and stronger connections' (ibid, p.38).

As a result of such enrichment programmes, data have been collected from schools like Douglas Elementary in Columbus Ohio, which show that it has resulted in 'achievement scores 20 points above the district norms in five of six academic [ie non-arts] areas . . . Other schools in the area . . . are experiencing similar academic success through an arts emphasis' (ibid, p.38).

Meanwhile, in this country, while recognising inconsistencies in its quantitative data, the NFER research nevertheless noted 'some positive associations between taking GCSE arts courses, especially for music, and general academic performance (as indicated by average scores in English, Maths and Science GCSE exams)' (NFER, 1998, p.5).

I have also gathered a great deal of anecdotal evidence about ways in which visual arts activities in Sandwell LEA's 'Quality Start' programme has extended children's language skills. In preparation for, or follow-up work from, practical art activities – drawing, painting, printmaking – either myself, or the teachers I have worked with, have engaged the pupils in speaking and listening and/or critical or imaginative writing work. In every case, the classroom teacher has expressed surprise at how many of the students have performed beyond their expectations of them. This has been particularly noticeable amongst those pupils who have English as an additional language. 'They have written more than ever before', 'they have used words I didn't know they knew', 'they have talked more than before', 'they have spoken in sentences', 'they have used adjectives correctly', 'they have used language in a really creative way', are just a few of the comments I have received. In each case, I suggested that the school used the lists set out in Figure 21.2 as the starting point for its art and language development.

Similar lists and ideas might support these links in other arts subjects and the attention of all teachers needs to be re-drawn to the SCAA publication 'Use of Language: A Common Approach' (SCAA, 1997b) and the individual subject papers that accompanied it, eg 'Art and the Use of Language' (SCAA, 1997c). These leaflets give subject specific examples to support the general statement about use of language across the curriculum contained in the new National Curriculum 2000 documents.

There is clearly much more research to be done in this area. However, it would seem more appropriate for a government to initiate such research, given the evidence currently available, before giving children more of the sterile academic diet which they are clearly failing to digest. We wait to see whether the Literacy and Numeracy strategies really are the most effective ways of dealing with this problem.

**Awareness of the 'elements' when making or analysing art can produce opportunities for infinite vocabulary consolidation and extension:**

| LINE | SHAPE/FORM | TONE | TEXTURE | COLOUR |
|---|---|---|---|---|
| short | circle | dark | rough | *primary* |
| long | square | light | smooth | yellow |
| thick | triangle | bright | soft | red |
| thin | rectangle | dull | hard | blue |
| straight | pentagon | mid-tone | bumpy | *secondary* |
| curved | octagon | monotone | pitted | orange |
| wavy | decahedron | gradation | raised | purple |
| zig-zag | polygon | shading | ribbed | green |
| undulating | sphere | shadow | shiny | *tertiary* |
| interrupted | cube | silhouette | matt | brown |
| incised | pyramid | black | prickly | |
| vertical | cuboid | white | spiky | warm |
| horizontal | spiral | grey | bobbly | cold |
| parallel | angular | opaque | grainy | loud |
| hatched | rounded | transparent | furry | muted |
| cross-hatched | sharp | etc | scaly | pastel |
| diagonal | jagged | | silky | complementary |
| hairy | elongated | | wrinkly | iridescent |
| branched | stretched | | woven | *colour names* |
| twisted | extended | | engraved | scarlet |
| filigree | squashed | | indented | vermilion |
| taut | internal | | surface | crimson |
| tight | mass | | lustrous | pink |
| slack | volume | | etc | mauve |
| etc | crystalline | | | ultramarine |
| | organic | | | cobalt |
| | conical | | | turquoise |
| | etc | | | ochre |
| | | | | umber |
| | | | | etc |

**From looking at other artists' work, many opportunities exist for language extension including:**

- poems and haiku arising from looking at art objects
- narrative text – 'what happened before or next' – arising from narrative art
- critical reviews using description and analysis of own or other artists' work
- letters to and from artists, to and from patrons
- instructions describing art processes
- biographical accounts of artists
- imaginary diaries of artists
- drama arising from the study of an art object
- letter/postcard home describing a landscape image to another person
- imagining a portrait as an 'identifit' picture, describing the 'wanted' character

*Figure 21.2*

Certainly an absence of understanding amongst policy makers of the potential of the arts to develop transferable skills and understanding and to contextualise knowledge from other curriculum areas has continued to dog education since Mr Gradgrind demanded 'Teach these boys and girls nothing but Facts. Facts alone are wanted in life' (Dickens, 1854).

## Conclusion

The arts in education are in crisis. There can be no doubt about that when even the General Secretary of the NAHT warns that 'A squeeze caused by the combined pressure of a focus on the basics and the expectation that teachers can remedy all the ills of an increasingly sick society . . . [can] lead to schools being forced to produce literate and numerate, but unfit philistines' (Hart, 1999).

However, definitions of crisis vary. I believe that in Chinese it is made up of two words meaning 'danger' and 'opportunity'. The intention of bringing together these articles for this edition of *Education 3-13* has been to focus on the opportunity which the next century holds. They all support the notion that the arts are essential to any meaningful curriculum. They argue that it is the current mechanistic approach to language, number and information technology teaching which must be challenged. Furthermore, the emphasis that such methods place on orthodoxies and norms is an anachronism which belies the richness and diversity of the world in which children live; which denies a child's entitlement to a broad and balanced curriculum; which perpetuates the outmoded and simplistic binary model of reason versus feeling or useful versus recreational; and which simply ignores the collective evidence of the last century.

'The old biases about music and art being "right-brained frills" are outdated' (Jensen, 1998, p.8).

## References

Atkinson, D. (1999) 'A critical reading of the national curriculum for art in the light of contemporary theorisations of subjectivity', *Broadside 2*, ARTicle Press, University of Birmingham.

Cohen, A. and Cohen, L. (Eds) (1986) *Special Educational Needs in the Ordinary School.* Harper & Row: London.

Council on Environmental Quality and Department of State (1982) *The Global 2000 Report to the President.* Penguin Books: London.

Dewey, J. (1934) *Arts as Experience.* Capricorn: New York.

DfEE/QCA (1999) 'The national curriculum: art and design', HMSO: London.

Dickens, C. (1854) *Hard Times.* Penguin Books: London (1995).

Eggleston, J. (Ed) (1998) 'Learning through making: a national enquiry into the value of creative and practical education in Britain', Summary of Research. Crafts Council: London.

Eisner, E. (1972) *Educating Artistic Vision.* Macmillan: New York.

Gardner, H. (1973) *The Arts and Human Development.* John Wiley: New York.

Goldsworthy, A. (1996) *Sheepfolds.* Michael Hare-Williams Fine Arts Ltd: London.

Hargreaves, D. (Ed) (1989) *Children and the Arts*. Open University Press: Milton Keynes.

Hart, D. (1999) in Smithers, R. 'School basics drive will produce unfit philistines', *The Guardian*, 5.6.99.

Holt, J. (1964) *How Children Fail*. Pelican Books: London (1969).

Jensen, E. (1998) *Teaching with the Brain in Mind*. Association for Supervision and Curriculum Development, Virginia.

Mortimer, A. (1999) 'Collage in Cumbria', unpublished Project Report for the Arts Council of England.

National Advisory Committee on Creative and Cultural Education (NACCCE) (1999) *All Our Futures: Creativity, Culture and Education*. HMSO: London.

National Foundation for Educational Research (1998) 'The effects and effectiveness of arts education in schools', summary of Interim Report for RSA, NFER: Slough.

Papanek, V. (1974) *Design for the Real World*. Paladin: London.

Read, H. (1945) *Education Through Art*. Faber and Faber: London.

Sandwell Local Education Authority (2000) 'Quality Start Project', Web-site on line in summer 2000, Sandwell LEA: Birmingham.

SCAA (1996) 'Art: exemplification of standards, KS3', SCAA: Hayes.

SCAA (1997a) 'Expectations in art at KS 1 & 2', SCAA: Hayes.

SCAA (1997b) 'Use of language: a common approach', SCAA: Hayes.

SCAA (1997c) 'Art and the use of language', SCAA: Hayes.

Wittgenstein, L. (1953) *Philosophical Investigation*. Oxford University Press.

Young, J.Z. (1978) *Programs of the Brain*. Oxford University Press.

# 22 The National Literacy Strategy: missing a crucial link?

## A comparative study of the National Literacy Strategy and Success for All

*Wendy Jolliffe*

## Introduction

The National Literacy Strategy (NLS) has been held up by authorities on international change to be the largest and most ambitious educational project witnessed since the 1960s (Fullan, 2000). As such, it has been the subject of fierce debate and much research. This article starts by exploring the background to reform in the UK and then compares it with research into another large-scale literacy reform, Success for All (SFA), using seven key differences between the two strategies. It then goes on to analyse the results of a comparative study.

## Background

A brief look at the background to the introduction of the NLS is illuminating. Before accession to power in 1997, the Labour party had set up a literacy taskforce which was charged with developing a strategy for substantially raising standards of literacy in primary schools over a 5–10-year period. The preliminary report cited international data, as well as local data, as being influential in the development of 'best practices' (DfEE, 1997). They also referred to New Zealand research and practices. Indeed, a taskforce had been set up in New Zealand with very similar goals, but there the similarities end, as the New Zealand taskforce drew upon a much larger range of experience and research expertise. The New Zealand taskforce recommended increasing teachers' and school-based responses and developing best practice. The whole thrust was for the development of teachers' skills and knowledge so that they could implement best practice in the teaching of literacy with a stress on strong professional leadership. These recommendations form a stark contrast to the UK taskforce's preference for a 'framework' to structure and sequence pedagogic activities and to specify the content that was to be taught during the 'literacy hour' (Soler, 2000).

The stated aims of the NLS were ambitious in terms of improving standards and are summarized in the *Framework for Teaching* (DfEE, 1998). It is also interesting to note that it aimed to promote literacy instruction which is 'dis-cursive, interactive, well-paced, confident and ambitious' (DfEE 1998, p. 8). The method of doing this was through the introduction of the Literacy Hour, which aimed to provide a balance between whole class, guided group and independent work. This brief statement, and a five-minute introduction included in the initial training for the Literacy Hour, provided the underlying pedagogy.

Success for All has been developed from work on cooperative learning by Robert Slavin in the US and it is underpinned by a philosophy called 'talent development', i.e. believing that *all* children have talents capable of being developed to meet high standards. The distinctive features of the programme are briefly:

- lessons last for 90 minutes per day and during this time pupils are grouped by reading ability, irrespective of age, and work cooperatively in pairs and groups;
- one-to-one tutoring is provided to support pupils who are judged to be falling behind their peers;
- eight-week assessments of pupils are carried out to determine any further regrouping and any intervention needed;
- an Early Years/Foundation Stage curriculum emphasises the development and use of oral language through themed units;
- a programme facilitator is given 50% non-contact time to oversee the operation, training and implementation in each school;
- teachers and tutors receive detailed manuals, supplemented by in-service training days throughout the year;
- each school creates a Family Support Team to work closely with pupils, parents and the community.

## Effective teaching of literacy

Before going on to compare explicitly these two strategies, it is useful to summarise what we know about the key characteristics of effective literacy teaching and recent research has shown the following.

1.  Effective teachers have coherent belief systems about literacy which are generally consistent with the way they teach. This relates to adequate subject knowledge and Wray *et al.* (2002) state:

    The clear implication of this finding is that to raise expertise levels in all teachers of literacy, some professional development opportunities at least need to be channelled to those teachers not already identified as expert. (p. 130)

2.  Further support is needed in order to develop genuinely interactive teaching skills (the recommended model by the NLS). Moyles *et al.* (2003) found that:

for the most part, whole-class interactive teaching remains a one-way teacher-dominated activity. (p. xiii)

3.  Understanding of the pedagogical theory is crucial to effective teaching, but as Fisher (2002) notes, during the introductory training to the NLS there was only a five-minute short explanation which looked at the rationale.

    Harrison (2002, p. 16) specifies the five underlying elements of the teaching sequence of the literacy hour, which, interestingly, is nowhere made explicit in the training, as follows:

    (i)    Identification of prior knowledge
    (ii)   Teacher demonstration of process
    (iii)  Shared exploration through activity
    (iv)   Scaffolded pupil application of new learning
    (v)    Consolidation through discussion of activity

4.  An explicit understanding of the links between theory and practice is needed (Bailey, 2002). Bailey's research centres on the effective teaching of writing, and describes a 'fragile link' (2002, p. 23) between research and practice. The implementation of the National Literacy Strategy has, she suggests, led to an 'anxious literalism' (p. 26) which has in turn meant a discrete teaching of language skills and concepts, and a diminution of written composition.

## Focus questions for research

The foregoing resumé of research into the effective teaching of literacy and key differences between the NLS and SFA has shown that the following are pre-requisites:

1.  an effective programme of professional development;
2.  teaching should be genuinely interactive;
3.  a deep-rooted understanding by teachers of the pedagogical process; and
4.  clear links made between theory and practice.

## Key differences between the NLS and SFA

How these strategies met these criteria was my next question. My review of existing research elicited the following seven key differences between the NLS and SFA:

### *1. A learning theory which is specified and incorporated*

In SFA, learning through the social construction of knowledge by cooperative learning is integral. Teaching staff are trained in using it and pupils work through a 'Getting Along Together' programme to develop cooperative skills. Cooperative learning (CL) has an extensive research base (Johnson & Johnson, 1989) which has shown three main categories of advantages: achievement, interpersonal relationships and psychological health and social competence. SFA uses one particular approach to CL: Student Teams Achievement Division (STAD) which rewards teams for the sums of its members' efforts. This approach has received criticism for introducing an element of competition and extrinsic reward (Johnson & Johnson, 1989; Brown & Thomson, 2000) rather than being based on intrinsic reward. However, Slavin cites numerous studies to show its success (1996).

For the NLS, the underpinning learning theory consists of interactive teaching and while there is a statement of desirability: 'The most successful teaching is . . . interactive' (DfEE, 1998, p. 8), how this to be incorporated is not explicit. Critics argue that the concept is not well defined and that it mainly results in traditional whole class teaching. The findings of the study of Mroz *et al.* (2000), which were supported by the extensive research of Galton *et al.* (1999), found an increase in whole-class teaching and that the majority of questions used by teachers were either closed or factual. Further research has been carried out into interactive teaching in the primary school, in the form of a project entitled the Study of Primary Interactive Teaching (SPRINT), by Moyles *et al.* (2003). It concluded that although the NLS extended the rate of pupil contributions, it actually reduced the opportunities for extended interactions.

### 2. A school-wide programme which requires full staff commitment and restructuring

SFA is a holistic school reform model requiring a minimum of 80% commitment by all staff and organisational restructuring, e.g. through the provision of a facilitator and pupils grouped by ability, not age. NLS is a curriculum-based reform and requires no prior commitment by the majority of staff, nor does the organisation of the school require any restructuring.

### 3. Comprehensive materials and resources

For SFA extensive materials are provided which incorporate cooperative learning and metacognitive techniques. For NLS, extensive materials are provided, although these do not explicitly incorporate 'interactive' teaching, apart from some surface features. In addition, a major omission in the introduction of the NLS concerned provision for Speaking and Listening. The study of Collins and Marshall (2001) cites substantial classroom-based research on the importance of exploratory talk for learning. Cordon (2000) argues that considering an extensive body of research which demonstrates the relationship between talk, academic empowerment and achievement, it is a 'shameful neglect' that 'having emphasised the centrality of talk, the DfEE chose to exclude speaking and listening.' (2000, p. 17). This has been addressed with the production of guidance on incorporating speaking and listening within the NLS Framework (DfES, 2003). It will, however, require extensive professional development in order for teachers to see this as integral and not merely an 'add on'.

### 4. Commitment to ongoing professional development

For SFA there is extensive training, particularly for headteachers and senior managers. Ongoing training for all staff is provided by SFA staff, together with support from 'expert' literacy teachers, or facilitators, in each school. For the NLS a cascade model of professional development has been used through centrally produced resources for literacy co-ordinators to deliver to school staff, plus ongoing training to co-ordinators and support from LEA literacy consultants.

### 5. Inclusion of home–school links

SFA includes a family support team set up in each school to address issues that may impinge on learning, such as poor attendance. No explicit provision is made for this in NLS. However, as part of the Primary National Strategy (PNS), the NLS is endeavouring to embrace issues of 'Partnerships beyond the Classroom' through work on supporting pupils with English as an additional language (DfES, 2005a).

### 6. Tutoring

An early intervention programme for children identified as falling behind is part of the SFA program, which consists of one-to-one tutoring support for the duration of need. For the NLS additional support for those pupils who are falling slightly behind for specific year groups is provided for set periods of time. A symposium of research on the strategy (Fisher *et al.*, 2000, p. 264) stated that there were valid concerns 'about the capability of the NLS to address the learning needs of *all* pupils which urgently needs to be explored. One size does *not* necessarily fit all'.

However, in December 2001, an intervention scheme, called Early Literacy Support, was introduced for year 1 pupils who were falling slightly behind their peers. Further intervention strategies have also been introduced for years 4 and 5. One of the key factors in instigating change in the teaching of literacy was the 'long tail of underachievement' and evidence that between one-sixth and one-eighth of adults experience problems with basic literacy, and this had persisted for 60 years (Brooks *et al.*, 1996). Interestingly, the much publicised report on reading standards from 35 different countries (NFER, 2003) highlights the improvement in reading in England, but indicates that the NLS has had little effect on this 'long tail of underachievement'.

### 7. The provision of a facilitator

This is in place in each school for SFA in the form of a teacher who monitors and co-ordinates the programme and is given approximately 50% off timetable time to carry this out. With the NLS, the literacy co-ordinators monitor the programme, but no non-contact time is specifically given.

# Hypothesis

The foregoing all led me to conclude that in order to produce an effective literacy strategy, on the scale of the National Literacy Strategy, it requires firm foundations, i.e. teachers need to understand the underlying pedagogy: not just what to teach, but why they are doing it. My hypothesis was therefore that the National Literacy Strategy had a missing link—no explicit professional development on the underlying pedagogy, nor what constitutes the effective learning of literacy. In other words, ironically for many of its critics, it could be described as not 'prescriptive' enough. I sought, therefore, to put this hypothesis to the test through a comparison with Success for All.

## *Methodology*

In order to collect information from schools on the quality of teaching and learning, which largely involved judgements by senior staff, I elected to use a qualitative research method of semi-structured interviews. These were carried out with two schools using NLS and two schools using SFA, all in the same socially deprived inner city area of Hull within an Education Action Zone. My specific research questions related to the impact on teaching and learning from adopting either of these strategies. Interview questions therefore specifically related to teaching, learning and management of the strategies. The interviews were carried out with headteachers and literacy co-ordinators from each school. From this a conceptual framework was devised which aimed to show a clear comparison of the impact on teaching and learning. This consisted of nine key indicators (see Appendix).

# Results

## *1. NLS schools*

Interviews were carried out during the summer of 2002. The following significant comments were made by School B (using NLS).

- Training had initially de-skilled teachers and caused a loss of faith in their professional expertise.
- Lessons were too passive.
- Matching pupils' needs was difficult.
- The work produced was inferior, there were too many 'bits of things'.
- The school did not understand it initially and the personnel required to disseminate it were not sufficiently skilled.
- The three-part lesson had led to a positive impact across the curriculum.

Among comments made by School C (using NLS) were the following.

- Training that was provided in-house was better than that provided by the NLS.
- A key weakness was matching pupils' needs.
- The NLS was not good at identifying pupils in need of support.
- Whole-class teaching was not always effective, as not all children were involved.
- There was inconsistency in teaching and application of the strategy.
- Key staff with expertise made a significant contribution.

Out of nine key indicators within the conceptual framework used for analysis of the interviews, both schools answered positively on only four.

### 2. SFA schools

School A (using SFA) made the following contrasting comments.

- Training had enhanced skills although there was an ongoing need particularly on the underlying ethos of cooperative learning.
- It ensured genuinely interactive whole-class teaching.
- The provision of a facilitator with non-contact time to monitor and enable the provision was crucial.
- It promotes the inclusion of all children in active learning, both less able and more able pupils.
- Learning was good with emphasis on oral work.
- It enabled good monitoring of pupils' progress.

School D (using SFA) commented that:

- training had enhanced teachers' skills;
- pupils were engaged in learning through team work;
- gender issues were better addressed, with boys less able to dominate;
- it was inclusive with classroom support assistants enabling the fast identification of pupils who were falling behind;
- the environment for learning was positive and active;
- pupils were much more engaged in their learning;
- high quality oral work resulted;
- a dramatic improvement in pupils' learning;
- it has empowered younger children.

Both schools answered positively on eight out of nine key indicators used from analysis of the interviews, with both showing some reservation about the danger of more able pupils becoming bored through the predictability of the programme.

## Discussion

My hypothesis was that the National Literacy Strategy had a 'missing link', i.e a failure to incorporate effective teaching and learning and also a failure to make explicit its underlying pedagogy. To what extent, therefore, has this research illuminated this issue? In a limited small-scale review of four schools, it had shown some significant shortcomings.

First, ineffective whole-class teaching: the two NLS schools interviewed both commented on the passive nature of lessons, with not all children involved. In contrast, the SFA schools referred to teaching being 'genuinely interactive' with all children 'engaged in their learning through team work'.

Ways forward could include staff examining what characterises interactive teaching. Some features are discussed in the PNS Excellence and Enjoyment learning and teaching in the primary years professional development materials (DfES, 2004a). However, there is a danger that teachers will focus on superficial gimmicks such as 'show me' or 'get up and go' activities requiring children to use mini-whiteboards to display answers or physical movement to respond to a question. The SPRINT project (Moyles *et al.*, 2003) highlights some of these problems and cites the research of Beard (1999) and Reynolds and Farrell (1996) into interactive teaching. This relates to a three-phase framework of questioning in which teachers use: (i) questions of increasing difficulty to solve a problem; (ii) rapid recall questions to assess pupils' knowledge; and (iii) slower higher-order questions within whole-class discussion to promote pupils' thinking. Alexander's work (2004) on dialogic teaching echoes this third point. The emphasis here is on extending pupils' thinking and learning and not focusing on speed and pace which may be detrimental to learning. In addition, for truly interactive teaching to take place, a radical rethinking of the role of the teacher needs to be examined. One example might be the work of early years teachers in the Reggio Emilia region of Italy where a teacher is seen as a co-learner and collaborator using Malaguzzi's (1993) metaphoric description of a ping-pong match.

Second, the inclusion of all pupils: the NLS schools referred to 'matching pupils needs' as a 'key weakness'. In contrast, the SFA schools referred to the 'inclusion of all pupils in active learning in literacy' with issues of ability and gender being well addressed. One of the principal ways in which this was achieved was through heterogeneous cooperative group work with a high emphasis on oral work. The PNS is endeavouring to address these issues, however; for example, by publishing research on boys and writing (UKLA, 2004) and guidance on inclusion (DfES, 2005b).

Third, inclusion of learning theory: both the SFA schools made reference to the 'underlying ethos' of cooperative learning and 'the philosophy behind it—cooperative learning' and its impact on teaching and learning. In addition, both schools referred specifically to the increased amount and quality of oral work. Neither NLS schools made any such reference and indeed referred to 'bits of paving stones' as if they did not fully appreciate the 'big picture'. A way forward for schools could be through the PNS Excellence and Enjoyment learning and teaching in the primary years professional development materials (DfES, 2004a) which does include a section on learning to learn. The key issue for many schools is having the time and capacity to do this effectively.

Fourth, professional development: both the SFA schools indicated that the provision of an off-timetable facilitator to provide ongoing support, plus central-ised training had been effective. With both NLS schools the quality of training relied on individual expertise of co-ordinators, who were not given as much time as the SFA facilitators to carry this out and with variable results. Setting up learn-ing networks of schools may present a new model of 'bottom up' and not 'top down' centralised training. The DfES describes networks as offering the potential: 'for genuine transformation based on the knowledge embedded in teaching prac-tice.' (DfES, 2004b, p. 2). The impact of these will make interesting future research.

## Conclusion

While SFA would seem from this to be more effective, it is important to bear in mind the high cost of the scheme, requiring a teacher to be off-timetable for at least 50% of the time. In addition, resources were considerably more extensive than those required for the NLS. The schools studied here received funding from the Education Action Zone to implement the strategies, but for many other schools this would not be possible. Nevertheless, this needs to be set against the centralised costs of implementing the NLS (£205.5 million in year 2000–2001 alone; OISEUT, 2003). Both schemes have therefore incurred considerable costs, with a large proportion of centralised costs in the case of the NLS.

To conclude, this research has presented some initial findings to show the greater effectiveness of Success for All for the teaching of literacy. Further research would be needed to verify these results, in particular to probe in greater depth the understanding of all staff of the underlying pedagogy. To reiterate, the main differences centre around two main issues:

1. Explicit understanding of the underlying pedagogy and how this impacts on learning through ongoing and effective professional development.
2. The inclusion of all pupils in effective learning.

These principle differences need to be addressed in order to improve the quality of teaching and learning in the NLS. The Primary National Strategy is seeking to address some of these issues in 2005, in particular through the Excellence and Enjoyment Professional Development materials (DfES, 2004a). However, it is an ambitious task and its success will require careful evaluation.

The results from this small-scale study bear out the original hypothesis that an improvement in teaching and learning requires an explicit understanding of the underlying pedagogy, i.e. teachers need to know not only what to do, but why they do it.

# References

Alexander, R. (2004) *Towards dialogic teaching: rethinking classroom talk* (Cambridge, Dialogos).

Bailey, M. (2002) What does research tell us about how we should be developing written composition? In: R. Fisher, G. Brooks & M. Lewis (Eds) *Raising standards in literacy* (London, RoutledgeFalmer).

Beard, R. (1999) *National Literacy Strategy: review of research and other related evidence* (London, HMSO).

Brooks, G., Pugh, A. K. & Schagen, I. (1996) *Reading performance at 9* (Slough, National Foundation for Educational Research).

Brown, D. & Thomson, C. (2000) *Cooperative learning in New Zealand schools* (Palmerston North, New Zealand, Dunmore Press).

Collins, J. & Marshall, T. (2001) Teaching the Literacy Strategy: a teacher's perspective, *Education 3–13*, 25, 7–12.

Cordon, R. (2000) *Literacy and learning through talk: strategies for the primary classroom* (Buckingham, Open University Press).

DfEE (1997) *The implementation of the National Literacy Strategy* (London, HMSO).

DfEE (1998) *The National Literacy Strategy framework for teaching* (London, Standards and Effectiveness Unit).

DfES (2003) *Speaking, listening and learning, working with children in Key Stages 1 and 2* (London, DfES).

DfES (2004a) *Excellence and enjoyment: learning and teaching in the primary years, professional development materials* (London, DfES).

DfES (2004b) *Primary strategy learning networks* (London, DfES).

DfES (2005a) *Raising achievement for bilingual learners: EAL pilot* (London, DfES).

DfES (2005b) *Leading on inclusion* (London, DfES).

Fisher, R. (2002) *Inside the literacy hour: learning from classroom experience* (London, RoutledgeFalmer).

Fisher, R., Lewis, M. & Davis, B. (2000) Progress and performance in National Literacy Strategy classrooms in England, *Journal of Research in Reading*, 23(3), 256–266.

Fullan, M. (2000) The return of large-scale reform, *Journal of Educational Change*, 1, 5–28.

Galton, M., Hargreaves, L., Coomber, C., Wall, D. & Pell, A. (1999) *Inside the primary classroom: 20 years on* (London, Routledge).

Harrison, C. (2002) *Key Stage 3 English: roots and research* (London, DfES).

Johnson, D. W. & Johnson, R. (1989) *Cooperation and competition: theory and research* (Edina, MN, Interaction Book Company).

Malaguzzi, L. (1993) For an education based on relationships, *Young Children*, 49(1), 9–12.

Moyles, J., Hargreaves, L., Merry, R., Paterson, F. & Esarte-Sarries, V. (Eds) (2003) *Interactive teaching in the primary school: digging deeper into meanings* (Maidenhead, Open University Press).

Mroz, M., Smith, F. & Hardman, F. (2000) The Discourse of the Literacy Hour, *Cambridge Journal of Education*, 30(3), 385–389.

NFER (2003) *Progress in international reading literacy study* (London, NFER).

Ontario Institute for Studies in Education University of Toronto (OISEUT) (2003), *Final report* (London, DfES).

Reynolds, D. & Farrell, S. (1996) *Worlds apart? A review of international surveys of educational achievement involving England* (London, HMSO).

Slavin, R. E. (1996) *Education for all* (The Netherlands, Swets & Zeitlinger, B. V. Lisse).

Solar, J. (2000) *Research evidence and the literacy hour: was the National Literacy Strategy the only option?* Paper presented to British Educational Management and Admin Society, 29–31 March 2000).

UKLA (2004) *Raising boys' achievements in writing* (London, UKLA).

Wray, D., Medwell, J., Poulson, L. & Fox, R. (2002) *Teaching literacy effectively in the primary school* (London, RoutledgeFalmer).

Appendix. Analysis of interviews using key indicators

| School | Section B | | Section C | | | | Section D | | | Overall |
|---|---|---|---|---|---|---|---|---|---|---|
| | B1 | B2 | C1 | C2 | C3 | C4 | D1 | D2 | D3 | No of positive responses |
| A (SFA) | Very enhanced teaching skills | Genuinely interactive | Improved | Good provision | More able stretched | High cost Improved attitude. | Positive impact | Pupils active. Danger of being boring. | Big improvement in reading | 8/9 |
| B (NLS) | Enhanced but initially deskilled. | More group work. Three part lesson now a model. | Improved especially through feedback | School own system. Later some provision | Due to teacher's initiative. | New resources have impacted. | Greater variety but no impact on learning | Pupils too passive. More on task. | Behaviour more positive but problems providing for different learning styles. | 4/9 |
| C (NLS) | Knowledge increased, still needs developing In house training more effective. | A balance of whole class and group work. | Developed anyway not due to NLS. | Not always effective in identifying pupils | This is still an issue. | Impressive response by pupils. | Objectives displayed Learning made clearer. | Danger some children dominate. Depends on teacher. | Overall improvment | 4/9 |
| D (SFA) | Knowledge increased especially phonics and vocabulary | Children are engaged all the time. Strengths of teamwork. | Improved— constructive feedback. | Individual tracking system – also diagnostic. | More able provided for— grouped by ability not age. | Big expense. Materials motivated quality and no of copies helped | Layout facilitated learning and co-operative learning | Children active. Work well in groups. Good for less able. | Definite overall improvment empowered younger children. | 8/9 |

Coding of key indicators:

Section B. Impact on teaching

As a result of this training, are teachers' skills in teaching literacy, enhanced? (B1)

What has been the impact on overall teaching style? (B2)

Section C. Management:

Has the monitoring of teaching shown an improvement in the quality of teaching? (C1)

Does the strategy provide guidance on pupils who are not making sufficient progress? (C2)

Does the strategy provide for the more able pupil? (C3)

Have new resources had an impact on pupils' learning?

Section D. Impact on learning:

Does the organisation/layout of the classroom impact on pupils' learning? (D1)

How does the structure of the lesson impact on pupils' learning? (D2)

What improvements have you seen in pupils' learning? (D3)

# 23 International perspectives on history education

*Hilary Cooper*

History is important in constructing a sense of belonging in time and place.

> The present is where we get lost
> If we forget our own past and have
> No vision of the future
>   (Ayi Kwei Armah, in Fryer 1989)

But there are potential dangers in teaching history:

> There are tensions between political ideology and history education. Identity is a complex concept which covers language, religion, a shared memory and a sense of identity – sometimes of historical grievance and injustice. It is rich in symbolism: heroes, battles lost and won, national anthems, songs, poetry, paintings, memorials, street names.
>
> (Stobart 1996)

As Bruner has said (1996), 'It is not easy, however multicultural your intentions, to help a ten year old create a story that includes him in the world beyond his family and neighbourhood, having been transplanted from . . .'

I have just returned from a symposium in Nicosia (still a divided city), where I was a guest of the Association for Historical Dialogue and Research. The symposium 'What is historical thinking?' aimed to explore ways of developing multi-perspectival approaches to teaching Cypriot history as part of reconciliation with Turkish Cypriots. This symposium reminded me yet again of the power of history education to manipulate or enhance our understanding of who we are, just as I have been reminded in history education conferences in post-fascist Western Europe, post-communist Eastern Europe, South Africa, Russia, and Northern Ireland – and I am a primary specialist. The papers in this special issue give a flavour of the questions being asked in a wide range of countries about the nature of history education, the problems arising, and of the extent to which younger pupils can engage with them. England has of course been deeply engaged in asking and answering these questions over the last two decades and has also experienced the ups and downs in the fortunes of primary history education during this time.

Prior to the statutory introduction of *History in the National Curriculum in England* (DES 1991) if history was taught in primary schools it was generally the grand, nationalistic, and moralistic master story, which was part of a curriculum dominated by behaviourist and didactic approaches. History was barely mentioned in the Plowden Report (1967), which emphasised learning through experience, because history was said to deal with abstract ideas and adult motivations, with which children could not actively engage. However, the National Curriculum aimed to be an enquiry based curriculum offering all pupils from 5 to 14 the opportunity to engage actively in the thinking processes at the heart of each subject, in increasingly complex ways (Bruner 1963). The age range extended to include three to five year olds with the introduction of 'areas of learning' in the *Curriculum Guidance for the Foundation Stage* (2000); the ambitiously named area, 'knowledge and understanding of the world' included finding out about the past, through families, stories, and the environment.

During the late 1970s and 1980s, when the idea of a national curriculum for history was first mooted in England, the purposes and content of and approaches to learning history were widely and hotly debated in the press, in national conferences (e.g. Ruskin College 1980, 1990), and political papers (e.g. Beattie 1987). A broad consensus on content was finally agreed and it was accepted that this content must be explored through the processes of historical enquiry. During the 1970s and 80s there had been research into what historical enquiry means at an academic level and ways in which these enquiry skills might be taught to pupils in school, applying constructivist approaches to history teaching (e.g. Elton 1970; Hallam 1975; Rees 1976; Dickinson and Lee 1978; Booth 1979; Ashby and Lee 1987; Shawyer, Booth, and Brown 1988; Knight 1989) and also, in embryonic ways, in the primary school (e.g. Blakeway 1983; Hodgkinson 1986; Cooper 1991). It emerged that enquiry in history essentially involves:

- making inferences from sources (any traces of the past which remain), understanding the varying status of sources, and that sources are often incomplete and so 'probabalistic thinking' is required, which is valid if it is in line with what is known of the period and there is no contradictory evidence;
- making suggestions based on evidence of how people in societies with different knowledge bases and belief systems from our own may have thought and felt;
- selecting and combining inferences in order to construct accounts of changes over time, causes and effects, similarities and differences, continuity, and change;
- understanding why accounts may be equally valid but different, depending on the time in which they are written, the evidence available, the perspectives and interests of the historian, in groups or individuals, in gender or ethnicity, in political or social history;
- and that therefore history is dynamic; there is no single permanent view of the past.

Initially publishers, museums, and heritage sites were stimulated to provide exciting resources based on the National Curriculum for history and books for teachers drawing on research into constructivist approaches to teaching history to young children.

Sadly, this was 'the golden age of primary history'. With the introduction of the Literacy Hour (DfEE 1998) and the Numeracy Hour (DfEE 1999), national tests in basic skills and school league tables, history in primary education has again been marginalised, although there is hope for a revised, more creative, and coherent curriculum soon.

Meanwhile, other countries around the world have also needed to rethink the nature and processes of history education, often influenced by the English research and experience. The nine papers in this issue give a flavour of the diverse reasons for this, the different problems encountered and research into children's historical understanding. For history is everywhere a powerful subject, which many have a vested interest in controlling.

The first two papers both identify current problems in very different countries, concerning training teachers who feel confident to teach history in primary schools: Lesotho and England. Mary Ntabeni writes about encouraging developments in the social studies programme in Lesotho. This is an aspirational, developing country which was previously, from 1886 to 1966, the British Colony of Basutoland. During this time education consisted of basic skills taught by missionaries. The African Social Studies Programme was set up with 10 other African countries, at Queen's College, Oxford. Mary Ntabeni explains the rationale, values, and objectives of the programme. The history of the Basutho clans and their culture is set within the context of the global community. Mary identifies some of the difficulties history education faces in her country and concludes with an interesting small-scale, experimental, history activity. This thoughtful paper illuminates the extent of the problem of developing both a curriculum and pedagogy rooted in the traditions, assumptions, expectations, and patterns of learning which Mary Ntabeni describes. Sue Temple's paper is an interesting snapshot of what is going on in schools in England through the lens of enthusiastic history teachers. It also identifies similar problems for English primary teachers to those Mary Ntabeni describes; the need for more continuing professional development to support primary history teachers and how to manage effective curriculum change.

The next group of papers describe research into children's thinking in history, based on constructivist approaches in four countries (South Korea, Turkey, Portugal and Brazil), where history education has changed rapidly over the past decade, supported by university research.

Sunjoo Kang describes research with nine year-old South Korean children to investigate what inferences and deductions they could make about the past from visual sources and the previous knowledge and experiences they brought to the activity. Gülçin (Yapıcı) Dilek describes research undertaken with 12 year olds in Turkey, using a combination of visual and written sources. In this cross-curricular study pupils' drawings were analysed using criteria based on theories of both visual and historical thinking skills; it reveals how these skills are interdependent and can enhance pupils thinking in history. In Portugal there has been a considerable amount of research into constructivist approaches to history education; this is seen as essential in creating and maintaining an open society. Isabel Barca, Júlia Castro, and Cláudia Amaral investigate the coherence of pupils' narrative frameworks. Maria Schmidt and Tânia Garcia, in Brazil, also explore pupils' constructions of narrative. In their fascinating and ambitious study they describe how primary pupils and their families constructed their own multifaceted account of their town using primary sources, which was published as a textbook. They then analysed the ways in which teachers used the book with other children.

The following two papers discuss the challenges which countries face in trying to change their primary history education by developing a competence based approach. In Romania, following the fall of Communism, there were debates about what and how history should be taught and over the past 15 years a number of revisions of the national curriculum and textbooks followed; in many counties changes are forged through textbooks. Laura Elena Capita describes her research investigating to what extent and in what ways the latest textbooks incorporate features of active learning: lesson objectives linked to content, learning through projects and activities, use of sources, historical concepts, and self-assessment. This paper deals with the major issue of the role of a subject which has a seminal place in education, shaped to meet the demands of the twenty-first century.

By contrast in Cyprus, divided since 1974 into Turkish and Greek areas, which both have a painful past, Lukas Perikleous and his colleagues at the Association for Historical Dialogue and Research, based in the 'green line' area between Greek and Turkish Nicosea, are looking for ways of teaching about the past through multi-perspectival and constructivist approaches which they hope will develop reconciliation between the two divided communities.

In a final, thought-provoking paper, which identifies a folk pedagogy grounded in deep-rooted cultural and ideological assumptions, Francois Audigier and Nadine Fink describe research studies in France and Switzerland which suggest why many pupils do not see history as contributing anything useful to their education.

I greatly appreciate the opportunity to edit this special issue of *Education 3–11* on history education and am very grateful to everyone who has contributed to it. I am also grateful to Dr Jon Nichol, who helped me with the editing of these diverse papers. I hope that this issue stimulates interest in the importance of history education for younger students, and develops some shared understandings of the ways in which colleagues around the world are working to implement challenging, relevant, and enjoyable ways in which children can engage with the past and the varying difficulties faced in doing so. We are trying to help children to see where they stand in relation to the past, present, and future and that we all have many histories. There is no single, unchanging view of the past and children need, from an early age, to begin to understand why. Maybe the next stage is to develop stronger global perspectives of the past.

# References

Ashby, R., and P.J. Lee. 1987. Children's concepts of empathy and understanding in history. In *The history curriculum for teachers*, ed. C. Portal. Lewes, UK: Falmer Press.

Beattie, A. 1987. *History in peril: May parents preserve it*. London: Centre for Policy Studies.

Blakeway, S.E. 1983. Some aspects of the historical understanding of children aged 7–11. MA Diss., Institute of Education, University of London.

Booth, M. 1979. A longitudinal study of the cognitive skills concepts and attitudes of adolescents studying a modern world history syllabus and an analysis of their historical thinking. PhD Diss., University of Reading.

Bruner, J. 1963. *The process of education*. New York: Vintage Books.

Bruner, J. 1996. *The culture of education*. Cambridge, MA: Harvard University Press.

Cooper, H. 1991. Young children's thinking in history. PhD Diss., Institute of Education, University of London.

Department for Education and Employment (DfEE). 1998. *The national literacy strategy*. London: DfEE.

Department for Education and Employment (DfEE). 1999. *National numeracy framework: Framework for teaching mathematics from reception to year 6*. London: HMSO.

Department of Education and Science (DES). 1991. *History in the national curriculum*. London: HMSO.

Dickinson, A.K., and P.J. Lee, eds. 1978. *History teaching and historical understanding*. London: Heinemann.

Elton, G.R. 1970. What sort of history should we teach? In *New movements in the study and teaching of history*, ed. M. Ballard. London: Temple Smith.

Fryer, P. 1989. *Black people in the British Empire: An introduction*. London: Pluto Press.

Hallam, R.N. 1975. A study of the effect of teaching method on the growth of logical thought with special reference to the teaching of history using criteria from Piaget's theory of cognitive development. PhD Diss., University of Leeds.

Hodgkinson, K. 1986. How artefacts can stimulate historical thinking in young children. *Education 3–13* 14, no. 2: 14–17.

Knight, P. 1989. Children's understanding of people in the past. PhD Diss., University of Lancaster.

Plowden Report. 1967. *Children and their primary schools: A report for the primary education*. London: HMSO.

Qualifications and Curriculum Authority (QCA). 2000. *Curriculum guidance for the foundation stage*. London: QCA.

Rees, A. 1976. Teaching strategies for the advancement and development of thinking skills in history. MPhil Diss., University of London.

Shawyer, G., M. Booth, and R. Brown. 1988. The development of children's historical thinking. *Cambridge Journal of Education* 18, no. 2: 209–19.

Stobart, M. 1996. Tensions between political ideology and history teaching: To what extent may history serve a cause, however well meant? *The Standing Conference of European History Teachers Association*, Bulletin 6.

# Part V

# Primary teachers' work and professionalism

# 24 The primary teacher as servant of the state

*John White*

## Teachers as professionals

A problem facing many primary teachers is the indefiniteness of their job – its lack of clear aims and methodology, as well as its increasingly uncertain 'professional' nature at a time when external bodies are claiming a larger say in determining curriculum content. Until recently things were more clear-cut, at least for teachers leaving their colleges of education with a belief in 'progressive' education. On a 'progressive' view, as I am using the term, educational aims are not things to be imposed on a child from without, but implicit in his own nature: the teacher's job is to create the conditions which best enable each child's individuality to unfold harmoniously. This picture of the 'progressive' teacher is very familiar and I need not elaborate it. What I do wish to emphasise is that progressivism gives the primary teacher *status*, indeed a remarkably high status. It makes her the unquestioned expert on how children should develop. How could external bodies, whether in the shape of the state, LEAs, Taylor Committee governors or whatever, decide on aims and content? The only person who knows what these should be must be both an authority on the laws of child development, and an expert on applying these sensitively to particular cases, i.e. the teacher-psychologist of the progressive tradition. How, too, could a teacher have doubts about her basic aims and methodology? Once again, the theory leaves no room for worries like these. It sees the teacher as a confident professional, the supreme authority on all classroom matters.

This model of professionalism has received some hard knocks in recent years and in my view rightly so. One cannot find out what the aims of education should be from any amount of child observation or psychological theory. Empirical facts do not embody ethical values. The teacher-psychologist of the progressives' model is not and could never be an authority on the broad content and aims of primary education.

The assumption that teachers should have the right to determine aims is unsound. Whatever aims teachers adopt must surely be intended to have *some* influence on the kind of person a pupil grows up to be, and thereby, however minimally, on the kind of society in which he grows up. Since decisions about the kind of society we should have are political decisions, the choice of this set of educational aims rather than that rests basically on a political judgment. The crucial question is: why should teachers be empowered to make such judgments? If they had some special expertise, which the rest of us lack, on the nature of the Good Society, things might be different. But they have not. There are *no* experts on this topic. It is because there are none that democrats believe that political decisions cannot be imposed on people in the name of authority: each man is potentially in as good a position as any other to contribute to political decisions.

For reasons like this many have been advocating recently that the aims of education and the broad framework of school curricula should no longer be determined by teachers, as they have been *de facto*, but democratically, whether at local or at national level. This demand seems to hold within it another threat to the notion of the primary teacher as a professional. She has already lost her credentials as an autonomous teacher-psychologist; and now, if the broad framework within which she is working is to be determined by the electorate, she is apparently to be reduced to no more than a functionary, an obedient executive of political decisions taken elsewhere.

Many non-teachers would welcome such a large circumscription of her role, as has become evident in public reactions to Tyndale and in the Great Debate. I myself have argued elsewhere against the excessive freedom given to teachers in the British system and in favour of greater public control over aims and content. But I have never made it clear, either publicly or to myself, how far I would wish this reversal of policy to be taken. *Is* the primary teacher to become a 'mere functionary' or is there still a place for professional autonomy?

I shall take it as read, as I have in the past, that the teacher should be indeed an authority on what teaching methods and detailed content she should use in specific situations; only she is in a position to know how publicly prescribed content is to be accommodated to the particular abilities, motivations etc. of each of her pupils. The difficulty arises not so much here but over the general framework in which she is working.

## Teachers as civil servants

Supporters of teacher autonomy sometimes speak disparagingly of teachers' 'being turned into civil servants' under a régime of public control, pointing to continental experience to show the very little scope teachers there have to make independent decisions on curricular matters. But perhaps we need to explore the concept of teacher as civil servant a little further. Civil servants in Britain operate at various levels of autonomy, from the tightly circumscribed work of a clerical officer to the very broad scope which, say, a Permanent Secretary has in interpreting government policy. I see no reason why, if teachers in Britain are to become a kind of civil servant, they will have to operate at the more restricted, rather than the less restricted, end of this continuum. Why cannot we reconceptualise the teacher (in our context the primary teacher) as a senior rather than a junior civil servant?

Now I do not want to get into disputes about the proper organisation of the civil service, about whether we should have the kinds of grades we do have, and so on. Perhaps present hierarchies should be scrapped, I don't know. I am only interested in the senior civil servant – national or local – as providing a possible model of what the primary teacher might be under a system of democratic control. First, both jobs would presuppose an acceptance, at least for professional purposes, of a democratically-decided policy forming a framework for all they did. One has, of course, to write in the qualification 'at least for professional purposes' since senior civil servants might *not* accept government policy as private citizens. Perhaps the same could be true of teachers. Problems of conscience will arise, of course. I say rather more about these below. Secondly, for all their subjugation to political authority, senior civil servants do not tend to complain about their lack of freedom. On the contrary: as we have seen, they have considerable room for autonomous interpretation of whatever guidelines are laid down. Teachers could be in a similar position. One might imagine it being publicly laid down, for instance, that such and such areas of science be normally prescribed as minimum achievements for children of such and such an age: this could well leave individual teachers of science considerable scope in deciding the best routes, given their particular constraints and opportunities, to lead to this destination. (This is only, of course, an illustration, not a prescription).

It may strike some as bizarre to compare, say, the teachers of reception classes with senior civil servants. These teachers themselves may be the first to ridicule this idea: the gap between the two sorts of work, the status gap, if you like, is just too enormous. But how far do we think like this because we have conditioned ourselves over the years to do so? Other cultures, other thinkers have had a more exalted picture of the teacher than the British (or, rather, the English and Welsh, since the Scots have tended in another direction). It is true that there is one sig-nificant difference between teachers and senior civil servants, but this should not obscure the way in which they are alike. They are alike in that there need be no one between them and their political masters who 'interprets', as I have put it, political policy, i.e. translates it into practical courses of action. In this way, teach-ers are different from, say, *clerical* civil servants, since the latter *do* have others above them who do this interpreting. The significant difference between teachers and senior civil servants is this: individual civil servants help to forge plans of action applying to the country (or county or borough etc.) as a whole, while individual teachers' translations of public policy apply only to the pupils they teach. No doubt this is one, and one well-founded, source of the ridicule which would meet the attempt to put the infant teacher and the senior civil servant under the same umbrella. But the difference here is only quantitative: *qualita-tively* the two kinds of job may still be similar, in that they can both embody the 'interpreting' role described above.

Many would want to argue, even so, that the civil servant's job is immeasurably more *complex* than the primary teacher's and so cannot be fruitfully compared with it. But *is* it more complex? Think for a moment of the difficult judgments parents constantly have to make about just *one* child's moral development. This problem is compounded many times over for the teacher, even if she has a small class. Add to this the many-sided judgments she has to make about the selection and presentation of material across the whole curriculum, as well as the fact (quite alien to the civil servant's situation) that while making many of these decisions she is at the same time functioning as a model for the children of how they should behave and think – and it should be abundantly clear just how very complex her job is.

In some ways, of course, the jobs of teacher and civil servant are very different. For one thing, teachers do not have hierarchies of subordinates working beneath them. But this will not be seen as a disadvantage by any but the more megalomaniac of teachers. At least teachers need not be tempted into any of the various types of authoritarianism which may entice those at the top of bureaucratic trees. Some of them *can* be so tempted, if they choose to organise their school in a rigidly hierarchical way, but the smallness of scale of the institutions in which they work makes democratic régimes, perhaps even without heads, a possibility. For this reason, primary teachers often have better opportunities to create such régimes than their secondary colleagues. In general, horizontal relationships between equals could become the dominant kind of bonding in the teaching profession, without the vertical, superior-inferior relationships found in the civil service. The need for such horizontal links among teachers, as I am now conceiving them, should be obvious. Teachers of children of different ages cannot be left to interpret officially laid down guidelines completely independently: the teacher of six year olds has some responsibility to see that what she teaches meshes in with what the teachers of the same children at ten, twelve or fourteen do with them. It is sometimes urged against the comparison between teachers and senior civil servants that the latter are small, close-knit bodies and that teachers can never hope to emulate them in their cohesiveness since they are so numerous and so scattered. But there is no reason why the teachers in different schools in the same local area should not dovetail their curricula and syllabuses, working as a single unit in much the same way as senior civil servants, with, for instance, far more mobility between different institutions in the system. There is, in fact, every reason why they should cooperate in this way; otherwise the education which any particular pupil will receive in the whole course of his schooling is likely to be the hit-and-miss, hotch-potch affair it too often is today.

I hope these various points are enough to show where I am laying the emphasis in the comparison between the primary teacher and the senior civil servant. Despite the several ways in which they are different, both of them are in the unique position of being the direct translators of political policy into more determinate courses of action.

## Teachers as reflective thinkers

The new role I have been sketching for the primary teacher is very different from that in the progressive tradition. She will above all be a person of wide horizons. She will need, first, to understand the aims of the whole education system as democratically laid down; she will need to reflect on how to fit her own teaching into this framework ensuring at the same time that it meshes in with what her colleagues are doing in other institutions. Her horizons can no longer be bounded by her school, let alone, as with some of our most autonomous primary teachers today, by her classroom. She must see her day-to-day activity ultimately against the political framework which is to give it its *raison d'être*.

I am aware that this conception of the primary teacher runs quite against everything that we have come to expect of her. Of all members of the teaching profession, she has traditionally been the least politically aware. Her typical milieu has been the world of art and crafts, of movement and drama, of learning to read and count. It has typically been a cosy, inward-looking world, quite cut off from the complexities of politics. The new primary teacher will need to be more knowledgeable, more reflective about society and its values than her present-day counterpart. It is difficult to draw a line round the kinds of knowledge one would ideally require of her. A deeper understanding of political realities necessitates some knowledge of economics, sociology, applied science, social and political history . . . one could go on and on. A deeper reflectiveness about aims and their realisation depends among other things on something of a philosophical understanding. All this imposes great intellectual demands on her, demands which her initial training can never hope to meet on its own, if at all. I shall come back to this point later.

Meanwhile let me take up in more detail the point just made about reflection on aims. Ideally one would hope that public prescriptions about aims and content were also backed by a public rationale, which discussed in full such matters as the justification of different proposals and the relative priority to be given to each. Teachers will have to be able to argue their way around such rationalia.

If this kind of educational ideal is ever to be realised, it is clear that primary teachers will have to be far more adequately trained than hitherto to reflect on the larger purposes of their job. Their current lack of sophistication in this field, which emerges, as we shall see in a moment, from the Schools Council's *Aims into Practice in the Primary School*[1], is not to be blamed on them. It is the product of a system in which discussion of aims has been, wittingly or unwittingly, discouraged, for fear of opening rifts between ideological positions and endangering a 'consensus' thought necessary for the system to operate.

A brief look at *Aims into Practice* will show more clearly the kind of reflectiveness required. The book is based on a survey of primary teachers' objectives. It discovered that their views on aims (I am using 'aim' and 'objective' interchangeably) tend to lie in a continuum. At one extreme teachers believe that 'education is the means used by society . . . to ensure that new generations will maintain it both practically and ideologically' (p.11). Such teachers 'rate as most important aims dealing the basic skills and with conventionally acceptable social behaviour' (p.12). At the other extreme 'is the view that education is a personal service to the individual' (p.11). Here the aims thought most important are 'concerned with developing independence, both emotional and intellectual, and with a much broader educational front, including art, music, movement, drama, and so on' (p.12). Few teachers, we are told, are exclusively attached to one of these extreme positions: 'the great majority hold both to some extent' (p. 11), but with differing emphases.

The tension described is immediately recognisable. So, too, is the compromise which many teachers seem to settle for, i.e. to pay a certain amount of attention to basic skills and in the rest of the time to foster the child's personal development by allowing him plenty of choice among *activities*, especially creative activities; a régime, for instance, of reading and sums in the morning, 'choosing time' in the afternoon.

The question now is: have those teachers – i.e. most teachers – who adhere to both ends of the continuum really thought things through in depth? I am sceptical. For if one looks at all closely at either of the competitors, one sees obvious deficiencies. Why should the society-centred view, for example, put such emphasis on basic skills and conventionally acceptable social behaviour? Why not on the arts, on science, on political understanding? If we are concerned with the well-being of society, why should this broader understanding be thought less important? Presumably it is because the society-centred aim is dominated, as in the 'Great Debate', by economic demands: we will not survive as an industrial nation without a workforce that is literate and numerate and also industrious, punctual and cooperative. But why should economic considerations be overriding? Citizens of a society are more than workers, and there is no reason why their education should be restricted in this way. Why, too, should the status quo be taken as a baseline? Perhaps 'conventionally acceptable social behaviour' is *un*acceptable from another, namely a moral, point of view. Just because conventional ways of doing things do exist or have existed, this is no reason for claiming that they *should* exist.

Narrowness of vision also affects the pupil-centred point of view. Why should creative activities in art, movement, music and drama etc. be especially highlighted? There are historical reasons for this, I believe, to do especially with Percy Nunn's aesthetically-inclined theory of 'individuality'. If we are concerned with the well-being of the individual, why are science or political understanding (again) to be played down? Won't the pupil need *all sorts of* intellectual equipment, and not just the aesthetic, properly to fulfil himself?

But now we are getting into difficult waters. What is to count as 'self-fulfilment' or as the 'well-being of the individual' is a philosophical problem of some depth. So, too, is the meaning of the 'well-being of society'. Whatever one finally says about both these matters, two things should be clear at the outset. First, there is no good reason to narrow them down in the way proposed. The compromise curriculum, of basic skills, social training and plenty of creative activities is too thin a diet. Second, the opposition of pupil to society is misconceived, simply because the pupil is a member of society. Of course, if 'social needs' are to be limited to the requirements of the industrial establishment, then the pupil may indeed have no part in this, except as a means to others' ends; and it is as a reaction to this that many teachers have taken up the cause of individual self-development. But if 'society' is to be understood in any less restrictive sense, which includes the pupil himself as one of its members, the whole continuum of aims on which *Aims into Practice* located so many of its teachers, simply collapses.

We would do well to abandon the continuum. It is rooted in conflicting attitudes to modern industrial society. Against those who see education as the handmaiden of industry are those unwilling to sacrifice individuals' potentialities to capital's demands. But their reaction is often too negative. It leads too readily to a fruitless escapism: if the 'real world' of industry is too inhuman to contemplate, let us turn our backs on it and paint and sing and do collages. Teachers who hold both attitudes – i.e. the majority discovered by the survey – must be riven by conflict, half chained to necessity and half desiring to be free of it. It would not be surprising if this conflict were transmitted gradually to their pupils. And is this not indeed precisely what we find in a large part of our adult population today: on the one side a resignation to industrial semi-serfdom, and on the other the vain hope that one may one day strike it rich?

The continuum merely mirrors the social status quo. It allows little or no place to any critical challenge to it. This comes out very clearly in the recent HMI survey of *Primary Education in England*.[2] This draws attention to the schools' general failure to teach pupils to argue a case, to reason things out. Social studies and science, both areas in which critical skills may be developed, are particularly ill provided for. (Political education is presumably so little in evidence in any of the schools surveyed that it is not mentioned even once).

This is not the place to go in detail into what should replace the continuum, assuming it is abandoned. But I have at least hinted at the need to see individual pupils as members of society, not as standing over against it; to reconsider how the 'good of society' and the 'good of the individual' are really to be opposed; to broaden the primary curriculum, whether approached from 'society' or from the 'individual'; to create a new kind of industrial society in which there is less escapism because there is less sense of servitude. This last remark, I believe, strikes at the heart of things. We need somehow to construct a society in which men can work without the thought that they are sacrificing their one, unique life for nothing; in which their work is freely and willingly undertaken as a condition of their own and others' self-fulfilment. How this will be possible without a wide-scale democratisation of industry and a political education to prepare one for it, I do not know.[3]

## Teachers as political activists

I have argued that *Aims into Practice* reveals that if the primary teacher's role is to be remodelled in the way described, she will have to reflect more deeply than at present on aims. She should not take for granted what passes as the conventional wisdom, but should follow through the logic of an argument to its underlying assumptions, challenge these assumptions, put forward less inadequate alternatives if the latter prove wanting. This will lead her inevitably to frame her own picture of the kind of society we should be working to create. If my intuition is correct, reason will guide her towards the vision of a participatory democracy in both industry and in local and national politics. Obviously more would need to be said in support of this view. But, if correct, it brings out the point that the kind of reflectiveness one may expect in a teacher about her aims is all of a piece with the reflectiveness one would look for in her as a citizen of a democracy: each role demands a sophisticated political awareness.

This came out also in another way. As the person directly responsible for translating politically-determined aims into practice, she has some obligation to try to ensure that these official aims *are* so translatable. They may fail to be realisable in several ways: there may be practical difficulties in doing so; they may be impossibly vague or inconsistent; if one follows through their implications, they may be seen to be at odds with certain basic moral principles, and so on. Of these three kinds of defect specified, the first might make the aims *practically* unrealisable, the second *logically* unrealisable and the third *morally* unrealisable, that is, unrealisable by one whose basic moral principles they offended. So there is some obligation on the teacher, arising not only from her role as executant, but also from her being an autonomous moral agent, to bring pressure to bear to ensure that the official aims are aims that she can – practically, logically and morally – teach to. She is not to be a passive recipient of aims from above, but must play an active part in helping to improve them. This means political involvement – of two kinds. She has a duty to draw the attention of policy-makers to any practical or logical defects in actual guidelines. There must be *official* channels enabling her to do this. As for the moral obstacles, she can attempt to influence the political community – by pressure group activity, work within a political party, journalism or whatever – to change the guidelines themselves.

All this is implicit, I think, in the new model of the primary teacher. Not that every teacher will live up to all the expectations in the model in every particular. Not all, for instance, despite what I seemed to say in the last paragraph, will be political activists. There is certainly, as I indicated, *some moral obligation* on them to be, if official aims are morally inadequate, in their view. But whether this obligation is to be overridden by other more important moral obligations is something that each individual teacher must be left to work out for herself. Certainly I do not mean to imply that the gifted teacher of music, who would be not nearly so good a teacher if she had to attend to political matters, should necessarily sacrifice her teaching. Whether she does so is a matter for own conscience. But at the very least, in *seeing* this as a matter for her own conscience, she must be aware of the conflicting obligations on her, the pedagogical and the political. And this means that she must possess the breadth of vision, the wide intellectual and moral horizons which I have been advocating.

Similar considerations apply to the teacher who has conscientious objections to official aims so great that she cannot teach to them. For her it is not a matter of accepting imperfect aims *pro tem*, trying meanwhile to improve them by political action: she just cannot in all conscience agree to them. For her, too, there will be a conflict of obligations, between accepting, on the one hand, that she is not arbitrarily to lay down her own aims, and being morally unable, on the other, to accept an actual democratically-arrived-at decision. For her, too, how she resolves the conflict – whether by bending the rules, by resignation, or however – must be left to her.

## The greatest challenge

The new portrait of the primary teacher is so far from present actualities that many will dismiss it as impossibly utopian: it is too intellectually, perhaps even too spiritually, demanding for the average teacher; theoretically, it may form a pretty whole, but from a practical point of view it is a non-starter.

I disagree. What I hope to have done is set up some kind of signpost, indicating a new direction in which to move. How far we can get along the road I don't know. The greatest challenge is to find practical ways of getting the primary teacher to accept this grander conception of her role. Something, no doubt, may be attempted in her initial induction into the job of teaching during her pre-service training. But horizons cannot be widened at a stroke. Years of deepening understanding and reflectiveness are necessary, acquired in intimate association with practical classroom experience. How the teacher achieves this deepened understanding – by in-service courses, by informal discussion with colleagues, by solitary reflection – is another matter. It is a pity that our status-oriented society opens few paths before the ambitious young teacher beyond the climb up to headships, the inspectorate, LEA work or similar better-paid jobs. *No* work in education could be so responsible as the classroom teacher's and no work potentially so intellectually challenging. If we could once get the conditions of work right – manageable classes, adequate time to think out what one is doing, and so on – what more 'successful' persons in the educational system could there be than the broad-visioned, practically competent classroom teacher?

## Notes

I would like to thank Pat White for her help in revising an earlier draft of this paper.

## References

1. Ashton, P. et al, *Aims into Practice in the Primary School* (London, University of London Press, 1975).
2. *Primary Education in England* (London, HMSO, 1978).
3. See White, P.A. 'Work-place democracy and political education' in *Journal of Philosophy of Education* vol. XIII, 1979.

# 25 Teachers studying classroom learning

## Stephen Rowland

Six years ago Michael Armstrong put forward a research proposal which was accepted by Leicestershire LEA to conduct fieldwork in order to gain some understanding of the quality of children's intellectual activity as it is evidenced in the classroom. His plan was to work as both a teacher and a researcher alongside another teacher and thereby gain access to the details of the children's work as it progressed. After considering various schools, he decided to spend most of the year working with me in my class of eight to nine year olds in Sherard Primary School, Melton Mowbray. Although we taught and 'researched' together, he took the major responsibility for the research, while I undertook the day to day running of the classroom. The results of this year's work were then written up in the book *Closely Observed Children*.[1] In this article I want to describe some of the developments that have taken place since then, the ideas behind this type of inquiry and the problems and possibilities it raises.

After that year together, it became clear that the value of two experienced teachers working together to teach and research into classroom learning did more than increase our understanding about the quality of children's thinking – most important though that is. It also provided me, as the class teacher, with a unique opportunity to increase my own awareness of the complex relationship between what I do as a teacher, the subject matter being studied and the resulting changes in the children's skills and abilities.

The central idea behind this work – one might say a research assumption which our evidence appeared to support – was that children's work is worth taking seriously, not merely as reflecting the fits and starts towards the ultimate goal of adulthood, but as a contribution in its own right. For example, if we consider the painting of a child in the same light as we would that of an adult artist, or their philosophical puzzlings as we would the thoughts of a philosopher, then, granted the limitations in experience which are bound to constrain the child more than the adult, we find children to be artists, philosophers.

Such a notion may sound somewhat fanciful, romantic and 'unscientific'. How could one set about verifying such a claim? Is it not just another bit of progressivist myth? But such criticism, I think, misses the point. We would not make this claim as a statement of objective fact, but as describing an approach, a stance from which we should view children's endeavours. Only by doing so were we able to make sense of their work and account for its development. Without an approach which conceives of the child as a rational and fully human being, their intellectual activity could only be explained as being the combination of arbitrary behaviour and mechanistic responses to the world in which they learn.

The philosophical discussion of this point could be pursued endlessly – and indeed it has been a central issue of the project as it is now developing in Leicestershire – but I wish instead to look at the implications for adopting such a stance as far as teachers doing research is concerned.

There is a wealth of research evidence which makes it quite clear that few classrooms provide the type of environment which is in any way similar to that in which we would expect the adult writer, mathematician or whatever to function in. Those of us who have tried (against all the odds, recently) to provide an 'informal' or 'open' education have seen the need to provide an intellectual space in which students can reflect, make choices and develop a critical awareness of their own activity. Only when the classroom atmosphere includes an element of this can we, as teachers or as researchers, begin to 'get into' the child's thinking. Only then can we perceive the rational human that is so easily submerged in the hectic teacher-centred organisations that many of us feel contrained to operate.

It was in the hope of finding such an informal classroom that Michael Armstrong came to work with me, and that, two years later I decided to work with Chris Harris in his class of nine to eleven year olds at Merton School, Syston. There, with the support of the LEA and Leicester University (to which I was seconded to do a research MEd), I aimed to continue the enquiry from where Michael had left off. I was particularly concerned to gain a clearer understanding of how children can provide a structuring of their own work, how their skill can develop in response to their perceived need for development, or, in general terms, how children are able to exercise a degree of control over their own learning.[2] Clearly, the exploration of such matters required a classroom in which the children were encouraged by their teacher to work independently to some extent, to value the contribution which they could make and to use their initiative. It was apparent that children working exclusively on programmed work schedules or on other activities rigidly structured by the teacher, were unlikely to provide much valuable evidence about the abilities of children to plan and organise their learning.

At this point the reader might criticise what we were trying to do as being merely to select a 'cosy' and informal classroom where our own convictions were liable to be supported, to staff it with two experienced teachers (teaching and researching together), and, hardly surprisingly, we would find the children working imaginatively and making responsible use of the autonomy offered them. The necessarily subjective nature of our analysis of the children's work left open to question whether our interpretations and findings would be supported by other teachers working under more normal conditions. In question here was not only the 'truth' of our findings (are children really as we depict?), but their value (if they are, how does it help me to teach?)

As 'pure researchers' we might only be expected to meet the first of these objections, it would be up to others to decide upon the value of our findings. But as committed teachers, it became vital to explore our ideas with other teachers not only as a check to their plausibility, but also to see if others found them useful. Furthermore, we felt that the process of gathering and analysing work from the classroom had increased our professional awareness. Might not others benefit from such experience?

It was in order to meet these criticisms and explore these possibilities that we set up a research consultative group in 1978. This group of about fifteen (and now grown to thirty) classroom teachers met together once or twice a term out of common interest in the work. Initially, Michael Armstrong and myself would present material we had gathered from the classroom – a child's painting, a series of stories, our description of a scientific investigation, etc. – together with our tentative analysis of it. Invariably our presentations were well received. People seemed to think our analyses were plausible enough. At first such agreement seemed to confirm what we were finding out about children. But underneath this comfortable agreement I became aware of an increasing unease with what we were doing. This unease was rarely articulated and took nearly two years of the group meeting before it came fully to light. It then became apparent to me that general agreement with our interpretations of children's work was not sufficient. Any descriptive account of what happens in a classroom is made in the light of a particular theoretical perspective. (This problem of the impossibility of theory-free data is not only applicable to qualitative or descriptive analysis. It applies equally, though this is too rarely recognised, to quantitative data. Even if we had made accurate measurements rather than a form of analysis which relies on judgement, the question still remains 'Why were those particular measures made?' which, to be answered, must lead back to a statement of theory or value.) Our particular problem was that unless the other teachers themselves contributed material which they had selected, described and analysed, we would not be able to confront the issues of the theoretical underpinning of our work. Up till that point people had agreed with our analyses largely because no alternative was available to the 'reality' of the classroom as viewed from our own theoretical perspective. Had others worked with the same children, they would have seen a different 'reality'. Only then could conflicting 'realities' lead to critical consideration of the theoretical perspectives themselves.

But all this is no simple matter. Like the question of our approach to children's learning, it has been the subject of hours of discussion amongst those in the group, and is never likely to be finally resolved. However, as far as our research and the professional development of teachers were concerned, it was clear that a more active part needed to be taken by all those involved. And so, in 1980, the local authority agreed to support the enlargement of the scheme. The consultative group was doubled in size, with four full day meetings per year during term time. Also, support was given for other teachers who might be interested to obtain secondment from their schools so that they could also work for a year alongside a colleague, teaching and researching as Michael Armstrong and I had done earlier. Leicester University has also been supportive in this, offering places at the School of Education so that these studies could be incorporated into research MEd degrees. While the encouragement and practical assistance that the LEA and the University has been able to provide have been vital to our development, we have also been fortunate in that we have been allowed the autonomy to develop the project according to the wishes of its participants. So far, five teachers have taken up the opportunity to conduct their own teacher/researcher studies on secondment, and others hope to start next year.

I would like now to look in a little more detail at the work that has been done, its methods and its concerns. Our central idea is that teaching itself involves an element of research – finding out how the student is thinking, what is important to him and so on – in order that we might be able to respond appropriately. It is this aspect of teaching which; as teacher/researchers, we wish to capitalise upon. Compared with more traditional forms of research, we do not have a highly developed array of techniques distinct from those strategies which we would use as teachers. Were we to enter the classroom armed with sophisticated recording devices, the danger is not so much that we would disturb the classroom which we are studying (our presence as teachers does that anyway), but that our relationship with the children as one of their teachers would be threatened. It is upon a relationship of mutual confidence and proximity that our access to data depends. In general, we have held to the principle that only those research techniques should be used which can be justified on teaching grounds and pose no threat to the open relationships involved. Thus we are not concerned to 'bug' our classrooms, but try to record activity in a way which helps the learning we are studying. For example, we have often found that audio tapes, photographs and fieldnotes made in the classroom as work progresses, become transformed into a valuable teaching aid when played back or read to the students involved. Moreover, their response often increases the value of such records as research material. This access which students have to our material and our thoughts on their work has been found to be crucial especially with secondary school students who might otherwise become suspicious of our activity.

As far as the work in the classroom goes, the activity of the teacher/researcher would appear to differ little from that of the 'host' teacher (where a teacher/researcher and 'host' teacher work together in a classroom). Ideally, both would equally teach together, using the additional human resource in order to follow the children's work in much more detail than would normally be possible. In practice, however, the teacher/researcher takes the responsibility for the research and so it is important that he is able to work with the children in a way which is unpressurised, free as much as possible from the minute to minute and external demands that occupy so much of the normal classroom teacher's time. Some have described the teacher/researcher process as being one in which they have been able to work as 'ideal' teachers, interacting with their students whenever this appears to be valuable and for longer stretches of time than is often practicable in the normal way.

For those conducting fieldwork on secondment, this daily teaching is followed in the evening by making detailed notes describing the work they have been involved in and analysing it. The object of this analysis will depend upon the focus of the particular investigation, but it will normally be concerned to uncover the purposes that students have in their work, the ways in which they interpret the various environmental 'inputs' and the ways in which growth in understanding takes place. As has been suggested, any such analysis is bound to be highly infer-ential and subjective, and so it is most important that these notes are discussed as widely as possible. Normally, the 'host' teacher will take an interest in this, per-haps contributing his own notes or comments of the field-notes. As co-ordinator of the project, I would also read and comment on the notes, and at times univer-sity supervisors will also add their comments. In addition, all those on second-ment meet once a week to discuss certain fieldnotes in more detail, and there are occasional opportunities to share them with the wider consultative group at its meetings. These opportunities to share the descriptions and interpretations of children's work not only provide the possibility of checking up on one's own ideas about the work, but also provide a forum in which further analysis takes place. However full a description of, say, a child's painting or mathematical investiga-tion, it is difficult, on one's own, to provide a very full or coherent analysis. It is often other teachers, with perhaps quite different teaching experience, who pro-vide the odd clues, the missing pieces, by which we can grasp a clearer idea of what the particular work signifies. For this reason, the weekly meetings of the seconded teachers and the meetings of the consultative group, have not been so much vehicles for disseminating the work (although they do have that function) but have become primarily a forum in which analysis takes place.

This integration of analysis and dissemination is an important characteristic of our work. Traditionally, it is the job of professional researchers to gather the mate-rial and conduct the analysis, then produce the 'findings' for the consumer. The consumer (often the teacher, in educational research) can then make use of these findings, or ignore them (as is often the case). In our work, the teacher is also the researcher: the roles of consumer and producer are combined. The teacher is no longer presented with a package to be acted upon or left, but is himself involved in its production. While we may not agree with a particular teacher/researcher's interpretation of a child's work, or the implications which are drawn from it, such disagreement becomes a positive and active attitude, one from which we can learn and from which we can contribute our own ideas into the dynamic of analysis. As this suggests, analysis is not a process which ends at some point, or one which is right or wrong in its entirety (though mistakes as well as insights are frequent). So often have we found that a particular piece of work has been written about and discussed with different groups of teachers, but then, in the light of a further teacher's experience, it becomes seen in a new light. In this way, the valuable resource of each teacher's experience is exploited in the process of research.

As suggested earlier, this critical reflection upon our research 'findings' ('con-cerns' might be a better word here), becomes possible only when the 'audience' are also involved in the research process. Amongst the group of teachers seconded to do a year's fieldwork, this involvement is absolute. But increasingly, the teach-ers in the consultative group – who represent a wide range of primary and second-ary schools in county and inner city areas – have begun to conduct their own studies. The 'fieldwork' for this is sometimes done within the normal teaching routine. At other times, it requires a colleague or myself to stand in and take care of the minute to minute needs of the children while the teacher, as 'teacher/researcher', concentrates on some particular aspect of the children's work which is to be studied in more detail. Discussion, and often some form of written documentation, of the work may then lead to a presentation at a meeting of the consultative group. In this way the meetings of the consultative group have changed from being a forum in which the results of full time teacher/researchers are scrutinised, to one in which the members of the group present and analyse material from their own classrooms. But as these small scale studies get under way, so the meetings of the consultative group become less central to its members, and the school itself becomes the place where discussion and analysis takes place. A teacher once described the consultative group meetings as providing what the ordinary staff room should provide – an opportunity and an atmosphere in which teachers can seriously discuss the work of their students. I think many of us would agree that staff rooms do not at present provide this opportunity (if they ever did), and that increasing pressure in terms of teacher/pupil ratios and curriculum demands make it less likely that they will do so. But if more of us can begin to conduct our own small studies, based upon the needs of our own classrooms as we see them, then perhaps this trend could be reversed. As we begin to do this – and I believe we are only just beginning – then the consultative group will change again from being a centre in which research ideas are generated, to a group which provides a supportive structure and meeting point for a wide variety of school-based research projects. This I see as being the final objective of our work: to stimulate and support school environments in which educational research – that is, the serious and disciplined study of learning and teaching – can be generated to meet the needs of the schools. Only then will the artificial distinction which has been made between 'researcher' and 'teacher' be eliminated, with the result that educational research becomes meaningful to teachers and its results affect their practice.

So far I have said little about the content of our studies. Since we see it as important that teachers pursue their own interests, the topics cover a wide area. One study attempts to describe the ways in which adolescent students, in writing from their own personal experience, seek at once to gain a greater sense of their own identity and at the same time to explore the broader social world. In another, a tentative model is suggested for describing the prescientific activity of young children in a primary school. Yet another examines in detail the ways in which scientific concepts are developed both through the science curriculum and through work in the humanities. Small scale studies conducted by classroom teachers in the consultative group cover such areas as the ways in which the social relationships of one child in a primary classroom affect the quality of her learning; the use that a group of young children make of a tape recorder as a medium for composing their own stories. The reader might wonder how it is possible to achieve a sense of unity with such a decentralised and wide ranging collection of studies.

Part of the answer to this lies in the research approach that we all adopt, that is, to view the child's activity and work as the starting point of our investigations, rather than the teacher's teaching. I know it would be facile to view teaching and learning as separate phenomena, as though one can exist independently of the other. However, almost all classroom research has focused on the teacher's teaching rather than the child's learning. It is often assumed that learning follows directly from teaching. Studies that have sought to correlate the pupils' achievements with the teacher's performance (eg ORACLE[3] and Bennett,[4] 1976) invariably use forms of standardised testing to measure the former – tests whose value is suspected by many teachers and which can reveal little of the quality, rather than the quantity, of what is learnt. Even the growing trend towards 'action research' (The Ford Teaching Project,[5] Action Research Network,[6]), which has many similarities with our own work – in particular the way in which the teacher has the role of researcher – normally sees the teacher as the main subject of study whose performance is to be improved through his own research. The risk that such studies run, is that without sufficient analysis of the learning process itself through close examination of the children's work, unjustifiable assumptions are made concerning the relationship between the teacher's behaviour and the child's learning. On the other hand our studies with their focus upon the children's work, run the risk of taking insufficient account of the teacher's influence in generating learning. We have, I think, been aware of this danger, and much of our time in the consultative group meetings is now spent trying to articulate the complex relationships between how the teacher teaches and the learner learns. We are in fact approaching a view in which learning and teaching are seen as inseparable activities. The view that knowledge is not a commodity which is 'passed on' from teacher to learner – and is thus not readily quantifiable – leads us to see learning as some kind of active construction or reconstruction which both the teacher and learner are engaged in each time they together confront 'a community of subject matter which extends beyond the circle of their intimacy'.[7] Perhaps it is the significance we attach to the child's contribution to this 'community of subject matter' which leads us to adopt such a 'constructive' – rather than imitative – view of learning, one according to which child learning is, in principle, no different from adult learning.

From what has been said, it should be clear that the consultative group, in its meetings, is largely concerned to articulate a framework which underlies our studies of children's work. But our attempts to develop a rationale for 'the nature of learning', 'the research methodology', 'the purpose of education', and other such grand issues which must underly any research endeavour – and they must – inevitably prove to be fraught with difficulties.

The first difficulty is evident in any discussion of an abstract and highly ideological or value-laden nature. The participants soon feel that they are, yet again, tackling the same old unresolved question and getting no further with it. Alternatively, the question is not tackled because the terms of the discussion cannot be agreed upon – hours are spent discussing these terms and one ends up in a semantic bog. This problem is most evident when the participants do not share central beliefs and values. But matters can be just as bad when they do share (or think they share) such understanding, for then the assumptions upon which they are working may not be brought into the open to be challenged. We have found this type of difficulty to be most evident when the starting point for discussion is a theoretical issue – for example, 'What is the value of student autonomy in the classroom?' We have found that, to some extent, the problem can be overcome if the theoretical issue is no longer seen as the starting point, but actual material from the classroom (work samples, descriptions, etc) is seen as the focus of the debate. While consideration of such material and its anlaysis inevitably leads to the discussion of theoretical concerns, we at least have the concrete material before us to refer to in order to clarify and illustrate the meanings that develop in the course of the discussion. Looked at in this way, presentations of classroom material may be seen not so much as providing evidence to support a particular theory about learning or teaching, but as a reference point from which a variety of theoretical perspectives might be developed. It is, I think, by this means that we can increase our level of awareness as teachers; by using specific instances of learning in order to develop a greater articulation of the theoretical ideas that underly our practice. We thereby bring to a conscious level what had been unconsciously assumed, transforming intuition (so often held to be the chief resource of the 'good' teacher) into deliberation which is thus open to change.

The second difficulty we have when it comes to sharing our teaching and research experience concerns the extent to which values are shared between us. On the one hand, we would not want to develop a doctrine which would necessarily exclude many teachers. On the other, too wide a divergence would make it impossible for us to communicate and so share our understandings. What we have tried to do is to develop a language for talking about classroom experience, a language rooted in the activity of the child, a language which permits the individual teacher to extend his own ideas rather than uncritically to take on board or reject the ideas of others. Careful observation of children at work can provide the start to developing such a language. But just as we can never absolutely share experience, so we can never absolutely share a language. This is the problem we shall always have as teachers learning together. It is also the problem we and our students confront in our classrooms as we strive to share experience of the world.

# References

1. Armstrong, M., *Closely Observed Children*, Writers and Readers, London, 1981.
2. Rowland, S., *Enquiry into Classroom Learning*, unpublished MEd thesis, Leicester University, 1980.
3. Galton, M., Simon, B., ed., *Inside the Primary Classroom*, and *Progress and Performance in the Primary Classroom*, Vols. 1 and 2 of the Observational Research and Classroom Learning Evaluation project, Routledge and Kegan Paul, 1980 and 1981.
4. Bennett, N., *Teaching Styles and Pupil Progress*, Open Books, London, 1976.
5. East Anglia, University of, Centre for Applied Research in Education, *Ford Teaching Project*, 1975.
6. Elliott, J., *Action Research: A Framework for Self Evaluation in Schools*, Working Paper No. 1 of the Schools Council Programme 2 'Teacher-Pupil Interaction and the Quality of Learning' Project, 1981.

7. Hawkins, D., *The Informed Vision: Essays on Learning and Human Nature,* Agathon Press, New York, 1974, 49.

Further examples of the qualitative analysis of children's work may be found in:

Rowland, S., *Ability Matching: A Critique* in Forum for the Discussion of New Trends in Education, 1979, Vol. 21, No. 3, 82.

Rowland, S., *How to Intervene: Clues from the Work of a Ten Year Old,* Forum, 1981, Vol. 23, No. 2, 33.

# 26 Educational reform and primary teachers' work

## Some sources of conflict

*R.J. Campbell*

## Introduction: the politics of educational reform in the United Kingdom

In this article I want to examine the relationship between education reform policy and primary teachers' work, exploring some of the dilemmas for teachers arising from the relationship. I want, in particular, to look at the dilemmas associated with the culture of primary schools, and then I would like to conclude by raising some questions about how far that culture has become anachronistic. Before doing that, however, I would want to make three introductory points about the recent politics of educational reform.

First, a few facts. In the seven years since the 1988 Education Reform Act there have been five different Secretaries of State for Education. Anthony Crosland reckoned that it took about two years for a good Minister to master his/her brief and develop policy effectively and with authority. There have been four permanent secretaries – the Sir Humphreys of the DfE. The National Curriculum Council and the Schools Examination and Assessment Council had between them, in four years, some six Chief Executives and/or Chairmen. In its short life – under two years – the SCAA has already had two Chief Executives. One impressive irony about this motley procession passing quickly across our national policy-making stage is that they were charged with, amongst other things, introducing greater continuity and consistency into the school system. But it also provides a picture of ephemeral involvement in policy making by politicians and others before they move on to something else, with apparently little concern for the impact of their decision making on the teachers and pupils. I remain shocked by the paragraph in Duncan Graham's book about his time as Chairman and Chief Executive of the NCC:

> Eventual reform of the curriculum was inevitable the moment it was decided to introduce it subject by subject. The appointment of individual subject working groups guaranteed that zealots outnumbered cynics – always a dangerous thing – and that no subject would be knowingly undersold. When the full enormity of the consequences became clear, complexity and over-prescription became the cry of those who had caused it.
>
> (Graham and Tytler, 1993, p 118)

He implies that he and others knew that the first National Curriculum orders would have to be revised – he knew *before* they became statutory that they would have to be revised – yet primary teachers were required to waste hours and hours of their time over three years implementing them. The consequences of this shifting and unstable policy making is that the central agencies for reform should have forfeited whatever professional creditbility they might once have had – so that the responsibility for real reform is now more clearly on the schools, back where it ought to be.

Secondly, before 1988 the word 'reform' had positive associations; it generally meant as a noun, 'the amendment of some faulty state of things', and as a verb, 'to renew, to re-build, or to convert into another and better form' (all from *Shorter Oxford English Dictionary*). Thus, educational reform meant, by definition, educational *improvement*.

Since 1988 the word 'reform' has been corrupted by the way it has been used in political discourse, promiscuously attached to any untried proposal for *change* in advance of the time when it could be known whether the change would lead to improvement. Thus the Act that brought in the changes was entitled the Education Reform Act 1988, and the changes in school governance, in curriculum and assessment, and in control over the education system, were typically referred to as 'the government's reform'. There was something Orwellian in this use of language in that it enabled opposition to the changes, or open-minded scepticism about them, to be presented as resistance to much-needed improvement.

It also created problems for those writing about the changes since it became increasingly difficult to write in a way that kept the concepts of change and reform technically distinct. I use the term reform to read as *'reform'*, the inverted commas implying that the worthwhileness of the outcomes of the change process remains in doubt.

Third, a simple claim which can be supported from much of the research into the impact of educational reform over the last 20 years or so, both here and else-where. Curruculum reform policies do not generally, or easily, lead to the cur-riculum change intended but they usually affect teachers' work and their work relationships, often in ways that they were unintended. Ten years ago I published a book (Campbell, 1985) on the work of what are now called 'curriculum co-ordinators' (or more frightfully, 'subject managers'). In it I argued that you could not create curriculum change in primary schools without creating changes in the work and work relations of the teachers and in the culture of the school, and I believe that continues to be the case.

## Conceptualising teachers' work

As a preamble to the main argument it may be helpful to provide a brief and rather simplified overview of the ways in which the work of primary teaching has been conceptualised and researched.

Until the early 1980s teachers' work as a concept was largely defined by rather arid arguments about the idea of a profession. Sociologists like Etzioni (1969) and Lortie (1975) conceived of teaching as only a 'semi-profession' because of its lack of clearly-defined skills and its inability to control recruitment and membership. Primary teaching in particular was seen, according to Lortie, as lacking any 'visible technical expertise', a view sometimes surfacing in politicians' judgment (Rumbold, 1986). There has been too a long-running debate about professionalism, strongly influenced by Hoyle's (1975) polarisation of 'restricted' and extended professionality: the former describing a view of teaching as largely confined to the classroom, the latter seeing the job as more broadly based, inevitably concerned with matters of educational theory and principle. In this respect Keddie (1971) designated the extra-classroom role as 'the teacher-as-educationalist', thereby anticipating the now widespread interest in the teacher as 'reflective practitioner' (eg Pollard and Tann, 1987; Nias, 1989). The 'teacher-as-researcher', which is one focus of this conference, is, of course, an extension of the reflective practitioner ideal.

This kind of theorising about teaching, in my view, has been highly problematic for two reasons, viz, a tendency to implicit moralising, and to romanticising teaching.

First, the theorising has become loaded with moral value: to be a 'full' profession has to seem preferable to being a semi- one; extended professionalism appears, by implication, better than the deprecatory 'restricted' version – and who wants to be thought of as an *unreflective* practitioner? The consequence of this moral loading is that it has become difficult to contest the ideas themselves despite the fact that some of them, especially the idea of extended professionality and the reflective practitioner, are highly contestable, as I shall argue a little later.

The second problem is that this theorising has been almost entirely devoid of empirical basis: it is a projection of 'what ought to be' with scant regard for 'what is'. One consequence is that it tends towards romanticising primary teaching. As an example, the teacher-as-researcher model has some obvious attractions, but it is worth noting that it has been promoted, and gained support, as funded opportunities for teachers to be seconded out of their classrooms for full-time research have been destroyed. From this, admittedly jaundiced, perspective, the teacher-as-researcher model is rendered as a second-best surrogate for the real thing – research conducted in a research enviroment with conditions that make research realisable.

Partly as a consequence of this kind of problem with theorising about the profession of teaching and also, I think, as a consequence of the effects of industrial action in the mid-1980s, and the reduction of autonomy in teaching after 1988, the focus has changed. Throughout the 1980s and 1990s an alternative view (see Ozga and Lawn, 1988; Apple, 1986; Evetts, 1990) was promoted largely by neo-Marxist sociologists, in which teaching was seen in a framework of politics and economics, as an occupation like any other job, shorn of value loading, to be researched, like any other, in terms of the labour market, of career opportunities, pay and conditions of work, work relations, including the exercise of power and control, of morale, and of the workplace culture. Alongside this have been other, less theoretically ambitious, attempts to map out and describe empirically the nature and patterning of the work of teachers (eg Campbell and Neill, 1994a; 1994b; Office of Manpower Economics, 1994) building on, amongst other things, a baseline established by Hilsum and Cane (1971). In both kinds of study the emphasis is upon issues such as the use of teacher time, and the nature of teachers' work, teacher careers, promotion, gender bias and discrimination, upon the intensification of teachers' work, casualisation of teachers' work through part-time, short-term contracts, and upon de-skilling. It is from this latter perspective that the arguments in this article are being made.

## Three contemporary pressures on primary teachers' work

I now want to trace three general pressures on primary teachers' work. I shall over-simplify them by doing so, but I think these pressures may be seen as shifts along three continua, viz,

(a)  from specificity towards diffuseness
(b)  from the generalist towards the specialist
(c)  from restricted to extended professionality

I will briefly illustrate these three pressures, both from the UK and from other educational systems, since I think that these pressures are operating in teachers in most industrial societies.

### From specificity towards diffuseness

By this I mean that there is increasing pressure on schools, and therefore on teachers, to take on an ever-widening scope or range of activites, in addition to the task of teaching or instructing pupils. Increasingly in modern societies teachers are expected to be concerned with the social and moral dimensions of pupils' lives, with welfare matters, with health, and with the pupils' communities. We might characterise it as a shift from being expected to take responsibility only or mainly for instructing pupils (specificity of the role) to being expected to be a teacher, cum secretary, cum social worker, cum community liaison officer, cum paramedic, cum priest (though given the recent activities of some priests there may be reservations about this last aspect). If the Home Secretary has his way, teachers will soon act also as surrogate Home Office staff, monitoring and reporting on the legitimacy, or otherwise, of the citzenship status of their pupils and their parents. You will recall the previous Secretary of State, John Patten, calling for teachers to promote a fear of hell and damnation into their pupils, taking for granted that teachers could be expected to act for religious institutions. More recently teachers have been expected to become teacher-trainers, expert spotters of child abuse, and advisers on safe sex. And in this conference we want them also to be researchers. It is not only the politicians who push this way: primary educationalists may be, in this sense, our own worst enemies. To take one example only, a recent book published by the Open University Press *Educating the Whole*

*Child*, (Siraj-Blatchford, J. and Siraj-Blatchford, I, 1995), attempts to place responsibilities on primary teachers for (in addition to teaching the National Curriculum subjects) citizenship, racial gender equality, awareness of economics and careers education, environmentalism, health and personal and social education. The main editors argue that:

> 'Social class domination and deference, racism, sexism, homophobia, the intolerance of disability, economic individualism and community and environmental recklessness are all reoccurring themes. Each negatively affects the self-image of some children in schools and perhaps ultimately and even more seriously, all children's images of 'others' are affected by these influences. The children of today will be the responsible and tolerant employers, employees, landlords, tenants and citizens of tomorrow, *or they may not*. The professional responsibility lies with us teachers, parents, and adult citizens ourselves, to create or *recreate* our society in the 21st century.
>
> (p 3)

It is always difficult to attack idealism, but there are two problems with the promotion of dreams such as these. The first is the failure to recognise that schools are under-powered to achieve such socially influenced aims; indeed, it could be argued that they have not yet convincingly achieved the much more limited specific educational aims of literacy and numeracy for all pupils. The second is that they induce guilt in a professional workforce noted for its conscientiousness.

These pressures are not restricted to the UK. A report in 1991 from the International Labour Office (ILO, 1991), based on an analysis of teachers' work in more than 40 countries, argued that the nature of teachers' work was changing in response to a range of new expectations being placed on the schools. Not only were curriculum reform programmes being put in place but there was an accelerating trend for moral and social responsibilities, previously exercised by other agencies (eg the home and family, the church, the welfare agencies, and local communities) to be transferred to schools. The reasons for this are obvious and banal; primary school is the only universally experienced institution in societies that are morally and socially fractured or fragmented. The schools thus become the prime site in which policies for the creation and reinforcement of a moral and social order can be implemented – the prime site, if you like, in which society attempts to create the identies it wishes. In some areas of these societies increasingly schools are the only site for such policies to be enacted, and teachers, willy nilly, are expected to take on the responsibility of ensuring that they work. The most obvious locations are in the 'underclass' areas where, for some pupils, school is the main locus of moral and social stability. But it is, nonetheless, a phenomenon common to all teachers.

In Northern Ireland, for example, teachers are expected to 'Educate for Mutual Understanding' pupils whose social world outside school – and sometimes inside it – has offered them little other than bigotry and stereotyped misunderstanding. In a more trivial, less dramatic form, I was in a classroom recently at registration time when a pupil came in with a note from her parent asking the teacher to punish the pupil because she had been kicking cars on the way home from school. In the same classroom a second parent came in and asked whether the teacher could clear up a squashed hedgehog, run over by a car, from the road outside the school because some of the pupils had been jumping up and down on the corpse.

There is, of course nothing wrong with the raft of increasing expectations individually. Collectively, however, they are impossible to realise in a set of working conditions that include reduced or level funding, inappropriate or poor training, and already high stress. It is surely time for teachers to start saying 'no': to establish priorities for their own professional sanity.

As a study of contemporary teaching for the OECD (1990) demonstrated:

> 'The broadening . . . of demands [on education] has its equivalent at the level of the individual teacher. What once would have been regarded as exceptional devotion to duty has now become viewed as normal practice.'

### From the generalist to the specialist

The second pressure arises from the curriculum reform programmes being almost universally adopted across the post-industrial world in the drive for higher stand-ards. This pressure, paradoxically in view of the social welfare pressure mentioned above, is pushing teachers into a more instrumental orientation, emphasising pupil cognitive achievement above everything else. Often this achievement is the only, or the main, area that is publicly tested and is a prime source for teacher appraisal. Under this pressure the valuing of the work of the generalist class teacher is being replaced by a concentration upon the value of specialist subject expertise. In this country we have seen it emerge in two Select Committee reports (House of Commons, 1986; 1994), in the literature on primary education (eg Campbell, 1985; Schulman, 1987), in HMI and OFSTED reports on the system and its schools (eg DES, 1978; OFSTED, 1994) and in the continuous revision of primary teacher training priorities at both initial and in-service levels, where the significance of subject expertise and the deficiencies arising from its absence (for example, Bennett and Carré, 1993) have been played up. The consequence is that subject expertise – despite the serious problems of definition – has become a defining characteristic of the skills required by primary teachers to do their work effectively.

Elsewhere similar pressure operate. In Italy (see OFSTED, 1994) for example, where curriculum reform programmes were defined in 1985 and introduced year by year from 1987, teachers who were previously generalist are now required to take responsibility for one of three specialist areas of learning (for example, linguistic – expressive, scientific – logical – mathematical, and historical – social – geographical).

> 'Until very recently, most Italian primary teachers worked as generalists – teaching all subjects to their own classes. However, the new systems involving

a shared curriculum and joint responsibility for classes . . . are forcing an element of semi-specialisation in that teachers are expected to remain with their assigned "areas of learning" for either two, three or five years. There is some debate within the system as to how effective these arrangements will prove. Teachers recognise the need to reduce their planning and assessment load, given the requirements of the national teaching programmes, but are unsure about narrowing their range of expertise for a prolonged period.'

In general there remains in the UK substantial resistance to this pressure, at least where 'specialist teaching' in a secondary school style is involved. The main reason is that it tends to 'go against the primary ethos'. However, as I shall argue later, from the point of view of the power relations between head and staff, the demonstrated possession of specialist subject expertise and its use in school planning has considerable advantages.

## From restricted to extended professionality

By this pressure I mean something slightly different from the original formulation by Hoyle (1975). I mean the pressure to work collaboratively and to discuss educational practice by reference to theories, ideas and research.

I shall spend less time on this pressure, partly because it has been widely recognised both here (Campbell, 1985; Osborn and Black, 1994) and elsewhere (eg Hargreaves, 1991). In this country Osborn and Black, for example, reported that in their sample of Key Stage 2 teachers one significant change in work was 'an increase in collaborative planning and working. This mainly took the form of planning initially with colleagues, sharing the distribution of resource materials and working with others on a consultancy/advisory basis' (p iv).

Likewise, Rosemary Webb's (1993) study of teachers' roles and responsibilities found them increasingly being expected to work in cooperation with colleagues, though her study revealed the contraints upon this happening effectively. In Italian primary schools (OFSTED, 1994) teachers are required to plan the work of year groups collectively at the beginning of the school year and to monitor progress collectively through regular staff group meetings. Campbell and Neill (1994b) found primary teachers spending substantially more of their time with other teachers than had been the case in Hilsum and Cane's study some 25 years earlier. They reported that:

'The teachers in our study spent 6.2 hours per week – 11 per cent of their working week – in contact with other adults, though whether this led to authentic or 'contrived collegiality' (Hargreaves, 1991) was unclear. This is a much larger time – whether absolutely or as a proportion of the working week – spent in the company of colleagues than was true for Hilsum and Cane's teachers in 1971.'

(p 213)

Part of this shift in the UK is explained by the way the National Curriculum pushed teachers into collaborative planning, part by earmarked funding for professional development and part by the statutory requirement on schools to create school development plans. But there is another reason, admitted by teachers, even though, as in the Osborn and Black (1994) study, reluctantly. It is that earlier notions of restricted professionality, in which the teacher traded in involvement in school-based decision making for isolation and classroom autonomy, were not in the interests of pupils.

## Primary school culture

Primary schools, like all organisations, create a culture that constrains and habituates the working lives of its members (see Pollard, 1985; Nias, 1989; Acker, 1990). Julia Evetts (1990) has analysed elements of this culture as follows:

- Primary schools are typically small institutions, with inevitably close working relations between teachers.
- Commitment to generalism, with little adherence to an identity based on subjects as in secondary schools.
- A numerical dominance of women.
- An emphasis on the social/emotional/pastoral dimensions of teaching.

Three consequences for the everyday working lives of teachers seem to be:

- Considerable intolerance of friction and of professional disagreement because of the closeness and regular face-to-face contacts; as Evetts puts it (p 48):

  'It is almost impossible . . . for teachers to avoid or distance themselves from other teachers . . . an outcast teacher would find life intolerable in the close confines of the primary staffroom'.

- When added to the pressure for 'collaborative cultures', in Jennifer Nias's (1989) phrase, this has led to primary culture being seen as cosy and insulated (White, 1982), inert and lacking in intellectual challenge.
- Imbalance in power relations between heads and teachers because of the lack of subject expertise which, in secondary schools, provides teachers with a base to resist the undue exercise of power by heads, particularly in respect of curriculum and teaching methods.
- A moral order in which conscientiousness and an ethic of care are rewarded and reinforced, arising from the values associated with predominantly female organisations (Acker, 1992; Evetts, 1990; Campbell and Neill, 1994b).

The occupational culture of primary schools is important for the reason that, as Peter Woods argued in 1980, teachers' culture is the medium through which educational reform must pass – 'Through their working practices teachers shape, transform, adapt or resist educational innovations' (cited in Evetts, 1990, p 43).

## Discussion

If these three values are characteristic of the primary school culture, what are the consequences for teachers' work of the three pressures I have outlined earlier? I shall deal briefly with four, though doubtless there are others.

First, the increasing scope of teachers' responsibilities will be very difficult to resist, partly because of the conscientiousness syndrome and partly because to resist would create considerable tension or friction in school staffrooms. Yet my judgement is that the most urgent priority for primary schools is to *reduce*, not increase, the scope of expectations on class teachers so that they can gain a sense of real achievement from teaching well instead of the current sense of doing nearly everything inadequately. The study for the OECD (1990) came to similar conclusions:

> 'Implementing real change may depend less on the constant introduction of still more reforms, and instead call for a concentration on priorities.'
>
> (p 99)

Of course, schools as organisations will continue to be subject to increased expectations, but it does not follow that individual teachers need shoulder them all.

One way forward may be by increasing the division in labour in primary schools, with teachers' work being progressively focused on teaching in its narrow sense, and a range on non-teaching para-professionals being allocated the responsibility for home–school liaison, pupils' welfare and social development. There is some evidence – from Italy, France and Japan – that, where the teachers' work is more narrowly focused in this way, higher cognitive achievement is made and job satisfaction is increased. The OECD study I have just cited raised as a major issue requiring attention 'the proper distribution of tasks between teachers as professionals with the principal responsibilities for instructional duties, and other personnel' (p 99).

Second, I would argue that the resistance within the profession to the pressure for more subject specialism in planning, teaching and assessing the curriculum should not be sustained. We should, on the contrary, embrace the concept of subject specialism – including not only the co-ordinator and semi-specialist roles but also the specialist teaching role where it can be provided – for two reasons. The first is a pragmatic one, that it should lead to a reduction in workload for individual teachers. The second is about power relations between heads and other staff. A subject specialism will help to redress the historic power imbalance, by pushing more power over decisions about curriculum and pedagogy away from the head down to the staff group as a whole. Subject expertise in the workplace of the school is not only a knowledge or information base, important though that is; it also offers the possibility of restraint upon the headteacher's exercise of professional control. If you are the science expert and the head is not, you become more powerful in defining good practice for yourself and your colleagues in respect of science. Changing the distribution of power in primary schools seems an especially important objective in institutions in which, disproportionately, the head is male and most of the other staff are female.

Third, we need to reduce our fear of open professional disagreement, or to put it another way, we need to stop pretending that there is an easy school-based consensus on curriculum and pedagogy. In the post-modern world, old certainties have dissolved and the essence of an intelligent professionalism is the recognition and valuing of the fact that professionals contest ideas and beliefs rather than accept them from on high. Being or becoming an extended professional, reflective practitioner or teacher-researcher does, of course, mean that you contribute to school development plans. But almost inevitably it also means that you will be challenging the existing, rather cosy, insulated culture of the primary school. You may then become styled as 'difficult', 'unhelpful' or, worst of all, 'ambitious', because in the short term at least you are disturbing long-settled habits.

Fourth, there is in the issue of conscientiousness and the deeply-caring ethic, associated in some commentators' views (eg Acker, 1990; Evetts, 1990) with the predominance of women in the culture. It is, of course, very difficult to argue against a conscientious attitude to work, especially when the work is with young children. But the care ethic does have some disadvantages. Let me mention the two main ones. There is some evidence from comparative studies that pupils perform more highly where teachers ignore their social and personal development. In Japan, for example, according to an OFSTED report (1994) teachers made no allowance for social background in the expectations they held for pupils, and offered this as an explanation of the higher standards in writing and reading, especially of the lower ability pupils. The other disadvantage lies in a culture in which overwork, and a strong sense of conscientiousness, are regarded as virtues. It starts in initial teacher training of course, where on teaching practice students are still encouraged or required to produce the great TP file in which every lesson plan is time-consumingly written out by hand, and lovingly evaluated by several pages of confessional style commentary. The use of extended colour coding is particularly rewarded. In the everyday culture of the school we still believe that the only virtuous teacher is the one who has written all her own workcards, writes more pages of lesson forecasts than any of her colleagues, and changes her displays almost as frequently as her underwear. Yet there are good commercial workcards, not to mention text books; forecasts can be standardised and still meet their purpose; and displays can be mounted by other people.

## Implications for teachers

Finally, two brief points about the implications for teachers. The first is fairly obvious but needs to be made explicit. I have presented the three pressures on teachers as though they were separate, but they are not. They frequently operate simultaneously, and this is part of the explanation for high stress levels in primary teachers. Take the example of the Code of Practice and the SENCO. Simultaneously here there is the pressure to diffuseness, to be concerned with a range of agencies and concerns outside the classroom, to become more specialised (though not in a particular subject), and to develop school policy and practice of work by reference to theories and principles about learning.

I have just published (Lewis et al, 1996) with Ann Lewis and Sean Neill a study of the implementation of the Code of Practice involving over 2,000 SENCOs, probably 1 in 10 nationally. There is a widespread perception among them that this is one more work requirement bolted on to existing demands without adequate time, resources or skills for its realisation. Here are three of their responses.

'I am absolutely exhausted. I am a deputy headteacher, have a reception class of thirty-four children, responsibility for the three core subjects in addition to being SEN co-ordinator. I therefore do not feel my school is treating special needs seriously. In April 1995 the headteacher informed me she had budgeted for an increment this year; by the 7th April I was informed this is not the case. I am on Point 2 of the deputies scale after four years and special needs responsibility, and I fully intend packing up.'

'As a full-time teacher of a Year 5/6 class in an inner city school with a lot of problems, and as maths co-ordinator with no free time, I find it almost impossible to fulfil my role as SEN co-ordinator. There is no time to liaise with other staff and very little support from outside.'

'I can see little point in a Code of Practice for SEN when it doesn't change anything except an increase in the workload of the SEN co-ordinator. To be told, "Yes, this child has a severe problem – No, we can't give you any real support", it is worse than useless.'

In many of the primary schools, because of the acknowledged heavy workloads of class teachers, heads have added the SENCO role to their own responsibilities. As far as I know, no school has yet said, 'No, we won't do it because we don't have the resources'.

Secondly, the message to heads and teachers is clear cut. If they do not establish priorities for their work, no-one else will. I started off by emphasising the way in which national agencies such as the SCAA have lost credibility. It is worse than this: their main function post-Dearing appears to be simply to identify more and more things for primary teachers to do to occupy their allegedly discretionary time – teach Latin, teach a modern language, teach spirituality, teach citizenship – have been some of the most recent offerings. Only at the level of the individual school and the individual teacher can priorities be established to reduce the overload on teachers, and headteachers in particular have an important role to play.

I finish with two vignettes of teachers interviewed for our book, *The Meaning of Infant Teachers' Work* (Evans et al, 1994). They seem to me to represent two positions over which teachers may need to exercise choice. I was interested in Fullan's (1990) idea that state-engendered reforms needed 'the passive professional' if they were to work.

One of the teachers, Tricia, had nursery and reception children, and argued that the heavy workload of implementing the National Curriculum and assessment had affected her relationships within her family. She thought she needed non-contact time to do all that was being expected of her but she would only accept non-contact time on conditions:

> 'Even though I have talked about non-contact time, I don't want non-contact time unless the person in my class is me, or a clone of me, or someone who is going to be able to go in there and carry on or do something which will enhance those children who are learning for half-an-hour a day or one day a week, or whatever. I don't want someone going in there just doing a holding job, because then, suppose somebody was to say, "You can have one day off a week to do record-keeping, to do administration work, that sort of thing, go on courses". I mean, unless I could really be sure that that person in my class for that one day was doing meaningful things, carrying on and continuing with the National Curriculum and bringing something to these children, I would rather do it in my own time at home if I had to, because then I'd cram five days into four.'

We called Tricia 'overconscientious' because she seemed ready to give in to what she saw as unrealistic and inappropriate demands, and did so out of an obligation to do her best.

The second teacher we called Christine and we characterised her as 'sane'. She was in a tiny minority. Christine had decided to limit her impulse towards overwork because she was anxious to protect her own time and her personal and family life. She discussed her strategy thus:

> 'I frequently have to say, "No, I can't do that", especially when other members of staff want my time for something, something that they are doing. I just haven't got the time. The headteacher doesn't get everything she wants either – if she asks me I say, "Yes, I'll try", and if she comes back a couple of weeks later I have to say, "Sorry, I haven't had any time".'

'How do you feel about that?', she replied:

> 'I would like to have more time to help other members of the staff but I think, when it comes down to it, your own class has to come first. You have to do your best for your own class, you can't take your time out to do things for other people in school if you haven't done what you should for your own class. We are all experienced teachers, we haven't got any probationary

teachers, so I don't feel that much of an obligation to do things for other members of staff.'

Christine had established a cool, no-nonsense approach to the new demands. If they took longer than people were expecting then to take, then people would have to put up with it:

> 'I still find it a very satisfying job, yes. Well, I can see that I can still teach the way I want to regardless of the National Curriculum – in fact, I won't allow the National Curriculum to change me that much. I always feel that you have to move forward, make progress with new ideas and so on, but I like to take the best of what's new and add to it what I have already got rather than going overboard for a new idea. And I think the National Curriculum is much the same, you know – we will be able to assimilate most of it and, hopefully, not make it too burdensome in the future. So, yes, I am very satisfied with the job – nothing would induce me to leave teaching and if they don't like the way I teach they will have to sack me, and that would be that.'

It has been conventional to analyse teachers' attitudes to teaching according to Hoyle's (1975) concept of 'restricted' and 'extended' professionalism; the former defining their work as primarily teaching, the latter responding to a broader set of professional expectations, including theorising and working in the professional development activities. The polarisation is, of course, somewhat false, and in any case relative, but it is interesting to turn the value assumptions of Hoyle's analysis on their head. For three of our teachers, restricted professionalism put a brake on otherwise unrealistic time demands and enabled them to obtain or regain a greater sense of control over their working time. For the others, an extended sense of professional obligation removed the brake and left the use of their time at the mercy of an unco-ordinated and confused multiple set of policy initiatives frequently mismanaged by LEAs or headteachers. For these teachers, their own conscientiousness was a source of exploitation.

There is a rumour – and its status is no more than that – that the Senior Chief HMI, Chris Woodhead, has complained to the Secretary of State that OFSTED is being given more and more inspection tasks to do, but that there are not enough inspectors to do them, and that it is unrealistic to increase demands on the Inspectorate whilst simultaneously reducing the workforce. I do not know whether the rumour is true but I would like to believe that it is. For, if it is, I can finish with two bits of advice I never thought I would offer: feel sympathetic toward Her Majesty's Inspectorate, and follow the example of Chris Woodhead.

# References

Acker, S. (1990) 'Teachers' Culture in an English Primary School: Continuity and Change', *British Journal of Sociology of Education*, 11, 3, 257–73.

Acker, S. (1992) 'Teacher Relationships and Educational Reform in England and Wales', *The Curriculum Journal, 2, 2.*

Apple, M. (1986) *Teachers and Texts.* Routledge & Kegan Paul: New York.

Bennett, N. and Carré, C. (1993) *Learning to Teach.* Laurence Ellbaum Associates: London.

Campbell, R.J. (1985) *Developing the Primary School Curriculum;* Eastbourne, Holt, Rinehart & Winston.

Campbell, R.J. and Neill, S.R.Stj. (1994a) *Secondary Teachers at Work.* Routledge: London.

Campbell, R.J. and Neill, S.R.StJ. (1994b) *Primary Teachers at Work.* Routledge: London.

Department of Education and Science (1978) *Primary Education in England: A Survey by HMI.* HMSO: London.

Etzioni, A. (Ed) (1969) *The Semi-Professions and Their Organisation.* Free Press: New York.

Evans, L., Campbell, R.J., Neill, S.R.StJ. and Packwood, A. (1994) *The Meaning of Infant Teachers' Work.* Routledge: London.

Evetts, J. (1990) *Women in Primary Teaching.* Methuen: London.

Fullan, M. (1990) 'Staff Development, Innovation and Institutional Development', in Joyce, B. (Ed) *Changing School Culture Through Staff Development.* ASCD: Virginia.

Graham, D. and Tytler, D. (1993) *A Lesson for Us All.* Routledge: London.

Hargreaves, A. (1991) 'Teacher Preparation Time and the Intensification Thesis', *Annual Conference of the American Educational Research Association,* Chicago, 3–7 April.

Hilsum, S. and Cane, B.S. (1971) *The Teacher's Day.* NFER: Windsor.

House of Commons (1986) Third report of the Education, Science and Arts Committee, *Achievement in Primary Schools,* Vol 1. HMSO: London.

House of Commons (1988) *Education Reform Act.* HMSO: London.

House of Commons (1994) Education Committee Session, 1993–4, 2nd Report, *The Disparity in Funding between Primary and Secondary Schools.* HMSO: London.

Hoyle, E. (1975) 'Professionality, Professionalism and Control in Teaching', in Houghton, V., McHugh, R. and Morgan, C. (Eds) *Management in Education.* Ward Lock/Open University: London.

International Labour Office (1991) *Teachers: Challenges of the 1990s: Second Joint Meeting on Conditions of Work of Teachers (1991).* International Labour Office: Geneva.

Keddie, N. (1971) 'Classroom Knowledge', in Young, M. (Ed) *Knowledge and Control: New Directions for the Sociology of Education.* Collier-Macmillan: London.

Lewis, A., Neill, S.R.StJ. and Campbell, R.J. (1996) *The Implementation of the Code of Practice in Primary and Secondary Schools.* National Union of Teachers: London.

Lortie, D. (1975) *Schoolteacher.* Routledge: London.

Nias, J. (1989) *Primary Teachers Talking.* Routledge: London.

OECD (1990) *The Teacher Today.* OECD: Paris.

Office of Manpower Economics (1994) *Report on a Study of Teachers' Working Hours for the School Teachers Review Body.* Office of Manpower Economics: London.

Office for Standards in Education (1994) *Teaching and Learning in Italian Primary Schools.* HMSO: London.

Osborn, M. and Black, I. (1994) *Roles and Responsibilities at Key Stage 3.* NASUWY: London.

Ozga, J. and Lawn, M. (Eds) (1988) *Schoolwork.* Milton Keynes: Open University Press.

Pollard, A. (1985) *The Social World of the Primary School.* Cassell: London.

Pollard, A. and Tann, S. (1987) *Reflective Teaching in the Primary School.* Cassell: London.

Rumbold, A. (1986) Interview in *Child Education,* November.

Schulman, L.S. (1987) 'Knowledge and Teaching: Foundations of the New Reform', *Harvard Educational Review*, 57, 1–22.

Siraj-Blatchford, J. and Siraj-Blatchford, I. (Eds) (1995) *Educating the Whole Child*. Milton Keynes, Open University Press.

Webb, R. (1993) *After the Deluge*. Association of Teachers and Lecturers: London.

White, J. (1982) 'The Primary Teacher as Servant of the State', in Richards, C. (Ed) *New Directions in Primary Education*. Falmer Press: Lewes.

# 27 Would schools improve if teachers cared less?

*Jennifer Nias*

Five responses to this question:

**Key Stage 1 Teacher** (appalled): 'Of course not! What a terrible thing to say! Children need more care from teachers, not less.'

**Governor:** 'Our school couldn't stay in business if teachers cared less. Our budget has been cut so much that if our teachers didn't work as hard as they do, we'd be stuck.'

**Teaching Head of Group 1 School:** 'Quite right! We shouldn't be so conscientious about everything. We'd probably teach better if we didn't, because we wouldn't be so tired.'

**Key Stage 2 Teacher:** 'Ours is a caring school and we try to run it so that children learn to care for each other. Would you want it any other way?'

**German Visiting Teacher:** 'The trouble with English teachers is that they care too much, and perhaps about the wrong things. I care if my pupils do not learn as they should. That's enough.'

These responses reveal the confused nature of 'caring' as a characteristic of primary teachers in Britain. Many teachers see themselves as 'caring' people and welcome this aspect of their jobs. However, the detailed and challenging work of Jim Campbell and his associates on teachers' workload (Evans et al, 1994; Campbell and Neill, 1994) claims that the 'ethic of care as a central value in primary teachers' occupational culture contributes to teacher overload' (Campbell and Neill, 1994, 220), and so to reduced teaching quality, job satisfaction and morale (op cit, 220–4). At the same time, there is a continuing public demand, reflected in the media and by politicians, that teachers should assume responsibility for a number of social ills, from child abuse to declining standards in athletics, that is, that they should 'care' about their pupils in an ever-broadening sense, with the implication that they are morally culpable if they do not. Together these clues build a sketchy and contradictory picture: teachers are impoverished as people and as practitioners because they care too much. By contrast their pupils suffer because they do not care enough. And, in any case, both problems are of teachers' own making because it is their choice to care.

We owe this confusion, in large measure, to the way in which as educators, we use the word 'care' without questioning its meaning or implications. In this paper I examine five sets of understandings associated with the term and explore areas of overlap with 'conscientiousness' and 'commitment'. Throughout, my aim has been to assist the school improvement debate by introducing greater conceptual clarity into a small area of it. I have not attempted to supply empirical evidence which might give definitive answers to the question with which I began: I do not know whether schools would improve if teachers cared less, but I argue that we need to question carefully what we care about and why, and who most benefits from teachers' 'caring'.

I also want to make one general point. In my analysis I have used terms such as 'maternal' and 'women's work'. I do not thereby wish to imply that primary teaching is an unfit profession for men, despite the well grounded fears of the TTA about declining numbers of male applicants for education places in higher education, or that men do not 'care' every bit as much as women about their pupils and about their own professional competence. However, the fact that historically there has always been a preponderance of women teachers in primary schools has left a legacy of beliefs about the nature of the job and of schools, the influence of which is still very powerful. As a result, cultural assumptions about women sometimes shape the way in which teachers of both sexes themselves perceive the job and interpret their responsibilities. Feminist thinking has much to contribute to the debate about 'caring' in schools, but does not apply simply to women.

## Caring: liking children

Most teachers 'care' for children in the sense that they like them, enjoy their company, have chosen to spend several hours a day with them. This is not always the case. Every teacher will be able to recall individual pupils whose personal characteristics they found disagreeable or offensive or whose behaviour was insupportable (as the current debate about exclusion suggests), and classes with whom a comfortable relationship was established only after repeated negotiation. Nevertheless, liking is the more or less universal backdrop to the other meanings of the term 'care'. Teachers who do not, in a generalised sense, enjoy working with children do not in my experience stay for long in the profession or, if they do, they become very unhappy people.

On the face of it, we surely cannot question the educational benefits of such a situation: teachers who enjoy their work are likely to be more stimulating and supportive; children who feel secure in an adult's affection can concentrate on learning. However, I have been in classrooms where the preservation of a warm social climate seemed to have become an end in itself (see also Broadfoot and Osborn, 1993), where teachers and children shared so much personal conversation, laughter and fun that little time was left for forms of learning other than the interpersonal. We have constantly to remind ourselves that the purpose of schools is to further children's learning. 'Fun', used as a shorthand term for a range of affective activities, is a legitimate means to an educational end; it is not an end in itself.

This is to argue not for a return in classrooms to the attitudes of Mr Gradgrind, but for a balance between the affective and the task-centred. Preserving such a balance is particularly important at the moment in view of the mounting evidence that it may be in danger (Pollard et al, 1994). Faced with a relentless intensification of their workload, teachers are reluctantly reducing the frequency of their affective interactions with individual children and cutting back on shared moments of banter, joking and talk about personal matters. They feel forced into such action to ensure both more time for curriculum coverage and some space (eg in breaks) for their own refreshment and recovery. But they are not comfortable with their behaviour, feeling that it reduces their own job satisfaction and may adversely affect children's motivation and sense of self-esteem. There is a deep conviction in the profession that teaching is interpersonal, in the sense that it involves communication between two or more people. In this sense the fact that teachers show their liking for children through their classroom behaviour is not a sentimental self-indulgence but a necessary condition for the latter's education. A non-teaching staff member recently said in my hearing, 'Is it possible that some people become teachers because they hate children?'. Whatever experience provoked this rhetorical question, it cannot have contributed to school improvement. So, although we may question the amount of time some teachers devote to 'fun', we need to preserve its existence. If the time were ever to come when teachers felt too pressured to demonstrate to children their liking for them, the lives of both would be impoverished. 'Care' in this sense is fundamental to all educational endeavour.

## Caring: altruism, self-sacrifice and obedience

Liking is not, however, the same as loving. Many teachers become deeply involved with individuals and classes. At a mundane level, they wipe away tears, attend to wounds, mop up vomit, mend broken toys, listen, arbitrate in playground squabbles – and much else besides. More profoundly, they lie awake at night worrying about individuals, weep when they are lost, hurt or go astray, rejoice with their successes. Men and women talk of a profound emotional relationship with whole classes as well as with individuals, although the extent of their involvement is normally masked by their assumed calm and what King (1978) calls their 'professional pleasantness'. They use the words 'love', and less often 'hate'; they feel bereaved at the end of an academic year (Nias, 1989).

There are several reasons why teachers 'care' in this way, all of which are relevant to the school improvement debate. Leaving aside the possibility that such a relationship meets the emotional needs of individuals and the fact that young children evoke strong, loving feelings in many adults, whatever their jobs, the ways in which primary schools are structured bears some responsibility. In particular, the one teacher-one class system encourages intensity of feelings especially when teachers are isolated for long periods with 'their' children in what Grumet (1988, 85) describes as their 'kitchen-like' classrooms.

I wish to emphasise three historical reasons. Each is so deeply embedded in the profession that we seldom acknowledge its existence, let alone question it. Together they contribute to two related trends in English primary schools: teachers' 'caring' often implies altruism, self-sacrifice and obedience; and pupils are perceived as whole persons, not simply as minds.

The first reason is the religious origin of most teacher education in England and Wales. Until 1870, the majority of schools were provided by the Anglican or, less frequently, non-conformist churches or by charitable individuals with religious sympathies. Teachers were prepared for their work through apprenticeship in the schools, notably the pupil-teacher system, or in a handful of Church of England colleges. As a consequence, teachers were socialised early in their professional lives into a view of their work as helping, serving and indoctrinating others. As a corollary, the satisfactions of their pupils' needs took priority both over their own needs and over the likelihood of material reward. Kay Shuttleworth, one of the most influential teacher educators in nineteenth century England, spoke of the students at St John's College, Battersea, as 'a band of intelligent Christian men (sic) entering upon the instruction of the poor with religious devotion to their work' who would 'go forth into the world humble, industrious and instructed' (Rich, 1972). This is a view that has persisted. There are still plenty of teachers in the system whose motivation is that of service (Nias, 1989) and even more outside it who feel that teachers' dedication should exceed their desire for reward or, sometimes, for reasonable working conditions.

Although I lack statistical evidence, I would guess that the number of teachers in the profession with a specifically religious education or commitment has long since been overtaken by those with a more secular desire to help others. In my lifetime I have known the generation of teachers who entered the profession in the 1940s and early 1950s, most with experience of the 1930s depression or World War 2. A large number of them were fired by a desire to build a better world. Later, I found that many of those entering teaching in the 1960s and 1970s had a similar vision, albeit inspired by different experiences (Nias, 1989); and during the years I spent working in two inner-city areas, I frequently met teachers who were driven by a strong sense of social justice. My recent impression is that now the wheel may be turning, that there is a rising number of people entering teaching with an explicit commitment to religious principles and an associated desire to help others. One way and another, altruism is still a powerful force within the profession.

In practical terms, such altruism leads to self-expenditure and self-sacrifice. Teachers with religious or socio-political motives for their choice of career frequently give themselves to their jobs without regard to personal cost, work very long hours in and away from school, blur the boundaries between their domestic and occupational lives, often giving the latter priority over the former, and are constantly preoccupied with individual pupils and their well-being. In addition, because they have broad aims for children's education and development, they undertake many tasks which go well beyond a strict definition of teaching – acting as social workers, counsellors, home and hospital visitors, not to mention cleaning, redecorating and renovating classrooms, unblocking drains, washing and dispensing second-hand clothes, and performing a range of other practical tasks in the interests of children's physical, moral, social and emotional welfare.

The second reason why teachers feel it appropriate to form deep emotional relationships with their pupils and to work altruistically for them is because their work has, historically, been likened to parenting. In particular, Froebel and Pestalozzi, early nineteenth century child-centred educators, did a great deal to establish a view of teaching as facilitation and informed intervention rather than instruction, and of learning as growth rather than memorisation. Their educational theories drew heavily upon what they saw as 'natural', for example, play, development, intrinsic motivation and the unity of mind, body and spirit. Accordingly they stressed the educational potential of parenting, arguing that teachers could promote children's learning by consciously extending the 'natural' attitudes and actions of mothers, in particular. Empathy, close observation, tactful intervention, compassion and concern are qualities that many parents exhibit. They lie at the heart of the educational methods advocated by Froebel and his followers.

Froebel's ideas were initially developed in Britain by men (eg Robert Owen) and there have been, and still are, many outstanding male 'child-centred' educators. Nevertheless, it is maternal language and imagery that are most often used in relation to primary teachers. This may be partly because in this country Froebel's influence was, for historical reasons, greatest in early years education, an area which has traditionally been the preserve of women. It may also be, as Grumet (1988) suggests, that, in the nineteenth century when women were reaching out towards independent employment, their claim to be morally superior to men supported their bid to become teachers. And, in time, sheer weight of numbers encouraged the elision of 'teacher' and 'she'.

Whatever the reasons, teaching young children is often perceived in this country as a form of mothering. According to some feminist writers (see, eg Lawn and Grace, 1987; Acker, 1995), 'mother's work' in its turn is a historically constructed idea, the origins of which lie in the industrial revolution and the rise of capitalist society. The supply of cheap labour needed for industrialisation depended on men's availability to work long hours and so upon women's capacity to sustain the home and care for children. As a result, these activities came to be seen as the work of women and particularly of mothers. Feelings such as warmth, compassion and affection were readily associated with physical caring, so these too became a mother's duty and prerogative. Girls were socialised early in their lives, as many still are, into an assumption that theirs was a caring role within the home and that this involved both doing and feeling, labour and love. Grumet's seminal book, *Bitter Milk: Women and Teaching* (1988) takes this argument further, emphasising both the dull, repetitive and tiring nature of much maternal work and the altruism and self-sacrifice that it involves.

When teaching is construed as an extension of this kind of mothering, the effects on the profession are depressing, in both senses of the word: teachers in primary schools should be women. They will love their pupils and cheerfully undertake tiring, repetitive, physical tasks on their behalf. They will willingly expend themselves on behalf of others to the point of exhaustion and often beyond. They will make do with scarce resources, and be content with low status and few material rewards. In return, they will receive the satisfaction of knowing that they have done their duty and, if they are lucky, will be blessed with the affection, esteem and gratitude of their pupils.

Since mothers care for the 'whole child' and missionaries usually have social and moral as well as religious objectives, it is easy to understand how the aims of primary education in Britain came to be defined as broadly as they are. Teachers' responsibilities were, by implication, not just to teach the curriculum, however that was defined, but also to ensure the healthy development of every aspect of the growing child. Teachers were expected to be aware of and capable of catering for all the needs of every child in their classes. The fact that it is impossible for them to do this has been repeatedly masked by the rhetoric of 'care' and 'commitment' (Alexander, 1984; 1995).

Moreover, there is ample evidence that this not simply a historical picture. Primary teachers have themselves internalised many of these expectations and have passed them on from one professional generation to another. Despite recent legislative changes, the classroom is still a workplace in which practitioners accept their accountability to everyone (Broadfoot and Osborn, 1993; 1995), their responsibility for everything (Nias, 1989; Evans et al, 1994; Jeffrey and Woods, 1996), a workload which expands without apparent limit (Campbell and Neill, 1994) and, underlying all of this, the constant burden of guilt which Hargreaves (1994) sees as characteristic of the profession.

The third cultural reason why many teachers accept, and even willingly espouse, these perceptions of their aims and responsibilities is associated with the other two. From the start teachers in the public education system, especially if they were women, were expected to live in social and economic dependence on their patrons and employers. Tropp (1957), Simon (1965) and Rich (1972) are among those who have vividly documented the low social status accorded to primary teachers in the nineteenth and early twentieth centuries, the control exercised over them by those who appointed, inspected or paid them, and their struggle for professional status and recognition. These were partly gender issues: in a patriarchal society women were expected to obey and defer to men. The struggle was also, however, class-related, especially in the nineteenth and early twentieth centuries. Most primary teachers were of working class origins; after 1870 they often taught in areas with poor, labouring populations. In the interests of social control, it was felt necessary to encourage them in habits of deference and dependency. As recently as 1965 a village school head in Hampshire told me that he had been asked to remain standing while being interviewed for his job by the seated managers. In the same year, a woman headteacher recalled that she had been threatened with dismissal by her chairman because he had discovered that she read the 'wrong' newspaper, copies of which she brought into school to cover desks during art sessions.

Such conditions could not apply today, but in my in-service work with teachers I have repeatedly been struck by their tenacious authority-dependence (Abercrombie, 1984). One of the hardest and most long-running struggles of my professional life has been to persuade teachers to question what they are doing and the reasons why, to discriminate between levels of priority in what is required of them, to suggest alternatives and to decide when it is professionally necessary to say no. I found it easier to understand this almost universal docility when I realised that it was in part a legacy from the past, a century-old habit of socially induced obedience which can be traced back to the origins of English public education.

## 'Conscientiousness'

It is in the context of these three historical aspects of teachers' work – religious or social idealism, quasi-maternalism and authority dependence – that Campbell's recent work on conscientiousness is particularly relevant (Campbell and Neill, 1994). It vividly and painstakingly documents the hours worked, at home and in school, by teachers at different key stages, ages and career stages, points out the inflating expectations which bear upon them without the protection (because of the open-ended nature of 'non-directed time') of contractual limits, and shows the mounting dissatisfaction and increasing ill health of many teachers. Moreover, a major component of their dissatisfaction is the increase in administration, paperwork and record keeping, activities which they know in their present form have limited professional value and which they sense are alien to their beliefs about the nature of 'caring' for children (Pollard et al, 1994; Campbell and Neill, 1994). Campbell and Neill (op cit 223) conclude:

> '"Conscientiousness", whatever its benefits to the pupils, has acted as a mechanism, actual or potential, for exploitation of teachers. Driven by their sense of obligation to meet all work demands to the best of their ability, the majority of teachers found themselves devoting much longer hours in their own time to work than they considered reasonable, and attempting to meet too many demands in order to achieve government objectives for educational reform. This was despite the fact that some of the demands. . .were structurally impossible. Others. . .were confused and unworkable.'

Campbell and Neill go on to document the fact that such over-conscientiousness is damaging the health of individuals, increasing the likelihood of early or sickness-related retirement and other forms of 'burnout', and in some instances diminishing the quality of teaching. Pollard et al (1994) and Croll (1996) have come to similar conclusions.

The situation is complicated by the large numbers of women in primary teaching and by their learnt inability to attend to their own needs. This inability arises partly from the manifold demands they face which leave them little time or energy for their own concerns. Many women now work 'double' or 'triple' shifts, juggling work, home and the responsibilities of child care (Acker, 1994) or of the care of elderly relatives (Evetts, 1990). However, Eichenbaum and Orbach (1983) suggest another explanation for women's neglect of themselves. There is, they argue, a cycle perpetuated through child-rearing practices which results in gender-related differences in the extent to which men and women express their needs and have them satisfied. Simply put, girls are brought up by mothers in ways which make them aware of their needs but lead them to expect that these will not be met. Boys, by contrast, learn that 'needs' belong to women; they therefore do not learn to identify or recognise their own. However, with the tacit collusion of their mothers, sisters and, later, wives, they grow up expecting that their needs will be met, usually by women. If Eichenbaum and Orbach are right, there are two additional reasons why women teachers are prone to over-conscientiousness and open to exploitation. They do not anticipate that their emotional or physical needs will be met, sometimes even noticed, by those with whom they work and they therefore continue to take on additonal burdens without complaint. At the same time, they are likely to protect and attend to others, especially if these are males, compounding with altruism their own neglect of themselves. That is, women staff members, like good mothers, put the children first and, like well socialised girls, look after men second and themselves a poor third.

What answers are suggested by any of this to the question: 'Would schools improve if teachers cared less?' Certainly, children need quasi-parental warmth, reassurance, concern and vigilant attention, both in their own right as dependent human beings and because appropriate levels of self-esteem and security are necessary conditions for learning. For their part, teachers' job satisfaction and with it their motivation are reduced when they feel too pressured to show concern for the 'whole child' or when they are no longer able to act in ways which are consistent with their educational values. In my experience, most teachers want to 'care' for children in a comprehensive sense, even when this involves doing relatively unskilled, boring work or when it results in their own exhaustion. Many still also gain pleasure and a sense of fulfilment from self-expenditure in pursuit of their ideals. When 20 years ago, I asked teachers, 'Why do you let the school take so much of you?', the typical reply was, 'I enjoy giving it' (Nias 1989, 197). Now, as then, many teachers are most fulfilled by their work when they are most depleted by its demands.

Moreover, physical nurturing may be an essential means to pedagogical ends. Nurses sometimes argue that they should carry out tasks which could easily be undertaken by less well qualified professionals (eg washing a patient's hair), because it is through this kind of personal, though relatively unskilled, service that they build up a therapeutic relationship with their patients. Similarly, unless pupils and teachers can relate as people, often in the first instance through the practical activities and quasi-parental behaviour of the teacher, little learning is likely to take place.

Perhaps most important of all, since it is in part through schools that pupils learn about their world and the adults in it, there is a continuing place for teachers who demonstrate to children that they are loved, respected and valued. Indeed, for some children school may be the only place in which they experience a sense of being cared for in a consistent and predictable fashion, by adults who do not habitually put their own interests first. It would be hard to argue that, for such children in particular, schools would be better if teachers were less actively concerned about the well being of individuals, less involved in their social, moral and emotional welfare and worked less hard on their behalf. There is surely also an important place in our competitive, materialist society for adults who model for children a life-style involving idealism and selflessness.

On the other hand, 'caring' as a diffuse concern for the 'whole child' or as altruistic self-expenditure can, like the enjoyment of children's company, become a substitute for thinking or talking about the cognitive aims of teaching and how they can be achieved. The purpose of schools is to ensure children's learning. This requires that teachers make intellectual demands upon their pupils and that they spend time and energy not on children's social and emotional needs but upon their own teaching. That teachers love children, are deeply involved with them, work selflessly for them and are aware of their need for development in all areas of their lives are not sufficient conditions for school improvement.

In addition, it is clear that teachers cannot do effectively all that others require of them and that, all too often, they expect of themselves. As Alexander (1984) made clear a decade ago, few have the knowledge and none have the curriculum time to meet the learning needs of a class of 'whole children' at differing levels of achievement, development and experience. More recently, Campbell and his associates have documented the impossibility of meeting the time requirements of the National Curriculum, even in its revised form. There are also the pressures of assessment, record keeping and reporting to parents and governors, and all the meetings and informal interaction required by these and other growing responsibilities. Leaving aside the patent problem caused for individuals by conscientiousness, never mind 'over-conscientiousness', and the pressures, especially for women, of domestic responsibilities, primary teachers cannot successfully meet the targets which so many people set for them. All too often, those who make the attempt wear out, burn out or leave the profession while there is still time to preserve their physical or mental health. My recent experience suggests practitioners are slowly and reluctantly learning that by caring too much, they may in time be unable to care at all.

In particular, early years' teachers need to be aware that to allow or to encourage a view of their work as maternal is to play into the hands of those who avowedly see the education of young children as a less-skilled, lower-status – and so less well rewarded activity than that of older pupils. For all its educational benefits, 'caring' opens teachers, especially women, to exploitation and may in the long run make effective teaching for all children more difficult to achieve.

There are no simple answers to these dilemmas. If teachers cared less about their ideals, less about the all-round well being and development of their pupils and were less conscientious in pursuit of both, it is possible that children might make greater cognitive gains in school. But as members of a troubled society we also have to consider what might be lost if teachers became less loving and altruistic and if a practical concern for children's social, moral and emotional welfare became the responsibility of others.

Open and public discussion of these issues is overdue. In the meantime, teachers, individually and together, must repeatedly ask themselves, in relation to all that they do in and out of school: 'Why am I doing this?', 'For whose benefit is it?', 'What educational value does it have?' and 'What would happen if I did not do it?'. They must habitually question what they are asked to do and be able to defend it in educational terms, if they wish to preserve the right and ability to care for children as a skilled professional activity.

## Caring: quality in human relationships

'Caring' is widely used in schools in a third sense: to refer to the nature and quality of relationships within the organisation as a whole and to the idea that those relationships should be pursued as ends in themselves. There is an obvious practical overlap between 'caring' of this sort and the notion that teachers feel and act towards their pupils as parents or moral exemplars. An observer in both cases would note similar behaviours and relationships. Nevertheless, there are differences in emphasis. In particular, in schools where 'care' is used to describe a shared ethos embodying mutual respect and concern, attention is paid to collective as well as individual goals (eg whole school discipline policies; the state of the school environment; and the nature of school assemblies). By implication 'care' extends beyond the relationship between teachers and 'their' children; the group is as important as the individual. Indeed, in such schools, it is rare to hear teachers speak of 'my' children. Pupils, and by extension problems, are 'ours' not 'yours' or 'mine'.

Teachers or headteachers who value collectivity as well as individuality have usually made a conscious moral choice to promote throughout the school social values such as trust, cooperation, tolerance and consideration. Moreover, teachers attempt to carry these values into their interactions with one another and with other adults. They do not care only for children and, unlike many mothers, they accept their own need to be supported and nurtured. To be sure, collaborative cultures of this sort (Nias et al, 1989) can arise in response to circumstances. For example, Acker (1995) describes an inner-city school in which the task of teaching was so stressful that teachers could cope with it only by depending heavily on one another. But even in this case much of their mutual support and joint action was due to the headteacher's leadership and the importance that she attached to interpersonal qualities such as compassion, empathy and appreciation of others' contribution to the work of them all. Children are also encouraged to care. Nel Noddings, who believes that caring should be at the heart of school improvement, suggests (Noddings, 1994), that in a mature relationship caring is reciprocal rather than one way. I have been surprised in some schools by the level of care which pupils will show towards their teachers if they are encouraged to do so. This too is an aspect of the high quality human relationships which many primary schools make central to their work and which have been glowingly commended in repeated HMI and OFSTED reports.

Feminist writers have suggested for a decade or more that 'caring', used in this sense, is a specifically female attribute. In particular, a number of North American psychologists and philosophers, sometimes described as 'relational' or 'cultural' feminists, have argued that women perceive, learn, reason and make moral judgements in ways different from those commonly practised by men (see, in particular, Noddings, 1984; 1992; Gilligan, 1982; Belenky et al, 1986). Women focus on connected relationships, emphasise an ethic of care, celebrate empathetic behaviour, interpersonal engagement, affectivity and trust. They are more interested in collaboration than competition, in ensuring everyone's well being than promoting the success of the few, and in preventing conflict than resolving it. These writers have been criticised for assuming that women 'naturally' have such ways of thinking and values, for making little allowance for diversity and change over time in 'women's ways' and for paying scant attention to the social contexts which may have formed them (see, eg, Acker, 1995). Nevertheless, relational feminists have made a considerable contribution to our thinking about 'care'. For example, they have challenged the idea that building and sustaining relationships between people are low-level, low-status activities. Instead they argue that the qualities traditionally associated with 'women's ways' (eg of working, managing and making judgements) should be celebrated and promoted as viable alternatives to established models, since these have almost always been shaped by 'men's ways' of thinking and behaving. Noddings (1992; 1994) in particular has vigorously argued that caring in this relational sense is central to teaching and should be consciously adopted as a moral basis for practice. It is not an adjunct or aid to the achievement of cognitive goals, but an inseparable part of the interpersonal relationship which is at the heart of any encounter between teacher and learner. The fact that women have 'natural' propensity to look for and promote connectedness and empathy and that they are numerically in a majority in the profession should help practitioners of both genders to promote ways of teaching and of running schools which embody these and similar qualities.

At first glance, it is hard to quarrel with the view that schools would improve as workplaces for adults and for children, and in terms of the moral and social education they offered, if teachers 'cared' more about the quality of their relationships with each other and throughout the school. In this respect the Burnage Report (1989) tells its own sad and significantly neglected story. I have had the privilege of working in schools which consciously taught this kind of collective caring and in which both men and women modelled mutual respect, empathy and consideration in their relationships with children and adults. Partly as a result of these affirming experiences, I am very sympathetic to the view that as teachers we should constantly seek to cultivate relations of trust, reciprocal confidence and collaboration, especially in a wider social climate which increasingly emphasises competition, mutual suspicion and division. I am also in favour of letting more women run educational institutions in 'women's ways', to offset escalating national trends towards vertically structured bureaucracies and formal accountability.

But there is another side to these aspirations. There are dangers in placing too much emphasis upon the help and support which teachers can give to one another or to children. There is less and less 'slack' within the educational system. Many teachers are overburdened in the classroom and overwhelmed by administrative and other duties outside it. We cannot assume that they will have the time, energy, resilience or desire to commit their own scarce resources to building or maintaining 'caring' relationships within the school as a whole. To make this assumption would be to increase rather than decrease their load. 'Collegiality' and 'collaboration', simplistically construed, are no answer to resource shortages and long-term social, economic and demographic problems. Once again, it is incumbent on teachers to ask: 'What am I being asked to do?', 'For whose benefit?' and 'Is it the best educational use of my time and energy?'.

## Caring: moral responsibility for children's learning

Teachers' 'care' is expressed in a fourth way. Whether or not they place the development of mutually respectful relationships high on their list of educational aims, most teachers regard their relationship with their pupils as a personal rather than an impersonal, bureaucratic one. They derive from the interpersonal nature of this relationship a moral, as distinct from a legal, responsibility for and accountability to pupils, and often to their parents. They are conscious that their work carries ethical obligations which stem from personal interaction with and knowledge of others. Indeed Elliott et al (1981) call this awareness 'answerability' to stress its interpersonal nature.

'Caring' in this sense includes but goes beyond concern for the safety, happiness, comfort and well being of pupils or for high quality human relationships. It also encompasses what the parents interviewed for the Cambridge Accountability Project (Elliott et al, 1981) called 'stretching' (extending individuals to their limits) and 'pushing' (making reluctant pupils work harder). In the view of these parents, teachers who 'cared' for individuals also 'stretched' and 'pushed' them. In other words 'caring' practitioners put learning high on their agenda and were concerned about their own professional expertise and development. Teachers themselves share this perspective. For example, Evans et al (1994) found that teachers' reactions to the introduction of the National Curriculum were determined in large measure by its effects on their sense of professional competence. Pollard et al (1994) documented similar concerns among practitioners, centring on loss of freedom and a feeling of being forced into an 'unnatural way of teaching'. Drummond (1993), Campbell and Neill (1994), Alexander (1995) and Croll (1996) all highlight the fact that teachers passionately want to have a sense of professional efficacy. Indeed, much of their job satisfaction depends on their ability to feel that they are promoting children's learning and development. In a longitudinal study of teachers I concluded: '[For these teachers] to care for children was to teach well and to accept the need for continuing self-improvement. . . "Caring" was not a soft occupational option' (Nias, 1989, 41).

On the face of it, it would be nonsense to argue that schools would be improved if teachers cared less in this sense. On the contrary, they would probably meet their primary goal – student learning – more effectively if more of them put pupils' curricular progress and their own pedagogy at the top of their professional agenda. I have no quarrel with this. Teachers' aims and their expertise are to do with learning. By all means let us have schools in which more learning takes place.

However, to argue that teachers who 'care' effectively promote children's learning is to beg two questions: 'What learning is it in children's best interests to acquire' and 'To which children do we refer?'. These are moral questions requiring moral answers (Kelchtermans, 1996). Despite, or perhaps because of, the introduction of the National Curriculum, we need a continuing debate about values in the curriculum. To quote Skinner (1996, 253):

> '[The National Curriculum] gives insufficient weight to values and experience through which students (of any age) grow and become critical persons. I refer to literature, music, drama, dance, art and even sport and physical activity . . . As presently conceived [it] is a disabling weapon in the hands of an insensitive and centralising government; it could become a deadly tool if used by a powerfully ideological one'.

Unless we continue to call in question and to debate the nature of the curriculum to which children are exposed, it is possible to envisage a time when teachers would best meet their moral obligations to their pupils by teaching them less. More learning does not necessarily mean a better quality education.

## Caring: personal investment, 'commitment' and guilt

Underlying each of these forms of 'caring' is the individual teacher's personal relationship with his/her job. Primary teachers identify very closely with their work (Pollard, 1985; Nias, 1989). Often indeed their personal and professional selves are so closely intertwined that the person with all his/her beliefs, values and priorities goes to work and the practitioner brings teaching back into the home, to occupy even the sleeping hours. Teachers 'care' about their work in the dual sense that they invest themselves heavily in it and that, as a result, their self-esteem is intimately bound up with their sense of success or failure in it. The daily work of the classroom and the staffroom matters to them because it reflects not only upon their sense of professional competence but also upon who and what they perceive themselves to be.

Partly as a result of this personal involvement in work, many teachers are 'committed' to it, in Lortie's (1975, 189) sense that they are 'ready to allocate scarce personal resources' (eg, time, money or physical effort) to their jobs. Now, it will be clear that individuals may be committed in this sense to many different aspects of their work. Given the fact that there are never enough human resources to meet all the personality and learning needs of pupils in any school, what matters to their colleagues, however, is not the precise nature of their aims, but whether or not they are generous, hard-working and capable of self-expenditure. The focus of an individual's 'commitment' is of concern only when it obstructs others' aims or the school's progress towards generally agreed goals, as the presence of someone single-mindedly dedicated to the pursuit of particular personal ideals occasionally does. In other words, to say that teachers are 'committed' is to reveal nothing about their individual values, judgements, priorities or sources of motivation.

This imprecise use of the term is particularly unhelpful to teachers because it places no limits on individuals' self-expectations. In a comparative study of English and French primary teachers, Broadfoot and Osborn (1993; 1995) demonstrated that the latter felt their professional responsibilities to be both more clear cut and more constrained than the former. English teachers expected more of themselves and imposed far more ambitious goals upon themselves, with the result that they took responsibility for a much broader range of outcomes than their French counterparts. In consequence they more often felt guilty or inadequate. Similarly, I found that teachers were often conscious of not living up to their own internalised standards of self-expenditure, but had seldom asked themselves or others if their aspirations were realistic, attainable or even educationally justifiable (Nias, 1989). Their failure to question, or sometimes to make conscious, the roots of their commitment created 'guilt traps' (Hargreaves, 1994) for them. These traps, he suggests, are due to the social conditions of teachers' work and in particular to the conjunction of: a general commitment to care; the open-ended nature of the job; the pressures of accountability and intensification; and self-imposed demands for perfectionism. Teachers caught in them easily fall victim to cynicism, ill health or exit; there is always more that they should be doing, they never do it well enough and it is their fault anyway for not giving as much as the job demands. In short, the corollary of ill defined and unexamined commitment is increased guilt and this can easily become 'personally unrewarding and professionally unproductive' (Hargreaves, op cit, 142).

It is possible then, that if individuals were less involved in their jobs, they would do them better. Once again, the key to school improvement is not that teachers should be more personally involved or deeply committed, but that individuals should rigorously ask themselves: 'To what do I feel it is worth giving my own resources?', 'Why?', 'Whose interests are served by my giving?' and 'What would happen – to my pupils, to my colleagues, to the school, to parents, to myself – if I were to be less personally involved in what I do?'.

## Conclusion

I have argued that the unquestioning way in which teachers use and are influenced by the complex notion of 'caring' adds to their responsibilities, and thus to their sense of guilt, without necessarily benefiting children proportionately. Teachers who enjoy their pupils' company and have a good relationship with them may unthinkingly give priority to affective rather than cognitive aims. Those who work unstintingly for the 'whole child' may, similarly, unwittingly overlook children's right to intellectual challenge and extension while wearing themselves out in pursuit of unattainable aims. Even the staff in a 'caring' school, well supported by one another, may be too depleted by the social and affective demands of the job to do full justice to children's learning. And the mere existence of 'commitment' guarantees nothing except fatigue and, with good fortune, a sense of individual fulfilment and accomplishment. Nor can teachers who feel responsible, as most do, for children's cognitive progress and for their own professional efficacy be confident that they are contributing to school improvement, unless they have equal confidence in the quality of the curriculum and the values which it embodies. By itself, to 'care' may be to confuse oneself, pupils, parents, governors and all those interested in education.

Accordingly, teachers who wish to see themselves as 'caring' owe it to themselves as informed professionals to know what and who they care about; what are the practical consequences and costs for themselves and others of wanting to care; what are the likely educational gains and the possible losses for children, for their parents and for society as a whole; and whether individuals can sustain the physical and emotional costs of caring or have been adequately prepared to do so.

In particular, it is crucial that we are honest with ourselves about our motives for choosing to 'care' in different ways, whether for pupils or for our own professional competence or skills. To 'care' in the sense of being altruistic, trying to build communities with high quality relationships or being concerned for pupils' learning and development is to make a moral choice, often in fulfilment of a felt moral responsibility. By contrast, sustaining a warm, encouraging relationship with children and investing one's own resources in work may be activities undertaken in order to maintain one's self-image or sense of self-esteem. Of course, this distinction is blurred by the fact that a moral choice to 'care' may be part of an individual's sense of identity. Nevertheless, it is worth reminding ourselves that 'caring' attitudes and behaviours sometimes reward the carer as much as or more than the recipient.

The relationship between 'care' and self-image is particularly relevant in the contentious areas where unquestioned 'care' merges into over-conscientiousness and a docile willingness to accept an unlimited extension of professional responsibilities. Bluntly put, it is easy to see 'care' construed as altruism and self-sacrifice, as a convenient way of exploiting teachers, especially those who are women; and also of conning them into taking on, unpaid, work which would be better done by other trained professionals such as counsellors and social workers. No-one's interests are served when the path to school improvement is paved with the ashes of burnt out teachers.

I should like to end, therefore, with a proposition which I hope will stimulate debate among educationalists at all levels: given that primary teachers cannot fulfil all the expectations that are held of them, and that some at least of their wounds are self-inflicted, they should decide to care less about those aspects of their jobs which seem to them individually to be least worthwhile, especially when the factors affecting these are outside their control. Instead, they should care more about their own professional skill and the impact that this can have upon their pupils' learning. Schools will 'improve' only if they succeed in their primary task – that of equipping children for life in the twenty-first century. Paradoxically, therefore, teachers who care more will have in the future to steel themselves to care less, especially when caring is a matter of self-image rather than moral obligation.

# References

Abercrombie, M. L. J. (1984) 'Changing Higher Education by the Application of Some Group Analytic Ideas'. Paper at the 8th International Conference of Group Psychotherapy, Mexico City.

Acker, S. (1994) *Gendered Education: Sociological Reflections on Women, Teaching and Feminism*. Open University Press: Milton Keynes.

Acker, S. (1995) 'Carry on Caring: The Work of Women Teachers', *British Journal of Sociology of Education*, 16, 1, 21–36.

Alexander, R. (1984) *Primary Teaching*. Cassell: London.

Alexander, R. (1995) *Versions of Primary Education*. Routledge: London.

Belenky, M., Clinchy, B., Goldberger, N. and Tarak, J. (1986) *Women's Ways of Knowing*. Basic Books: New York.

Broadfoot, P. and Osborn, M. (1993) *Perceptions of Teaching: Primary school teachers in England and France*. Cassell: London.

Broadfoot, P. and Osborn, M. (1995) *Primary Schooling and Policy Change in England and France*. SCAA: London.

Burnage Report (1989) *Murder in the Playground*. Longsight Press: London.

Campbell, R. J. and Neill, S. (1994) *Primary Teachers at Work*. Routledge: London.

Croll, P. (Ed) (1996) *Teachers, Pupils and Primary Schooling: Continuity and Change*. Cassell: London.

Drummond, M-J. (1993) *Assessing Children's Learning*. David Fulton: London.

Eichenbaum, L. and Orbach, S. (1983) *What Do Women Want?* Michael Joseph: London.

Elliott, J., Bridges, D., Ebbutt, D., Gibson, R. and Nias, J. (1981) *School Accountability*. Blackwell: Oxford.

Evans, L., Packwood, A., Neill, S. and Campbell, R. J. (1994) *The Meaning of Infant Teachers' Work*. Routledge: London.

Evetts, J. (1990) *Women Teachers in Primary Education*. Routledge: London.

Gilligan, C. (1982) *In a Different Voice*. Harvard University Press: Cambridge, Mass.

Grumet, M. (1988) *Bitter Milk: Women and Teaching*. University of Massachusetts Press: Amherst.

Hargreaves, A. (1994) *Changing Teachers, Changing Times: Teachers' Work and Culture in the Postmodern Age*. Cassell: London.

Jeffrey, B. and Woods, P. (1996) 'Feeling De-professionalized: The Social Construction of Emotions during an OFSTED Inspection', *Cambridge Journal of Education*, 26, 3, 325–43.

Kelchtermans, G. (1996) 'Teacher Vulnerability: Understanding Its Moral and Political Roots', *Cambridge Journal of Education*, 26, 3, 307–24.

King, R. (1978) *All Things Bright and Beautiful: A Sociological Study of Infant Schools*. Wiley: Chichester.

Lawn, M. and Grace, G. (Eds) (1987) *Teachers: The Culture and Politics of Work*. Falmer: London.

Lortie, D. (1975) *School Teacher*. University of Chicago Press: Chicago.

Nias, J. (1989) *Primary Teachers Talking: A Study of Teaching as Work*. Routledge: London.

Nias, J., Southworth, G. and Yeomans, R. (1989) *Staff Relationships in the Primary School: A Study of Organizational Cultures*. Cassell: London.

Noddings, N. (1984) *Caring: A Feminine Approach to Ethics and Moral Education*. University of California Press: Berkeley.

Noddings, N. (1992) *The Challenge to Care in Schools*. Teachers' College Press: New York.

Noddings, N. (1994) 'An Ethic of Caring and Its Implications for Instructional Arrangements', in Stone, L. (Ed) *The Education Feminism Reader*. Routledge: New York.

Pollard, A. (1985) *The Social World of the Primary School*. Cassell: London.

Pollard, A., Broadfoot, P., Croll, P., Osborn, M. and Abbott, D. (1994) *Changing English Primary Schools? The Impact of the Education Reform Act at Key Stage One*. Cassell: London.

Rich, R. (1972) *The Training of Teachers in England and Wales during the Nineteenth Century*. Cedric Chivers: Bath.

Simon, B. (1965) *Education and the Labour Movement, 1870–1920*. Lawrence Wishart: London.

Skinner, J. (1996) 'Reflections . . . on Experiences, 1971–1996', *Cambridge Journal of Education*, 26, 2, 251–4.

Tropp, A. (1957) *The Schoolteachers*. Heinemann: London.

# 28 Doing school differently

## Creative practitioners at work

*Mandy Maddock, Mary Jane Drummond, Ben Koralek and Idit Nathan*

## Introduction

In March 2004 Cambridge Curiosity and Imagination[1] and Shape Cambridge[2] were invited to organise, manage and support pilot creative projects in two regions of Essex as a precursor to the launch of the Creative Partnerships[3] initiative in this authority. Ten interdisciplinary creative practitioners were recruited, who all had experience of working in schools and who would approach the projects from outside the usual structures of schooling within which teachers are required to work. The aims of the projects were to introduce the settings to the rationale and potential of Creative Partnerships; to maintain the momentum of the local community towards Creative Partnerships; and to excite further interest from the local schools and communities. The approach of the individual projects was to involve children, young people, their teachers and other educators in a creative response to issues around twenty-first-century schools and communities. At the heart of this '21st Century Schools' project was a belief in the power of the collaboration between the creative practitioners (visual artists, architects, writers, engineers, photographers, dance and movement therapists), and the teachers and other educators with whom they worked.

There were 11 projects in total; they took place in infant, primary and secondary schools, an applied learning programme, a pupil referral unit and an after-school club for looked-after children. Some of the schools and community groups were self-selecting, and some were selected by the project steering group (consisting of Arts Council and local authority members), having first been identified as being in areas of multiple deprivation, with substantial numbers of underachieving pupils, in order to qualify for involvement in the Creative Partnerships initiative. Twenty-two creative practitioners worked in pairs in each setting for two or three observation days and four or five activity days. The projects concluded with a formal presentation to members of the local community including parents.

This paper presents a selection of material from three of the 11 projects: one primary and one secondary school, and the looked-after children's club. These three were chosen to illustrate a range of settings and the themes that seemed to have most significance for the future development of Creative Partnerships. The data in this paper are drawn from a combination of sources:

- memory scrap books kept during the activity days by the adults and the children;
- reflective journals kept by the creative practitioners;
- participant and non-participant observations by the researcher;
- photographs taken by adults and children;
- project comments books open to all participants (adults, children and visitors to the projects);
- comments collected at the final presentations;
- focus group discussion of creative practitioners held mid-project;
- creative practitioners' presentations at a review and evaluation meeting at the close of the project.

## The three settings

### *So Near So Phare[4]: two visual artists in a primary school*

This large community primary school is situated on the edge of an estuary; the sea can be seen from the windows of the school. The creative practitioners took time to observe the school and its environment and were particularly struck by a lighthouse in the estuary, the cranes on the dockside and the staircase leading to the room where they worked. Their aspiration was to explore links between learning and the environment. Their aim was to reconnect human beings (children and adults) with their natural desire to discover within their domain of expertises. Their strategy was to use a combination of 'Signs Words Visuals Languages' to deconstruct the conventional connection between children and the written word. The children's activities progressed from two dimensions (words on paper, photographs, maps, banners) to three-dimensional structures conjuring up the built environment using a variety of symbolic languages, drama and music. They worked with Year 2 children (6- and 7-year-olds).

### *Be brave and do the unexpected: a visual artist and an architect in a secondary school*

The head teacher greeted the creative practitioners with the invitation to be brave and unpredictable. Their aspiration was to practise a questioning and exploratory approach to the built environment of the school, in order to inspire a Year 9 class (13- and 14-year-olds) to take a similar approach to their own learning. Their strategy was to subvert the everyday environment by changing aspects of it; turning tables upside down, wrapping furniture, covering floors, threading the room with elastic. The intention of these disruptions was to invite people to look at taken-for-granted, everyday aspects of their environment with renewed vision, and to engage in creative thinking, questioning and dialogue in response to the surprises and the shock of the new.

*A roller coaster experience: a writer and a visual artist
at an after-school club for looked-after children*

The after-school club is held in a resource centre which supports looked-after children, their families and carers. The creative practitioners worked with two groups of children, one for eight to ten year olds who were required to attend as part of their personal care plans, and the other for young people aged 11 to 15 who attended on a voluntary basis. The creative practitioners started with the big idea that the way a place looks can change the way we feel. Their aspiration was to empower the learners and the centre workers to think creatively about where and who they are. Their strategy was to facilitate the children and young people to make spaces that were meaningful to them and that they could explain to others. They provided huge quantities of card of every size for making shapes and structures, many of them large enough for the children to inhabit.

## Emerging themes

From the mass of data collected across all 11 projects, three major themes emerged: the use of space and time, the constraints and opportunities for creative practice and the possibility of continuity into the future. Running across these themes were common threads: the richness of chaos, learning and unlearning, challenge and confrontation. In this paper we illustrate each of the themes and threads from the perspective of the creative professionals, with some supplementary material contributed by the student participants and centre workers.

### *Space and time: different ways of seeing at the primary school*

In the primary school the visual artists' observation visits included time to wander about the building. As they explore this new environment, they do not see what the teachers see, the familiar sights and sounds of the workplace, the routine trappings of schooling, the taken-for-granted spaces in which children and teachers travel through the day, following their detailed timetables. The visual artists see signs and symbols that foreshadow the focus of their project, which they describe as the use of writing in the environment and the ways in which the environment might be transformed by establishing a new relationship with it. They notice photographs of the gigantic cranes in the port on the horizon; they are reminded of the title of their project (So Near So Phare). They write up their impressions in their project journal:

> There are charts (in several places) showing 'High Frequency words', which sound like radio waves. Echoes of the environment: messengers, time-keepers, trackers, high frequencies, a ship on the weather-vane on the roof of the school, seagulls and beach huts painted on the walls of the corridors inside. So near and so far, inside and outside, here and there/elsewhere, the claustrophobia inside the school and the vastness of the port and the sea, so close so phare.

On the way to the room upstairs where they will be working, the artists take photographs of the corridors and staircase—places that may never have been looked at in this way before. They arrive in their designated workshop area and start to rearrange the space, moving tables and chairs. They are politely informed that the furniture must not be moved; the room is being used for the Standard Assessment Tests, taken by the 10- and 11-year-olds, which are still in progress. The artists restore the room to its former arrangement; the school system reclaims its space, for its proper purpose. The time for transformation is not yet ripe.

Before the project begins the artists prepare a CD of photographs, mostly of the staircase leading to their workshop area; these are to be used by the children in preparation for the four activity days of the project itself. At a planning meeting with the teachers, the school project leader opens the CD; the artists note 'he seems intrigued by the spaces he is looking at, (they are empty for once and not full of children) and rediscovers the school's interior'. Perhaps the sought-for transformation is beginning to be a possibility.

Only a week later, the activity days of the project begin. The first day passes, and the artists reflect in their journal:

> We talk between ourselves later about the 'floating' quality of certain moments during the day. G remarks that this 'losing it' feeling at times is necessary. In these uncomfortable moments, new connections are beginning for everyone, [educators] and [artists] alike. We feel that some moments are empty, maybe it's not the moments but us, because a new door is open and we face an empty space that we have to fill. Confidence is the key of this door.

This is a fascinating passage of reflection. It is hard to imagine a busy Key Stage 2[5] teacher experiencing a feeling of emptiness or facing a space that needs to be filled. There are so few empty spaces in a school day—or week—or year. There is no room for emptiness in the current structures of schooling; small wonder that the teachers appear to be unsettled by the artists' plans and predictions, by the project as a whole. The demands on teachers' professional confidence are multiple: curriculum coverage, classroom organisation, pedagogical interactions; their confidence is not usually deployed in unlocking new doors, opening on to unknown spaces.

On the second activity day the artists become aware of another difference between a teacher's way of seeing and their own. One of the teachers seems distracted, even disinterested, in the activities and chooses not to be involved; the children become disorganised and noisy. The artists comment that the teacher does not seem to be aware that the work they are doing now is research, preparation, sketches, like plans for a building. They find it difficult to explain their alternative perspective, their relish for the uncomfortable moments, their wish to open the door into a new space, in which preparatory sketches are more important than the polished product. Again it seems as if there is little time or space in the busy school day for what the artists see as a necessity, not a luxury: the need for slow thinking, and yet slower re-thinking, as gradually, bit by bit, new connections are made between curriculum areas normally neatly slotted into their proper spaces on the timetable, which can be seen, in a sense, as a map of space as well as time. 'As we connect writing/reading/geography/plans/history/languages, maybe we tread on [the teacher's] toes', the artists ruefully conclude.

Maybe in the contemporary climate of schooling, such differences are predictable, even inevitable. The distinction so forcibly made by Dweck and her colleagues may be relevant here. In *Self-theories* (1999), for example, Dweck differentiates between a learning orientation and a performance orientation in children; she demonstrates their characteristics through a brilliant series of carefully designed experimental situations. These two contrasting orientations seem to have parallels with the differences in the adults' perspectives that the artists record in their journal. While they themselves prioritise the challenge of the unknown, the empty space, the sketch, the rehearsal, the unpredictability of learning, teachers are constrained to orient themselves towards the predictable, the familiar, normative standards and public accountability. The experience of education as performance, in the semi-public place of the classroom, is by no means confined to the teachers in the project schools.

## Space and time: responding to the unexpected at the secondary school

The characteristic pressures of the school timetable are also experienced by the creative practitioners in the secondary school. Every moment of the day is spoken for by lesson periods, assemblies, time-fillers, study time, tutorial time and so on. Even the lunch break has been shortened to 30 minutes as a strategy for managing pupils' challenging behaviour; there is less time to misbehave in 30 minutes than in 60. The creative practitioners observe that there is little free thinking space during the day: 'The pace of this school's daily life was frenetic, both of us . . . found it difficult just to sit and think'. The absence of thinking time reminds us of the concept of the empty space that the visual artists in the primary school were trying to open up.

The artist's and architect's response is to provide time and space and an abundance of simple, inexpensive materials; as a result, there are abundant opportunities to engage in creative play, research, thinking and non-directed learning. The visual artist writes in his journal: 'What to do with free time and how to be within it are important elements in learning'. He continues to muse, noting the learners' need for nourishing food and concludes 'there is [also] the digestion of learning and experience'. But before the learners can participate fully in these new ways of thinking and doing, there is a substantial degree of unlearning to do. The creative practitioners note that many of the learners appear to have forgotten how to play, to innovate, to question: 'They found it so hard to be creative, even when we told them to play with the materials . . . [they were] ingenious in trying not to learn'.

The creative practitioners are sensitive to the needs of the learners, responding flexibly to the space and time the students can manage. Building on the students' crumbs of participation, the creative practitioners change their plans and offer additional inputs as the students' concentration waxes and wanes. Gradually, the students' focus broadens as they become involved in the project, and take ownership of the space and the work. They become more willing to think for themselves and to question. In a discussion of the work of Joseph Beuys[6] one student asks: 'I wondered why [Joseph Beuys] went from war to art. Why couldn't he do both war and art?'

Another student responds to an installation created in the space by the artist and the architect with a profound personal observation: 'It makes you think without meaning to'.

By the fourth day the students are working in the outdoor environment in ways that are excitingly different and enticingly engaging: for example, altering the space outside the front of the school building using pallet wrap. The crumbs of participation are reconstituted as something more substantial. The creative practitioners note that: 'This task was very popular, the students . . . were very keen to discuss the experience and even turned the clearing up into an extension of the process'. The next day the students extend the activity indoors: 'One boy suggested suspending the ball of [waste] pallet wrap over the atrium space using the elastic [left over from a different activity]' and 'a number of students helped to make a sculptural work by wrapping furniture'. The architect reflects on: 'How different it was working outside with the plastic. Such fun, so many different stimuli, especially with the wind . . . all the kids loved it and the sounds were fabulous'. The students also comment on their changing perspective, not only of the activity itself:

> I didn't notice how big the space is.
> It's a giant web.

but also their changing experience of learning:

> It's really fun.
> Do we have to stop?
> Can't we finish off?
> The smile on his face when we said it was a brilliant idea.

The usual demands that schooling makes of students are very different from the demands of the provocations offered by the creative practitioners. Learners are normally required to learn what teachers intend them to learn, to learn 'the right thing'. In this project the learners were surprised into thinking for themselves. They claimed spaces, took control and ownership of the environment and the activity; they enjoyed being themselves, and succeeding in their learning.

### Constraints and opportunities at the primary school

In a beautiful essay on the dignity of labour, Simone Weil, the great French philosopher and mystic, writes: 'In human effort the only source of energy is desire'

(1941, p. 265). Reflecting on this thought in the light of the artists' journal entries, and their observations of children, one is forced to admit that the source of energy in schools is more often the powerful principle of accountability, in its thousands of daily manifestations, the pressure not just to do it right, but to be seen to be doing it right. This is the source of the energy that goes into creating and sustaining a quiet class, a busy hum, a brisk pace and the satisfying completion of each orchestrated movement of the school day. The pressure to complete activities on time, the necessity of sticking to the complex choreo-graphy of the timetable: these are forces powerful enough to preclude the possi-bility of desire.

And yet, by the third activity day of the project, when the artists meet with the teachers to review what has been happening, there is a shift in perspective. At this hour-long encounter ('the best we have had so far'), the artists ask if the children are changing in any way. In the ensuing discussion, one teacher reports that the children are more able to analyse, and, at the same time, are thinking in a more abstract way:

> We discuss this and conclude that when the children are free of pressures to write in a rigid academic way, the desire to write is stronger than the desire to write correctly. Since we are not expecting a necessarily 'correct' reply (nothing is right, nothing is wrong) the children are freer to express themselves.

One of the teachers follows up this insight with the words: 'the children are no longer bored with pressure'—a brave new world of learning may be opening up here. It seems that the task of switching on the energy of desire, in place of the boredom of pressure, is difficult but not impossible. Indeed, one of the children commented '[I didn't realise] everything can be right'; and another, in response to the same prompt 'I didn't realise', wrote 'so fun so complicated'. When adults, teachers, or artists, or both, offer children opportunities, activities, tasks that are designed to increase the learners' autonomy, rather than reduce it in the interests of performance, the children are energised; they are, the artists note, 'concentrated and eager, helpful and imaginative'. These words are a fine description of successful learners, a vivid contrast to some of the children's earlier scrapbook entries:

> I was worried that it all went wrong if our work didn't go right.
> I was worried that I did not get my work done in time.

In a paper given to the British Psycho-Analytical Society towards the end of her life, the pioneering educator Susan Isaacs (1943) argues that learning depends upon interest, and that interest is derived from desire, curiosity and fear. We can see all three of these forces at work in the encounters between artists, teachers and children. It is not the arrival of the artists in the school that triggers fear. According to Isaacs, the possibility of fear is a permanent human condition; it is a necessary component of interest and its grand outcome, learning. For fear is the trigger for courage. And in responding to the new opportunities the project gave them, the children are courageous as well as fearful. The artists watch them attentively, and document their achievements: the children connect, build, experiment, stabilise, write, invent, complete, cooperate, succeed. So fun, so complicated; such learning!

### Constraints and opportunities at the after-school club: different ways of responding to challenge

Apprehension and fear were also observed in the responses of the centre workers to the unstructured, apparently chaotic, artist-led sessions. The workers were concerned that 'we'd got them so structured and things got really unstructured'. The visual artist and the writer agreed, noting further that 'staff felt that the session had been chaotic, yet were really pleased with the efforts by individuals'. Whereas the centre workers saw structure and control as important elements of pedagogy, the creative practitioners saw the relaxing of boundaries as necessary in order to liberate learners from their preconceptions, thus creating the space in which creative thinking can happen. The creative practitioners worked without observable structures or boundaries. They offered learners the gift of 'space and listening', valuing 'process' over predetermined outcomes.

This difference in perspective was initially challenging for both creative practitioners and centre workers. Throughout the project they continued to reflect, discuss and negotiate; there was sustained shared dialogue about the relaxing of boundaries, and the transfer of control from the centre workers to the learners. But different ways of seeing persisted. For example, while the rest of the group were using masking tape to make simple 3D constructions with strips of card, one boy wound the masking tape round his leg. The artist was concerned that the centre workers would read this as non-cooperation, or going off-task, and would want to confront him. She commented: 'I feel [he] needs adult time following his lead and pushing him to develop anything he comes up with to constructive outcomes'.

The centre worker also observed a similar moment when another child was wrapping masking tape round his hand. She reflected on the way the artist responded:

> [the child] changed the focus from what he had been asked to do, to an idea of his own. Whereas I might have challenged him for not sticking to the task, [the artist] praised his creativity, which the child responded very well to, and the incident was reframed from a negative to a positive.

This minor moment of handing power and control of learning to the learner had a major impact on him. The outcomes of motivation and desire were more significant than the creation of a predetermined end product, which the centre worker recognised would have been her priority: '[The boy] actually wanted to show his carer his work. Usually he either destroys it or puts it into the bin on his way out. This was a great achievement for him'.

Although centre workers initially found the letting go of boundaries and control very difficult, by the end of the project they reported different perceptions; they realised that to relinquish control is sometimes to gain it:

> I thought [he] would just run around [but he] didn't because no boundaries or structure [gave him] more room.
> Being in control and being able to use any materials and imagination allowed them to achieve.
> No limitations made it easier, [we] could co-opt what they did that was naughty.
> The children were able to express themselves without any boundaries in place and this could potentially be therapeutic.
> I am determined to be more careful about what I see as destructive.

Although eventually successful, the journey through the project had been an emotional one for the workers. The creative practitioners wrote that: 'The success of the project depended on the readiness of the staff to go along with the work and initially they found it very challenging'. They called it a roller coaster experience for the centre workers, whose comments included:

> We were baffled.
> I felt over my head.
> I had no control.
> I learned a lot from this.
> Next week they'll be raving about what they did.
> I look forward to another new experience that will challenge the way I think!

Just as they had changed their ideas about the need for control, they had also shifted in their perceptions of children. One comment from a centre worker suggests a deficit view of children: 'I didn't think the children would have the imagination'. By the end of the project this had been replaced with a wealth or credit view:

> I was amazed to see the children's and visitors' faces when they were showing their projects. The children were proud, confident and expressive . . . they showed a great interest in one another's projects.

The artists' view of the children as essentially active, purposeful, powerful learners, which was successfully communicated to the centre workers, ensured the positive outcomes of the project.

### Perspectives on the future

The 11 Creative Partnerships projects, of which three have been examined here, were designed as pilot projects from which lessons could be learned, lessons which would enrich and sustain the launch of the full-scale Creative Partnerships initiative in the regions in November 2005. From the schools' perspectives the four or five project days were a sudden intervention, discontinuous with the past, unconnected to the future. But from the perspective of Cambridge Curiosity and Imagination and Shape Cambridge, and the creative practitioners who were recruited, the projects were invitations to speculate on the shape of things to come, and to invent a longer term relationship between the educational and artistic communities. What might be the enduring characteristics of such a relationship?

One aspect of all 11 projects that cries out to be carried forward to further close encounters between the communities is the dramatic possibility of cross-disciplinary learning, as teachers and other educators are given time to explore and permission to adopt conceptual and experimental structures from other disciplines (for example, architecture, writing, sculpture, photography, dance and movement, music). The pilot projects demonstrated that educators offered such opportunities did more than learn to participate in unfamiliar pedagogical approaches; they began to respond to the challenge of challenge, as it were, building their capacity to accept and welcome the unexpected, the unfamiliar and the unscripted. The various creative practitioners who introduced these challenges into the educational settings see their role as 'facilitating the chaos. Not controlling it but letting it happen'. In one sense chaos simply means untidiness, a messy classroom or paint on the floor. But in another, the chaos the artists facilitate is the deliberate juxtaposition of contrasting values and approaches. Faced with this kind of chaos, the teachers and other educators began to realise that they can both speak and act off-script; they can unlearn some of their tried and tested teacherly ways and means, and think more adventurously about their role in building a culture of creativity. Released by the creative practitioners from the highly regulated rhythms of the classroom, the teachers began to see the possibility of a different kind of professional development, where their engagement with the creative process was the desirable outcome, more important than any number of pre-specified learning intentions, for themselves or their learners.

The benefits of a continuing relationship between the artists and the schools are not, of course, confined to the adults. The value of the experience for the children and young people taking part was plain to see: their evaluative and reflective comments were refreshingly frank, and overwhelmingly positive. They expressed their profound appreciation of the richness of their experience; the abundance of materials (bucketfuls of paint, acres of paper, miles of string and elastic) stimulated their exuberance, their enthusiasm for learning, their unbridled imagination. Furthermore, the artists tentatively identified the therapeutic benefits of these experiences for the learners, especially for those who seemed to have a troubled educational history, and those facing social or personal difficulties in their homes or communities. The opportunities these young people were given included the possibility of ownership and authorship, another thread running through all 11 projects. In future projects, it will be important to listen still more attentively to the voices of the student participants, giving them still more space and time to speak for themselves, creating their own patterns and pathways of learning in their purposeful engagement with the richness of chaos, the safety of freedom.

It is too early to go very far in attempting to describe how 'doing school differently' will unfold as the education and artistic communities improve and deepen their relationship. We can be certain, though, that the themes we describe here, the use of space and time, the constraints and opportunities for creative practice, the richness of chaos, learning and unlearning, challenge and confrontation, will continue to be significant. In this brief paper, we have done little more than describe the beginning of a beginning, the preface to a book yet to be written or the overture of an opera still unscored. But from this perspective, the future looks bright. A beginning has been made. The Creative Partnerships approach has been devised and tested, documented, analysed and trawled for hidden treasure; the participating actors, teachers, artists and young people, may now be ready to commit themselves to the promise of tomorrow.

## Acknowledgements

The authors would like to thank the staff and students in the 11 settings, and the creative practitioners. We also acknowledge the invaluable contributions of Delyth Turner-Harriss (Project Manager at Shape Cambridge) and Ana Percival (Project Administrator). The projects and research were funded by Arts Council England, East.

While this article was in preparation one of its authors, Ben Koralek, died after a brave battle against cancer. All his colleagues will remember him with great affection and will sorely miss his commitment to the cause of the fruitful and creative collaboration between artists, architects, educators, families and children.

## Notes

1. For information on Cambridge Curiosity and Imagination see www.cambridgecandi.org.uk/home/
2. For information on Shape Cambridge see www.shape-cambridge.org.uk
3. Creative Partnerships 'provides school children across England with the opportunity to develop creativity in learning and to take part in cultural activities of the highest quality . . . the idea behind Creative Partnerships is . . . to animate the national curriculum (the sciences as well as the arts!) and to enrich school life by making best use of the UK's creative wealth' (Creative Partnerships, 2005).
4. Phare is French for lighthouse.
5. In the UK, Key Stage 2 refers to the four years of upper primary schooling for children from 7 to 11 years old.
6. Joseph Beuys (1921–1986) is one of the influential figures in post-war German and European art. An artist, teacher, curator and activist, a generation of artists were influenced by his ideas about art and social utility.

# References

Creative Partnerships (2005) Available online at www.creative-partnerships.com/aboutcp/ (accessed 1 October 2005).

Dweck, C. (1999) *Self-theories: their role in motivation, personality and development* (New York, Psychology Press).

Isaacs, S. (1943) The nature and function of phantasy, in: M. Klein, P. Heimann, S. Isaacs & J. Riviere (1952) *Developments in psycho analysis* (London, The Hogarth Press).

Weil, S. (1941) Prerequisite to dignity of labour, in: S. Miles (Ed.) (1986) *Simone Weil: an anthology* (London, Virago).

# Index